COMBAT FLYING EQUIPMENT

COMBAT FLYING EQUIPMENT

U.S. Army Aviators' Personal Equipment, 1917–1945

C. G. Sweeting

Smithsonian Institution Press • Washington and London

Designer: Alan Carter
Editor: Catherine Schwartzstein

Library of Congress Cataloging-in-Publication Data

Sweeting, C. G.
    Combat flying equipment : U.S. Army aviators' personal equipment,
1917–1945 / C.G. Sweeting.
        p.   cm.
    Bibliography: p.
    Includes index.
    ISBN 0-8747-894-1 (cloth); 1-56098-502-X (paper)
    1. United States. Army Air Forces—Equipment—History. 2. United
States. Army Air Forces—Aviation—Safety measures—History.
I. Title.
UG1173.S94 1989
358.4'181'0973—dc19   88–18623

∞The paper used in this publication meets the minimum requirements of
the American National Standard for Permanence of Paper for Printed
Library Materials Z39.48-1984.

A paperback reissue (ISBN 1-56098-502-X) of the original cloth edition

8 7 6 5 4 3 2
09 08 07 06 05 04 03 02

Manufactured in the United States of America

Frontispiece: AAF waist gunner, equipped with typical flight gear, in action
aboard a B-17 bomber during the winter of 1943–44. (Courtesy of U.S.
Army)

Contents

Foreword

In *Combat Flying Equipment*, Glen Sweeting employs the same clear writing, attention to detail, and meticulous research that distinguished his companion volume, *Combat Flying Clothing*, and his work as Curator of Flight Materiel at the National Air and Space Museum. I had the pleasure of being a colleague of Glen's for some twelve years at the Museum, and without question he can be called The Compleat Curator. No one ever worked harder at collecting, conserving, organizing, and studying the myriad items in his field.

As an Army Air Forces and U.S. Air Force pilot, I used many of the items of equipment described in the book, but I had no idea at all of how they came to exist. I vividly recall two incidents involving combat flying gear, one amusing and one nearly fatal, which occurred when my fighter squadron was in China during World War II. In the first, one of the squadron pilots happened to be flying my P-40 and wearing my parachute on a strafing mission. The oil cooler was hit by ground fire and he was forced to bail out. He did so successfully and landed between the Chinese and Japanese lines. He wisely decided to wait until darkness fell before making his way to the Chinese lines. Late in the day, he became hungry and opened the jungle kit on the back of the chute for the emergency chocolate bar, only to find that I had already eaten it. When he returned, he was more than somewhat irritated with me, until a survey revealed that virtually all the pilots had eaten their bars too.

In the second mishap, one of our P-40s was badly shot up by Japanese fighters. The airplane was trailing heavy black smoke and the pilot was preparing to bail out, when the smoke decreased to a trickle and he decided to try and make it back. He reached the field, but his hydraulic system was shot out so he could not lower the wheels. He made a good belly landing, and except for a cut on his scalp from the gunsight, was unhurt. An hour or so later, the parachute rigger came up to him and said that it was lucky he hadn't tried to bail out, because an incendiary bullet had come up into his seat pack and had burned away most of the nylon. Had he jumped, he would surely have been killed.

That last tale just goes to show that even the research, huge technical advances, and discoveries detailed in this book cannot meet all the exigencies of wartime. Nevertheless, the flyers of the mid-1940s went up with protection that makes what was worn only thirty years before appear neolithic in comparison. Glen Sweeting's effective prose and his selection of rare photographs lead the reader along the difficult, often tortuous, development paths of the equipment that kept our aircrews alive and efficient in combat.

Current and future generations of historians and other researchers will be spared a great deal of extensive inquiry by referring to this excellent book.

Donald S. Lopez
Deputy Director
National Air and Space Museum

Preface

Over four decades have passed since the end of World War II, and we are still learning about the tremendous effort that was required to achieve final victory over the Axis powers. We know now that the margin between victory and defeat in that complex world-wide struggle was often narrower than many realized at the time.

The campaigns and contributions of the great commanders, air aces, and other heroes, have been well documented; often overlooked are the important but lesser known technical accomplishments that made victory possible and laid the groundwork for postwar progress. The story of how American airmen became the best clothed aviators of any air force during the war may be found in the book; *Combat Flying Clothing: Army Air Forces Clothing During World War II*, published by the Smithsonian Institution Press in 1984. This companion volume is intended to describe the development and use of the many types of individual life-support equipment, a Herculean task that had a direct bearing on the efficiency of America's air arm and the successful outcome of the conflict.

To appreciate fully the significance of this accomplishment, the story must be traced back to World War I. The many difficulties and problems encountered in providing flight materiel for Army flyers, in an era of rapidly changing technology, continued through the 1920s and the decade of the Great Depression. The events of the hectic World War II years are, by comparison, a success story, but one that was achieved only through the dedicated efforts of the many unsung heroes of the Army Air Forces, the medical profession, the scientific community, and American industry.

It will be noted that many of the items of personal equipment in service during World War II were actually developed long before the United States entered the conflict. It is, of course, impossible to include every item used by flying personnel of the U.S. Army Air Forces and its predecessor organizations: the Army Air Corps, Army Air Service, and Aviation Section, Signal Corps. The following chapters do cover the main types of individual flying gear used since World War I. Navigation instruments have been omitted, because of the great number involved, and the fact that these specialized devices have been described in numerous other publications. U.S. Navy, commercial, and foreign equipment has been mentioned when it influenced development overall, or Army materiel in particular. Space limitations unfortunately preclude a detailed description of the operation and use of most items. This information may be found in the references included in the notes and bibliography.

This study deals primarily with the personal equipment carried and used by the individual Army flyer, but some items of essential aircraft equipment have been included in order to make the history more complete and understandable. The entire oxygen apparatus, for example, including masks, regulators, and cylinders, is described because the components were designed to function as a part of a specific, overall system.

The preparation of this book involved the examination of many documents and photographs from a variety of sources. Little has been published concerning many important types of equipment, and I relied mainly on official manuals, technical reports, and studies. Also available for examination were actual specimens of flight materiel in collections, including that of the National Air and Space Museum (NASM), the U.S. Air Force Museum, and Robert Lehmacher of Burbank, Illinois. Unless otherwise indicated in the captions, the photos were produced originally by the United States Air Force (USAF) and its predecessors, and many were obtained from the NASM archives. Some photos of flyers' armor were provided by the Army Ordnance Museum and the Army Natick Research and Development Laboratories. The U.S. Air Force Museum and the Office of Air Force History were, of course, invaluable sources of information and photos on every aspect of military aviation.

Most of the people responsible for the development of flight materiel before and during World War II received little public recognition for their effort. Unfortunately, many are now deceased and others could not be located, however, much of value was furnished by participants and experts in various fields.

I would like to extend my sincere thanks to the many people who provided information, assistance, and encouragement during preparation of this study. Lt. Col. Donald S. Lopez, USAF (Ret.), NASM Deputy Director, was particularly helpful during my research, because he actually used many of the items of personal equipment in air combat during World War II, and was always willing to share his flying experiences and intimate knowledge. Don kindly consented to review, and comment on my manuscript, and to write the foreword. Robert Lehmacher, expert on survival gear and flight materiel in general, provided much valuable information for Chapter VI, and important advice on equipment of all kinds. Chapters VI and VII include photographs of items in his splendid collection. Col. A. Pharo Gagge, Ph.D., USAF (Ret.), of the Pierce Foundation, Yale University, was assigned to the Aero Medical Laboratory at Wright Field throughout the war, where he was involved in the development of many items of flying equipment. As the originator of pressure-breathing oxygen equipment for the Army Air Forces (AAF), his suggestions were very beneficial during preparation of Chapter II.

I especially appreciate the generous contributions of the following individuals, who furnished expert opinions, and valuable historical and technical material on a great variety of subjects: Jack Hilliard, Curator, and Vivian White and Charles Worman of the Research Division, U.S. Air Force Museum; Bill Heimdahl, Archivist, Office of Air Force History; Dr. Robert Smith, Chief Historian, USAF Logistics Command; and Kenneth Zimmerman, USAF Aerospace Medical Research Laboratory.

Particular thanks go to aviation pioneers Brig. Gen. Harold R. Harris, USAF (Ret.), Russell S. Colley, retired Goodrich engineer, and Ernest H. Schultz, Wiley Post's chief mechanic; also to several former AAF flyers who shared with me a wealth of wartime experiences: Brig. Gen. Charles E. Yeager, USAF (Ret.); Lt. Col. David Toplon, USAF (Ret.); Warren Keating; Morgan Rawlins; Carl R. Thompson; Fred Huston; W. L. Warren; and the late Brig. Gen. Benjamin S. Kelsey, USAF (Ret.).

Others who helped in diverse ways include Richard Morris, former Goodyear Aerospace Washington Representative and ex-B-17 pilot; the late David Gold, former parachute engineer and historian with Irvin Industries; David Cole, Army Center of Military History; Daniel E. O'Brien and Armando E. Franiani, Army Ordnance Museum; Leonard F. Flores, Army Natick Research and Development Center; Col. Robert Benford, M.D., USAF (Ret.); Col. Leonard W. Lilley, USAF (Ret.); Lt. Col. John Shatz, USAF (Ret.); Dr. John C. Schmitt; George A. Petersen; and Mrs. R. C. Dunn.

I want to offer special thanks to my former NASM colleagues including Dr. Von. D. Hardesty; Dr. Tom Crouch; Dr. Howard Wolko; Robert Mikesh; Paul E. Garber; Louis S. Casey; Robert B. Meyer; Robert van der Linden; Russell Lee; Rick Leyes; Sybil Descheemaeker; Dana Bell; Edward J. Pupek; Mary Pavlovich; Dale Hrabak; Alfred Bachmeier; and Carol Lockhart.

Last, but certainly not least, I want to thank my wife, Joyce, for all her efforts. Her help made the completion of this book possible.

C. G. Sweeting
Clinton, Maryland

Introduction

The fragile human body is adapted to life on the surface of the Earth, at the very bottom of our atmosphere, while the modern aircraft is designed to operate efficiently in the thin, cold, upper atmosphere. On these two facts and their interrelations hang most of the problems of aviation medicine, and the challenge to human engineering in attempting to resolve them. Today, as in the past, problems arise primarily from rapid changes to which earth-conditioned man is subjected by flight: changes in atmospheric pressure and temperature, and changes in the rate and direction of motion.[1]

The impressive recent progress in aerospace development and in solving the human problems of flight, tends to obscure the fact that very little was accomplished prior to World War II in preparing the airman to operate efficiently the modern, high-performance aircraft then entering service. By the time Pearl Harbor thrust the United States into war, there existed a great need for rapid design and production of modern combat aircraft. A lack of fundamental research applied to the human aspects of flight meant that aircraft were still designed and constructed in a way that took little note of those who were to operate them. This resulted in airmen frequently performing complex tasks under conditions which led to discomfort, inefficiency and often unnecessary danger. During the course of the war, it became increasingly evident that it was the man-machine complex that must be made into an efficient fighting element, rather than the aircraft alone.

This problem dictated three fundamental approaches: (1) a consideration of human requirements in the design of aircraft, which must include assessment of needs in the light of human limitations as well as application of those requirements in equipment; (2) selection of aircrew members on the basis of those human qualities that make for efficient combat airmen; and (3) training of aircrew members in the techniques which would enable them to survive and perform efficiently under the unusual stresses produced by high speed, high altitude, and contact with the enemy.[2] It was finally realized that emphasis on human requirements in the design of aircraft decreased proportionately the effort otherwise necessary to meet requirements for personal equipment. This concurrently increased the efficiency of the flyer.

A much closer collaboration was developed between the aeronautical engineers, who designed the planes and equipment, and the medical men and specialists, who were responsible for the maintenance of the flyer at the highest pitch of efficiency. In 1943 Brig. Gen. (later Maj. Gen.) David N. W. Grant, Air Surgeon of the U.S. Army Air Forces, stated that "In the last few years, the aero-physician has taken on the additional duties of assisting the engineers and designers. The awakening of the engineering and medical professions to the great benefits to be derived from co-operative research has brought about a new era of aviation in the United States Army."[3]

It had taken almost three decades of effort before the favorable situation described by General Grant was finally realized.

Human Engineering

THE EARLY YEARS

The first aero-medical interest in the physical well-being of the military aviator in the United States can be traced back to February 1912. That is when the U.S. Army Surgeon General, at the direction of the Secretary of War, prepared a special preliminary physical examination for candidates who were to receive instruction in the Aviation School of the Signal Corps.[1] With the exception of the purchase of weather-resistant leather flying coats and football-type helmets for head protection, the special needs of the aviator were generally unrecognized or ignored. There was also little research in the United States into the special medical or physical problems of flyers during the years before World War I.

Army and navy air medical services were established, however, more or less along parallel lines by each of the major powers in Europe. By 1914, both the Western Allies and Germany were doing much research into the problems of aircrew selection, the design of flying clothing and equipment, and other related subjects. The United States Army was almost completely unprepared for modern war when America entered the conflict in April 1917, although World War I had been in progress for over two and a half years. Fortunately, the Allies shared their knowledge, experience, and equipment when the United States became a belligerent, greatly expediting America's contribution to the war effort.

The entry of the United States in the war led to a great amount of effort being devoted to pilot-candidate selection for the rapidly expanding air arm. By July 1917, 67 examining units had been established in cities all over the country, each supervised by officers of the newly formed Air Medical Service. The improvements in the methods of pilot selection were developed as an urgent priority, because of the great number of accidents in training and active service attributed to unsuitable pilot candidates. Col. (later Brig. Gen.) Theodore C. Lyster, MC, of the Office of the Army Surgeon General, had early recognized the need for physical and mental standards for the flyer. He was assigned as the first Chief Surgeon, Aviation Section, Signal Corps, on September 6, and in that capacity guided the development of American aviation medicine during World War I. Under Brigadier General Lyster's direction, flight surgeons were assigned, as soon as they

The first type of U.S. Army flying outfit. Flying Cadet D. G. Logg posed proudly for the photographer, while in training at the Signal Corps Aviation School, North Island, San Diego, California, about 1916. Note the hard, leather football-type helmet for head protection, goggle, and brown leather flying coat worn over regular olive-drab (O.D.) wool uniform. Either russet leather riding boots or high-top service shoes and leggings, as shown here, were worn when flying. Parachutes were not worn, and in case of engine failure, the pilot was expected to guide his plane down safely to an emergency landing. (SI Photo A1376)

1

could be trained, to each flying school and air base, to look after the health and special medical problems of aviators.[2] Flight surgeons helped to markedly reduce the number of flying accidents and deaths among aviators.

The Air Medical Service was transferred, in May 1918, to a section of the Surgeon General's office assigned as part of the new Division of Military Aeronautics. This was just one of the many organizational changes which were to occur over the years, due to the Army's efforts to find the best command structure and to keep pace with changing events and circumstances.

Large quantities of special flying clothing and accessories were purchased for Army aviators during World War I. Winter flying clothing was given priority, so that training and operations could continue even in the coldest months of the year. Procurement was first made by the Committee on Supplies of the Council of National Defense, but the function was soon transferred to the Army

U.S. Army flying clothing in World War I. Crew of Handley Page 0/400 bomber built by Standard Aircraft Corp., after a crash in late 1918. Left to right: Crewman in winter flying suit of O.D. fabric, brown leather gauntlets, winter hat with combination goggle and face pad on top, and high-top service shoes; airman with brown leather flying jacket, leather winter flying helmet with fleece lining, scarf, and service shoes; man wearing leather flying jacket (note map pocket on front) over O.D. service uniform, winter flying helmet with goggle, service shoes and leather leggings; fourth man wearing same combination, except for moccasin flying boots worn over shoes and leather leggings; man in same fabric winter flying suit as number one, with winter helmet and "Resistal" goggle; last man wearing same winter flying suit and brown leather football-type protective helmet. Parachutes were not carried by airplane crewmen until after World War I. (Courtesy U.S. Army)

Quartermaster Corps. After a short time the responsibility was again reassigned, this time to the new Bureau of Aircraft Production, where it was handled by the Aviation Clothing Board established by the Army on September 17, 1917. No record has been found of any cooperation between the Aviation Clothing Board and the Air Medical Service concerning the design or suitability of flying clothing.[3]

The U.S. Army initiated its first scientific program for the study of special aero-medical subjects in October 1917, with the establishment of a Medical Research Board and a Medical Research Laboratory. This first Medical Research Laboratory, which opened officially on January 19, 1918, was located at Hazelhurst Field, Mineola, Long Island, N.Y. The first director was Col. William H. Wilmer, an ophthalmologist. The laboratory experienced the usual wartime difficulties in obtaining the necessary personnel, equipment, and facilities; but it eventually included the first decompression or low-pressure chamber in the United States where flight at high altitude could be simulated and studied. This was the beginning of the School of Aviation Medicine and much useful knowledge was gained through research during the critical months of the war. There is no doubt that this research and its practical application resulted in the saving of the lives of hundreds of American airmen.[4] The Medical Research Laboratory was the medium through which aviation medicine in all its ramifications was placed on a sound scientific basis.[5]

The laboratory at Mineola had, until 1920, devoted most of its effort to determining the various effects of flight upon aviators and to actually designing equipment to obviate those effects that proved adverse to the health, comfort, and efficiency of the flyer. The whole problem of oxygen, for use in high-altitude flight, including the amount required and the special equipment for supplying it, was a new field, and it dominated the activities of the research group virtually to the exclusion of other considerations.

The scientific study of the physical standards for flying and the selection of qualified aviators was another important contribution of the laboratory. The term "flight surgeon" was officially adopted by the laboratory on March 11, 1918, to identify those physicians assigned specifically to oversee the selection, health and well-being of flyers. On May 8, 1918, America's first three flight surgeons graduated from a new training program, which was also conducted by the research staff.

The Medical Research Laboratory was destroyed by fire in 1921, and was reorganized the following year, and redesignated as the School of Aviation Medicine (SAM). The SAM moved from Mitchel Field, Long Island, to Brooks Field, Texas, in 1926, and finally to larger quarters at Randolph Field, Texas, in 1931. During this period little attention was given to research in aviation medicine.[6] When the SAM moved to Texas, the low-pressure chamber that had been at Mineola was declared surplus and eventually relocated to the Equipment Branch of the Materiel Division at Wright Field, Ohio, where it was utilized for instrument testing. The development of aircraft and the training of pilots in the early 1920s were advancing at such a rapid pace that they demanded the full attention of all of the branches of the small postwar Air Service. The SAM became fully occupied in instructing flight surgeons and in the selection and physical care of flying personnel. With the exception of goggles, the study of personal equipment was gradually discontinued.[7]

The SAM continued to perform valuable services to the Army air arm and the medical profession through the lean years of the 1920s and 1930s, and especially during the turbulent days of World War II. Beginning in 1941, new facilities were constructed and the school began a vast expansion of its activities, including an enlarged research program under the direction of Maj. Harry G. Armstrong, MC. By the end of the war over 500 research projects had been completed, more than 4,200 medical officers graduated, and several thousand flight nurses and aero-medical technicians trained. By 1946 the School of Aviation Medicine had already embarked on its postwar mission of training jet-age medical and technical specialists, and conducting its program of research into the problems of aerospace medicine.

WRIGHT FIELD IN PEACETIME

World War I provided a momentum to aeronautical research and development that continued for several years after the Armistice. The Air Service Engineering Division at McCook Field, Dayton, Ohio, was the center for military experimentation, and significant progress was made during the early 1920s. Army engineers designed, and actually built, 27 new airplanes of all types at McCook Field between 1919 and 1922, as well as experimenting with many other types of equipment. Research activities gradually declined for lack of funds after 1923, and commercial manufacturers, guided by Air Service specifications, took over most of the work of aircraft design and construction. Limited fund appropriations were, of course, a problem shared by the entire Army.

Brig. Gen. William "Billy" Mitchell made the headlines as a flamboyant exponent of air power, and other aviators set new and impressive records, but a small nucleus of dedicated officers and civilians carried on with their vital work in aeronautical development. In 1927, with the closing of McCook Field because of its proximity to downtown Dayton, the new Materiel Division with most experimental and testing activities were consolidated at nearby Wright Field. In this location the Division also enjoyed the benefits of newly constructed facilities in place of the inadequate buildings at McCook dating from World War I.

The Air Service was reorganized and designated as the U.S. Army Air Corps in 1926, and the functions of the Air Corps were divided into three major divisions: Training, Operations, and Materiel. The Materiel Division, formerly called the Engineering Division, was established on October 15, with Brig. Gen. William E. Gillmore as Chief. It was responsible, not only for the development and procurement of aircraft, but also virtually all of the gear used by the Air Corps including engines, armament (in cooperation with the Ordnance Department), communications (in conjunction with the Signal Corps), and ground equipment.

The Equipment Branch, formerly called the Equipment Section, was assigned to the Experimental Engineering Section after the reorganization. The Aerial Photographic Unit was responsible for cameras and accessories; the Electrical Unit handled equipment for aircraft as well as beacons, lights, batteries and, during this period, heated clothing. The Instrument and Navigation Unit handled instruments for aircraft, navigation devices, and liquid and gas oxygen equipment. The Radio Unit took care of aircraft radios in conjunction with the Signal Corps, while the Administrative Unit coordinated the efforts and activities of the branch, handled reports, files, and similar duties. Most items of flight materiel were the responsibility of the Parachute and Miscellaneous Unit. These included parachutes, safety belts, flying suits, helmets, gloves, moccasins, flotation gear, and numerous other items, even tow targets, special vehicles, and equipment. Maj. Edward L. Hoffman served for many years as Chief of the Equipment Branch, providing creative leadership for the small but dedicated staff. He was personally involved with the development of parachutes, clothing, and other types of personal gear, and in 1926 was awarded the Collier Trophy for his accomplishments in parachute development. Maj. Oliver P. Echols, who was Chief of the Equipment Branch in 1928, ultimately became famous in his own right and as a major general served as Army Air Forces (AAF) Assistant Chief of Air Staff, Materiel, Maintenance and Distribution, during World War II.

Six air depots for supply and maintenance, and six procurement offices, were also operated by the Materiel Division at selected points around the country, but Wright Field became home to the laboratories, shops, and testing facilities that were to contribute so much to the technical progress of the Air Corps as well as to civil aviation.

In spite of meager budgets, new and improved aircraft, engines, and equipment were obtained in limited quantities during the 1920s, to replace obsolete and worn out World War I materiel which was becoming dangerous to fly. By the early 1930s, the performance of military aircraft had increased significantly, including higher speeds and

Pilots of a Keystone B-4A bomber of the 9th Bombardment Squadron, March Field, California, in late 1932. Lt. C. D. Shaw (left) wearing Type B-1 winter flying jacket and A-2 trousers combination, of horsehide lined with lamb shearling, Type B-3 winter helmet with earphones, Type B-6 goggle, and Type A-2 moccasins. Lt. J. D. Hutchinson wears a version of the Type B-7 full leather one-piece winter flying suit, with coney-fur gauntlets, Type B-3 helmet with U.S. Navy goggle, and A-2 moccasins. Parachutes are the Type S-1 seat pack. (Courtesy U.S. Army)

greater altitude through supercharging, heavier armament, and longer ranges for normal operations. Pilots complained of the loss of fillings in their teeth, "blacking out" during maneuvers, headaches, and nausea from breathing large amounts of carbon monoxide, inadequate oxygen equipment, and uncomfortable flying clothing and seating; little was done, however, to supply improved equipment that would resolve these problems.[8]

Testing and experimental work on flying clothing, parachutes, oxygen equipment, and other types of flying gear, continued to be conducted by personnel of the Equipment Branch. This work was based mainly on empirical grounds, usually on trial and error rather than on scientific research. The need for a research laboratory of the type operated during World War I at Mineola became increasingly clear to Maj. Malcolm C. Grow, MC, then flight surgeon of

Patterson Field, near Wright Field. He was probably the first to recognize the human element as an important factor in aircraft design, and thus to pioneer what was one of the major contributions to aviation medicine. Major Grow began performing some research work at Wright Field on his own initiative in the spring of 1933, in addition to his regularly assigned medical duties at Patterson Field. Equipped only with a desk and no laboratory facilities, he worked on the problems of flying clothing, and prepared a monograph on carbon monoxide and internal combustion engines. Among recommendations by Grow that were adopted by the Equipment Branch, was the design of flying trousers of the ski pants type with tight cuffs in place of the old tapered garments. Grow was transferred in 1934 to the Office of the Chief of the Air Corps in Washington, D.C. as Chief of the Medical Section. In that position he was able to convince Air Corps officials of the necessity of continued research, and the importance of a laboratory for the study of the effects of high-performance and high-altitude flight on the human organism, and other related subjects.

Capt. Harry G. Armstrong, MC, a young flight surgeon with a personal interest in improving flying clothing and equipment, was assigned to the Equipment Branch of the Engineering Section at Wright Field on September 16, 1934, for the purpose of assisting in the improvement of flight gear for aviators. After studying the magnitude of the problem for a few months, he developed a proposal for the establishment of a much-needed physiological laboratory to provide formalized medical research in support of Engineering Section activities. The laboratory plan was approved by the Chief of the Air Corps who issued a directive on May 29, 1935, establishing the Physiological Research Laboratory. Thus began Armstrong's long and productive association with what was to become the Aero Medical Laboratory (AML), the facility that played such an important role during and since World War II.[9]

Armstrong's own contributions in the field of research during the following years were to add a new dimension to aviation medicine, which ultimately made him stand without peer in the field.[10] It should be noted that Grow, and co-founder Armstrong, in keeping with the concept of the interrelationship of man and airplane, placed the Physiological Research Laboratory in the "hardware department" of the Engineering Section of the Materiel Division.[11]

Among the important problems under study from the mid-1930s, none was more important, or more complex, than the requirements of high-altitude flight. These included the development of the pressurized-aircraft cabin, and a modern oxygen mask and system, for use by crewmen of the new fighters and bombers with supercharged engines then entering service. The Aero Medical Laboratory was eminently qualified for this type of research,

but it would be several years before full responsibility for developing oxygen equipment was transferred to the AML.

Armstrong frequently utilized the old Air Service low-pressure chamber, in the course of his high-altitude research. This chamber was originally at Mineola, and had been reactivated in Building 16 at Wright Field. It had mostly been used by the engineers for testing aircraft instruments; an exceptional use was the testing of Wiley Post's pressure suits in 1934. The following year a larger and more elaborate low-pressure, or altitude, chamber was installed in Building 16, and it became one of the most important tools used by personnel of the new Physiological Research Laboratory.

The effects of the Great Depression in the early 1930s, as well as the needs of the ground forces and Navy, caused restrictions in Air Corps appropriations. This situation improved somewhat during the next few years, partly as a result of the recommendations of the Baker Board, which was established in the wake of the controversy caused by the poor performance of the Air Corps while temporarily flying the airmail.

The organization of the Materiel Division changed gradually, and by 1934 the Engineering Section was divided into eight branches: Aircraft, Power Plant, Armament, Equipment, Materials, Repair, Specifications, and Drafting and Records. An Engineering Procurement Branch was added the following year. A total of 454 civilians were working in the Engineering Section at the end of January 1935. Sixty of them were working in the Equipment Branch; of these eight were working in the Parachute Unit and only seven in the Miscellaneous Equipment Unit, which had responsibility for almost all types of flying clothing and accessories.[12] Much time and effort during this period was devoted to the development of an improved winter flying suit, resulting in the introduction of the sheep-shearling outfits beginning in 1934. The Equipment Branch was responsible in the mid-1930s for research, development, and standardization of 500 items of air and ground equipment. By the end of 1936, the Equipment Branch under Maj. F. S. Borum consisted of the following main units, often referred to as laboratories: Instrument and Navigation; Electrical; Parachute and Clothing; Aerial Photographic; Miscellaneous Equipment; and Physiological Research. The Equipment Branch was assigned to the Engineering Section, directed by Lt. Col. Oliver P. Echols, who reported to Brig. Gen. A. W. Robins, Chief of the Materiel Division.

It should be noted that during the early years much of the flying clothing and personal equipment used by aviators consisted of commercial products. Items were often made for the Army air arm at their request, but they were usually designed by civilian manufacturing companies. From the mid-1920s, the Army began to standardize all types of aeronautical equipment, including flight materiel, and procure items made in accordance with Army specifications. Pressing requirements sometimes necessitated the purchase of substitute or non-standard items, however, especially during wartime. The urgency of increased production and easier distribution in wartime was one of the primary reasons for the establishment of the Army-Navy "AN" standardization program of World War II.

Many commercial companies had modern laboratories and workshops for performing research and development in connection with aeronautical equipment. Most of the prototype or experimental pieces of personal gear under study at the Equipment Branch during the 1930s were actually constructed by the commercial companies that specialized in manufacturing these types of items. These included both original designs and items made in accordance with Air Corps specifications. If the prototype passed the laboratory tests, a small quantity of a design was procured for field or service tests. Any changes or modifications recommended as a result of testing were then made, and the standardized design was placed in production by the contractor, when funds were available. This system had changed by the middle of World War II, and many prototype or experimental items of personal equipment for aviators were made in the shops of the Personal Equipment Laboratory, the Aero Medical Laboratory, or some other branch of the Engineering Division. After successful laboratory testing, a limited quantity was ordered from an appropriate manufacturer for service testing, and the item as finally approved was then authorized for procurement and placed in production by one or more contractors in their factories. (Pressure suits were among the exceptions to this procedure.) Wright Field authorities continued to monitor the performance of the item in the field to insure satisfactory service and compliance with specifications, and recommend any necessary modifications suggested by experience.

The Materiel Division was also responsible for operating the Air Corps Engineering School, which graduated many of the officers who were to play such an important role in the conduct and equipment of future wars, and the development of the U.S. Air Force. The entire Wright Field organization was an important military and civilian training activity, however, and it is no exaggeration to say that Wright Field professionals guided the technical development that provided the great quantities of superior equipment that helped win World War II.

Wright Field, as the home of the Materiel Division, was always even in peacetime a busy base, with many fascinating activities in progress. Visitors might, on any given day, have found several new and experimental aircraft in the hangars, on the flight line, or undergoing flight testing high above the 4,600 acre installation. Perhaps they would have observed parachutists descending during testing of an experimental chute design. Engines would be roaring on test stands in various research buildings, and propellers, guns, radios, navigation instruments, and other complex items of equipment would have been involved in experiments in the wind tunnels and other facilities of the Engineering Section. A tour of the laboratories would have revealed many busy scenes: a civilian technician behind the control panel of a giant high-speed wind tunnel directing a man-made tornado; frost-covered men, bundled up in winter flying clothing, sitting in a test chamber that simulated the thin air and 50-below-zero temperatures at 40,000-feet altitude; woodcraftsmen carefully putting the finishing touches on detailed models of new planes; specialists adjusting the fine internal mechanisms of gun or bomb sights with a watchmaker's care; and engineers directing the loading of thousands of pounds of lead on the wings of a combat plane until ribs and spars crumpled and snapped.

Test pilots and other Wright Field personnel also participated in the making and breaking of many important records for speed, altitude and distance. New speed records were always exciting, but the major efforts went into long-distance and endurance flights. America's vast distances required long-range aircraft before military and civilian aviation could truly come of age. The experience gained in long flights also helped establish the requirements for clothing and personal equipment so important to the health, comfort, and efficiency of the aviator.

Shortly after war in Europe began in September 1939, Wright Field commenced its transformation into the elaborate air base and technical development center, which would continue to grow at a phenomenal rate during World War II. However, an investigating board in 1939 found "an appalling lack of qualified personnel . . . particularly in key positions." Another study at the same time described the "pitifully inadequate" technical staff then available in the Materiel Division. To correct this situation an aggressive program was launched to recruit a vastly larger professional staff.[13] Many of the new engineers and technicians that were hired were long on enthusiasm but short on experience. Some, however, were already experts in their own right, and brought to their new jobs a wealth of talent that considerably aided the Materiel Division in accomplishing its growing mission. Joining the experienced cadre at Wright Field, there was soon a remarkable team in place for the great wartime effort which was soon to come.

The specialists at Wright Field directly concerned with research and development of personal equipment and clothing, were learning to cooperate more effectively to produce improved items of flight materiel. The units of the Engineering Section of the Materiel Division were assigned to six technical laboratories. This arrangement was formalized on February 10, 1939, with the official establishment of the following major laboratories: Aircraft, Power Plant, Armament, Equipment, Signal, and Mate-

The introduction in the mid-1930s of modern aircraft, with closed, heated cabins allowed more extensive use of lighter-weight flying clothing. Pvt. Edward F. Kayser of the Station Company, Mitchel Field, Long Island, N.Y., is shown here in front of a Martin B-10B bomber in August 1936. He is wearing a Type A-3 summer flying suit of O.D. cotton and probably a Type A-4 summer flying helmet of cape leather, with earphones. His parachute is the widely-used Type S-1 seat pack. (Courtesy USAF)

rials. The Equipment Laboratory included the Aero Medical Research Unit (as it was then called) under Capt. Harry Armstrong; the Miscellaneous Equipment Unit under Maj. Rudolph Fink, in charge of breathing oxygen and ground support equipment; the Parachute Unit; and the Clothing Unit under Paul Manson, who was responsible for development of all flying clothing and some types of personal equipment. The Equipment Lab. was sometimes called the "Gingerbread Department."

Although Captain Armstrong began work on the Physiological Research Laboratory in September 1934, it was not established until 1935, and not officially completed until January 1, 1937. The laboratory was originally located in the basement of Building 16, the main engineering experimental laboratory building at Wright Field. Armstrong's first assistant was Sgt. Lloyd Stevens, a medical technician, assigned in 1935. The crowded basement lab-

oratory eventually included a massive low-pressure chamber and other scientific equipment. A centrifugal force laboratory was established in the balloon hangar in 1936. With this equipment, Armstrong was able to conduct research into anoxia, and undertake the first studies in the United States on the effects of acceleration on human beings in a centrifuge. In addition to the initial experiments on the effects of gravity, or G-forces, the laboratory also assisted in the development of the pressurized aircraft

Air Corps fighter pilot in winter flying outfit, late 1940. He is wearing the bulky Type B-3 winter jacket and A-3 trousers combination, made of sheep shearling. The shearling outfit in this photo is still in the "raw," however, by 1941 most shearling garments were finished with the brown Korsseal waterproofing treatment, introduced in the late 1930s. Other items of flight materiel include a Type B-5 shearling winter helmet, B-6 goggle and A-8 oxygen mask, also A-9 gloves and A-6 flying shoes, both of shearling. The seat-type parachute is the Type S-1 with harness equipped with bayonet-type fasteners. The Curtiss P-40B fighter is the fifty-first aircraft assigned to the 35th Pursuit Squadron (Fighter), 8th Pursuit Group, Langley Field, Virginia. (Rudy Arnold Collection, NASM)

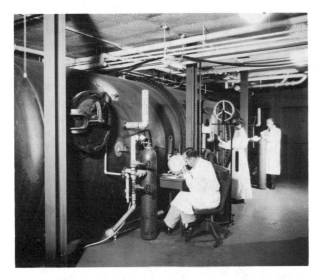

Capt. Harry G. Armstrong, Chief of the Physiological Research Laboratory (left), S/Sgt. Lloyd Stevens, laboratory technician (center), and Dr. John W. Heim, physiologist (right), performing research in the new high-altitude chamber located in the basement of Building 16, Wright Field, December 1938. The low pressure encountered at any desired altitude up to 80,000 feet could be simulated in this chamber, and it could be refrigerated to −65° F. Subjects participating in medical experiments, or testing new types of oxygen equipment or clothing, inside the three-compartment chamber, remained in communication by telephone and were viewed through portholes. (Courtesy USAF)

cabin, which resulted in the successful flights of the Lockheed XC-35, for which the Air Corps was awarded the Collier Trophy in 1938.

Captain Armstrong and his small staff had already brought the laboratory world-wide eminence by the late 1930s. Armstrong then moved to the School of Aviation Medicine in Texas where, under the sponsorship of Brig. Gen. David N. W. Grant, he developed a comparable research and training facility to meet the expanding medical research requirements of the national defense program. Armstrong was succeeded as director of the Aero Medical Research Unit, later named the Aero Medical Laboratory (AML), by Capt. Otis O. Benson, Jr. in September 1940. As war drew nearer, plans for expansion of the laboratory were accelerated. The plans included a new laboratory building and an increase in personnel that eventually comprised an impressive staff of specialists. Among those joining the staff before America entered the war were Dr. John W. Heim, who began work in 1936, Pvt. Raymond Whitney in 1937, Dr. Ernest Pinson and Mr. John Hall in 1939, and Sgt. Harold Lichty in 1940. Dr. Bruce Dill, Dr. A. Pharo Gagge, and Mr. Steve S. Horvath arrived in 1941.

Thus by the time America entered World War II, there was a systematic aero-medical research program that was separate and distinct from the traditional clinical research activities of the medical profession. During the war, the program's theoretical and applied research efforts resulted in such developments as improved oxygen equipment, electrically heated flying clothing, anti-G garments, body armor, the ejection seat, and in pressurized-cabin aircraft. The AML was also responsible for such innovations as the first aerosol "bomb" for the dispersal of insecticides. Clinical research, especially at the School of Aviation Medicine, continued to be concerned with the development of physically and mentally fit flyers.[14]

WRIGHT FIELD AT WAR

The events of Sunday, December 7, 1941, were as shocking to the personnel at Wright Field as they were to the rest of the American public. Military and civilian employees reported immediately to their duty sections and, during the chaotic months following Pearl Harbor, the staff worked day and night to handle the staggering burden of work confronting the Materiel Division. The procurement activity alone was a prodigious task, which soon saw the ever-growing staff working in hallways and in every other available space. Thousands of contracts, including those for clothing and personal equipment, threatened at first to swamp the available manpower. The tremendous growth in the size and responsibilities of the Materiel Division caused many problems in training, space allocation, coordination, and operations during the war years.

The Materiel Division underwent numerous organizational changes as a result of the increase in activities and requirements, necessitated by the great expansion of the Army Air Corps—from June 20, 1941, included in the Army Air Forces (AAF). In 1939, Gen. Henry H. Arnold, Chief of the Air Corps, in anticipation of greatly increased aircraft procurement, directed that a Production Engineering Section be established in the Materiel Division. The remainder of the Engineering Section became the Experimental Engineering Section from August 1939 until October 1942, when it became the Engineering Division under Brig. Gen. Franklin O. Carroll. In recognition of its increased importance, the Aero Medical Research Unit, under Colonel Benson, was removed from the Equipment Laboratory on July 1, 1942, and reorganized as an independent laboratory. It was renamed the Aero Medical Research Laboratory in March, and the Aero Medical Laboratory in December, 1942.

The AAF underwent a series of complicated reorganizations in the months following Pearl Harbor, which had an important, if indirect, bearing on the development of personal equipment for aviators. The Materiel Division became the Materiel Command (MC) in the War Department reorganization of March 1942, with its commanding gen-

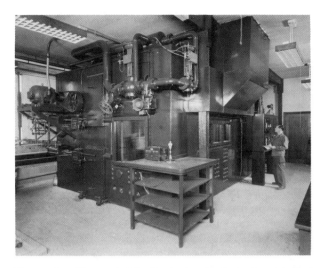

The small, refrigerated high-altitude chamber in the Aero Medical Laboratory, ready for another experiment on October 10, 1944. This facility was used extensively for research, development, and testing of aviator clothing, pressure equipment, oxygen gear, and other items of flight materiel. (Courtesy USAF)

eral moved to Washington, D.C. The Wright Field organization under Brig. Gen. Arthur W. Vanaman became the Materiel Center until March 1943, when it again became the Materiel Command under Maj. Gen. Charles E. Branshaw.

In early 1943, the Materiel Command had three separate operating components: the Engineering Division, Procurement Division, and Production Division. An Inspection Division was added later that year. Divisions were divided into sections, the sections split up into laboratories, and further subdivided into branches and units. The section was a self-contained operating group with its own manager, offices, foremen and workers, and shops where the work was carried out. The duties of the Materiel Command and its respective divisions and sections were administrative and technical. The administrative sections handled the necessary paper work, including the Technical Data Section with its vast files of information. The technical sections ran the machinery and turned out the product—the best possible warplane and all of the equipment and accessories to go with it. The number of civilian employees at Wright Field had grown to more than 10,000 by mid-1943, and this figure was rapidly increasing.[15] The Air Service Command (ASC) had been established in 1941, to issue aircraft to units and maintain them in the field. In September 1944, Materiel Command merged with the Air Service Command to form the Air Technical Service Command (ATSC), under the direction of Lt. Gen. William S. Knudsen.

The Engineering Division of ATSC, already looking towards the jet age by 1945, was essentially a collection of nine aeronautical and five electronic laboratories. All were located at Wright Field except the Watson Electronic Laboratories at Eatontown, New Jersey. The Engineering Division organization included important installations, and liaison offices for cooperation with other government and nonmilitary research agencies in several states and Alaska. Of the many subdivisions of the Engineering Division in 1945, the one of most interest to the history of flight materiel is the Aircraft and Physical Requirements Section, under Col. Paul H. Kemmer, which contained the Aircraft, Aero Medical, Materials, and Personal Equipment Laboratories.

Personal Equipment Problems

Some improvements and modifications in flying equipment had already been recommended to the Materiel Division, as a result of experience gained by the European powers since the outbreak of hostilities in 1939. But as the tempo of the war increased after Pearl Harbor, and AAF operations expanded around the world, an increasing number of complaints and unsatisfactory reports were received concerning the suitability of many standard items of flying clothing and personal equipment. The shearling winter flying clothing, in particular, was reported to be too bulky, stiff, and cumbersome, and it did not allow easy access for tending the wounds of injured airmen. Electrically heated clothing was undependable due to frequent breakage of the wires, and flying shoes and gloves were proving unsatisfactory, resulting in frostbite. Oxygen equipment was said to be inefficient. Better survival gear was urgently needed by flyers who were in action over the Arctic, the jungle, the deserts, and the wide expanses of the oceans.

The Wright Field engineers and specialists responsible for developing flight materiel wanted the latest and best items of clothing and personal equipment, procured as soon as possible for issue to the units in combat. Problems of a complex nature sometimes caused delays in addition to lead time, however, exacerbated by the frequent shortages of materials, trained workers and manufacturing capacity. The supply and maintenance people in the Air Service Command (ASC) had, for example, to satisfy the growing demand for quantities of personal equipment for the tactical units, and at the same time they had to resist the introduction of too many models, if they hoped to simplify maintenance and training, as well as provide up-to-date technical orders and instruction manuals for the equipment they sent out. To attain these ends, ASC sometimes refused to order a newly developed item or asked for it only in small quantities. This was not

only uneconomical, but also lowered the morale and efficiency of combat personnel. It also caused frustration among the engineers and specialists at Wright Field who had worked so hard to develop the new and improved items.[16]

The small staffs responsible for the development of personal equipment were augmented to cope with the increasing workload and urgent wartime demands, but it took time to train new personnel, obtain equipment, perform the necessary research, and service-test and standardize new and improved designs. By the summer of 1942, flying clothing had become such a subject of controversy that special consultants such as Bradford Washburn, noted authority on the Arctic, were called in, and an investigation was conducted that resulted in a reorganization and several changes in personnel. Progress was being made on a wide variety of projects, but the lead time from drawing board to operational use often seemed agonizingly slow.

Gen. Hap Arnold accompanied by (then) Col. Malcolm Grow, surgeon of the Eighth Air Force, made an inspection tour of AAF units in England in the fall of 1943, including a visit to the U.S. Army General Hospital at Oxford. General Arnold was deeply moved by the sight of so many frostbite casualties, attributed to the failure of the electrically heated garments, such as the Type F-1 suit, and other inadequate items including the sheep-shearling clothing. He issued a direct order to Maj. Gen. Charles E. Branshaw, Commanding General, Materiel Command, to place all clothing development temporarily under his personal supervision. Lt. Col. A. Pharo Gagge of the Aero Medical Laboratory was appointed acting chief of the reorganized Clothing Branch. The development of improved electrically heated clothing and the new multilayer, fabric, winter and intermediate flying suits was given high priority. During this period of intensive effort, closer cooperation with other Army branches, agencies, and services was initiated, but the earlier overtures by the Quartermaster Corps to acquire responsibility for flying clothing continued to be opposed. This position was based on the belief that the AAF could best satisfy its own special requirements for flying clothing, and was in accordance with the continuing policy of seeking self-determination for the Army Air Forces.

The AAF armada was growing, and combat missions over Europe sometimes involved more than a thousand bombers plus several hundred supporting fighters and reconnaissance aircraft. Air warfare on that scale, under the severe conditions found at 25,000 feet in the wintry skys over Europe, placed significant pressure on the personnel and facilities at Wright Field to provide the technology for improved human performance and protection.

In January 1944, Lieutenant Colonel Gagge was sent to England to demonstrate a wide variety of newly developed items of flying clothing to Brigadier General Grow and others at Headquarters, Eighth Air Force. These included prototypes of the multilayer Type B-10 jacket and A-9 trousers, with the new gabardine outer shell and wool pile inner layer, and the newly designed and tested Type F-3 electrically heated flying outfit. Operational flight tests of these new garments were made by the Eighth Air Force Central Medical Establishment, first organized in the fall of 1942 by (then) Col. Harry G. Armstrong.

It was during this visit that Gagge observed that the number of AAF bombers going out on a combat mission was determined more by the amount of adequate clothing available than by any other factor.[17]

General Arnold attempted to solve the continuing clothing problem in the same manner as he had many other critical operational deficiencies. In February 1944 he assigned Col. John P. Fraim, one of his special troubleshooters, to Wright Field as coordinator of flying-clothing development, procurement, and production. In the spring of 1944, clothing and personal equipment development was incorporated into the newly organized Personal Equipment Laboratory (PEL) under Col. Millard Haskins. Colonel Fraim was later assigned as coordinator of all procurement and production of personal equipment for aviators at nearby Patterson Field. During the transition, the Aero Medical Laboratory, which had officially relocated its headquarters to the new Building 29 on January 1, 1943, continued its mission of investigating the effects of flight on man and all medical problems associated with AAF materiel. The AML retained a joint responsibility for altitude chamber, all-weather chamber, and flight-testing of all flying clothing in development by the PEL, along with its continuing responsibility for the development of oxygen equipment, and anti-G garments used by fighter pilots. (Early in 1943 the AML's new human centrifuge for the study of acceleration and the development of anti-G devices became operational.) With its capable personnel and special equipment, the AML also contributed significantly to other programs, including the development of improved electrically heated clothing, which helped to eliminate frostbite as a major health hazard among flyers.

When Col. Otis O. Benson, Jr. was assigned overseas in April 1943, as surgeon of the newly organized Fifteenth Air Force, he was succeeded as Chief of the Aero Medical Laboratory by Lt. Col. W. Randolph Lovelace II, who performed outstanding service in that position through the remainder of the war. Throughout the war years, there was close collaboration between the Clothing Branch and the Aero Medical Laboratory, first in 1941 under Paul Manson of the Branch, and later under Maj. F. E. Miller and Donald Huxley. Lovelace, who had a wide range of experience in early civil aviation, was pragmatic and direct at getting action and solutions. He personally tried out all individual flying equipment in flight whenever possible. He was also responsible for establishing closer cooperation and rapid lines of communication between the AML branches; Administration, Medical Detachment, Medical Specialty, Oxygen, Biophysics, Physiology, and Services Liaison. At that time the staff included 46 officers, 82 enlisted men and 73 civilians. A Psychology Branch was added in 1945.[18]

Mention should also be made of the Army Air Forces Board, which operated with the AAF Tactical Center at Orlando, Florida. Also called the Combat Laboratory, the AAF Board conducted tactical research and experimentation to determine military requirements. In addition to developing improved tactics and operational techniques, the Board evaluated the operational suitability of aircraft, and performed tests on equipment, such as oxygen masks, radios, weapons, and rations under combat conditions. The AAF Board frequently utilized the personnel and facilities of the Proving Ground Command at Eglin Field, Florida, and its Cold Weather Testing Detachment at Ladd Field, Alaska. Close liaison and cooperation with all of the service organizations and activities became an important function of the testing organizations, including the new Personal Equipment Laboratory.

The Personal Equipment Laboratory

April 13, 1944, is an important day in the history of flight materiel in World War II. On that day, the Personal Equipment Laboratory (PEL), under the direction of Col. Millard

The large, low-pressure cold chamber in Building 29, Aero Medical Laboratory, Wright Field, in November 1943. Often called the high-altitude chamber, it was used for a great variety of research projects dealing with anoxia and aeroembolism, as well as experiments that led to the development of improved oxygen equipment, pressure suits, flying clothing, and accessories. This chamber could accommodate up to sixteen fully equipped airmen, and could simulate the reduced air pressure at 80,000 feet and a temperature of −85° F. These men are dressed in Type B-3 shearling winter flying jackets, A-3 trousers, A-6 flying shoes, and B-6 helmets. All are wearing Type A-14 demand-oxygen masks connected to Type A-12 diluter-demand regulators. Note the portable oxygen unit for emergency use under the seat at right. Chambers similar to this were used at various bases for instructing flyers as part of the Altitude Training Program. A large, low-pressure chamber was located at Randolph Field, Texas, and used by personnel of the School of Aviation Medicine for indoctrination and research in aero-medical subjects, including the neurologic and psychiatric factors involved in operational or combat fatigue among flyers. (Courtesy USAF)

Personnel of the Materiel Division participated in numerous scientific experiments, including many of a dangerous nature. Some laboratory and flight tests were in the interest of basic research, while others were vital to the successful development of new items of flight materiel. This photo, dated August 22, 1944, shows Lt. Col. W. Randolph Lovelace II, Chief of the Aero Medical Laboratory, during an explosive-decompression experiment in the altitude chamber. He is wearing a Type A-14 demand-oxygen mask while seated in the special cabin utilized in the tests. (Courtesy USAF)

and the RCAF Aeromedical Group at Downsview, Toronto, Canada, the RAF Institute of Aviation Medicine at Farnborough, England, and the newly formed Eighth Air Force Central Medical Establishment at High Wycombe, England, under Col. Harry Armstrong. There were continuous interchanges of AML personnel with these groups and operating air forces throughout the war. The exchange of technical and test information was rapid and rarely burdened by red tape. Lovelace reorganized the AML in September 1943, and expanded it to seven

Haskins, was officially organized within the Engineering Division of the Materiel Command at Wright Field.

The PEL incorporated the Clothing Branch and other branches responsible for personal equipment. The staff of the Laboratory must be given credit for the successful development of much of the improved flying clothing and equipment during the last years of the war. They performed an outstanding job of research and development, resulting in many new and innovative designs, which continued in use for many years after the end of the conflict. It should be noted, however, that the work of the PEL included many on-going projects that were initiated long before the laboratory was established.

The director of the Personal Equipment Laboratory reported to the chief of the Aircraft and Physical Requirements Section. To accomplish its vital work, the Laboratory was initially organized into six branches: Emergency Rescue, Clothing, Service Liaison, Administrative, Miscellaneous Equipment, and Parachute. By the fall of 1944 Col. W. C. Warner had replaced Colonel Haskins as director, and by the end of the war the organization of the PEL had been revised again in the interest of increased effi-

The new all-weather room in the basement of Building 29, Aero Medical Laboratory, was used frequently to test flying clothing and personal equipment under all types of climatic conditions. In this 1944 photo, a group of volunteers breathing oxygen, are testing various items of winter flying clothing and equipment, at the low temperatures normally encountered at high altitude. Hail, snow, heat, wind, and sand storms could be simulated, and it was also possible to create humid conditions and rainstorms of varying intensity. (Courtesy USAF)

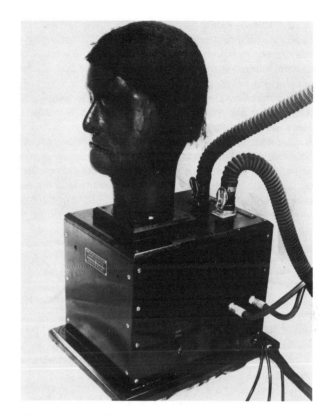

ciency. The new organization included three engineering branches; Parachute, Clothing, and Rescue and Survival, and three service branches; Administrative, Service Liaison, and Test Coordination.[19]

A full program of research in human engineering could be implemented within the Materiel Command, once the Personal Equipment Laboratory and the Aero Medical Laboratory were operative. The staffs of both laboratories worked in close cooperation, utilizing the modern scientific facilities of the AML to expedite the research and development of improved flying clothing and personal gear. This was accomplished in conjunction with engineers and specialists from other branches of the Engineering Division working towards functional improvement in the design of aircraft cockpits, controls, turrets, gun and bomb sights, and other important items of equipment. Facilities in the AML of particular value in the development of clothing and personal equipment, included the all-weather room and the refrigerated altitude chamber. In these chambers it was possible to reproduce any climatic condition existing on the ground or in the air anywhere in the world. Many natural conditions could be studied in the climatic chambers, including the effects on clothing and flying gear of heat, cold, sun, rain, humidity, fungus, sand, dust, salt, and fog.

Work in the PEL also continued on a wide variety of basic projects, including the substitution of less critical materials, such as rayon and nylon, for the silk used in parachute canopies. Progress in parachute design included a modified harness with a quick-release box. Emergency kits featured improvement of specific articles of survival and signalling gear, and there was a consolidation and consequent reduction in the number of kits.[20]

There were many special items of laboratory equipment utilized by personnel of the PEL and AML; one of the most interesting was the "thermal man" or "copper man." Originally constructed by the General Electric Company for use in testing electrically heated clothing, this device was shaped like an average man, five-feet, ten-and-one-half inches tall. It had a copper skin one-sixteenth-of-an-inch thick, consisting of fifteen parts or areas, each with separate heat controls. A complicated system of electric wires connected the separate areas of the copper head, torso, hands, and feet to reproduce the temperature variations that occur in different parts of the human body. The temperature of the thermal man could be made to vary from subnormal to above normal. A dummy head was provided to "breathe" air with a controllable moisture content. Thus, it was possible to determine what clothing was adequate under specific controlled conditions, without subjecting human beings to long, tedious periods in high-altitude or refrigerated test chambers, under uncomfortable or even dangerous conditions. By eliminating the human variable, the testing of various articles of clothing

"Horace the Head" was a research device, made late in World War II by the General Electric Company for use by the Aero Medical Laboratory. This model of a man's head could "breathe," run a "fever," and even smoke a cigarette. It was used in a series of tests, to determine performance characteristics of new types of headgear and oxygen equipment, during simulated trips to the substratosphere. Horace could reproduce the temperature and humidity of human breath, while tolerating conditions in the high-altitude cold chamber beyond anything a man could endure. The replica of a head was built around a semi-rigid shell covered with sponge rubber and a thin latex "skin." Veins were represented by tiny electric heating wires, for warming the rubber skin to the temperature of human skin, in the bitter cold encountered at high altitude. An automatic "lung" operated through a series of cams could make Horace inhale, exhale, and even pant and gasp. The breathing was accomplished by a bellows located in a separate cabinet outside the chamber, and could be measured scientifically at any altitude up to 70,000 feet and under a variety of atmospheric conditions. (Courtesy USAF)

and other personal equipment could be conducted more accurately and systematically, and in a much shorter period of time.[21]

The insulative qualities of fabrics and complete items of clothing were of great importance in developing improved garments for aviators. The amount of insulation provided by an item was measured in "clo" units. One clo is the insulation necessary to maintain comfort under the following conditions: an ambient temperature of 70°F;

relative humidity of less than 30 percent; air movement at a rate of 20 feet per minute; and a metabolic rate of 50 calories per square meter of surface. In addition to the thermal man, a "clometer" was developed for use in testing clothing.

Personal equipment and clothing received final laboratory tests under simulated flight conditions in the low-pressure chamber at the Aero Medical Laboratory. But some tests involved conditions that were difficult or impossible to duplicate on the ground, and required actual flight testing aboard an aircraft. These conditions included engine noise, vibration, air turbulence, extreme changes in temperature within short intervals of time, centrifugal force, glare, wind, movement in a limited space, emotional stress, and nervous fatigue.

In order to carry out such flight tests on a systematic basis, a Boeing B-17E bomber was obtained by the Engineering Division in September 1943 for extensive use in testing of clothing and equipment with personnel at crew positions. The plane had previously been used by the Boeing Aircraft Company for its high-altitude test flights, and could reach altitudes of 43,000 feet. The name "Nemesis of Aeroembolism" was painted on the nose, as a reminder of the many important experiments with oxygen equipment and the problems of high-altitude flight. Personal equipment and clothing used by fighter pilots was tested aboard fighter aircraft, including a Lockheed P-38 specially modified into a two-place configuration.[22]

All items of clothing and equipment were given a type designation number and systematically recorded on "Type Designation Sheets." These forms were maintained by the Materiel Division from the mid-1920s, when the standardization system was begun, until the early 1950s when card forms were introduced. The Type Sheets constitute a valuable record of when different types of garments and other items of aeronautical equipment peculiar to Army aviation were tested, standardized for use, listed as substitute or limited standard, and finally declared obsolete. In practice, the stock of an item was usually exhausted long before it was finally listed officially as obsolete. However, some individuals continued to use obsolete gear, particularly clothing items, because of personal preference. In other cases, the item was standardized for use, but never procured. The Type Designation Sheets also indicated the specification and drawing number for each item.[23]

Most items of flying clothing were classified as either "summer" or "winter." Summer flying clothing was originally given type numbers in the "A" series, and most winter garments were assigned "B" series numbers. The type A-2 summer flying jacket and the Type B-2 winter flying jacket are examples. There were exceptions; winter flying shoes for instance, were given numbers in the "A" series, probably because there were no standard summer

flying shoes when shoes were first assigned type numbers in the 1920s. In addition, the official nomenclature for many items changed over the years.

The worldwide deployment of the AAF after Pearl Harbor meant that the limited variety of clothing available soon became inadequate to provide proper protection under all kinds of climatic and operational conditions. Some of the new types of items developed did not fit properly under the old nomenclature and categories, so a revised system of type designations was introduced. Effective October 26, 1944, all assignments of type designations in the Personal Equipment Laboratory were changed to comply with the new program of flying clothing development, which classified garments by the "temperature zone" for which they were best suited. The new designations were as follows:

Type K—very light garment (86° to 122°F, 30° to 50°C)
Type L—light garment (50° to 86°F, 10° to 30°C)
Type M—intermediate garment (14° to 50°F, −10° to 10°C)
Type N—heavy garment (−22° to 14°F, −30° to −10°C)
Type P—very heavy garment (−58° to −22°F, −50° to −30°C)
Type Q—electrically heated garment (−58° to −22°F, −50° to −30°C)

This system proved to be very practical and remained in use for many years after the establishment of the U.S. Air Force.

HUMAN ENGINEERING COMES OF AGE

Hardship was always believed to be an inescapable part of a soldier's life, but Army Air Forces planners realized during World War II that discomfort lowered the airman's efficiency and often adversely affected his health. It was agreed that every effort should be made to eliminate physical hardship where possible, but this was often easier said than done. The increasing performance and complexity of modern aircraft would have made conditions for the airman impossible, without the efforts of the many engineers, scientists, and medical specialists working in the field of human engineering.

Most of the improvements in aircraft and equipment and much of the advantage offered by mass production were wasted when the devices overtaxed the capacities of men. Man had become the weak link in the man-machine partnership by World War II, and without assistance, would have been the limiting factor in the future development of aircraft. It was recognized that two methods of seeking improved operating efficiency were possible. The more fundamental approach was to improve the design of the equipment so that the machine fit the man, and so the effects of pilot stature on aircraft design and performance were studied at the Physiological Research Laboratory as early as 1935. The second approach was to fit the man to the machine by development of improved operating procedures, training methods, and classification devices. The techniques developed during World War II for dealing with these vital problems lead to improved aviator efficiency in the increasingly complex technological environment of the postwar world.

The concept of human engineering that evolved during World War II included the full range of applications and not just those appropriate for personal equipment, flying clothing, and accessories. The human problems which had to be overcome for the efficient operation of modern, high-performance aircraft stemmed from the following facts: (1) Man in flight is differentiated from man on the ground because of the effects of lowered barometric pressure and temperature on the body. (2) Aircraft flying at speeds of nearly 1,000 feet per second had to be controlled by a body, some of whose reflex reactions required a fifth of a second—time for the aircraft to travel about 200 feet. (3) The centrifugal accelerations encountered, even in a heavy bomber, might transiently impose upon the body a force equal for a moment to twice that of gravity, so that a man weighed, with full equipment, 400 pounds instead of 200 pounds.[24]

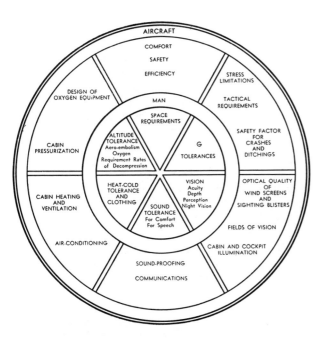

Human factors in aircraft design. (From Mae Mills Link and Hubert A. Coleman, Medical Support of the Army Air Forces in World War II, Office of the Surgeon General, USAF, Washington, D.C., 1955)

The importance of solving the problems of the airman in World War II can be better appreciated, in this much more technical age, by considering the difficulties encountered by a pilot of a Boeing B-17 bomber, a relatively simple aircraft in comparison to those that succeeded it. The efficient operation of all of the controls and instruments, in those days before automation, would have been difficult in the optimum comfort of an air-conditioned office. The difficulty was multiplied when the "office" was a cockpit about the equivalent of a five-foot cube. It would be engulfed in the roar of four 1,200 horsepower reciprocating engines, its height above the ground was often four or five miles, the atmospheric pressure was reduced by one-half to two-thirds and the outside temperature was 40 or even 50 degrees below zero. There were also the threats of frostbite, airsickness, and the possibility that the aircraft, or equipment such as the oxygen gear, could malfunction at any time. The stresses of air combat and antiaircraft fire were additional factors with which the airman had to contend. The maintenance of the mental and physical efficiency of the flyer in the face of continual stresses and strains was confirmed as a vital task of aviation physiology and human engineering. In 1943, Brig. Gen. David N. W. Grant, the Air Surgeon, stated that . . . "The solution is to select and train the individuals best fitted for this trying duty and to then provide them with devices, methods and training to assist them and protect them against their limitations."[25]

The AAF did everything practicable within the state of the art at that time to pick the best people for flying training. The next tasks included making them expert in the mechanical and tactical operation of an airplane. High-altitude flight imposes physiological stresses demanding exacting application on the part of the flyer to maintain his efficiency, and the AAF attempted to prepare the aviator to overcome these difficulties. A vital portion of his training concerned the body in flight. This important training in the fundamentals of physiology familiarized the flyer with the dangers of high altitude and other factors in operational flying, and the necessary means of guarding against them.

The "Altitude Training Program" was in operation in the Army Air Forces by 1942. This grew out of the study of the physiological effects of atmospheric pressure changes dating back to World War I. In addition to the usual lectures, films, and demonstrations, the program featured the use of low-pressure chambers to simulate flights to high altitude. This training was conducted by specialists in aviation physiology at the Aero Medical Laboratory and the School of Aviation Medicine. Maj. Otis O. Benson, Dr. John W. Heim, and other prominent members of the staff of the Aero Medical Laboratory, developed and taught the first courses for instructors at Wright Field. Each airman was required to make three chamber flights during his flying training, one to the equivalent of 30,000 feet and two to 38,000 feet. Training covered the dangers of insufficient oxygen and the proper operation of oxygen systems, especially the demand system. This included actual demonstrations of the effects of oxygen lack. Other subjects covered included fatigue, air sickness, and medical considerations, and the practical problems of operational flying. Unit oxygen officers were appointed in all flying units, beginning in June 1942, and performed valuable service in training personnel in the proper use of oxygen equipment.

The value of the Altitude Training Program can be appreciated when it is remembered that the safe operation of thousands of bomber missions over Europe was largely dependent on oxygen discipline. During the last year of the war, the total anoxia-accident rate among heavy-bomber crew members was cut by 80 percent. This was accomplished in the face of more than a hundredfold increase in man-sorties and an overall increase in average bombing altitude of 5,000 feet—from 22,000 to 27,000 feet.[26]

The Altitude Training Program was eventually coordinated and integrated with the work of the Personal Equipment Officer (PEO) assigned to each flying unit, beginning in May 1943. The PEO was, in effect, the person responsible for seeing that the teachings of aviation physiologists were heeded by members of operational units. The Personal Equipment Officer was a ground operations position, originated in March 1943 by the 1st Central Medical Establishment of the Eighth Air Force in England. PEO personnel were trained by that organization and later at the AAF School of Applied Tactics, Orlando, Florida. Most wartime aviation physiologists were also trained as PEOs, and some were engaged jointly in both fields. In addition to training aircrewmen in the proper use of oxygen equipment, parachutes, clothing, and other flying gear, the PEO was responsible for maintaining the personal equipment of his unit. This was a very responsible job, in view of the fact that the very lives of the crewmen depended on the reliable and efficient operation of personal gear.

Personal equipment included all types of flying gear used by aviators to withstand the effects of altitude, heat and cold, and G-forces, as well as parachutes and survival equipment. The personal equipment problems encountered by an operational unit depended on supply and repair facilities, but also on the nature of its mission, and geography of its area of operation, the seasonal and climatic conditions in that region, and the competency and experience of its service staff. By 1943, personal equipment was in a state of change as new materiel began arriving in the combat theaters to alleviate shortages and replace unsatisfactory items. Careful instruction in the use of the new demand-oxygen system and other equipment was essential to the survival of aircrew personnel and to the reduction of the large number of aircraft forced to return to base early because of oxygen difficulties. In early 1943, less than one percent of American airmen forced to land in the waters around England were saved. By comparison, with greater activity and largely at night, the RAF saved nearly 30 percent of their ditched personnel. Another example of the importance of efficient personal equipment and proper training in its use, can be found in the Eighth Air Force casualty figures for the first six months of 1943. During that period, there were more casualties among American airmen from frostbite than there were from enemy action.[27]

The development and procurement of improved equipment, improved maintenance, and better training helped to overcome these personal equipment problems. By the end of 1943, nearly 70 percent of American airmen who ditched around England were saved and equally impressive figures in the Pacific theater resulted from improved survival gear and training, and increased air-sea rescue activities. During the same period, the number of aircraft forced to abort missions because of oxygen problems was greatly reduced, while frostbite cases declined from first place as a cause of casualties to nearly last. This dramatic improvement was attributed to a number of factors, including the installation of waist-window enclosures in bombers, provision of adequate face protection, vastly improved types of electrically heated suits, gloves, and shoes, and the combined efforts of flight surgeons, personal equipment officers, and aviation physiologists to indoctrinate airmen in the methods of preventing frostbite.

Significant progress was also made, by the end of 1943, in developing improved personal equipment for flyers. One of the most notable successes in reducing the number and severity of combat wounds was accomplished through the introduction of body armor for aviators. The use of armor, commonly known as "flak suits" or "flak vests," and the special steel helmets for aircrew, drastically reduced the number of casualties, especially in the air war over Europe.

The Boeing B-29 bomber is perhaps the best-known aircraft of World War II, featuring advanced design characteristics developed through the cooperation of aeronautical engineers, aviation physiologists, and also flight surgeons. The B-29 cabin pressurization produced a relatively constant air pressure in flight from sea level to the stratosphere. The greatest practical advantage of pressurization was to free the flyer from dependence on the oxygen mask at altitudes below 30,000 feet. Pressure disturbances of the middle ear, the sinuses, and the gastrointestinal tract were also greatly minimized. It was found that pressurization prevented aeroembolism, or "the bends," which became a problem at altitudes above 30,000 feet. Noise levels in the sealed cabin were lowered, and the heat resulting from air compression reduced the danger of high-altitude frostbite.

Countless scientific experiments have been performed by the specialists of the Aero Medical Laboratory. In this view of the Physiological Branch on October 19, 1944, the man seated at left wearing the special oxygen mask, and the third from left riding the stationary bicycle, are participating in an experiment conducted by the Respiration Unit. (Courtesy USAF)

Aircraft designers developing the B-29 and other new aircraft had available in 1943 three sizes of synthetic men—transparent plastic mannequins—which proved of great value in human engineering. Each articulated mannequin represented an average-sized crewman, a tall, a short, and a medium size, as determined from the dimensions taken from 2,954 aviation cadets at Kelly and Maxwell Fields. They were developed at the Aero Medical Laboratory by 1st. Lt. Francis E. Randall and 1st. Lt. Albert Damon, with the cooperation of Dr. Earnest A. Hooton of Harvard University, a leading anthropologist. The mannequins, named "Slim," "Shorty," and "Roger," were used as standard yardsticks for the design of cockpits, turrets, emergency doors, and passageways. They were also valuable in solving problems in the location of instruments, proper placement of controls, adjustable seats, and hundreds of equipment items involving proper eye level, adequate elbowroom, height clearance, legroom, seat width, and so on. The adjustable mannequins, representing typical sizes of airmen, along with seven standardized heads sculptured in plaster, were also used by the staff of the Personal Equipment Laboratory as aids in designing and sizing helmets, oxygen masks, flying suits and accessories. The anthropological surveys of body sizes helped greatly to adjust the production of clothing sizes to eliminate shortages and surpluses of certain items of flying clothing.

The development of efficient flying clothing, for use at all altitudes and in every theater of operation around the world, was a priority project by the middle of World War II. It was recognized that low temperature was second only to lowered atmospheric pressure as a physio-

logical hazard in high-altitude flight. During the previous twenty years, almost every conceivable design and material had been tried, in attempts to produce a really satisfactory winter flying suit, but none had proved totally successful. The two-piece sheep-shearling suits, introduced in 1934, had proven to be too stiff, bulky, and cumbersome, and when men perspired in shearling clothing

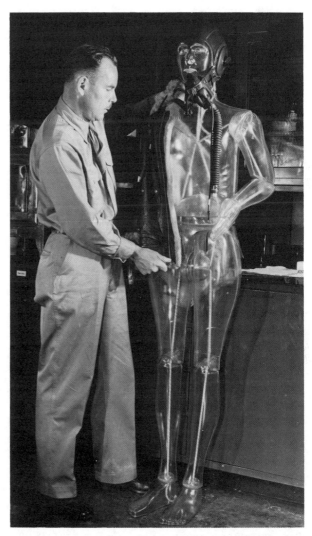

This "Plastic Man" was built during World War II, for use by the "Human Engineers" of the Aero Medical and Personal Equipment Laboratories at Wright Field. Articulated mannequins, such as this one, were used during the development of flying clothing and equipment, and also by aircraft engineers for determining the proper sizing and layout of airplane cockpits and turrets to accommodate various physiques. In this November 1943 photo, Pvt. J. H. Thomas is shown fitting "Roger" with a Type B-3 winter flying jacket. The helmet may be the Type B-8 with a prototype of the Type A-13 pressure-demand oxygen mask. (Courtesy USAF)

18 on the ground and at lower levels, it posed the danger of frostbite when the aircraft climbed rapidly to higher, colder altitudes. Shearling also could become compressed when worn, resulting in a marked decrease in insulating efficiency. The problem of the natural absorbency of the raw shearling material was resolved, in the late 1930s, by the development of the Korsseal waterproofing treatment. This process consisted of coating the flesh side of the skin with a brown, polyacrylate leather dye and a lacquer top finish. While this made shearling clothing more resistant to moisture, fuel, oil, and dirt, it tended to make the material stiffer and slightly heavier.

The great expansion of the Army Air Forces required mass production of clothing, but improved designs had also to be found. The Clothing Branch of the Personal Equipment Laboratory solved persistent problems through the cooperation of engineers, anthropologists, physiologists, and the clothing and textile experts. Wind-resistant fabric clothing was developed that not only reduced bulk but also provided variable multilayer insulation. The use of manufactured pile for the lining of body clothing marked a great advance over shearling and other animal-skin garments. The new generation of multilayer fabric clothing was both less cumbersome than shearling and stronger, easier to clean, warmer, and resisted crushing during long periods of wear. The use of outer jackets that could be donned over other layers helped control the degree of insulation, according to the demands of the situation in a way hardly possible with a single, heavy, leather garment.

Using the same principle, a rayon inner liner for gloves was evolved, based on RAF experience during the first two years of the war. The rayon insert served also to protect the hand if the heavy outer glove was removed for brief periods at high altitude, to perform detailed work requiring manual dexterity.

Electrically heated clothing is another example of the value of perseverance in the never-ending quest for perfection in flying clothing. Electrically heated suits, gloves, and shoes had been tried in limited quantities by the U.S. Army Air Service as early as World War I. Those early garments and all subsequent types proved to be unreliable, because of the recurrent breakage of the wiring. This problem persisted even after the introduction of the well-designed Type F-3 flying outfit in February 1944. Three months later the situation changed dramatically, with the development of a new type of wire capable of 250,000 flexings. Composed of silver, beraloy, and BB bronze, the wires were produced in both flat and round form for use as heating elements. The new wires were incorporated immediately into the F-3 suits then in production, and proved so successful that electrically heated clothing gained a new importance for wear during the remainder of the conflict and well into the postwar era. The new,

flexible wire was utilized in the manufacture of electrically heated blankets for the civilian market after World War II.

Although the design of fighter cockpits improved during the course of the war, they remained very small and compact. The canopy of the Lockheed P-80, America's first combat jet, was so small that the protective or ''hard'' helmet had to be reintroduced for use for the first time since World War I. Even a pilot of average size found it

This AAF airman is wearing an interesting mixture of old and modern items of flying clothing in a photo taken during the last year of World War II. His lightweight clothing indicates that the picture may have been taken in the Pacific theater of operations. He is probably a pilot, because of the numbers written on the top of his left hand, which may be his times for takeoff, arrival on target, or dead-reckoning computations required during his mission. He appears to be wearing a Type K-1 very light flying suit, introduced late in 1944, under the popular Type A-2 summer flying jacket, standardized in 1931. Other items include the Type B-5 life vest, a pair of Type A-6 flying shoes, Type B-8 goggle and probably an AN-H-16 helmet, A-14 oxygen mask, and white scarf. (Courtesy USAF)

difficult to operate the controls of a fighter effectively while wearing a parachute, life vest, one-man pneumatic life raft, personal emergency kit, anti-G garment, and other items over his protective flying clothing. Aircraft heaters were improved by late in World War II but they had to be turned off in combat as a safeguard against noxious gases.

Fighter and bomber missions over Europe usually had to be carried out at higher altitudes than in the Pacific because of the effectiveness of German antiaircraft fire. Winter flying clothing was, therefore, of greater concern in the European theater than in the Pacific. The development of lightweight summer flying clothing was also necessary, however, to allow crewmen to remain healthy and operate at full efficiency in the humid heat of the tropics.

Aviation physiologists had experimented for years in efforts to develop protective anti-G devices and techniques, for use by fighter pilots engaging in high-speed maneuvers. Studies on the effects of acceleration on the human body had begun at the Aero Medical Laboratory as early as 1936. Successful anti-G garments were developed and used in combat by the AAF during the last year of the war, and this significant accomplishment is credited with giving American airmen an important advantage over enemy fighter pilots during air-to-air combat. The program for developing a full pressure suit for use at very high altitude was less successful, and a usable pressure suit was not produced until after the end of the conflict. Details of anti-G garments and pressure suits are covered in Chapter V.

Army Air Forces Manual No. 25-2, "Physiology of Flight: Human Factors in the Operation of Military Aircraft," dated March 15, 1945, was a directive which emphasized the necessity of basing the design and construction of aircraft and equipment upon human physical factors.[28] Anthropometric surveys were conducted to present requirements for personal equipment based on variations in the dimensions of relevant portions of the anatomy. In addition to the measurements of total body proportions in 3,000 aviation cadets and 800 aerial gunners, about 2,000 airmen were measured for dimensions applying solely to head and face. Additional data was collected from approximately 1,400 crewmen, in order to establish clothing size requirements, and to investigate and solve specific problems. These data greatly expedited the development, and especially the procurement, of properly sized items of clothing and personal equipment.

Specialists in the design and construction of flying equipment working at the Personal Equipment Laboratory took into consideration both the physical dimensions and the physiological requirements. The complexity of the equipment that was worn made the complete integration of individual items essential for maximum safety and ef-

ficiency. Anthropometric data was translated into tailors' measurements to establish basic requirements. Jackets, trousers, helmets, and gloves were sized and charts prepared which were utilized routinely in the design, sizing, procurement, and issue of clothing for AAF flyers. Master charts demonstrated the adequacy of any one type of clothing, and the percentage distribution of sizes which had to be procured. Thus, the number of sizes required, and the dimensions for each size, were tentatively established for a proposed garment, based on knowledge of its function, design, material, and associated clothing. A sample of each size was made and tested on subjects of known dimensions, and the size schedule modified as indicated. These dimensions were included in the specifications prepared for each item. Finally, the percentage of each size in the total production was determined. By 1944 this process helped to eliminate the shortages of some sizes of flying clothing experienced during the first two years of the war.

Oxygen masks presented an important and often intriguing problem. Oxygen masks involved the first attempt, early in the war, to apply anthropometry to aviation medicine, and its emphasis, at first on analysis and evaluation, soon shifted to original design. Even before head models were employed, all available masks were thoroughly tested for fit on a series of individuals measured according to a facial survey. This study of sizing in relation to facial dimensions resulted in recommendations for redesigning and resizing, which eventually produced better fitting and more comfortable masks. It was finally decided that only three carefully determined sizes of oxygen masks were required for AAF use, and the percentages of these sizes were established for general production and for issue to specific groups of flyers. Strangely enough, it was found that fighter pilots, and especially photographic reconnaissance pilots, required a greater proportion of small and medium sizes than did members of bomber crews.[29] The basic dimension on which the size requirements were based was the nasion-menton, obtained by measuring the distance from the root of the nose to the base of the chin.

The routine application of the knowledge gained from the systematic study of the sizes and shapes of flying personnel, was just one of the many examples of successful human engineering carried forward into the postwar national defense program. By the close of the war, aeronautical engineers were cooperating with aviation physiologists, medical officers, and other specialists to insure that human characteristics, capabilities, reactions, and limitations were taken into consideration in the design of cockpits and almost every other type of equipment, including personal gear. Not only did this increase the efficiency of the airmen operating advanced aircraft, but

it also helped to simplify the manufacture and procurement of equipment of every type. This process of human engineering, as evolved during World War II, set a precedent, which is still followed today in the production of America's most modern weapon systems.

All in all, with the exception of parachutes for use when bailing out at high speed, research and development of personal equipment by the AAF, paralleled, and in many cases exceeded, corresponding efforts by the German, British, Soviet, and other air forces during World War II.

The Army Air Forces, with its global operations, required efficient flying clothing and personal equipment in great variety and immense quantity. Many difficulties were surmounted in developing and producing the flight materiel necessary to equip the largest air force in history. The successful accomplishment of the overall program required teamwork among the military, other government agencies, industry, universities, and the medical profession. The wartime achievements and innovations were carried forward into the jet age with the establishment of the United States Air Force in 1947, and formed the basis for mastering the tremendous challenges yet to come.

AAF combat crewman, c. 1944. This efficient outfit protected American flyers against climate and calamity. The popular Type B-15 intermediate flying jacket and A-11 trousers combination, of multilayer alpaca and wool-pile construction, was usually worn over the Type F-3 electrically heated two-piece suit, QMC wool service uniform and underwear. The electrical cord with PL-354 jack can be seen hanging down the right leg. Trousers featured thigh pockets, and the green ball of a bailout oxygen bottle can be seen in the left-leg pocket. The full-length zipper on the left leg permitted easy removal of trousers, even under water. The Type A-11 intermediate flying helmet with ANB-H-1 earphones, B-8 goggle with heated lens, and A-14 demand-oxygen mask with microphone, integrated to provide face protection from cold, wind, and flash fire. Other items of equipment included the Type B-4 "Mae West" pneumatic life vest. Hands were protected by electrically heated gloves with rayon inserts. Electrically heated shoe inserts were often worn, but QMC high-top G.I. shoes were recommended for wear under Type A-6A flying shoes shown here. The harness for the Type A-4 quick-attachable chest parachute has the Irving quick-release device. A Type C-1 sustenance vest can be seen, with the butt of a pistol in the holster under the left arm. (SI Photo A4847J)

Oxygen Equipment

A B-17 bomber landed after a training flight at an Army airfield in Florida, during World War II, with one of the crew dead of anoxia, or oxygen starvation. Before taking off, the pilot had carefully instructed his crew of four—a copilot, crew chief, sergeant, and private—in the use of the demand-type oxygen system. The private was seated in the radio compartment, while the sergeant climbed into the ball turret to test its operation.

The total flight time was little more than forty-five minutes, of which about fifteen minutes were spent above 20,000 feet, and less than thirty seconds at the maximum altitude of 28,000 feet. When the sergeant crawled out of the turret at 10,000 feet on the homeward descent, he found the private lying dead on the floor. His mask had been disconnected from the regulator hose, and his portable oxygen unit stood in the rack beside his seat, unused.

This true account, documented in Army Air Forces Manual No. 25–2, "Physiology of Flight," dated March 15, 1945,[1] provides a graphic example of the deadly cost of carelessness in the use of oxygen equipment. Oxygen equipment was (and is) the barrier that stands between a flyer and death at high altitude. If oxygen gear is used properly, high-altitude operations are no more hazardous than low-level operations, but even the best oxygen equipment is only as efficient as the person who uses it.

SCIENTISTS AND AERONAUTS

Oxygen is an abundant chemical element, occurring free in the atmosphere as a colorless, odorless, tasteless gas. It forms 20.94 percent by volume of the atmosphere, and is the only gas able to support respiration. Oxygen is the most vital of the bodily requirements, and the immediate cause of death when flying is most often lack of oxygen in the body tissues. There are many conditions which may bring about a decreased oxygen supply to the tissues, but we are concerned here only with that which results from a decrease of partial pressure of oxygen in the inhaled air during aircraft flights at high altitudes.

Oxygen must be under a certain pressure to pass through the lung membranes and into the bloodstream. The percentage of oxygen remains constant for all practical purposes at all altitudes, but since the total air pressure decreases with the increasing altitude, the partial pressure of oxygen likewise decreases. When breathing air, the partial pressure of oxygen in the lungs is sufficient until about 12,000 feet above sea level, and when breathing pure oxygen, about 40,000 feet. These levels, therefore, are the practical limits to which a person can fly, breathing air or pure oxygen. Beyond these altitudes, the blood arterial saturation drops sharply, tissue function is impaired, and the individual flyer develops symptoms of anoxia. (Anoxia literally means no oxygen at all, hypoxia—deficiency of oxygen—is a more accurate term, but one less often used.)[2]

The problem of oxygen lack at high altitude was recognized long before the invention of the balloon or airplane. For centuries natives thought that the condition known as "mountain sickness" was the result of evil spirits, metal ores in the hills, or other causes, while early European explorers and mountain climbers often attributed the symptoms to fatigue, intense cold, and hunger. Joseph Priestley, an English chemist, was one of the first scientists to discover oxygen, in 1774, and gave it the name "dephlogisticated air." A. L. Lavoisier of France repeated Priestley's experiments and named the gas "oxygène." The word comes from two Greek words meaning "acid-producing." The vital role of oxygen in human function was only suspected for many years, but in the early 1870s Denis Jourdanet, a French physician, suggested that a lack of it could prove fatal in ascents to high altitude.

The invention of the balloon by Joseph and Jacques Montgolfier, and especially the first manned flight by Pilâtre de Rozier and the Marquis d' Arlandes near Paris in November, 1783, created considerable interest in the characteristics of the atmosphere. Dr. John Jeffries, an American physician, made balloon flights with French aeronaut J. P. Blanchard as early as November, 1784, as a means of studying the properties of the upper atmosphere. These flights were followed by other scientific ascensions during the following decades including experiments for measuring the oxygen in the atmosphere. During some flights to high altitude, breathing difficulties and even unconsciousness were experienced.

In 1874, one hundred years after the discovery of oxygen, two young scientists, Theodore Sivel and Joseph Croce-Spinelli, made their first high-altitude ascension to nearly 24,300 feet outside Paris in their balloon *Etoile Polaire.* During this flight they intermittently used "bags" of oxygen, furnished them by Paul Bert, the pioneering French physiologist, who had designed and built the first low-pressure chamber.

The following year, they joined aeronaut Gaston Tissandier in the basket of the balloon *Zenith* for the high-altitude flight which ended in tragedy. The purpose of the flight was to ascend to a very high altitude and try out an oxygen breathing apparatus, previously tested successfully in Dr. Bert's altitude chamber. The oxygen device consisted of a mouthpiece connected by tubing to one of three 200-liter bladders filled with a mixture containing 65 percent oxygen and 35 percent nitrogen. The apparatus was first used when the balloon reached 22,800 feet, and had such a restorative effect that the balloonists decided to throw out ballast and ascend higher. Their plan to use the limited oxygen supply only at the last moment when they considered it necessary was a fatal decision. When they finally felt themselves being overcome, they were paralyzed and unable to grasp the oxygen tubes. The balloon reached 28,200 feet before descending, and during this time all three occupants of the basket became unconscious. Only Tissandier survived. The disaster revealed the danger of depending on an inadequate oxygen supply for intermittent use at high altitude. This tragic experience led eventually to the development of the oxygen mask and improved oxygen equipment. The fact that Tissandier survived while his two companions perished from anoxia was attributed, at the time, to his physical fitness and long aeronautical experience, which acclimatized him to flight at high altitude. A more important factor may have been his lack of physical exertion during the flight, for individual tolerance of altitude flying depends predominantly on the oxygen saturation of the blood.

The many subsequent high-altitude flights included that of Professors Reinhard Suering and Artur Berson in the giant German balloon, *Preussen*, which reached a record altitude of 34,500 feet in 1901. In all the German ascents in the early 1900s, oxygen was carried in steel cylinders equipped with a valve, but was still inhaled through a rubber tube and a dangerous hand-held mouthpiece. This crude arrangement caused both Berson and Suering to loose consciousness for a time on their record ascent to what was believed by many, at the time, to be "the greatest height at which existence is possible."[3]

The Austrian physiologist Hermann von Schroetter, who had instructed Berson and Suering, is credited with developing the first oxygen face mask for aeronauts in about 1900. His device consisted essentially of a fairly snug-fitting covering for both the nose and mouth, and the oxygen flowed through a tube into the face piece in a steady stream. A small opening in the mask allowed the expired air to pass out to the atmosphere. This type of mask and the plain tube were very inefficient, since the oxygen, during the pause at the beginning and end of respiration and throughout expiration, passed directly to the atmosphere and was lost. This loss amounted to approximately two-thirds of the oxygen carried, and meant that for every liter of oxygen used, two were wasted. Von Schroetter and Berson were also the first to make a high-altitude balloon ascent using liquid air.

Other early oxygen systems for balloonists (such as the first German Draeger model of 1909, which used compressed oxygen in a tank) featured a mask that covered only the nose. An improved 1913 Draeger model offered an oxygen mask that covered both the nose and mouth.[4] The discomfort of wearing a mask, however, ensured that before World War I, the most common device used by balloonists for receiving oxygen remained the simple rubber tube held in the mouth, with or without a mouthpiece. This tube and mouthpiece, often called a pipestem, would continue to see service with flyers until the eve of World War II.

The tethered observation balloon was used to a limited extent by several armies, beginning with the French as early as 1794. The U.S. Army employed balloons in the American Civil War, in Cuba during the Spanish-American War, and in World War I. Oxygen equipment was not required for use by Army balloon observers.

High-altitude balloon flights resumed in the 1920s with more sophisticated equipment, but the record altitude reached by the *Preussen* was not surpassed until 1927, when Capt. Hawthorne C. Gray of the Army Air Corps reached 42,480 feet in a basket equipped with compressed oxygen equipment. Unfortunately, this record was not recognized by the Fédération Aéronautique Internationale (F.A.I.), because Gray was forced to bail out during the descent when the balloon gas valve jammed open. He was killed in November of that year, when he ran out of oxygen during another attempt to set an altitude record.

Record-breaking balloon ascensions using sealed gondolas with artificial atmospheres included the flight of three Russian aeronauts, who reportedly reached 62,230 feet on September 30, 1933, with the balloon *USSR*. A new altitude record of 72,395 feet was set by Capt. Orvil A. Anderson and Capt. Albert W. Stevens of the Air Corps on November 11, 1935, with the *Explorer II* balloon and pressure gondola, fitted out as a scientific laboratory. The gondola was constructed in Building 16 at Wright Field. Capt. Harry G. Armstrong, MC, chief of the new Physiological Research Laboratory, provided the physiological data and served as flight surgeon. The artificial-atmosphere equipment in the gondola was more sophisticated than the regular liquid oxygen gear previously used. To eliminate the fire risk associated with pure oxygen, 53 pounds of a liquefied mixture of 46 percent oxygen and 54 percent nitrogen was carried in a double-wall 25-liter container. Helium under pressure forced the mixture through an evaporating coil, which converted it into a gas.[5]

This was the last record high-altitude balloon flight prior to World War II.

OXYGEN FOR AVIATORS

Orville and Wilbur Wright designed, built, and flew the first successful, powered, controllable airplane in 1903, and it was then just a matter of a few years until aircraft of various types were being flown widely in the United States and Europe. The U.S. Army purchased the first military airplane from the Wright Brothers in 1909, and soon afterward several European nations bought aircraft for military use. Aviation was to command far more serious attention in Europe during this period than it did in the United States. In December, 1913, just ten years after the Wrights flew at Kitty Hawk, the Frenchman, Georges Lagagneux, flew to a height of 20,014 feet in a Nieuport, and for the first time used oxygen in an airplane.[6] In 1913, a speed record of 127 miles per hour was also set in France.

Oxygen Equipment in World War I

By the time World War I began in August 1914, all of the major powers had small air services that increased greatly in size and capability during the course of the conflict. Rapid improvements were made in aircraft and engines because of the war, and by 1919, the altitude record had increased to 32,450 feet, and the speed record to 167 miles per hour. This high-altitude flight was made by Maj. Rudolph W. Schroeder of the U.S. Army Air Service who, of course, used oxygen while piloting a Le Pere biplane.

Military aircraft were employed during the first few months of the war, mainly for scouting and observation, and most flights were made at altitudes under 7,000 feet. The rapid improvement in antiaircraft defenses, and the arming of pursuit planes with machine guns, soon made it necessary to fly at altitudes of 10,000 feet and higher. Flying at those heights required not only improved winter flying clothing, but planners also had to consider oxygen equipment for service use. It was learned that at altitudes above 15,000 feet the efficiency and physical condition of aviators were seriously affected by lack of oxygen, unless artificial means were provided to supply the deficiency. The physiological symptoms reported included headache, numbness of the limbs, ear pains, weakening of the attention, diminished sense of stability, vertigo, faintness, fatigue, and finally, loss of consciousness. Many casualties among aviators during the war were attributed to loss of control of the airplane because of oxygen shortage.

The first real operational use of oxygen by any air force probably occurred in early 1917, when Zeppelin airships of the German Navy, capable of flying at high altitude, entered service for the purpose of carrying out raids against the British Isles. Several types of oxygen equipment were used by the German Army and Navy air services during World War I. Gaseous oxygen was used aboard airships and bombers initially, but was soon replaced for most purposes by liquid oxygen. Airship crewmen were originally issued individual bottles of compressed oxygen, so that each man could "suck air" as he felt the need. Some men considered it a sign of weakness to do so, but commanders eventually ordered the use of oxygen by all airship personnel flying above 16,000 feet. There were complaints that the "air" tasted strongly of oil and caused nausea, even long after the flight had ended. It also caused cracked lips and a hangover the next day. Gaseous oxygen cylinders were eventually replaced by special, insulated "bombs" containing liquid oxygen, and this was considered a big improvement. The so-called bomb was a vaporizer, mounted around the neck of a container, and its function was to evaporate the liquid oxygen and raise the temperature of the gas so that it was comfortable to breathe. There was no feeling of hunger or thirst reported after using liquid oxygen, and instead of feeling fatigued, the airship crewmen felt extraordinarily alert and energetic.[7]

A U.S. War Department translation of a French War Ministry document, dated October 31, 1917, described the Draeger Type B portable gaseous oxygen apparatus found on board a German Zeppelin brought down in France.[8] In addition to emergency high-altitude use, it could also be worn while inspecting the inside of an airship's envelope or hydrogen gas cells.

Liquid oxygen apparatus, in addition to being the main oxygen system on board airships, was also carried on bombers such as the Gotha G.IV and G.V, and giant "R" series aircraft such as the Staaken type. Similar equipment was also used aboard Rumpler C-VII photo reconnaissance planes, which routinely flew long-range missions at high altitude, and by some pilots of single-seat fighters including the Fokker D-VII of 1918. The most widely used system was made by the firm of Ahrend and Heylandt, in models for one or two persons. Both models were similar; the small size held 1.3 liters of liquid oxygen in a special, double-wall copper evaporating container, while the large held 2.3 liters. Both used the same type of flexible tube, which could be warmed, and the gaseous oxygen, formed through evaporation, was delivered through either a mouthpiece or a cone-shaped celluloid oxygen mask.

German directives stated that oxygen was for use at or above 4,000 meters (13,123 feet).[9] The liquid oxygen was placed in the spherical vacuum container immediately before a flight in any type of aircraft. The apparatus was

German Fokker D-VII pursuit pilot with an Ahrend and Heylandt liquid oxygen apparatus, summer 1918. Weighing about 11 pounds, this equipment was used aboard German airships as well as airplanes. The delicate coils and spherical, double-walled, copper vacuum flask were protected by a pierced metal covering, which also prevented anyone from accidentally touching the super-cold evaporating chambers and coils. The gaseous oxygen produced by the vaporizer was fed to the flyer through a flexible tube and pipestem, as shown here, or an oxygen mask. Note the nose clamp and Heinecke parachute harness. Ahrend and Heylandt equipment was tested extensively in the United States by the Army Air Service and the Bureau of Standards. (SI Photo 84– 8484)

more difficult to handle, dangerous in an accident, required special plant for its manufacture, and insulated vacuum containers for temporary storage and transportation at a temperature below its boiling point of -182.5° C. (-296.5° F.) It could not be shipped long distances or stored for extended periods because of the evaporation loss. The Allies did not use liquid oxygen in aviation during the war, and compressed oxygen in steel cylinders was used exclusively. However, the use of liquid oxygen was under study by the Allies, and captured German equipment was tested extensively.

By 1917, the importance of using oxygen during high-altitude flight was recognized by most aviation commanders and medical experts, and was generally accepted by a majority of the crewmen of bomber and reconnaissance aircraft of both sides. They understood that the lessened efficiency and other problems of aviators at high altitude were directly traceable to the effects caused by changes in the density of the atmosphere at higher altitudes. It was increasingly realized that supplemental oxygen could sustain a flyer's health and prevent the loss of efficiency and the risk of loss of consciousness, during long flights above 15,000 feet. Large aircraft usually had the extra space and load-carrying capacity to accommodate oxygen equipment, when such equipment was available.

The situation was different with pursuit or fighter pilots. Speed, a high rate of climb, and maneuverability were of the utmost importance, and every pound of extra weight carried aloft in those small machines had to be compensated for by carrying less fuel or ammunition, or by a decrease in aircraft performance.

The symptoms of oxygen starvation were usually very subtle and not easily recognized however, because the initial giddiness or exhilaration might be easily attributable to the excitement of combat flying. Many young, healthy pursuit pilots did not believe that oxygen lack at high altitude reduced their efficiency, and this view was supported by some officials. Arguments against the use of oxygen included the fact that pursuit planes (of that day) seldom remained at maximum altitude for more than a few minutes. Some pilots complained that an oxygen mask or tube made it more difficult to turn their head rapidly, and therefore dangerously restricted their vision in certain directions during combat patrols. Others said that oxygen equipment "hampered" them, and that a tight-fitting oxygen mask and hose interferred with their flying during the critical seconds of a dogfight.

The oxygen mask was often uncomfortable, but it did protect the face somewhat from the cold blast of wind in an open cockpit. It also had the advantage of delivering oxygen without the necessity of holding a tube between the teeth or fitting a mouthpiece between the teeth and gums. There was less likelihood of the mask coming off

covered by a perforated metal cage, designed to protect personnel from frostbite through touching the super-cooled evaporating chambers and coils. The rate of delivery of the oxygen was determined by adjusting a needle valve. Most liquid oxygen equipment developed at a later date, including American equipment, was similar in operation to the German apparatus.

The German liquid oxygen systems had the considerable advantage of being lightweight and compact, and made a smaller if no less dangerous target than the high-pressure gaseous oxygen cylinders. However, liquid oxygen was

during combat than there was of the tube falling out of the mouth, and the other disadvantages of pipestem delivery were also avoided.

An essential feature of oxygen-supply equipment was (and is) the device for controlling the amount of oxygen delivered to the aviator. This consisted in the early apparatus merely of a hand-controlled reducing valve attached to the oxygen-supply tank which the flyer operated to deliver oxygen according to his perceived need. A great amount of research was conducted in efforts to develop a dependable automatic pressure regulator that could maintain the pressure of the oxygen supplied, independent of the pressure in the tank, and an automatic control for regulating the amount of oxygen supplied to the aviator according to his altitude. It was also considered necessary to develop an oxygen-pressure gauge when compressed oxygen was used, to indicate the pressure in the supply tank, and a flow indicator to show when oxygen was passing through the apparatus.

The French developed oxygen equipment for high-altitude flying, and after considerable experimentation, finally standardized on a gaseous system for their aviators, featuring a rather elaborate automatic regulator. This equipment was designed by Dr. Paul Garsaux and manufactured by the firm of Panhard and Levassor. The system consisted of a regulator and gauge, usually attached to the long, thin, compressed-oxygen cylinder, rubber tube, and mask. The mask was oval-shaped, and covered the nose and mouth. It was made of aluminum, with inflatable rubber sections covering the edges that touched the face. The oxygen tube was attached to the bottom of the mask, which was held in place by an elastic strap. According to the official French manual for this system, the aluminum mask was malleable and could be formed by hand, to a limited extent, to fit better the contour of the wearer's face. The Garsaux equipment weighed 11.5 pounds for one person, and 20 pounds for two. Illustrations in the manual show it in use aboard Nieuport and Spad pursuit planes where it was carried on the left side of the seat, however, the equipment was also used on some reconnaissance and bomber aircraft.[10]

Little, if any, of this equipment was delivered to the American Expeditionary Forces with the aircraft purchased by the United States. Examples were provided by the French, however, for testing by the U.S. Army and other government agencies. Tests by the U.S. National Bureau of Standards determined that because of the faulty design of certain parts of the regulator mechanism, the device was undependable in the delivery of oxygen at various altitudes.

By the summer of 1918, a new and improved Garsaux oxygen regulator had been introduced for use by the French Air Service. This modified design was also tested by the U.S. National Bureau of Standards, but none of the new models are believed to have been purchased for use by the U.S. Army Air Service in France.

Experiments by the British Royal Flying Corps (RFC) convinced many that the provision of oxygen equipment for pursuit pilots would definitely give them an edge at high altitude over their German opponents. They found that oxygen not only maintained their efficiency and judgment, but often allowed RFC pilots to climb above the high-flying German aircraft and attack by diving out of the sun—an extremely valuable tactic in air-to-air combat. The problem, in the British view, was therefore not whether extra oxygen should be supplied to pilots flying at high altitudes, but how to develop an efficient, dependable, lightweight oxygen apparatus.

The first "official" oxygen equipment to be used by the RFC was produced by the firm of Siebe, Gorman and Company. It was a rather crude device for one or two persons, with a simple regulator valve and three manual altitude-settings. It included a rubber mask, without valves, which loosely covered both the nose and mouth, and utilized either one or two cylinders containing 500 liters of compressed oxygen. One tank provided enough oxygen for two men for about four hours each. The Siebe, Gorman equipment weighed 24.5 pounds when used for one person, and 54 pounds for two. In addition to being heavy, it had the disadvantages of decreasing oxygen delivery at higher altitudes, and frequent leaks in the high-pressure system. Because of its weight, the Siebe, Gorman equipment was used mainly by bomber crewmen. The British abandoned the use of the same apparatus for two men, after a year and a half of experimental work, and began supplying each crewman with his own individual oxygen apparatus.

The Dreyer Oxygen Equipment

Lt. Col. George C. Dreyer of the British Royal Army Medical Corps is credited with designing the first successful automatic oxygen system used by the Royal Flying Corps. Dreyer, assigned to the RFC Zone of Advance in France, in cooperation with Jacques de Lestang, a French manufacturer, studied all existing types of oxygen equipment, including that developed for the French Air Service. The Dreyer design was considered superior, and after tests of the prototype, the new system was adopted by the Royal Flying Corps, and placed in production at the de Lestang factory in Paris in April 1917. Jacques de Lestang acquired the patents for all parts of the Dreyer equipment.[11]

The Dreyer apparatus was based on the mechanical principle of a constant static pressure and a variable orifice area, and was entirely automatic in operation. The Dreyer oxygen regulator was aneroid-controlled and automatic, in contrast to the Siebe, Gorman regulator which was hand-controlled. All the flyer had to do was to turn on the oxygen at the tank and put on his oxygen mask. The oxygen from the cylinder was reduced from a high to a low pressure through a special reducing valve, and then delivered in increasing quantities as the plane rose in the air, by means of the aneroid-controlled valve. The equipment was designed to be regulated in such a manner that the deficiency of oxygen in the air at any altitude, was always just compensated for by the oxygen delivered by the apparatus.

The Dreyer equipment consisted of the oxygen regulator with high-pressure gauge, a flow indicator, a manual control, a reducing valve and a distributing valve, low- and high-pressure tubing and connections, oxygen tank, and an india-rubber mask.[12] A 300-liter cylinder provided about 2¼ hours of oxygen, if consumed at the rate of two liters per minute. To operate satisfactorily, the workmanship had to be precise, requiring that each apparatus be practically handmade. Most parts required hand-fitting and were not interchangeable, so production at the de Lestang factory was very slow.

The first Royal Flying Corps combat unit at the front to receive the Dreyer equipment was No. 25 Squadron,

The original Dreyer oxygen regulator, designed by Lt. Col. George C. Dreyer of the British Royal Army Medical Corps, and made for the Royal Flying Corps during 1917 and 1918 in the factory of Jacques de Lestang, Paris, France. This photo of the regulator, with the cover removed, shows the high-pressure gauge at left, which indicated the supply remaining in the cylinder. The oxygen-flow indicator at right showed the flow to the crewman. The flow-regulating valve at center was used to set the regulator to provide oxygen for one or more persons, and to turn it on and off. (Courtesy USAF)

9 Wing, equipped with DH-4 aircraft. According to various accounts, the pilots who used the new equipment were very enthusiastic. Major Birley, the officer commanding, is quoted as saying, "The oxygen apparatus enables my squadron to do six times the amount of work that any other squadron is doing without oxygen."[13] The demand for the equipment was soon so great that a military automobile was kept waiting constantly at the factory door to rush each apparatus, as soon as it was finished, to the battle front for immediate use.[14]

Although considered superior in comparison to other British and French designs, the Dreyer equipment was far from perfect. A French technical report, quoted in a U.S. War Department Circular (Stencil), described problems encountered during test flights at the front on October 25, 1917. The defects included leaks, weak connections, and poor mask fit. However, the apparatus was said to be very strong and was not affected by vibrations.[15]

American military-purchasing commissions were assigned to European countries soon after the United States declared war on the Central Powers. These officers were responsible for selecting and purchasing the best available items of Allied war materiel for equipping the U.S. forces as they arrived in France. Aviation-procurement officials were favorably impressed by demonstrations of the Dreyer oxygen equipment, and recommended that it be adopted for use by the Aviation Section of the Signal Corps. They recognized that oxygen equipment would be needed by the American airmen, who would soon be entering combat, but they also realized that obtaining the Dreyer equipment in quantity would be unlikely in view of the slow rate of production at the de Lestang factory in Paris.

The American Dreyer Oxygen Equipment

It is difficult to realize the utter unpreparedness of the United States when it entered the war in April 1917. The U.S. Army had practically no modern aircraft, trained personnel, or experience in military aviation, and American industry was equally unprepared to produce modern aeronautical equipment. Only 142 airplanes had been delivered to the Aviation Section of the Signal Corps prior to 1917, and not one of them was suitable for use on the battle front in Europe. No American aircraft had ever been built to carry a machine gun, and none was equipped with oxygen equipment.[16] The United States was dependent on its Allies to provide knowledge as well as all needed equipment until American war production could get under way.

The slow rate of production at the de Lestang factory in Paris and the urgent demand from the Royal Flying Corps meant that it was months before even one sample of the Dreyer oxygen equipment could be acquired for testing by the U.S. Army. On October 6, 1917, a cablegram signed "Pershing" reached Washington, stating that it was ". . . necessary to immediately start American production . . . of oxygen equipment." On October 13, the first sample of the Dreyer gear was shipped from France, followed by a letter dated October 15, from Maj. E. S. Gorrell, Aeronautical Engineer with the Bolling Mission, who reported that the Dreyer–de Lestang equipment was ". . . the best in Europe . . . and none can compare with it in any way, shape, or form."[17] Based on the reports and tests of the Dreyer equipment, it was adopted on December 5, 1917, as the first standard oxygen gear for use by the U.S. Army Air Service.

Plans were formed immediately to start quantity production in the United States. Col. Raynal C. Bolling, Assistant Chief of the Air Service, Overseas, and Jacques de Lestang, signed an agreement on October 27, 1917, whereby de Lestang would transfer to the U.S. government all manufacturing and future patent rights as far as American manufacturing was concerned, for a minimum guaranteed royalty of $17,500. De Lestang further agreed, for a fee, to proceed to the United States with two skilled employees, to supervise the work of putting the apparatus into quantity production. The group arrived in New York City on December 8, with two sample instruments, and immediately conferred with the American representatives. Brig. Gen. Theodore C. Lyster, MC, the Chief Surgeon of the Aviation Section, Signal Corps (later Army Air Service), was responsible for the overall direction of the program because oxygen equipment was considered to be a Medical Corps responsibility. Capt. E. A. Hultz, Chief, Electrical Section, was directly in charge of the engineering development and production program, and other officers and officials also participated in the discussions. By December 19, a formal contract for the manufacturing rights had been signed and approved, expedited by the receipt of an urgent cable from General Pershing on December 15, requesting that "production of 5,000 apparatii, 25,000 single-man tanks, and 15,000 masks should be commenced at once."[18]

It might seem to us now that the manufacture of the Dreyer oxygen equipment should have been a simple project, accomplished easily by any one of a dozen companies. Such was not to be the case in the wartime America of 1918. The early optimism and confidence was soon tempered as a result of a multitude of unexpected problems and delays.

It became apparent that no exact duplicate of the Dreyer–de Lestang handmade equipment would be feasible, and that very considerable redesign would be necessary for mass production in the United States. It was agreed that all parts would have to be standardized, interchangeable, and of a design easily handled by American workmen and machinery. It was also desired to give real efficiency and reliability to the equipment by eliminating

certain mechanical features which were considered "bad construction." This included reducing the weight of the apparatus while making the tanks, valves, aneroids, flexible tubing, and connections more leak-proof. The equipment had to supply two crewmen, and the face mask had to be redesigned to accommodate a radio microphone or interphone transmitter, without hindering the free flow of oxygen or unduly binding the aviator's head movements.[19] These modifications to the original design produced many unexpected complications and difficulties, which would delay production for months.

Contracts for modification and production were awarded promptly to the Julius King Optical Company of New York and to A. C. Clark and Company of Chicago, a firm with skilled craftsmen, which had specialized in the production of oxygen equipment for hospitals. Production was painfully slow because of design and manufacturing difficulties. A. C. Clark and Company gave its utmost in patriotic energy, and must be given credit for finally attaining quantity production.

The design of the oxygen face mask was a problem never satisfactorily solved. The redesigned mask was made mainly of leather and rubber, and included a microphone. Because of the size of the microphone, oxygen feed, and other elements, it was awkward and did not fit comfortably or securely on the average face. Many aviators scorned the use of the mask and pursued the primitive procedure of simply taking the oxygen tube in their teeth, sucking in enough to last for a while whenever they felt in need of it.

The production effort to perfect this equipment was, from January to May, 1918, a succession of metallurgical and mechanical experiments and readjustments, enthusiastic efforts, and scientific disappointments. Considerable argument and disagreement was experienced among the scientists, manufacturers, military specialists, and even flyers. Innumerable meetings and conferences were held to try to resolve the problems. The new drawings and designs were all approved personally by Jacques de Lestang, but the early models did not function properly. The aneroids proved faulty above 20,000 feet, and months were spent in improving this elemental part of the instrument for high-altitude work. Jacques de Lestang remained to render assistance, and on April 1, Lt. Col. George C. Dreyer, the original inventor, came to the United States as liaison officer to try to help expedite production.[20]

A number of completed sets of equipment made by A. C. Clark and Company were submitted in April, for testing by the Experimental Engineering Section at Wilbur Wright Field, Ohio, and by the U.S. National Bureau of Standards. On May 3, the first six complete sets, including supply tanks, masks, and all accessories, were sent to France by special messenger for service tests at the front. On May 18, six sets were sent to Hazelhurst Field, Mi-

28

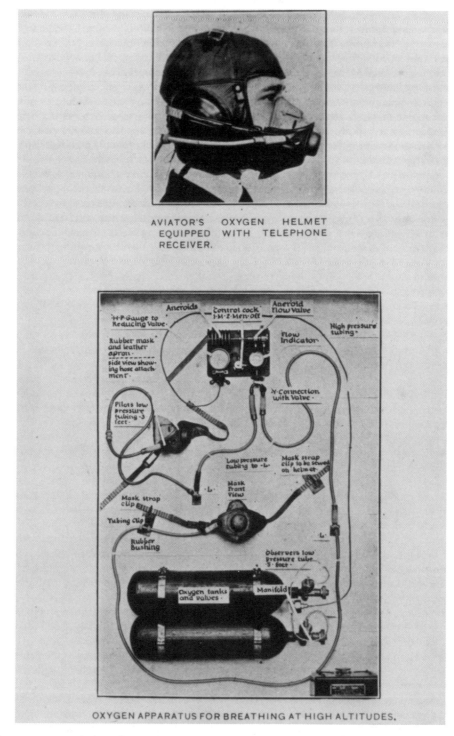

AVIATOR'S OXYGEN HELMET
EQUIPPED WITH TELEPHONE
RECEIVER.

OXYGEN APPARATUS FOR BREATHING AT HIGH ALTITUDES.

American-built Dreyer oxygen equipment of 1918. This was the first oxygen system adopted for use by the U.S. Army Air Service. The complete system as shown included the high-pressure oxygen tanks, high-pressure tubing from tanks to regulator, oxygen regulator (with cover removed), later designated as the Type A-1, gauges, and low-pressure tubing to masks. The leather oxygen mask also accommodated a microphone. Most sets were manufactured by A. C. Clark & Company of Chicago, Illinois. (Courtesy USAF)

neola, Long Island, N.Y., for scientific testing in the Army Air Service Medical Research Laboratory. The bell jar and other tests in the laboratory at Mineola were checked carefully by Lieutenant Colonel Dreyer himself. At Wilbur Wright Field, high-altitude tests were made in June aboard a de Havilland 4 aircraft with favorable results. Lieutenant Colonel Dreyer and American officials finally approved production of the much-modified Clark-Dreyer equipment, including the mask, with certain last-minute changes which were immediately incorporated into the equipment being produced.

By the spring of 1918, combat missions in France were being flown at ever-increasing altitudes, and oxygen equipment assumed rapidly growing importance. Thirty-five French-made Dreyer sets were delivered on contract to the American Expeditionary' Forces (A.E.F.) by August. However, the first American-made equipment to be received and tested in France did not make a very good impression and additional modification was required.[21]

By early July, 1,033 sets of improved equipment had passed the U.S. government tests and 446 sent to the port of embarkation for prompt overseas shipment. The production of 1,000 sets per month was expected to increase to 1,500. By the Armistice on November 11, 5,609 regulators had been approved, of which 2,946 had been shipped to France.[22]

The oxygen mask, assembled by the Western Electric Company, although approved by the Medical Corps and flying instructors in the U.S., was rejected by an A.E.F. cable on August 6. This necessitated a prompt redesign, and production of a modified model. It had been impossible to copy either the British or French types of masks because they made no provision for the radio receiver or telephone, which were considered essential by the Air Service because of the increasing use of radio aboard new American aircraft. By the Armistice, 2,600 masks had been shipped overseas.

Problems with other items also hindered the use of the equipment including a three-month delay in the delivery of high-pressure tanks. Only three factories in the United States could produce such lightweight, high-pressure oxygen containers, and they were subject to the priority rulings of the War Industries Board. Somehow, other war materiel had been given preference in production.

Five planes properly equipped with oxygen equipment were provided at every aviators' advanced-training field in the United States, so that each flyer would have complete instruction and experience in the use of oxygen, expediting training. Professional training of aviators dispelled most of the opposition to oxygen use before the Armistice. Although not always popular, oxygen use was generally accepted as a necessary part of military aviation.[23]

Had the war continued into 1919, American production would have provided all of the oxygen equipment required by the European Allies as well as the U.S. Army Air Service. By the end of the war A. C. Clark and Company had produced a total of 5,200 sets of oxygen equipment, Julius King Optical Company 400, and Van Sicklen and Company 10.[24]

Despite the tremendous effort made by all concerned, it appears that few aircraft equipped with oxygen gear were actually used by American aviators at the front prior to the Armistice. According to an account of the Oxygen Equipment Division, A.E.F., during the summer of 1918 it was necessary to purchase "a certain amount of equipment in France, but at the close of hostilities oxygen equipment was beginning to arrive from the United States."[25] However, on October 17, 1984, five members of the American World War I Overseas Flyers Association visited the National Air and Space Museum in Washington, and each member was asked independently if he was ever equipped with oxygen equipment while flying over the Western Front in 1917–18. Each member stated that he never used oxygen equipment during the war, and had never seen any oxygen system at the front.

George Vaughn (13 victories) flew Sopwith Camels with the Royal Air Force in 1918 and stated: "The Camel could not fly high altitude patrols because the castor oil would congeal at heights over 10,000 feet, so we never used oxygen equipment." Former Spad XIII pilot A. Raymond Brooks (6 victories) said: "When assigned a high altitude mission, all the participants smeared grease on their faces because face masks were in short supply. No oxygen equipment was used." The other pilots in the group concurred with the statement of Ray Brooks.[26]

The story of the American Dreyer oxygen equipment has relevance for us even in the technological world of today. The design, development, production, and distribution of complex equipment takes time and a great deal of work. It would be gratifying to record that the program was crowned with success, but unfortunately, it simply challenged the state of the art and came up short. The truth is that the American-built Dreyer equipment never really performed fully according to the specifications. It failed to perform certain functions properly when subjected to the full pressure of operational use. The mask was quite unsatisfactory, but most importantly the regulator finally proved in use to be undependable and, according to a report by the Bureau of Standards, the Dreyer control apparatus was very erratic at low temperatures. This does not imply criticism of the people or organizations involved, because much that they could be proud of was accomplished in a short period under severe wartime conditions.

Had the war continued, the American-built oxygen equipment would, of course, have been pressed into use because this gear was the only type in mass production, and oxygen equipment would have been absolutely es-

30

The Dreyer automatic regulator made by A. C. Clark, installed on the right side of the pilot's cockpit of the first American-built DH-4 aircraft. The red-painted, 500-liter oxygen cylinder was located in the observer's cockpit, on the rear of the bulkhead separating him from the pilot. Oxygen entered the regulator through a tube at approximately 2,200 pounds, depending upon the pressure in the cylinder. This initial pressure was reduced to nearly atmospheric pressure, and could not exceed 17 pounds to the square inch. The regulating valve, operated by aneroids, adjusted the oxygen flow to the altitude, the flow to the crewman increasing as the machine went higher. This photo was taken in 1980 during restoration of the DH-4 at the National Air and Space Museum. (SI Photo 80–16174–5)

sential in air combat during 1919. It should be noted that the French equipment and the original British Dreyer apparatus also experienced frequent failures during the war. According to a postwar RAF publication, it was not unusual for the pilot or observer of special DH-4 photo-reconnaissance aircraft of the Independent Force to be flying above 19,000 feet and to lose consciousness due to oxygen failure. The other crewman would then fly the aircraft down, using dual control, to 14,000 feet where his companion would revive.[27]

OXYGEN EQUIPMENT IN THE POSTWAR ARMY AIR SERVICE

The deficiencies in the American-made Dreyer equipment became all too obvious, as the Air Service demobilized

and reorganized in the United States during the months after the Armistice. The lives of test pilots at McCook Field, Ohio, and other high-altitude flyers depended on the proper functioning of their oxygen equipment. Brig. Gen. Harold R. Harris was a lieutenant and chief of the Flight Test Branch at McCook Field during the early 1920s, and recently described the situation concerning the American Dreyer equipment in use immediately after the war:

The reason the test pilots had no great enthusiasm for the regular oxygen mask stems from Major R. W. Schroeder's work at high altitude while setting a new world's altitude record just about the end of the war. This was with the Le Pere, French designed but American built, that proved to be a very satisfactory test aircraft in which Schroeder and later Macready increased the world's altitude record. Schroeder had a failure of the regulator in one of his earlier experiments and, I believe, had abandoned the face mask prior to that because it kept slipping around his face. His unhappiness was inherited by the other younger test pilots. Discontinuing the equipment was absolutely necessary because the mask had a tendency to slip around sideways and block your vision and the regulator had a bad habit of not regulating. So, rather than go through any monkey business of fiddling with these things while we were up at great altitude requiring oxygen, we simply threw the theoretically fine devices overboard and went back to the simple pipestem. I know because I was one of the test pilots that had to do it at McCook Field from 1919 to 1926.[28]

The removal of the American Dreyer oxygen equipment from regular use in 1919 left the Air Service without an automatic oxygen system. The original type of hand-operated regulator, tank and tube system was utilized for most flights which had to be made at high altitude, in a manner similar to that employed by the balloonists and aviators up to the latter part of World War I. When the official "Type Designation System" of nomenclature for aviation equipment was established in the mid-1920s, the old American Clark-Dreyer regulator, which had long since been removed from service use, was given the designation of "Type A-1," and so recorded on the "Type Designation Sheets" maintained by the Materiel Division.[29]

A. C. Clark and Company continued their efforts to develop an automatic regulator that would overcome the disadvantages of the Dreyer device. They designed a new regulator with two filters to prevent moisture and other impurities in the oxygen from interfering with the action of the aneroid control valve. Unfortunately, the Clark apparatus was heavier and more complicated than the old Dreyer type and contained more parts. Although considered an improvement, Clark regulators were not standardized for Air Service use, and only a limited number were acquired for testing.[30]

Other U.S. and foreign oxygen regulators of improved or different design were tested by the Air Service at the Medical Research Laboratory at Mineola, the Engineering Division at McCook Field, and the U.S. National Bureau of Standards, Washington, D.C. Among the designs tested were the French Munerelle, and two models designed by the American inventor, W. E. Gibbs.

A device of radically different design was invented by an American engineer named T. C. Prouty, and built in prototype form by the firm of Van Sicklen and Company of Elgin, Illinois. The Van Sicklen–Prouty apparatus featured a high-pressure chamber and reducing valve and a low-pressure chamber and reducing valve, the latter controlled by an aneroid capsule, This equipment differed from the Dreyer in that the required amount of oxygen

was obtained by forcing the oxygen through an orifice of constant area by varying the pressure of the oxygen, instead of maintaining the driving pressure effectively constant and varying the orifice in the aneroid-control valve. Tests by Maj. Rudolph W. Schroeder and Lt. G. W. Elsey of the Engineering Division at McCook Field on September 24, 1919, proved satisfactory. The tests indicated minor problems and it was reported that more oxygen was actually used than was necessary. This was possibly because of the instrument's maladjustment and more rigid tests were recommended. Although the lightest and most compact of the instruments tested, and rated as the best high-pressure regulator thus far developed, the Van Sicklen-Prouty apparatus was not immediately adopted for standard use by the Air Service, but a small number were acquired and extensively tested, beginning in 1919.[31]

The basic hand-operated gaseous oxygen system used during the 1920s. It consisted of an oxygen flask with pressure-reduction regulator, gauge, and flexible hose or tubing to the mouthpiece inserted into an aperture in the winter face mask, such as this Type B-2. The pilot shown here at McCook Field, Ohio, in 1925, is wearing a Type B-3 winter flying helmet, goggles, coney-fur gauntlets, and early one-piece leather winter flying suit, possibly the experimental electrically heated Type B-3. (SI Photo A4861F)

In 1921 the U.S. National Bureau of Standards conducted exhaustive tests of all available types of oxygen equipment in cooperation with the National Advisory Committee for Aeronautics (NACA) and the U.S. War and Navy Departments. In addition to testing all of the equipment previously described, the original Dreyer gear was tested again, along with the wartime French Garsaux equipment, and the modified Garsaux apparatus. A newer French Gourdou oxygen device built by Aera of Paris was also examined and, like the others, found to have undesirable limitations. While almost every type of regulator had some good features, none was considered entirely satisfactory.[32]

Along with the various types of gaseous oxygen apparatus, liquid oxygen equipment was also studied carefully. German wartime Ahrend and Heylandt gear, which weighed 11 pounds 14 ounces, and a newer but similar German apparatus, were examined in detail. In addition, a British Siebe, Gorman device of similar design to the German one, but weighing 17.25 pounds, was tested with fairly good results. The same drawbacks to the use of liquid oxygen still remained, however, including the need for special handling and the inevitable loss of oxygen due to evaporation. It was also noted that in case the apparatus was inverted, the rate of delivery could not be controlled.

The Bureau of Standards also developed its own liquid oxygen apparatus. The liquid was evaporated at a nearly constant rate by heat from the atmosphere, transmitted through the layer of insulating material. A gauge was provided to show the amount of liquid in the container, and the device could be inverted without liquid being delivered with the oxygen (provided the container was filled not more than half full and the valve on the top was turned so that gas passed out through the tube extending to the center of the container).[33]

Some tangible results were achieved through the various experiments and tests conducted during the first few years after the end of World War I. In 1922 a slightly modified version of the Prouty oxygen apparatus was finally standardized for use by the Air Service. This equipment was manufactured by the Gaertner Scientific Corporation of Chicago, Illinois. According to the Air Service Specification published on June 6, 1922, and revised April 10, 1923:

> This apparatus is designed to so control the supply of oxygen from the high-pressure tank to the mask that the aviator will automatically receive the proper amount of gas at all altitudes within the range of the regulator. Regulation is required through all altitudes between 10,000 and 32,000 feet. . . . The weight of each apparatus . . . shall not exceed 1¾ pounds.[34]

The Prouty equipment was entirely automatic and the pilot was only required to open the stud valve on the

The Prouty Oxygen Regulator, manufactured by the Gaertner Scientific Corp. The aluminum case, at left, had a glass window that covered the high-pressure gauge. A shut-off valve with a knurled ring, at lower left corner under the regulator base, was provided to cut off the supply of oxygen to one mask, in case the plane was being operated by one aviator. This regulator was designated by the Air Corps as the Type A-2. (Courtesy USAF)

oxygen tank. Oxygen was automatically supplied to either one or two aviators, beginning at 10,000 feet. It was preferable for the Prouty regulator to be attached directly to the oxygen-supply tank by a bracket and adjustable clamp, but it could also be mounted in the cockpit at a distance from the tank by the use of high-pressure oxygen supply tubing. The use of the tube was to be avoided whenever possible as it offered a possibility for clogging due to the gradual accumulation of frost on the inside.

The Prouty regulator was well made and little oxygen was wasted during operation. It had no parts subjected to excessive wear through rapid rotation, and therefore could be expected to operate for a considerable period of time before showing any deficiencies. In fact, the Prouty proved fairly dependable in service, and although changed to limited standard status on August 10, 1927, it continued to see some use until the end of the decade. The Prouty regulator was designated as the Type A-2 when the Type Designation System for flying equipment was established in the mid-1920s.[35]

The Prouty regulator itself was light in weight, but the complete oxygen system, including the high-pressure steel tanks, continued to present weight problems when installed in aircraft. This was an especially important concern in airplanes carrying several persons and designed for long-distance flight because of the number and size of the cylinders required for gaseous oxygen. Designers began to consider the definite advantages that could be gained by the use of lightweight, compact, liquid oxygen systems then under development.[36]

In addition to the Type A-2 Prouty, hand-operated gaseous oxygen regulators, including the "Rego" type, continued to see service during the 1920s. An Air Service Circular from 1925 advised that great care should be taken with hand-operated regulators, to insure that the user did not open the valve wider than necessary and thus waste his oxygen, perhaps expending his supply before the flight at high altitude was completed. One oxygen cylinder filled to a pressure of 1,700 to 2,250 pounds per square inch (psi) would normally be enough for a two-hour flight. For longer flights or those to extremely high altitudes, several cylinders could be connected to the same system with high-pressure oxygen manifold connections. Two men could also take oxygen from the same system.

The impurities and moisture found in the oxygen were usually removed during the filling of the cylinders by passing it through a purifier. This was a seamless steel tube, three inches in diameter, containing alternate layers of glass wool and phosphorus pentoxide, as well as mesh screens.[37]

It is interesting to note from the Air Service Circular of 1925 that there was still no standard oxygen mask available for issue. It was stated that if one was made (by the units themselves), no metal parts should come in contact with the face. A small tube, preferably of hard rubber, could be fastened into the mask opposite the mouth, ending in a sort of button. The rubber connection on the oxygen tubing could be slipped over the outside of the tube fastened in the mask. The pilot then did not have to hold anything in his mouth.

The most common conduit for receiving oxygen in the mid-1920s was still a tube, made of rubber or flexible metal, and a mouthpiece, often called a pipestem. The usual type of mouthpiece was made of wood, included a round flange, and resembled a baby's pacifier. Wood was a good nonconductor of heat, did not frost up easily, and did not have a disagreeable taste which was often present in a rubber mouthpiece. If a winter face mask was worn, the mouthpiece could be passed through the mouth hole of the mask, and the round flange inside the mask would keep the mouthpiece in place.

An important decision was made in 1923 by the Chief of the Engineering Division at McCook Field, and approved by the Chief of the Air Service in Washington, D.C. After careful consideration, liquid oxygen was adopted for use by the Air Service, along with gaseous oxygen, and a long period of testing and experimentation began. The new liquid oxygen equipment had several advantages over compressed oxygen, as we have seen, including its comparative lightness and small size. It was estimated that the complicated, undependable equipment, and large, heavy steel cylinders needed to supply a given quantity of gaseous oxygen, weighed at least twice as much as the gear required to supply the same amount of oxygen carried in liquid form. This was important considering the relatively small size and low performance of the military

aircraft of that period. Liquid oxygen was also free of the impurities and moisture found in gaseous oxygen.

Liquid oxygen was available commercially in almost every city at which an Army airfield was located, but was difficult to locate in the countryside. It could not be shipped long distances or stored for extended periods because of the evaporation loss. Liquid oxygen had to be kept at a temperature below its boiling point of -182.5 degrees C. (-296.5 degrees F.), and had to be carried in a special vacuum flask similar in construction to a large Thermos bottle. It required special handling to prevent accidents, and the aircraft needing oxygen had to be serviced immediately before flight. The early equipment provided no means of determining the amount of oxygen in the container during flight and no accurate method of controlling the rate of oxygen flow. Liquid oxygen vapor is also very cold, and proved uncomfortable to breathe with some equipment unless a supplementary heater was provided. Despite these drawbacks, the use of liquid oxygen at that time was considered to have important advantages over the use of compressed oxygen.

The first time liquid oxygen was used for an altitude flight in the United States was on June 1, 1923, when Lt. George W. Polk and P. N. Sutton, a civilian employee from McCook Field, took a DH-4B for a two-hour flight to 13,000 feet. The purpose of the flight was to test the experimental apparatus designed for the Air Service by the Bu-

A pipestem attached to the end of an oxygen-supply tube, was often inserted through the mouth aperture of a protective face mask, in the days of open cockpit flying. The oxygen tube, with or without a mouthpiece, was used by many Army aviators until the introduction of the modern oxygen mask in 1939. The goggle in this recent NASM photo is of the Resistal type. (SI Photo 84–12156–6)

34

reau of Standards, and later designated as the Type B-4. On June 4, a second flight of two hours with the same equipment was made to an altitude of 20,200 feet. These flights were described in an article by A. M. Jacobs, in the April 1924 issue of the magazine *U.S. Air Service,* and it was stated that in both cases the apparatus functioned perfectly, the supply of oxygen was sufficient, the gas was absolutely dry, and not cold enough to cause discomfort. When four-fifths full, the 2½-liter container held a little more than six hours' supply for two persons. The liquid oxygen used in these and subsequent test flights and experiments was produced in a Heylandt-type plant set up at McCook Field in 1923.

In addition to the Bureau of Standards apparatus, liquid oxygen equipment similar to the German wartime gear was tested. It consisted of a combined regulator and tank, usually called the vaporizer or evaporating flask. The first three models to be type-numbered were commercial products of German type with a capacity of 2.5, 5 and 15 liters. Under the new type designation system introduced in the mid-1920s, they were designated as the Types B-1, B-2, and B-3 respectively. These models were not adopted or procured as standard equipment.

OXYGEN EQUIPMENT IN THE ARMY AIR CORPS

The U.S. Army Air Corps superseded the Air Service in the reorganization of 1926. For those personnel in the Materiel Division concerned with providing oxygen equipment this was a learning period during which new gear was tested, handling techniques perfected, and personnel trained in the use of liquid as well as gaseous oxygen. The next type of liquid oxygen vaporizer to be developed, and tested extensively by the Air Corps, had double vacuum-walls, and was solenoid-controlled. It was designated as the Type B-5, and remained in experimental status.

By 1926, designers were planning to use high-pressure gaseous oxygen equipment on one- and two-man planes, and liquid oxygen gear on large, long-range aircraft carrying a number of men, because it was more compact and lighter in weight. However, because liquid oxygen equipment was still experimental, was taking longer to develop than expected, and funds for procuring new materiel were limited, gaseous oxygen equipment remained the standard type in operation. It should be noted that only a limited amount of high-altitude flying was performed routinely during the 1920s by Air Corps tactical units. Most flights above 20,000 feet and to really high altitudes were experimental, and both liquid oxygen equipment in test status and gaseous equipment were available for such special missions.

Air Corps Technical Order 03–10, published on November 5, 1927, stated that the Type A-2, or Prouty, was the only standard oxygen regulator in Air Corps use. The Type A-1 high-pressure steel oxygen cylinder, Type A-1 drier and purifier device (and necessary valves and tubing), were also described along with maintenance instructions. The T.O. advised that the average person required oxygen above 15,000 feet, but the amount varied considerably with the individual depending on how much he was exerting himself. It also said that it was impossible to maintain normal oxygen pressure in the lungs above 20,000 feet even when breathing pure oxygen, but it was not harmful, as was once thought, to breathe pure oxygen above that altitude. No mention was made of liquid oxygen equipment.[38]

Technical Order 03–10–1, dated June 30, 1928, advised that it had been found that the Prouty regulator, Type A-2, was not suitable for flights over 22,000 feet because of insufficient oxygen flow, nor was it suitable for flights where an intermediate altitude was maintained for any length of time before reaching higher altitudes. This was because oxygen flow started at about 5,000 feet, when no intermediate shut-off valve was used, and thus the oxygen supply might be nearly exhausted before the higher altitude was reached. When flying was to be accomplished under either of the two above-mentioned conditions, the Prouty regulator was to be replaced by a standard hand-operated oxygen-welding type of regulator. A Rego regulator had been found to be satisfactory.[39] This manual regulator was adopted as substitute standard for Air Corps use on August 9, 1927, and designated as the Type A-5. It was not declared obsolete until February 15, 1944. According to the Type Designation Sheets, the Prouty Type A-2 regulator was officially transferred to limited standard status on August 10, 1927. (The Type A-3 manually operated regulator was an experimental design that was not adopted.)

T.O. 03-10-1 also provided drawings for a wooden mouthpiece that was recommended. It resembled a baby's pacifier, and the round flange was said to prevent the cold air from the oxygen tube reaching the lips and chapping them. Mouthpieces were to be made locally where their use was desired. According to this T.O., a standard oxygen face mask was still not available, but masks could also be made locally.

Shortly after T.O. 03-10-1 was published, a loose-fitting oxygen face mask designated as the Type A-1 was adopted, and made available as limited standard issue. Of rubber construction, it had a metal nipple in the mouth area for attaching the oxygen supply hose, and was used as an optional item by some aviators. The Type A-2 was another design which remained in experimental status at the Material Division. It was an oxygen face-mask-and-helmet combination service-tested in the late 1920s but not adopted for use. The Type A-3 was almost the same design as the Type B-2 winter face mask except that provisions were made for insertion of a rubber nipple for the oxygen hose. The A-3 remained in service-test status from October 21, 1929, until January 13, 1931, when it was declared inactive.

The first annual report of the Chief, Materiel Division, for fiscal year 1927 (FY1927), discussed the move of the Division from McCook Field to Wright Field, Ohio. It advised that work had been started on a new and improved type of automatic gaseous oxygen regulator, to replace the Type A-2 (Prouty) and the manually operated type of regulator. In the second annual report for FY 1928, it was stated that test results for the new regulator designed by the Division were promising, and that it had been designated as the Type A-4.

The main principle of this new aneroid-controlled regulator was a yoke type of valve seat, mounted on a diaphragm actuated by a Sylphon bellows through a linkage mechanism. Two different rates of flow were obtained, depending on whether one or both outlet tubes were opened. In cases where more oxygen was needed (as in formation flying, or when performing physical duties such as swinging a flexible machine gun in the air stream) the flow of oxygen could be doubled by giving an auxiliary valve one-quarter turn to the open position. Although automatic in operation, the A-4 did not start to deliver oxygen until an altitude of about 15,000 feet was reached. This was later reduced to 10,000 feet. The amount of flow thereafter increased in ratio with the altitude. The flow

automatically decreased in descent, and cut off at about the same altitude as that at which it had started. The Type A-4 was designed for the use of only one person, and it was therefore necessary to install a separate regulator for each occupant of an aircraft. After service-testing, the A-4 regulator was standardized for Air Corps use on March 20, 1930. Unfortunately, the A-4, like its predecessors, could not be depended upon to automatically provide an adequate flow of oxygen at altitudes above 20,000 feet. With the increase in service ceilings and operating altitudes in the mid-1930s, this was no longer acceptable, and the A-4 was declared obsolete on July 10, 1936, when stock was exhausted. At that time the Air Corps returned to the use of the manually operated regulator for dispensing gaseous oxygen.

Liquid Oxygen Enters Air Corps Service

Progress was made during the late 1920s in developing new and more efficient vacuum-walled liquid oxygen equipment. Laboratory tests were conducted during 1927, and successful flight tests were performed in 1928. Five models were procured for service test, one of each type being allotted for evaluation to five different Air Corps organizations. These units depended upon superpressure above the liquid oxygen to give an increased flow of gas, the same principle that was used in the German-type vaporizers. Their construction, however, differed from the German type in the following ways: vaporizing and container units were separate, making it unnecessary to dis-

The Type A-4 automatic gaseous oxygen regulator, standardized for Air Corps use on March 20, 1930. This photo shows a complete regulator at right, and the device in center with cover removed. The Type A-4 replaced the Type A-2 (Prouty) regulator, and was designed for use by only one person. It began to deliver oxygen at an altitude of about 10,000 feet, and from there on the amount of flow increased with the increase in altitude. When the aircraft descended, the flow automatically decreased, and cut off again at about 10,000 feet. The gauge indicated the gas pressure in the oxygen-supply cylinder. (Courtesy USAF)

card the whole apparatus because of damage to one unit; silica gel was used in the absorbent blister between the walls, in place of charcoal, to eliminate the danger of explosion and fire if hit by rifle or shell fire; the flow was controlled by means of a needle valve at the end of the superpressure line placed where the pilot could reach it; and the superpressure gauge was located near the needle valve, where the pilot could see it.

The Type B-6 was a liquid oxygen device with a five-liter capacity that featured a double-wall container with a coil-tube-type vaporizer. It was standardized for Air Corps use on May 9, 1929, and although little used after 1936, it was not declared obsolete until January 27, 1944. The Types B-7 and B-8 were of the same construction as the B-6, but had a ten- and fifteen-liter capacity respectively. Their main use was aboard bombardment aircraft. Both were standardized and declared obsolete on the same dates as the B-6 equipment.

The next type, the B-9, was an experimental design by the Bureau of Standards, which had a capacity of five liters. It was actually a redesigned Type B-4, and did not enter the Air Corps inventory.

The Type B-10 vaporizer had been undergoing tests for almost two years before it was standardized on October 13, 1930. Some of the compact B-10s remained in the inventory until finally declared obsolete on January 27, 1944. They had a 2.5-liter capacity, and were developed for use with pursuit planes. The B-10 had sufficient oxygen capacity for a two-hour flight to 30,000 feet. The Types B-6, B-7, B-8, and B-10 were all redesignated as limited standard on April 1, 1932, when the improved Types B-11 and B-12 vaporizers were standardized for use.

The development of liquid oxygen equipment continued, resulting in the 2.5 liter Type B-11, which was similar to the B-10 except for minor improvements to facilitate installation and filling. The modifications were such that the two units were not interchangeable. The B-11 was standardized on April 1, 1932, and declared obsolete on January 27, 1944. The improved Type B-12, with a five-liter capacity, was very similar to the B-11, and was standardized and declared obsolete on the same dates. The B-12, like the B-6, was used mainly in two-place aircraft.

The last design in the series to be standardized, the Type B-13, was also similar to the B-11 and B-12 vaporizers except that it had a capacity of ten liters of liquid oxygen. The B-13 was standardized on December 18, 1934, and officially declared obsolete like most other items of liquid oxygen equipment, on January 27, 1944. It should be noted that the above three units were changed to limited standard status on May 9, 1936, when the Air Corps returned to the use of gaseous oxygen equipment as its standard and primary type.

The Type B-6 and later liquid oxygen vaporizers, the standard models developed and procured for Air Corps use, were all similar in operation. These vaporizers consisted of three units: a container, a series of vaporizing coils and a superpressure line. The spherical container was of the double-walled type, having the space between the steel walls evacuated almost to a perfect vacuum. The vaporizing coils unit was made up of three coils, a sump, a neck piece and a safety valve. This unit was mounted upon the neck of the container. The superpressure line attached to the top of the coils unit and consisted of a length of copper tubing, a pressure gauge and a needle valve.

A summary of the principle of operation of the standard vaporizers used by the Air Corps was outlined in a technical report prepared by the Equipment Branch of the Materiel Division on April 28, 1931:

> The container element is filled or partially filled with liquid oxygen. The coils element is then mounted on the container and the superpressure line is attached. The valve in the superpressure line is then closed. As oxygen cannot be kept as a liquid it is constantly evaporating. This evaporation then slowly builds up a pressure above the liquid as indicated on the pressure gauge. This pressure forces liquid oxygen up the end of the coils element which reaches down nearly to the bottom of the container. The liquid oxygen then evaporates in the coils and comes out the coil outlet as a gas, from where it is carried to the crewman through a flexible tube.[40]

The storage and shipping container was an important item of equipment for use with super-cold liquid oxygen. The types developed for Army use were spherical, had double-vacuum steel walls, and an additional protective metal housing. The first model to be given a type designation, the Type A-1, was a German commercial 25-liter container purchased in limited numbers in 1923, and declared obsolete on November 25, 1925. It was replaced by the Type A-2, a very successful Purox commercial 25-liter model standardized on August 23, 1924, changed to limited standard on May 6, 1936, and finally declared obsolete on March 31, 1944. The A-2 was manufactured by the Purox Liquid Gas Company of Denver, Colorado. The Type A-3 was very similar to the A-2, but had a 50-liter container. It was in experimental status from November 18, 1924, until standardized on October 31, 1927.

The last type of container to be adopted for Air Corps use was the A-4, similar to the above but of only 10-liter capacity. Standardized on December 2, 1933, it was intended to hold liquid oxygen in small quantities, when only a limited amount of high-altitude flying was planned. Both the A-3 and A-4 containers were transferred to limited standard status, and declared obsolete, at the same times as the Type A-2. A long-stemmed funnel was used

Capt. Albert W. Stevens (left) and Capt. St.Clair Streett before a high-altitude photographic test flight on October 10, 1928. At left is the aerial camera carried aboard the Engineering Division XCO-5 aircraft; at center is the Type B-6 liquid oxygen vaporizer, with a Type B-7 at right, both of which were then in experimental status. The aviators are dressed in Type B-7 winter flying suits, for protection against the severe cold encountered above 30,000 feet. Stevens is wearing experimental electrically heated gloves, and his Type B-1A goggles have 0.375-inch holes bored through the glass in front of each pupil, to allow vision in case the lenses fog or frost up. His oxygen face mask is probably the Type A-1. Streett is testing electrically heated goggles and also wears an early oxygen-face mask. Both masks have a metal nipple for attaching supply tubes from the oxygen vaporizers. This type of mask freed the wearer from having to hold the oxygen-supply tube between his teeth. (Courtesy USAF)

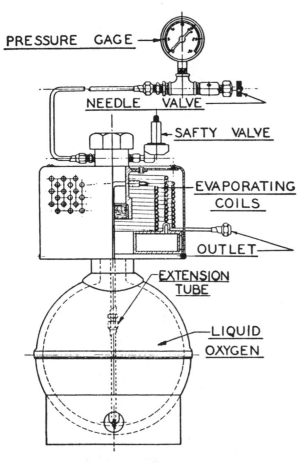

PRESSURE GAGE

NEEDLE VALVE

SAFTY VALVE

EVAPORATING COILS

OUTLET

EXTENSION TUBE

LIQUID OXYGEN

Schematic view of a typical liquid oxygen vaporizer. The apparatus comprised three main units: a double-walled, spherical, vacuum, liquid oxygen container, a series of vaporizing coils protected by a pierced metal covering, and a superpressure line. The amount of pressure built up above the liquid in the container, was indicated by the pressure gauge at the end of the superpressure line. The gaseous oxygen produced through the vaporization of the liquid in the coils, was delivered to the airman through a flexible tube and either a pipestem or mask. (Courtesy USAF)

in pouring liquid oxygen from the storage container into the vaporizer.

The status of Air Corps oxygen equipment at the end of the decade was nicely summarized in Technical Regulations No. 1170–50, "Aircraft Instruments," dated November 1, 1929.[41] By this time experience had shown that "The average person requires oxygen at altitudes above 10,000 feet." T.R. 1170–50 further stated that the Prouty regulator (Type A-2), had been reworked to give the higher flow of oxygen required by the revised Air Corps standard. It reiterated that the Prouty gave insufficient oxygen above 22,000 feet, that its screen should be cleaned of dust and moisture after each five hours of

use, and that the performance of the instrument should be checked by a laboratory test after each twenty-five hours of operation. The Type B-4 liquid oxygen vaporizer was not recommended for use above 20,000 feet, but the Types B-6, B-7, and B-8 vaporizers of vacuum-wall construction were recommended for use at higher altitudes, and remained in Air Corps service for several years.

The position of the Materiel Division on the use of gaseous and liquid oxygen at high altitudes, was clearly stated in a letter to the National Advisory Committee for Aeronautics (NACA) from Maj. C. W. Howard, Chief of the Experimental Engineering Section. In reviewing a NACA report recommending the use of gaseous oxygen, Maj. Howard stated that the use of compressed oxygen above 28,000 feet was "positively dangerous." He emphasized that only liquid oxygen equipment was safe for use above that altitude, because of the many failures experienced by personnel of the Division while using gaseous oxygen gear. Moisture-free gaseous oxygen was almost impossible to obtain, and the moisture in the available oxygen posed a danger due to the chance of its freezing in the lines or regulator. Liquid oxygen was recommended as there could be no possibility of plugging of the equipment.[42]

Air Corps personnel continued to set new high-altitude records during the 1920s. These records were earned the hard way because crewmen flying at great heights not only had to contend with possible failure of the engine or oxygen equipment, but also faced the constant threat of frostbite. Airmen had only their winter flying clothing, including face masks and helmets, to protect them from the brutal cold at high altitude while flying in the unheated, open-cockpit aircraft of that day. The notable accomplishments during that period included a record-breaking flight by 1st Lt. John A. Macready on January 29, 1926, over McCook Field. Macready set an American altitude record of 38,704 feet on that frigid winter day, during which he suffered from the severe cold and also experienced symptoms of hypoxia. He was still using the inefficient pipestem mouthpiece, and the oxygen equipment available to him just could not maintain normal blood-oxygen levels at extreme altitudes.

U.S. Navy aviators also set records during high-altitude flights. Lt. Apollo Soucek reached 39,140 feet on May 8, 1929, and 43,166 feet on June 4, 1930, while flying a Wright "Apache." Soucek wore an oxygen mask that covered his nose and mouth, but suffered some impairment of function at maximum altitude. This might have been expected, for without positive-pressure breathing, the ambient pressure at that height was insufficient to maintain normal blood oxygenation. This was the last United States altitude record during this period, and almost the last in an open-cockpit aircraft.[43]

The decade of the 1930s was a time of great change for the Army Air Corps. Despite financial limitations during the depression, new all-metal, high-performance monoplanes were introduced, bringing the biplane era to a close. The steady improvement in aircraft performance gave a new impetus to the development of better personal equipment for the aviators, who had to work efficiently during long flights at very high altitudes. Some knowledgeable individuals realized that it would take more than the trial and error method of developing personal equipment in the workshops of the Materiel Division, to produce the improved flight gear required in the coming years.

It was at this propitious time that Maj. Malcolm C. Grow and Capt. Harry G. Armstrong of the Medical Corps established at Wright Field what was eventually to be called the Aero Medical Laboratory. As described in Chapter I, the cofounders of the laboratory knew that a comprehensive scientific research program was necessary to study the entire subject of high-altitude flight and the physiological problems encountered at great heights. In 1933, Major Grow and, in 1934, Captain Armstrong, began the special medical research required to solve the many complex problems involved in flight at high altitude, and to develop the types of modern oxygen equipment and other devices, necessary to keep pace with the rapid progress in the design and performance of modern aircraft.

One of the first items of equipment utilized by Captain Armstrong for the study of flyers' oxygen requirements, and hypoxia in general, was the old Air Service low-pressure and temperature chamber dating from World War I. In March 1935, Captain Armstrong visited Pittsburgh, Carlisle, Pennsylvania, and Washington, D.C., in order to make a detailed survey of all literature on oxygen and related subjects, on which to base the development of new gaseous oxygen equipment. Armstrong conferred with the Air Corps Chief Flight Surgeon and other appropriate officials inside and outside the Army, but his trip report disclosed that the available literature failed to provide the information necessary to proceed with Materiel Division development projects on oxygen equipment and supercharged cabins. Basic research was simply lacking in many vital areas, and it was recommended that the necessary research be conducted at Wright Field.[44]

Old-style oxygen face masks were among equipment under development by the Equipment Branch during the early 1930s. Based on experience with the Type A-1 mask, and the experimental Types A-2 and A-3, an improved design was produced and designated as the Type A-4. Standardized on April 6, 1931, it was actually a combination winter-and-oxygen face mask, that consisted of a wind-resistant leather outer shell with a chamois lining. An oxygen-deflector connection was placed opposite the mouth cover, with exhaling tubes extending from the sides of the nose area and across the cheek part of the mask. The lower sides of the eye openings were padded with kapok to prevent fogging of the goggles. The A-4 was

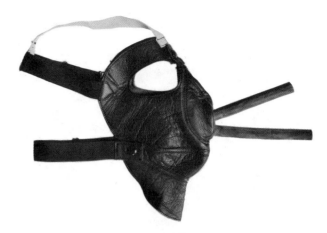

The Type A-4 combination winter-and-oxygen face mask, standardized in 1931, consisted of a leather outer shell with a chamois lining. An oxygen-deflector connection was placed opposite the mouth cover, with exhaling tubes extending from the sides of the nose and across the cheek part of the mask. The lower sides of the eye openings were padded with kapok to prevent fogging of the goggles. This mask stayed in the inventory as limited standard from 1933 until 1942. (Courtesy USAF)

changed to limited standard on March 21, 1933, and continued to see some use for several years. It was not dropped from the inventory until 1942, after all stocks were exhausted.

Another oxygen face mask developed during the same period featured full-face protection, with an oxygen compartment that included a deflector to prevent the cold oxygen from flowing from the supply tube directly into the mouth. It was composed of horsehide with a chamois lining cemented to the shell. The eye openings were made large to permit insertion of goggle cushions on the inside. The A-5 was standardized on April 1, 1933, changed to limited standard on May 31, 1935, and not officially declared obsolete until August 11, 1943.

The last of the old-style oxygen face masks to be developed was the Type A-6. It was made of flexible leather with an intermediate lining and a chamois inner lining. The A-6 covered only the lower part of the face, and had an opening in the nose and mouth area for attaching a metal oxygen distributor, which formed part of the mask, and connected with the single inlet to the supply tube from the liquid oxygen vaporizer. This not only obviated the need for placing the tube in the wearer's mouth, but also permitted natural breathing and improved vocal communication. This mask could also be worn without the oxygen distributor and tube, to provide protection from the cold and wind-blast in an open cockpit or crew position. The A-6 was standardized on May 31, 1933, transferred to limited standard on July 15, 1939, and declared obsolete

Type A-5 oxygen face masks were service-tested during high-altitude photographic mapping flights over the state of Maine in March 1932. The A-5 was basically a protective full-face mask, with an oxygen compartment that included a deflector to prevent the oxygen from flowing from the supply tube directly into the mouth. Composed of horsehide with a chamois lining, it remained in the inventory from 1933 until 1943. The helmets are probably the Type B-3, and the goggles the Type B-6. Capt. Albert W. Stevens (left), veteran high-altitude flyer, and Lt. J. F. Phillips are wearing Type B-7 winter flying suits, and Stevens is carrying a portable gaseous oxygen flask with manual regulator and gauge. The aircraft is a Fairchild C-8. (Courtesy USAF)

along with the Type A-5 mask on August 11, 1943. However, the revisions dated April 1, 1944, to the AAF Illustrated Class 13 Catalog listed the Type A-6 mask as still available, but non-standard and expendable.

The End of Liquid Oxygen in Air Corps Service

Laboratory and flight testing is important, but the ultimate test of equipment is how it performs in active service over a period of time. By the mid-1930s, the Materiel Division had about seventeen years of experience in developing and testing gaseous oxygen equipment, and about twelve

years of experience with liquid oxygen gear. Liquid oxygen equipment had performed quite well during the many test flights flown by personnel of the Materiel Division. They were usually single flights originating at Wright Field, where conditions were optimum and support was provided by an experienced ground crew. Air Corps tactical units around the country had by that time been using liquid oxygen, with varying degrees of success, for about five years, and through experience, certain inherent problems and difficulties in its use had become apparent.

An Equipment Branch study prepared in March 1935, by a committee headed by Capt. Armstrong, examined the merits of liquid and gaseous oxygen for Air Corps use.

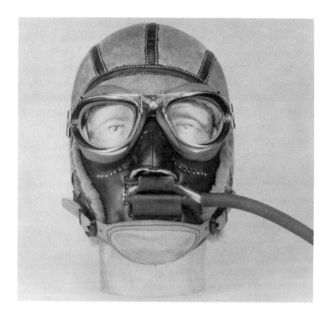

The Type A-6 was the last old-style oxygen face mask. It was made of flexible leather, with an intermediate lining and a chamois inner lining, and covered the lower part of the face. The A-6 had an opening in the nose and mouth area for attaching a metal oxygen distributor, which formed part of the mask and connected with the single inlet to the supply tube from the liquid oxygen vaporizer. This design obviated the need for the wearer to retain a tube in the mouth, and permitted natural breathing and talking. The A-6, which could also be worn without the oxygen distributer and tube, for protection from the cold, remained in service from 1935 to 1943. The winter helmet is the Type B-5 shearling, and the goggle is the Type B-6 (SI Photo 82–6582)

It included a detailed account of the difficulties with liquid oxygen experienced by the 2nd Bombardment Wing at Langley Field, Virginia.[45] The study clearly outlined the main objections to the continued use of liquid oxygen in regular service:

1. *Availability and Storage:* Liquid oxygen was not as available as gaseous oxygen. Only one portable liquid oxygen generator was in Air Corps service at that time, and it required up to twelve hours to commence production after relocation by truck or by air. All other liquid oxygen must be purchased on the open market, and it was usually necessary to order it days ahead to allow time for manufacture. It had to be used shortly after procurement, because of evaporation, regardless of weather conditions or changing mission requirements. Liquid oxygen was not always readily available away from cities, and would be quite difficult to obtain in case of war or national emergency. Gaseous oxygen, on the other hand, could be purchased in advance, and transported and stored at almost any location for long periods of time.

2. *Servicing of Aircraft:* Servicing with liquid oxygen presented problems not easily overcome, even with continuous practice. Due to the high evaporation rate, it was poured into containers in the airplane immediately before flight, and usually one to two pounds were lost in each filling. Servicing was much faster with gaseous oxygen. Even experienced personnel took about 15 minutes to service 18 airplanes with liquid oxygen, and this had to be done immediately before takeoff. An airplane could be serviced with gaseous oxygen days ahead of the contemplated mission, and it took only about five minutes to service 18 airplanes, simply placing the storage cylinders on board and making the few connections. This greatly affected the combat readiness of units, especially interceptor squadrons, because only aircraft equipped with gaseous oxygen could be made ready for rapid takeoff at unpredictable moments.

3. *Weight of Equipment:* The Type B-11 vaporizer weighed only 22 pounds and contained approximately four hours of oxygen if used at 20,000 feet. By comparison, four gaseous oxygen cylinders containing a total of four hours of oxygen weighed 76 pounds. However, it was noted that newer metal-alloy gas cylinders weighing much less than the ones then in use had been developed, and if adopted, the weight difference between gaseous and liquid oxygen equipment would not be so marked.

4. *Cost:* It was stated in the study that gaseous oxygen could now be procured in purer form than liquid oxygen, and at much lower cost, for one liter of liquid oxygen at that time cost about $0.058, while one liter of gaseous oxygen cost $0.02.

The study stated in conclusion that the liquid oxygen equipment then in service was poorly designed for servicing, while gaseous oxygen equipment was essentially the same as that used in 1922. It recommended that all equipment be carefully examined, and that a project be initiated to develop improved gaseous oxygen equipment.

All factors involved were considered by the Materiel Division and Air Corps headquarters, and liquid oxygen equipment was gradually phased out of regular service use from 1936. Some equipment remained in the inventory for experimental and special use. Larger, more powerful aircraft such as the Boeing B-17 had the room and performance capability to carry the bulkier gaseous oxygen gear, and new aircraft entering service were equipped with gaseous oxygen systems. With the greater service ceilings attained by the planes of the late 1930s, high-altitude flight by tactical units became a normal, daily routine.

The advantages of liquid oxygen were never forgotten completely, and during the last two years of World War II a new liquid oxygen research program was initiated. This resulted in the development of a new generation of highly efficient liquid oxygen equipment that finally entered service in the 1950s.

Air Corps Gaseous Oxygen Equipment

The discontinuance of the use of liquid oxygen by tactical units and the introduction of modern, high-performance aircraft meant that the Air Corps had a pressing need for improved gaseous oxygen equipment. The development of this equipment was given priority, and progress was made during the next few years by the small staffs of the Equipment Branch and the Physiological Research Laboratory at Wright Field.

A new, compact, manually operated regulator, for dispensing a metered quantity of gaseous oxygen to flyers at altitude, was one of the first items to be produced. Designated the Type A-6, it was standardized on May 8, 1936, and placed on procurement. It was changed to limited standard on August 13, 1940, but not declared obsolete until January 27, 1944. With dial settings for 20,000, 25,000, 30,000 and 35,000 feet, the A-6 was simple to use. Crewmen, such as gunners engaged in physical activity, could use the next higher altitude setting to obtain additional oxygen when needed. It was intended to dispense large quantities of oxygen, which were necessary in conjunction with the pipestem. Later used with the more efficient oxygen mask, the setting was fixed at 20,000 feet. The standard Navy automatic regulator (the Gaertner MK.1A) was given the Type A-7 designation and used in service-test status from November 12, 1936, until January 28, 1938.

New, lighter weight, high-pressure oxygen cylinders of various capacities were also developed, and procured for use with the continuous or constant-flow oxygen system. Oxygen was stored in these cylinders at a pressure of about 1,800 pounds per square inch. High-pressure oxygen fittings and lines carried the oxygen from the storage cylinders aboard the aircraft to the regulator. A low-pressure flexible rubber hose conveyed the oxygen from the regulator directly to the crewman.

The most urgent requirements at that time were for improved oxygen regulators for use at high altitude and for an efficient, modern oxygen mask. Capt. Armstrong and Dr. John W. Heim, of the Physiological Research Lab-oratory, worked closely with Maj. Rudolph Fink and other personnel of the Equipment Branch to develop a successful oxygen mask. Several experimental types were fabricated or obtained for tests, but none proved to be fully satisfactory.[46] The successful flight of the Lockheed XC-35 airplane led some officials to believe erroneously that the need for an individual oxygen mask and equipment would be eliminated by the use of the pressurized cabin on future military aircraft.

Experiments concerning the problems of high-altitude flight were also conducted in cooperation with aircraft manufacturers, civil airline personnel, and researchers at medical research facilities including the Mayo Clinic and Foundation in Rochester, Minnesota. The low-pressure chamber was made available for use by outside researchers, and assistance was provided on a variety of projects, including the development of oxygen-inhalation apparatus.

The Development of the Modern Oxygen Mask

Over twenty years had passed since the introduction in 1918 of the first oxygen mask for use by U.S. Army aviators. The mask designed for use with the American-built Dreyer oxygen system proved to be unsatisfactory, and during the following two decades, countless different types of oxygen masks were devised and tested both in the United States and abroad. In fact, oxygen masks of almost every conceivable style had been tried since the first mask was invented by Dr. Hermann von Schroetter about 1900. They had been made of leather, chamois, fabric, metal, celluloid, plastic, rubber, and various combinations of these materials. All sizes, shapes, and suspensions were tried, but all were either inefficient, wasteful of oxygen, or uncomfortable. Man has traditionally preferred to have his face uncovered, even in cold weather, not only because it is uncomfortable to have a garment touching or pressing on the face, but because there appears to be an inherent fear of suffocation if the nose and mouth are covered.

The inhaling of oxygen through a plain low-pressure supply tube or hose, with or without a mouthpiece, eliminated this objection but proved in practice to be both wasteful and dangerous. If the oxygen tube slipped from the mouth at 30,000 feet, unconsciousness could result within 30 to 60 seconds, often leading to death. The user had to wear an uncomfortable nose clamp, or remember to breath through the tube and not his nose. This was not always easy during times of stress or physical activity. It was tiring to hold the tube or pipestem between the teeth for long periods and very difficult to talk. The tube was also messy because ice usually formed around the user's lips and chin as a result of drooling. The flow of cold oxygen from the tube was much akin to having an icicle in the mouth, and, as such, was both unpleasant and caused excessive drying and irritation of the tissues of the mouth and throat.

The direct flow of the oxygen pouring continually into the mouth tended to puff out the cheeks requiring that the mouth be opened to allow excess oxygen to escape. Use of the tube was, above all, very wasteful of oxygen in the continuous flow system because from one-half to two-thirds was simply lost to the atmosphere. This necessitated carrying additional heavy cylinders of oxygen on long flights. When the mouthpiece was not used, some flyers would "bite off" the oxygen by closing the teeth on the tube at the end of every inhalation, thus stopping the flow of oxygen during exhalation. However, this procedure was detrimental to the oxygen regulator.

These negative factors were partially resolved through the use of the oxygen face masks, standardized by the Air Corps during the late 1920s and early 1930s; however, these masks were both uncomfortable and inefficient. They were basically warm winter face masks, which protected the face from cold and wind when flying in an open cockpit. In the new aircraft with enclosed cockpits, this was, of course, no longer such an important factor. In addition to discomfort caused by the masks, they tended to interfere with voice transmission. There was a tendency for moisture in the breath to freeze on any cold parts, such as the orifices or metal valves, often rendering the mask useless. Also, up to two-thirds of all the oxygen carried was wasted during breathing.

The quest for a more efficient oxygen mask can be traced back as early as 1917, when Prof. John S. Haldane of Great Britain developed an improved type of mask. It was an oronasal mask, to which was attached a small rubber oxygen reservoir bag featuring a rubber flapper valve activated during breathing. Although efficient in the use of oxygen, the Haldane mask was little used by aviators because the valve and reservoir tended to freeze in cold temperatures, when the moisture in the breath collected to form ice. The reservoir bag suspended from the mask also fluttered in the slip stream and could tear itself away.

During the 1920s and 1930s several experimental masks were tested, based on the rebreather method used in mine-rescue work. Although efficient in theory, none were found suitable for use in aviation.[47]

The development of an oxygen mask that was both efficient and comfortable proved to be one of the most intractable problems associated with high-altitude flight. This problem was among those studied during the 1930s by Dr. Walter M. Boothby, Dr. W. Randolph Lovelace II, and Dr. Arthur H. Bulbulian of the Mayo Clinic and Foundation in Rochester, Minnesota. The experiments of Boothby and Bulbulian resulted in the development of a

new type of nasal mask, which could be used for administering gaseous oxygen to patients in place of the old oxygen tent, which was not only inefficient but constituted a fire hazard.

In 1938, the development of a new type of oxygen mask for aviators was announced by the Mayo Clinic, and promptly demonstrated to representatives of the airlines, the military services, and the press. The new mask, called the "B.L.B." from the initials of the names of its designers: Boothby, Lovelace, and Bulbulian, performed impressively during a number of high-altitude test flights closely observed by aero-medical experts.

The B.L.B. oxygen mask consisted principally of a latex face piece that fit snugly over the nose, and a rubber oxygen reservoir or rebreather bag that hung under the chin. The nasal cover was designed to avoid interference with the wearer's vision, and permitted talking, eating, or drinking with the mask in use. It was available in two sizes and was retained on the head by an adjustable rubber strap. The B.L.B. mask was designed with two hollow rubber tubes, which ran from the nose piece around each side of the mouth, terminating in a single supply tube below the chin. In the original design the rebreather bag was attached to the supply tube just below a metal relief or exhalation valve, and a small air regulator provided for oxygen intake from the oxygen-supply hose. This valve had a tendency to freeze up, and was replaced in a later modification by two sponge rubber disks for inhaling and exhaling. The mask was shaped so as to be an almost exact anatomic counterpart of the portion of the face with which it was in contact, and was therefore quite comfortable to wear. The smooth rubber bearing surfaces were relatively wide, so that an airtight fit was assured, without undue pressure at any point.

The best feature of the B.L.B. mask was the rebreather bag, which conserved much of the continuously flowing oxygen that had previously been wasted. By the late 1930s, most commercial and military aircraft had enclosed crew compartments, which protected the rebreather bag from damage by the slip-stream. The small valve or plug at the bottom of the rebreather bag was for the purpose of draining off any water that collected in the bag.

The B.L.B. mask was intended to be worn with a normal continuous-flow oxygen system and a manually adjusted regulator. The operation of the original mask, as described in a study course for students attending a high-altitude training program at the Aero Medical Laboratory, was as follows:

> When in use, oxygen enters the mask from the tube attached at the inlet and is delivered through a tube to the lower end of the reservoir re-breathing bag. It is then inhaled by the flyer. The exhaled gases pass

44

down into the bag. When the bag becomes distended with the mixture of expired air and incoming oxygen, the pressure thus produced causes the remaining portion of the exhaled gases to pass out through the exhalation valve and through the port holes contained in the metal air regulator of the mask. The expired air thus escaping is from the later part of the expiration and contains the most carbon dioxide and the least oxygen, whereas the expired air which passes into the bag first and contains the least carbon dioxide and the most oxygen is available for re-breathing, thereby helping to increase the efficiency of the apparatus. On the next inhalation, the mixed oxygen and expired gases are again drawn in and further admixed with atmospheric air entering through the port holes. Without a rebreather bag, all of the exhaled gases, the first portion of which is still relatively rich in oxygen, would pass out into the atmosphere and be entirely wasted.[48]

Both the original B.L.B. nasal mask and the oronasal development were made by the Ohio Chemical and Manufacturing Company of Cleveland, and were used to a limited extent by commercial airlines for a number of years before cabin pressurization became common. The basic principle of the B.L.B. mask is used today in the emergency-oxygen masks for passengers carried over each seat in commercial airliners. The improvements made in the B.L.B. masks for military use were also incorporated in the masks produced for commercial sale.

When Captain Armstrong, chief of the Aero Medical Research Unit, first heard about the B.L.B. mask, he asked Maj. Rudolph Fink, head of the Miscellaneous Unit, Equipment Laboratory, to visit the Mayo Clinic and discuss the new development with the inventors. An example of the B.L.B. mask was obtained and carefully tested at the Aero Medical Research Unit by Captain Armstrong and members of the Equipment Branch staff. With its rebreather feature, it was considered to be the closest approach to the ideal mask of any developed up to that time.[49] In fact, the B.L.B. nasal mask, and its oronasal modification, which covered both the nose and mouth, could be considered the first truly modern American oxygen masks.

The B.L.B. nasal mask was adopted for Air Corps use and standardized as the Type A-7 on July 15, 1939. Its status was changed to limited standard on May 1, 1940, when the Type A-8 oronasal mask was standardized, and it was declared obsolete on August 11, 1943. Development of the Type A-7 continued for several years in an effort to make it even more efficient, and an improved version was standardized as the Type A-7A on June 5, 1943. It had sponge rubber inhalation and exhalation discs, mounted in rubber turrets on each side of the supply tube, in place of the troublesome metal valve and air regulator.

The first modern American oxygen mask, the B.L.B. nasal mask, standardized by the Air Corps in 1939 as the Type A-7. It is shown here in its original form, with the Type A-6 regulator and Type E-1 646-cubic-inch oxygen cylinder, during a demonstration by Pfc. Raymond Whitney of the Aero Medical Laboratory. Called the "Human Guinea Pig," Whitney was awarded the Distinguished Flying Cross, for his efforts in high-altitude chamber research and the XC-35 pressure-cabin airplane development project. (Courtesy USAF)

It was also no longer necessary to adjust the air regulator to open the portholes depending on the altitude. A final modification, the Type A-7B, was standardized on June 9, 1945. It also had the sponge rubber discs above the rebreather bag like the A-7A.

Either the Type A-6 or A-8 oxygen regulator could be used with the Type A-7 masks. Because the mask was much more efficient, it did not require the large quantity of oxygen required for the old pipestem. Therefore, when the Type A-6 oxygen regulator was used with the mask, the regulator was set at the 20,000 foot altitude mark and left at that setting for all altitudes.

The Type A-7 nasal mask proved to be generally satisfactory below 20,000 feet for use by transport and courier pilots and passengers, and for special purposes. However, it was found that the mask that covered only the nose was actually very dangerous when used by crewmen aboard combat aircraft operating at very high altitudes. Under stress or during energetic physical activity, it was just too easy to forget to breath only through the nose. Above 25,000 feet, breathing outside air could quickly result in hypoxia, with disastrous results. Nasal passages also frequently become congested in low temperatures. The A-7 covered only the nose, consequently the oxygen supply stopped whenever the flyer talked, since he inhaled through his mouth while talking. A modified version of the B.L.B. mask that permitted breathing through either the nose or mouth was desired for general Air Corps use in view of these findings.

At a conference held at the Equipment Laboratory on October 19, 1939, Captain Armstrong and other staff members discussed the principal requirements for any future oxygen mask with Dr. Boothby and Dr. Lovelace of the Mayo Clinic, and representatives of the firms manufacturing the B.L.B. and Type A-7 masks:

> The requirements for a new oxygen mask should insure that it is comfortable, of the oronasal (oral-nasal) type, and capable of transmitting voice to a hand-held microphone for radio communication without appreciable distortion or muffling. In addition, the mask should be simple or automatic in operation, free from the danger of freezing, and closely approaching 100 per cent in efficiency of oxygen utilization.

Boothby and Lovelace presented for consideration a new means of using the rebreather principle without valves. Armstrong and his colleagues exhibited a method by which voice could be transmitted through an oronasal mask without appreciable distortion or muffling of the voice. This consisted of an oronasal mask which contained a rubber diaphragm, only one millimeter in thickness, opposite the mouth. This type of vent was incorporated in the design of the new oronasal mask adopted by the Air Corps as the Type A-8.[50]

The Type A-8 oronasal oxygen mask was essentially the same in its principle of operation as the Type A-7. Like the A-7, it permitted rebreathing of part of the unused oxygen expired from the lungs and respiratory passages. The A-8 fit tightly over the nose and mouth, and oxygen flowed into the rebreather bag at a constant rate that was fixed manually at the oxygen regulator according to need. The design consisted of a moulded rubber covering for the nose and mouth, a large covering case of phenolic compound which supported the mask, and a turret-like protrusion containing a sponge-rubber disk in front of the mouth which functioned as an air-mixing valve. Fastened to the base of the mask was a connector sleeve to which was attached the flexible rubber rebreather bag, provided with an oxygen-intake tube. There were straps for securing the mask in position on the head, so that the A-8 and

A-8A masks could be worn with or without a flying helmet. The Type A-8 was standardized on May 1, 1940, and procured promptly for general use. It was designated as limited standard on February 13, 1941, when the Type A-8A was standardized, and declared obsolete on August 11, 1943.

One of the complaints encountered with the Type A-8 was that moisture from the breath collected on the sponge-rubber disk in the mask turret, and in an unheated cabin was likely to freeze up. Users of the A-7 and A-8 masks were advised that the freezing of the masks could be corrected by simply pinching the sponge-rubber disks between the fingers. The mask turret in front interfered with the bombardier's sight, and it was difficult to carry on an interphone or radio conversation easily and distinctly through the sponge-rubber disk. Improvements were made in late 1940 and early 1941 to correct the deficiencies,

Lt. Delbert V. Mitchell wearing the Type A-8 oronasal oxygen mask in the cockpit of a Bell P-39 on December 23, 1941. An HS-38 headset is being worn because earphones were not installed in his Type B-5 winter flying helmet. Goggle is Type B-7. This photo may have been posed, to show how crowded a fighter cockpit was, when wearing the bulky shearling winter flying clothing, such as the Type B-3 jacket and A-3 trousers. (SI Photo 10620)

46 and the A-8 was quickly superseded in production by the Type A-8A, standardized on February 13, 1941. It in turn was declared limited standard on November 3, 1941, when the improved Type A-8B was standardized. The A-8A was declared obsolete on October 29, 1944. All of the A-8 series masks were similar in operation. The Types A-8A and A-8B can be differentiated easily from the Type A-8 because they had a sponge disk inhalation and exhalation valve in a rubber turret on each side of the front of the mask. Rubber covers for the turrets or a fleece-lined cloth bag provided insulation against freezing when the mask was worn for extended periods in low temperatures. A different type of connector for the oxygen inlet was also incorporated in the A-8A and A-8B masks, making them sturdier and reducing excessive wear and tear on the rebreather bag.

The Type A-8B mask had a new type of suspension that attached the head straps to hooks on the flying helmets. This allowed for installation of a microphone in the face piece, which was modified for the purpose. During the war, an auxiliary head-strap arrangement called a "Juliet" was again introduced so that the mask could be worn with or without a flying helmet. The A-8B was standardized on November 3, and changed to limited standard on December 9, 1941. The Type A-8B was procured in far greater numbers than its predecessors, and remained in use aboard transport and cargo aircraft for many years after the end of World War II. There was one final minor modification of the mask, which was standardized as the Type A-8C on January 26, 1945. It is believed that few of these were procured.

According to an official 1943 catalog of aeronautical equipment, the Type A-8B mask could be converted into a demand-type mask by using a conversion kit. The conversion was accomplished by replacing the rebreather bag and oxygen-intake tube with a corrugated rubber tube, which was provided with a standard rapid connect (slip-in-fit) fitting. Each sponge-rubber disk was replaced with a valve insert, valve flap and a rubber insulating shield, all contained in the conversion kit.

The Type A-7 and A-8 oxygen masks quickly replaced the pipestem and the old Type A-5, A-6, and B-5 oxygen face masks that were in general use until the summer of 1939.

The new oxygen regulator provided for use with the Type A-7 and A-8 rebreather-type oxygen masks was designated as the Type A-8. It was manually operated, like the A-6 regulator, and was similar except for an increase in capacity in the sensitive flow-metering device combined with a more accurate indicator. The flow-metering mechanism was designed to provide a reduced oxygen flow to the more efficient masks. According to the Type Designation Sheets, the A-8 was designed for 3,000 psi.

Type A-8B oxygen mask, being worn with head straps in this photo taken on September 1, 1943. The rubber covers over the two turrets containing the sponge-rubber disk inhalation and exhalation valves, provided insulation against freezing when the mask was worn for long periods in low temperatures. The oxygen tube from the continuous-flow regulator is attached just above the rubber rebreather bag. Airman appears to be wearing the Type B-6 winter flying helmet, Type B-6 goggle, and Type B-3 shearling winter flying jacket. (Courtesy USAF)

It could not be used with the old tube or pipestem, because the restricted orifice would not provide sufficient oxygen flow. The knob was distinctly marked "USE WITH MASK ONLY." The A-8 was standardized on March 15, 1940, and although changed to limited standard on August 13 of that year, it remained in service through the end of the war. A modified version, the Type A-8A, was similar to the A-8, except that the flow valves were increased and the needle-valve control changed. It replaced the A-8 as the standard regulator on August 23, 1941, but was quickly changed to limited standard on September 8, because of the new models then entering service for use with the low-pressure oxygen system.

Other new items of equipment developed and procured in the late 1930s and early 1940s included the Type A-1 gaseous oxygen purifier, standardized on April 11, 1936, declared limited standard on February 27, 1937, and obsolete on January 29, 1944. The Type A-2 was an improvement that was standardized on February 2, 1937. It, in turn, was changed to limited standard on April 13, 1942 when a new model was adopted, and finally declared obsolete on January 29, 1944. These devices gained in importance during the war years, because oxygen obtained from Allied sources overseas often contained more impurities and moisture than that produced in the United States.

Personnel of the Aero Medical Laboratory and other organizations in the United States and abroad, in addition to providing valuable assistance in the development of new and improved oxygen equipment, continued to make progress in the study of the basic problems and conditions associated with high-altitude flight. Capt. Armstrong and R. E. Huber, for example, investigated the long-held belief of many aviators that oxygen use had a deleterious effect on their teeth and dental work. This was variously attributed to the action of oxygen itself, to cold, and to changes of barometric pressure. Their studies led them to the conclusion that none of these factors, nor any combination, produced evidence of injury to teeth or to dental restorations.[51] Other studies were made to determine the toxicity of pure oxygen on experimental animals at various altitudes.

Based on research at the Aero Medical Laboratory and the School of Aviation Medicine, Air Corps Technical Order No. 01–1H–1B was published on April 20, 1938, clarifying the use of oxygen at various altitudes:

Except in urgent, unforeseen emergencies, all personnel will use oxygen at all times while participating in flight above 15,000 feet. Oxygen will also be used when remaining at an altitude below 15,000 feet but in excess of 12,000 feet for periods of two hours or longer duration and when participating in flights below 12,000 feet but at or in excess of 10,000 feet for periods of six hours or longer duration.[52]

It was later determined that in night flying, oxygen should be used at all altitudes from the ground up. This was necessary to preserve maximum vision and efficiency and prevent night blindness.

The limits of high flying while using oxygen at ambient pressures were determined and mentioned in the list of accomplishments included in the annual report of the Chief, Materiel Division, for FY 1939. Armstrong and Heim discovered during that year that above 33,000 feet with aviators breathing 100 percent oxygen, there was a marked decrease in the arterial oxygen saturation, which determined the preservation of normal bodily function, and at 40,000 feet this fell to 88 percent. Armstrong stated that:

Flights at 25,000 feet must be considered as definitely hazardous and 30,000 feet should be the absolute allowable limit of high flying in any except the most unusual circumstances. In no instance should anyone ever be allowed to fly above 40,000 feet.[53]

Other related work at the Aero Medical Laboratory included the study of aeroembolism, the "bends," a serious and painful condition, caused by the formation of nitrous bubbles in the bloodstream at high altitude due to rapid changes in pressure. Breathing pure oxygen for half an hour before takeoff was recommended for crewmen scheduled to fly above 30,000 feet. This was at first administered while the airmen were exercising, but the exercise was eventually discontinued by the Army Air Forces and the Royal Air Force. The bends fortunately did not turn out to be as great a problem in high-altitude flying as many expected.

The tempo of European aeronautical research increased dramatically during the 1930s, resulting in the reequipment of all the major air forces. German efforts resulted in such advances as the pressurized aircraft cabin and the introduction of the demand-oxygen system in the German Air Force. Experimental full pressure suits were developed in England, France, and Italy, and the altitude record was broken almost every year, before peaceful competition was ended by the outbreak of war in Europe on September 1, 1939.

The U.S. Army Air Corps in the summer of 1939 was poorly prepared to fight a modern air war. The few first-line combat aircraft available at that time were equipped with continuous-flow oxygen equipment that consisted essentially of:

1. High-pressure, light-weight steel cylinders for storing gaseous oxygen at about 1,800 psi.
2. High-pressure oxygen fittings, and lines for conveying the oxygen from the storage cylinders to the dispensing equipment.
3. A regulator for dispensing a metered quantity of oxygen to the flyer at altitude. The standard regulator was the manually controlled Type A-6.
4. A low-pressure flexible rubber hose for conveying the oxygen from the regulator directly to the flyer. The pipestem and oxygen face masks were just beginning to be replaced by the Type A-7 oxygen mask.

All of the above equipment proved to have serious shortcomings, but just how serious was not yet realized.

THE CHANGE TO A LOW-PRESSURE OXYGEN SYSTEM

Fortunately for the United States, over two years were to pass after the beginning of World War II before American forces entered combat. Not only did this period of time allow American industry to prepare for war production, but it also permitted our armed forces to expand, to train, and to benefit from the combat experience gained by the Allied and Axis powers. During 1940 and 1941, U.S. Army experts visited England and observed the Royal Air Force and German Luftwaffe in action. These observers included Capt. Harry G. Armstrong and Capt. Otis O. Benson, who had replaced Armstrong as Chief of the Aero Medical Laboratory in September 1940. Armstrong first visited Canada, and then went to England as a "Canadian" observer during the Battle of Britain, because of United States neutrality.

One of the conclusions formed by the American technical personnel was that the high-pressure oxygen system in use by the Air Corps was undesirable for modern aerial warfare. It was recommended that the high-pressure system be replaced by a low-pressure system in combat aircraft. The high-pressure oxygen system stored compressed oxygen in steel cylinders at a normal charge of 1,800 pounds per square inch. Even in peacetime, difficulty and delay were encountered in servicing the high-pressure cylinders. The Air Corps practice was to remove cylinders from airplanes after flight at high altitude, and take them to the filling location, where they would be recharged directly from commercial 220-cubic-foot oxygen cylinders. These commercial cylinders were only charged to a pressure of between 1,800 and 2,000 psi, and filling was tedious, sometimes requiring the use of an oxygen compressor. The cylinders were then returned to the aircraft and reinstalled.

The slow and inconvenient servicing was sufficient reason to change from a high-pressure to a low-pressure system, but the change was considered mandatory after the results of gunfire tests were available. When a high-pressure oxygen cylinder was punctured by a .30 caliber bullet, the steel around the entrance hole burned in the oxygen atmosphere, yielding a short-lived but extremely hot and long flame. Even worse than this, when a charged high-pressure oxygen cylinder was punctured by a .50 caliber bullet, the cylinder exploded into two parts with great violence and was capable of completely disabling the airplane![54]

Combat reports from the Battle of Britain, and comparative gunfire tests at Wright Field, Ohio, Aberdeen Proving Ground, and Edgewood Arsenal, Maryland, led to the decision for the change from a high- to a low-pressure oxygen system for the Air Corps. As an interim measure, a method was devised to prevent the high-pressure cylinders from exploding, though not from burning, by winding piano wire around the cylinders. This, however, increased the weight of the cylinders.

Action was initiated by the Air Corps to change over to the low-pressure oxygen system, however, the U.S. Navy, like the Royal Air Force, decided to continue to use the high-pressure system. The new low-pressure cylinders consisted of two deep-drawn stainless steel hemispherical cups welded together to make a complete cylinder. The early types, like the Type G-1, had exterior steel strapping which sufficiently supported the stainless steel so as to withstand the stress produced by impact of a .50 caliber projectile. A great improvement was made in 1943 when low-pressure cylinders were developed, made of low-alloy steel, so fabricated that the exterior steel strapping was eliminated, and the cylinders were less affected by gunfire than the older stainless-steel cylinder design. This made possible greater production, a reduction in cost ranging from 60 to 90 percent of that for the stainless-steel cylinder, and an improvement in overall strength of the cylinder. The cylinders were sprayed with a coat of zinc-chromate primer, except for the A-4 cylinder for the portable (walk-around) unit, and the H-1 and H-2 bailout bottles, which were sprayed with green lacquer. The normal operating pressure of the cylinders was 400 pounds per square inch, and they were safe for use up to pressures of 500 psi.

The new aircraft cylinders carried oxygen at lower pressure than the high-pressure cylinders, so they inevitably had to be larger in size. However, because the low-pressure permitted a smaller wall thickness, they were lighter per quantity of oxygen carried than the high-pressure cylinders.

All the cylinders were manifolded together in some airplanes and filled from a single filler valve, normally located conveniently in the skin of the aircraft. To fill them it was only necessary to bring up to the airplane several commercial 220-cubic-foot cylinders on carts, plug into the filler valve, and charge up the airplane system. This efficient method was similar to that used for fueling the plane. This system, although found in some heavy bombers through the end of the war, became non-standard for combat aircraft, because a puncture of any manifold would exhaust the oxygen supply for two or three flyers.

Several schemes for low-pressure oxygen installation were used in AAF aircraft during the war. In addition to multi-place combat aircraft with the common manifold system, there were multi-place aircraft with individual manifolds at each station outlet; multi-place aircraft with a four-line (dual source) system; and single-place aircraft with an individual system. The systems in combat aircraft always included check valves for protection against oxygen loss from gunfire. Check valves permitted a rapid flow of oxygen in only one direction.

Problems were encountered occasionally during the war when AAF aircraft had to recharge their low-pressure oxygen systems at a U.S. Navy or British Royal Air Force base because both the Navy and RAF continued to use high-pressure oxygen systems. As a matter of interest, the German Air Force also used a high-pressure system through the end of the war.

The regulator developed for use with the low-pressure oxygen system was the type A-9. It was little different in design from the A-8 except that the maximum cylinder pressure was changed to 500 psi. The A-9 was standardized on August 13, 1940, and changed to limited standard on August 23, 1941. The Type A-9A regulator was almost the same as the A-9, but the flow valves were increased and the needle-valve control changed. It entered service as the standard regulator on August 23, 1941, but was declared limited standard less than a month later on September 8, because of the standardization of the Type A-12 demand-type regulator. The continuous-flow regulators were manually operated, and as such had to be adjusted

by the user at various altitudes. The Type A-10 regulator with automatic operation was similar to the A-9 in capacity, and entered service-test status on September 7, 1940. It was not adopted for use, and was declared obsolete on December 20, 1941, at which time the remaining stock was retained and used for experimental purposes.

Another regulator developed about the same time was similar to the A-10, except that the specification was written around particular performance requirements. This was the Type A-11 which was standardized on February 2, 1942, but changed to limited standard on May 8, 1944. The A-11 was superseded on that date by the Spec. AN-R-15, AN6010–1, intended for use by both the Army and Navy. The A-11 and its successor were used mainly in cargo or transport aircraft and supplied one to fifteen passengers, wearing Type A-7A or A-8B masks, with oxygen from an automatic continuous-flow system.

According to Col. A. Pharo Gagge, Chief of the Biophysics Branch of the Aero Medical Laboratory during World War II, there were second thoughts after the war

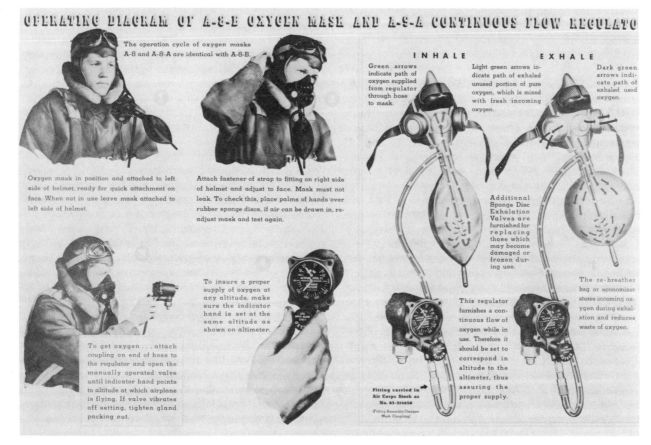

AAF instruction chart dated May 9, 1942, for the Type A-8B oxygen mask and Type A-9A continuous-flow regulator used with the low-pressure oxygen system. (Courtesy USAF)

concerning the decision to change from the high-pressure to the low-pressure oxygen system: "The final opinion was that the change over was not worth the effort because of the great amount of time required to develop and produce the new equipment, the waste of space required by the system aboard aircraft, and the fact that the high-pressure bottles were sufficiently resistant to 'flak,' which destroyed almost twice as many aircraft as fighters."[55]

The Demand-Oxygen System

The high oxygen consumption of the continuous- or constant-flow systems used aboard Royal Air Force (and American) aircraft was apparent to Captain Armstrong and other American observers during the Battle of Britain. It was obvious that much of the air combat in Europe would continue to be fought at great altitude, and the rate of oxygen consumption, as well as the capacity of the aircraft to carry oxygen in sufficient quantity, would be limiting factors on future combat missions. These problems had already become apparent on RAF bombing raids over Germany, where the amount of oxygen carried proved to be inadequate on some missions, even when oxygen was not used below 15,000 feet.

Major Benson was in England in 1941, and studied the oxygen equipment found on captured Luftwaffe aircraft; he was impressed with the German demand-oxygen system. The automatic demand regulator used with this advanced system appeared to provide an important advantage over the manually operated types used by the United States with the continuous-flow system. The Auer Company of Berlin developed the first demand-type regulator in 1936. The demand-oxygen system, including high-pressure oxygen cylinders and a quick-disconnect mask, was used as standard equipment by the German Air Force during World War II. The German regulator featured the Draeger demand valve designed by H. Seeler. Benson obtained several of the demand masks and regulators that had been removed from German aircraft shot down over England, and forwarded them to the Aero Medical Laboratory at Wright Field. They arrived on June 20, 1941, and after being carefully examined and tested, examples were turned over by Major Fink of the Equipment Laboratory to the Eclipse-Pioneer Instrument Division of the Bendix Aviation Corporation and to the Air Reduction Sales Company, to serve as a basis for the development of an American counterpart.[56] This work was successfully accomplished in a remarkably short time, and the demand regulators developed were both of the diluter type, resembling the German design only in the use of the venturi principle of dilution and the air-mixture valve, which included an aneroid for controlling the amount of air introduced at different altitudes. The other components of the mechanism were based on proven designs used in previous American regulators. After considerable modification, the designs of both companies were standardized on September 8, 1941, and identified as the Type A-12 diluter-demand regulator. The most sensitive and effective of the American-made demand regulators was developed by Bradford Holmes, a creative engineer at Pioneer-Bendix. With the introduction of the Type A-12, the Army at last had the automatic oxygen regulator that had eluded engineers since World War I.

The diluter demand-type regulator was essentially a suction-operated valve which released oxygen upon inhalation. When the auto-mix lever was in the "on" position, this regulator automatically mixed varying quantities of air and oxygen, the ratio depending upon the needs of the altitude, and delivered the quantity demanded upon inhalation. Above 30,000 feet pure oxygen was released. When the auto-mix was "off" pure oxygen was delivered regardless of altitude. To prevent confusion, markings on the A-12 and AN6004–1 diluter-demand regulators were eventually changed to read "normal oxygen" and "100% oxygen." The regulator supplied as much oxygen as demanded by the momentary physiological needs of the user, that is, the greater the rate of respiration, the greater the amount of oxygen supplied. There was also a red emergency knob, which when turned on, allowed the oxygen to bypass the demand mechanism and enter the mask in a steady flow, regardless of breathing and altitude.

The diluter-demand regulator incorporated neither a pressure gauge nor a flow indicator; these instruments were auxiliary equipment in a demand system and were mounted on a special panel at each station. Adjustments during flights were not required, and the regulators were installed as permanent fixtures at each crew station in the plane. Operation of the demand regulator was fully automatic, and normal breathing was all that was required to operate this economical type of regulator.

In order to speed up production, Type A-12 regulators of the two different patterns were manufactured by several companies. The Eclipse-Pioneer Division of Bendix Aviation Corporation produced the Pioneer designs 2850-A1 and 2852-A1. The Aro Equipment Corporation, Air Reduction Sales Company, Johnson Fare Box Company, and National Die Casting Company produced regulators to Aro design 0–511–214. This design replaced the Air Reduction Sales Company design 8800100.

The Type A-12 regulator was changed to substitute standard on July 4, 1942, and limited standard on February 5, 1945. It was replaced as the standard regulator by the similar Army-Navy Spec. AN-R-5, AN6004–1 on July 4, 1942, and this was in turn changed to limited standard on February 5, 1945, for AAF use, when the Type A-12A was standardized. The A-12A was similar to the A-12, except that the ratios of air and oxygen and the amount of emergency flow permitted were altered. Capacity was increased to reduce hazards imposed by mask leakage.

One other demand regulator was developed during 1941: the Type A-13, for use with portable oxygen cylinders (walk-around bottles). It will be described later in this chapter along with other items of portable oxygen equipment.

Only a demand-type oxygen mask could be used with a diluter demand-type regulator. The Type A-9 was the first production demand-oxygen mask designed for use with the Type A-12 diluter-demand regulator. It consisted of a rubber face piece, usually gray in color, connected to a flexible, corrugated oxygen hose, which, in turn, was attached by a rapid-connect fitting to the regulator outlet. An extension hose was usually required, depending on the proximity of the regulator. An operating diagram and description of the A-9 mask and A-12 regulator dated 1942 is included in this chapter. According to the instructions

that accompanied the mask, issued March 30, 1942, the pocket in the nose section was designed for the MC-253 or MC-254 microphones, which could be installed by removing the rubber sealing plug. Squeezing or manipulating the mask would break loose any ice formation that might form in the rubber mask. Similar instructions were provided for freeing the A-8 series of masks from ice, which continued to present a serious problem at high altitudes.

The Type A-9 mask was issued in only two sizes, large and small. It was normally attached by short straps and hooks to the flying helmet, and a set of hooks came in the box with the mask, in case the helmets available were not so equipped. An auxiliary headstrap, or Juliet, was also supplied, so that the mask could be worn without a helmet or with other types of headgear. The A-9 mask was standardized for use on December 9, 1941, and changed to limited standard status on April 20, 1942, when the improved Type A-10 demand mask was standardized. Only a limited number of A-9 masks were procured, and

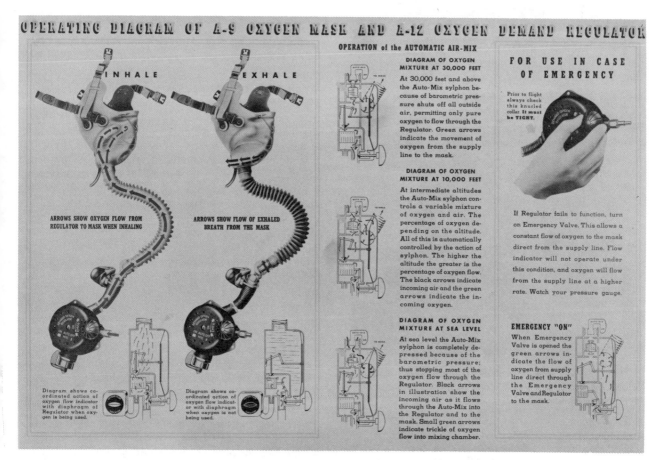

AAF instruction chart dated May 9, 1942, showing operation of the Type A-9 demand-oxygen mask and the Type A-12 diluter-demand regulator. The demand-oxygen system was a great improvement over the wasteful continuous-flow system. (Courtesy USAF)

the type was declared obsolete on August 11, 1943, because of the availability of improved demand masks. It was soon found that the suspension of the A-9 was not adequate to hold the mask in place during high "G" maneuvers, the expiratory valve was small, and the mask was difficult to fit, especially about the nose, contributing to excessive leakage. The demand-oxygen system required a tight-fitting mask to function well. Beards were, of course, not allowed, and crewmen were instructed to have a clean shave before using this type of oxygen mask in order to improve the fit.

The new demand-oxygen equipment was radically different, and far superior to the continuous-flow gear in use for so many years. It automatically provided the user with the proper amount of oxygen, up to approximately 40,000 feet. The demand system included low-pressure, shatterproof oxygen cylinders manifolded together using check valves and distribution lines, filler valves, diluter-demand regulators, pressure gauges, pressure-signal assemblies, indicator lamps, and the demand-type oxygen mask. In addition, a portable recharger hose was required at each crew position in bombers for recharging portable (walk-around) oxygen equipment from the main system in the airplane.

Demand-oxygen equipment was complicated in comparison to earlier gear, and required careful instruction of flying personnel through the "Altitude Training Program" and other indoctrination initiated in 1942. Considerable time was needed to develop and produce all of the components, install the equipment in the aircraft, and instruct support personnel in its proper maintenance. And in the fall of 1941, time was rapidly running out.

AAF OXYGEN EQUIPMENT IN WORLD WAR II

The year 1941 was a time of intense activity in the Army Air Corps—from June 20, 1941, Army Air Forces (AAF). New models of aircraft and equipment were beginning to arrive during this period of rapid expansion. The AAF was in the process of changing over from the high-pressure, continuous-flow oxygen system that used the Type A-8A regulator and A-8 series masks as standard, to the new low-pressure, continuous-flow system utilizing the Type A-9A regulator and A-8 series masks. The development of the new demand-oxygen system was also under way. Unfortunately, plans for a smooth transition were thwarted by the Japanese attack on Pearl Harbor.

It soon became apparent that the continuous-flow system was not adequate for extensive combat operations. The main reasons were: masks freezing at low temperatures; poor oxygen economy; and insufficient flexibility of the system to prevent oxygen waste at low altitudes and to insure an adequate supply at high altitudes under conditions of activity.[57] The early Boeing B-17E bombers of the U.S. Eighth Air Force, for example, were flying from England in 1942 equipped with the old high-pressure continuous-flow system. Mask freezing proved to be a serious problem on day-bombing missions requiring flight in the intense cold at altitudes between 25,000 and 30,000 feet. Many aborted missions, accidents and deaths were attributed to anoxia, reflecting not only faulty equipment but also carelessness and mistakes resulting from inadequate indoctrination. It was always necessary for the pilot to notify the crew of any change in altitude, so that they could adjust their regulators accordingly. Extra masks were carried along, in case the original ones froze up, but there remained the problem caused by the Type A-8A manually operated regulators, which frequently demanded more attention than the crewmen in combat were able to give them.

The first American demand-oxygen mask was the Type A-9, designed for use with the Type A-12 diluter-demand regulator. Standardized on December 9, 1941, it was replaced the following April as the standard demand mask by the Type A-10. Note method of attaching mask, by the use of short straps and hooks installed on helmet. When the A-9 mask was worn with a helmet and goggle, the entire face was covered as protection against frostbite and flash fire. The Type B-7 goggle is being worn with the Type B-6 winter flying helmet in this photo, dated February 2, 1942. (Courtesy USAF)

The AAF had a real need in all theaters of combat operation for a dependable, automatic, demand-oxygen system, but months would pass before aircraft equipped with this improved system entered action in significant numbers. Defective equipment and inexperienced personnel were to present a hazard even after the general introduction of the new demand-oxygen system, in the early spring of 1943.

Former Capt. Carl R. Thompson, who flew thirty combat missions over Europe as a B-17 copilot and pilot, recently recalled his experiences with oxygen equipment, especially the faulty quick-disconnect fittings on the oxygen hose:

> Oxygen checks were taken very seriously. On one mission to Wilhelmshaven, Germany, on February 3, 1944, we were flying at 27,000 feet when our ball turret gunner's oxygen mask connector came loose from the supply hose several times. On the intercom oxygen check he would insist that he was OK but Lenoski, the waist gunner, would say; "Gollaher is still going around and around," and we knew he was partially out. Mings and Lenoski, the waist gunners, would turn off the turret power, crank the guns down, open the door, and get him back on oxygen. This happened three or four times that day and it was a terribly frustrating situation to us in the cockpit for we could not see what was going on; just reports from the others in the rear of the plane. In another squadron a bombardier was brought back dead. He passed out and when the navigator tried to assist him he also passed out. Another crew member took portable oxygen equipment into the nose but was able to revive only the navigator.[58]

The AAF Altitude Training Program and the oxygen indoctrination presented by the Unit Oxygen Officers, and later by the Personal Equipment Officers, greatly reduced the number of casualties from anoxia and frostbite. A training course for noncommissioned officers who maintained and repaired personal equipment was also initiated during the war.

The urgent efforts to develop and manufacture the more economical and efficient demand-oxygen equipment resulted in a gradual replacement of the continuous-flow system with the demand system on some new combat aircraft by late 1942. The Allied strategy of defeating Germany first insured that units in Europe would receive priority over units in the Pacific when it came to the issue of new and improved aircraft and equipment of all types. Many new combat aircraft reaching Europe were equipped with the demand system by the spring of 1943, and most crews were trained in the proper use of the equipment before leaving the United States. The demand

system with the Type A-9 and A-10 masks reduced the need for an extra mask for each fighter or bomber crewman, but it introduced a number of other problems, and did not entirely remove the danger of masks freezing on long high-altitude bombing missions.

The type A-9 demand-oxygen mask had proven in use to be less than ideal because of its poor fit and excessive leakage—it drew outside air into the mask during inhalation. The Committee on Aviation Medicine of the National Defense Research Committee (NDRC) assigned Dr. C. K. Drinker the problem of designing a new type of demand mask, based on criteria agreed upon by all interested organizations, including the Aero Medical Laboratory. In cooperation with the Acushnet Process Company, the L-12 mask was hurriedly developed by Mr. Frank Mauer. It was similar in design to the A-9, but featured revised suspension, fuller face coverage, and an increase in the expiratory valve. After subsequent revisions, it was standardized by the AAF on April, 20, 1942, as the Type A-10.

The Type A-10 mask consisted of a rubber face piece that was easily recognizable because of the unique support or retention strap, which ran from the mask body up between the eyes to the top of the forehead, where it attached to the front of the helmet or auxiliary headstraps. This was the only standard American mask with this feature, and in this respect it resembled the German oxygen masks. It also had unusually high sides that curved up behind the eyes on each side of the face, for increased protection and a tighter fit. A corrugated-rubber inlet hose was attached to the bottom of the face piece. Oxygen from the inlet hose entered the mask proper through two openings at nose level. A housing for a T-42 (carbon) or a T-44 (magnetic) microphone mounting was provided in the front of the mask. The opening from the microphone housing was closed by a rubber plug when no microphone was installed. These mask microphones could also be used with other demand masks, but if no integral microphone was used, the T-30 throat microphone was employed. When the wearer exhaled, a rubber check valve allowed the carbon dioxide to leave the mask through an opening in the bottom. During inhalation, this valve closed, and prevented the outside air from entering the mask. The A-10 was attached to the flying helmet with short straps and hooks, or a Juliet could be used so that the mask could be worn without a helmet.

The new A-10 mask was quickly placed in production by the Acushnet Process Company as a wartime priority, and entered action with combat crews within a few months. The A-10 was first supplied to fighter pilots in late 1942. Reports from the front, including the China-Burma-India theater, stated that while it seldom froze, it fitted too high on the face for clear "moving vision," and frequently slipped down over the face of the fighter pilots during pull-outs from dives or other maneuvers involving

The Type A-10 demand-oxygen mask, worn without a helmet by use of the auxiliary head straps. Note the unique nose strap and uncomfortable nose clip. The mask seems to be poorly fitted to the B-17 crewman in this photo, dated September 7, 1942. He is wearing a radio headset, probably a Type HS-38, and a Type A-4 summer flying suit. The corrugated oxygen tubes and connection, and cord to microphone in the mask, can be seen on the crewman's chest, while the cord from the earphones is on his left. (Courtesy USAF)

"G" forces. The resulting loss of oxygen could have severe consequences.[59] Efforts to improve the design were only partially successful, mainly because of the poor fit and the complexity of the suspension. Fighter pilots, who were frequently required to be in the air within a few minutes after the signal to "scramble," were in general agreement that it could not be put on quickly enough.

The new Type A-10 oxygen mask was also uncomfortable, like so many of its predecessors. Fred Huston, wartime bomber pilot, well remembers his experience with the A-10 mask during flying training:

The only drawback to the demand system as first introduced was the A-10 mask. The A-10 did what it was supposed to do; deliver oxygen to the user, but

it had one real drawback. A spring clip at the top of the mask was supposed to insure that it fit tightly, and it sure did the job. It also rubbed all of the skin off the bridge of your nose. We had these at Dyersburg, Tennessee when going through phase training, and you could always spot the people who had been flying higher than 10,000 feet the day before by the red marks on either side of their nose. After about four hours they became terribly uncomfortable, to say the least, but only managed to really draw blood once.[60]

The Type Designation Sheets show that the Type A-10 demand mask was changed to limited standard status on July 1, 1943, when the Spec. AN-M-3, Part No. AN6001–1 mask of similar design was adopted for use by both the Army and Navy. The Type A-14 demand mask was also standardized on this date for AAF use. The A-10 was not officially declared obsolete until March 1, 1946. The AN-M-3, AN6001–1 mask was changed to limited standard on October 15, 1943, when the improved Type A-10A mask was standardized for service with the AAF.

Recommendations received from users, and continued experiments at the Equipment Laboratory and Aero Medical Laboratory, resulted in modifications to the A-10 mask, intended to correct some of the deficiencies found in the original design. A limited number of A-10 masks were modified and referred to as the Type A-10 (Converted). The first major improvement in the A-10 was designated as the Type A-10 (Revised), or Type A-10R, and standardized in late 1942. The Type A-10 (Revised) was similar in operation to the A-10 but the nose strap was eliminated and the face piece was reduced in size. Technical Order No. 03–50B-1, dated February 5, 1943, stated that the A-10 (Revised) could be identified by its nose design, which included four bridges in each of the two rolled-in gussets on the nose. It was further identified by the letter "R" stamped or molded into the rubber mask under the manufacturer's trade mark on the chin area. The A-10 (Revised) was supposed to give adequate oxygen, even during exercise in extreme cold, at altitudes up to 37,500 feet, and—used with extreme care—to an altitude of 40,000 feet, if the mask was adequately fitted (less than five percent leakage in all leak tests). A leakproof fit for the mask was essential for use with the demand oxygen system. The T.O. further stated that the A-10 (Revised) was made in four sizes, and must be worn only with a helmet; all helmets must be fitted with studs (snaps) to which the mask fastened. The A-10R used the two-point suspension like the A-14 mask. The T-44 (magnetic) or ANB-M-C1 (carbon) microphones could be installed in the front of the Type A-10 (Revised).[61]

Most items developed under the pressure of wartime urgency had problems, and some were reported during

GENERAL VIEWS OF A-9 AND A-10 OXYGEN MASKS WITH HELMET AND JULIET

Illustration shows the A-9 Oxygen Mask in position at left side of helmet ready for quick attachment on face. When not in use leave mask attached to helmet as shown.

Here the A-9 Mask is being attached with straps in uncrossed position on helmet. This method recommended for broad or full faces. Mask must not leak. To check this, hold thumb over end of mask hose. If leaks occur around face, adjust straps or nose wire to fit mask more securely and test again.

Illustration shows the A-10 Oxygen Mask being attached with straps in crossed position to the rear of the "Juliet". This cross position of straps is recommended for small, or long and narrow faces, as it makes a firm and leak-proof fitting.

Here the nose strap (distinguishing difference between the A-9 and the A-10 Masks) is being fixed to the front of the "Juliet" in regular supporter-like manner. This helps to hold the mask in position. Check for leaks, following the method suggested for testing the A-9 Oxygen Mask.

For normal operation the "Auto-Mix" should always be turned to "ON" position as noted here. This assures a proper mixture of oxygen with the outside air.

To get oxygen, place the end connection of mask hose into the fitting, on end of feeder hose coming from the Demand Regulator.

If regulator fails to function, turn on emergency valve illustrated above.

EMERGENCY GAS ABSORBING CANISTER

Gas canisters are furnished for all flying personnel to provide for protection against gas attacks while in flight or when landing on gassed terrain. Grasp canister near bottom and pull loose. This will automatically release both seals, making it ready for immediate use.

Before detaching oxygen mask hose from regulator connecting hose, take a deep breath. Then, before attaching the mask hose to the gas canister, exhale the mask and hose itself of any possible gas accumulation. Immediately thereafter, attach gas canister to mask hose, by inserting connection end into top of canister. Fasten canister to clothing by means of clip affixed to it.

To use the regular chemical warfare service training canister, attach a small section of rubber tubing to it, replacing the cork stopper to end of tube. This should be done before ascent. In attaching it to the oxygen mask remove the corks, top and bottom, and thus proceed in the same manner as with the aircraft gas canister.

AAF instruction chart, dated May 9, 1942, showing how the Types A-9 and A-10 demand-oxygen masks could be worn, either attached with hooks on the helmet or with auxiliary headstraps called a "Juliet." Note the information on use of gas-absorbing canister with the oxygen mask, for protection against gas attack. Later tests conducted by the Aero Medical Laboratory, in cooperation with the Chemical Warfare Service early in 1944, disclosed that the use of the oxygen mask as a gas mask was impractical, because the poison gas could injure the eyes regardless of which type of service goggle was worn. The regulator shown is the Type A-12. (Courtesy USAF)

use of the A-10 (Revised) mask. However, despite the drawbacks in the A-10 (Revised) design, a workable demand-oxygen mask was essential, and it was important to have a mask available in quantity as a backup, in case the new Type A-14 mask under development proved unsatisfactory for any reason. AAF combat units in 1943 needed all the demand-oxygen masks they could get, even masks that were less than fully satisfactory. The A-10 (Revised) mask was in production, and so it was safer, easier, and quicker to modify and improve it than to discontinue it and begin manufacturing an entirely new and unproven mask. Efforts to improve the design of the A-10 (Revised) continued, even after the design of the new Type A-14 mask had been standardized and it was entering production (production of the A-14 was initially slow). The modified mask was designated as the Type A-10A and, according to the Type Designation Sheets, it was "Superior to Type A-10 and AN-M-3 mask." The Type A-10A was adopted as substitute standard on October 15, 1943,

and used in decreasing quantities through the end of the war.

The A-10A mask had improved construction features, based on experience with its predecessors and knowledge gained from experiments at the Aero Medical Laboratory. It differed from the A-10 (Revised) mainly in the shape of the rubber face piece, which had an integrally constructed microphone pocket, and was furnished in only three sizes. The A-10A used the two-point suspension system, as did the A-10R and the A-14 masks. Even with the improvements, reports of masks freezing were received from the Eighth Air Force. Wearers of both the A-10 (Revised) and A-10A continued to suffer from freezing of the moisture in the breath, which partially blocked the oxygen-inlet ports. Additional experiments at the Aero Medical Laboratory resulted in rubber baffle flaps being devised, which did not prevent frost formation in the mask, but effectively corrected the blockage problem of the ports. It was recommended that the flaps be provided to all

The Type A-10 (Revised) demand-oxygen mask entered wide-spread use among flying personnel during the summer of 1943. Like the original A-10, it operated with the A-12 diluter-demand regulator. The A-10R mask fit more snugly, and was attached by snaps (studs) to the left side of the flying helmet. It was hooked on to the right side of the helmet by a quick-detachable ring device as shown in this June 1943 photo. The Type B-7 or AN-6530 goggle is being worn on this Type B-6 winter flying helmet. The jacket is the Type B-3 shearling. (Courtesy USAF)

theaters where these masks were in use, so that modifications could be made locally.[62]

It should be noted that the seriousness of the oxygen situation and the difficulties in developing adequate equipment during this period prompted the transfer of engineering responsibility for all breathing oxygen equipment from the Equipment Laboratory to the newly established Oxygen Branch of the Aero Medical Laboratory on April 5, 1943. Capt. Loren D. Carlson was appointed chief of the new branch. This important organizational change in responsibility greatly facilitated the development of oxygen equipment during the remainder of the war. The development of improved oxygen masks was assisted by the use of seven standardized sculptured heads, developed at the Aero Medical Laboratory in 1942 by 1st. Lt. Francis E. Randall and Harvard University anthropologist, Dr. Earnest A. Hooton. They studied 1,871 young airmen and prepared precisely measured composites of all types of faces. When

eventually produced in plaster, the heads proved to be very useful to AAF technicians and commercial contractors designing masks that could be mass-produced, in as few sizes as possible, while fitting different facial types with a minimum of oxygen leakage.

Research on masks and other items of oxygen equipment continued at an accelerated pace at the Aero Medical Laboratory, and experiments were also conducted by manufacturers, the Mayo Clinic, the U.S. National Bureau of Standards, and other organizations. Among the many projects were experimental helmet-and-face-mask combinations intended to provide protection to the head as well as oxygen, while eliminating the need for wearing a helmet, goggle, and mask. One of these oxygen helmets constructed of plastic was given the designation Type A-11, but its development was finally discontinued on November 10, 1943, along with that of another variation designated as the Type A-12. A more fully developed mask-helmet combination, the Type C-1, will be described later in this chapter.

The Type A-10A demand-oxygen mask adopted as substitute standard for AAF use on October 15, 1943. Although an improvement over the Types A-9, A-10, and A-10R masks, it was still subject to freezing and leakage, and had other deficiencies. This recent NASM photo also shows the AN-6530 goggle and Type A-11 intermediate flying helmet with ANB-H-1 earphones. (SI Photo 86–1753–44A)

The Type A-13 was a partial face pressure demand-oxygen mask that became part of an extensive pressure-breathing research project under intense development during the period 1942–1946. It will be discussed later in this chapter because the Type A-14 demand mask, under development since 1941, was standardized and procured more than six months earlier than the first A-13 masks.

The design of demand-oxygen masks turned out to be a physiological and mechanical problem of considerable complexity. Experience with the A-9 and A-10 series of demand masks proved that a tight fit of the mask over the contours of the face was critical, and the compromise between fit and comfort was a constantly perplexing problem. A separate development project for a demand-oxygen mask was carried out during this period by the Ohio Chemical and Manufacturing Company, based upon designs of Dr. Arthur H. Bulbulian of the Mayo Clinic.[63] In 1938, Bulbulian had been one of the codesigners of the original B.L.B. oxygen mask with rebreather bag used with the continuous-flow system. The first model of this new demand mask was completed in October of 1941, but many modifications were required before it was finally standardized for AAF use as the Type A-14, on July 1, 1943. Tests of the prototype indicated that it was the closest thing yet produced to the optimum oxygen mask, which Army aviators had been seeking for over 25 years.

The Type A-14 demand mask consisted of a medium-green rubber face piece, corrugated oxygen-delivery tube, and attaching straps. An integrally constructed microphone pocket was located just above the mouthpiece, to accommodate the T-44 or ANB-M-C1 microphone. The A-14 operated on the intermittent-flow principle, by which oxygen was supplied only when the aviator inhaled. The slight suction created on each inhalation operated the demand regulator, causing it to open and deliver oxygen to the mask. When the wearer exhaled, the demand regulator automatically shut off, and the exhaled gases passed out of the mask through the flutter valve.[64]

Time was so crucial during those critical months of the war, that production and distribution of the A-14 mask began in the spring of 1943, even before it had been officially standardized. Compared to previous masks, it was easier to fit, more comfortable, provided better visibility, and the suspension could be more easily attached to either the summer or winter flying helmet by snaps and buckle tabs on the left side. A hook and tab on the right side permitted the flyer, even with a gloved hand, to remove the mask from the face as desired.

The Type A-14 was first issued to pilots of the VIII Fighter Command who found the mask very satisfactory. Because the A-9, A-10 and A-10R masks had produced freezing problems and had been found rather ineffective by bomber crews, approval was given for use of the A-14 on bomber aircraft, before service-testing on such

The Type A-14 demand-oxygen mask, one of the best masks produced in World War II. This comfortable mask first entered use during the summer of 1943, and saw service in every war theater. The A-14 in this photo is being worn with the popular Type A-11 intermediate flying helmet, with ANB-H-1 earphones installed in the improved sound-insulated mountings. Note hook and tab on right side of mask (wearer's right side), for quick attachment and removal of mask from face. The goggle is the Spec. AN-6530. (Courtesy USAF)

planes. After three deaths due to anoxia occurred, it was reported by the 3rd Bombardment Division that freezing of the A-14 mask "was our greatest problem early in December" (1943).[65] This defect had not been discovered in the tests with fighter squadrons because of the absence of freezing conditions in most fighter cockpits. Modifications were made immediately, including "weep holes" in the masks to allow moisture to drain out, but causing the neck and Mae West to be coated with ice. Most men wore a towel around the neck, to keep the ice from forming, and to protect the jaw from being rubbed raw by the filler hoses on the Mae West.[66] A member of the Central Medical Establishment in England devised a more suitable modification in the form of a rubber baffle trap inside the mask, which protected the lower portion of the inlet ports from water vapor. The installation of the baffle reduced the danger of freezing, but did not completely overcome it; however, the Eighth Air Force reported no fatal anoxia incidents among the wearers of the modified A-14 masks during 1944.

Action was also taken to remove the excessive moisture found in oxygen obtained from British sources, in an attempt to prevent the freezing of the masks worn by bomber crewmen.

A small electric heater was developed to prevent ice formation in the A-14 mask. It fit between the mask and the mask harness, and was standardized as the Type E-1 on July 8, 1944. A similar heater was developed for the Type A-13A mask, and standardized as the Type E-2 on April 20, 1945. These heaters only functioned when an

The mask hood or face-mask cover being worn over the Type A-14 demand-oxygen mask and under the Type B-8 flying goggle. The cover was intended to protect the face, and help prevent the mask from freezing in exposed crew positions. This photo was taken at the Engineering Division, Wright Field, on June 6, 1944, and is believed to show a prototype. An insulated cloth bag was also issued for use with the Type A-8B mask. It covered the lower part of the mask and the entire rebreather bag. (Courtesy USAF)

electrically heated flying suit with the proper socket on the chest was being worn, or some other source of electricity was provided.

Among other ideas was a combination face and oxygen-mask cover that was tested at the Aero Medical Laboratory with the A-14 mask and B-8 flying goggle. The cover, called a "mask hood," was intended to provide protection to the wearer against fire, wind, and cold, and to reduce the chance of the mask freezing in extremely low temperatures. Tests of the fabric cover disclosed that it pushed the B-8 goggle out from the face, thus reducing significantly the total peripheral field of vision in all directions.[67] Fluttering of the cover was also a potential problem when the wearer was in an open crew position. After the closing of the open waist-gun positions in bomber aircraft, mask freezing became a minor hazard and mask hoods were no longer needed by gunners. The hood did give good protection to the face in case of an engine fire in a fighter aircraft. Some of the mask hoods were procured during 1944, but use is believed to have been limited. A photograph of this item and other issue oxygen equipment appears in AAF Manual 25–2, "Physiology of Flight," dated March 15, 1945.

The A-14 mask was generally considered at the time to be the finest mask available for use, however, experiments to perfect it continued at the factory, the Aero Medical Laboratory, and the National Bureau of Standards. These efforts resulted in the development of the Type A-14A mask, standardized for use on January 27, 1945. On that date the Type A-14 was changed to limited standard.

The Type A-14A was a demand mask very similar to the A-14. The main improvements were internal modifications made to prevent icing at very low temperatures. It was also made available in four sizes instead of three to insure the best possible fit. The A-14A mask remained in use for many years by the Army Air Forces and, after 1947, by the U.S. Air Force. This mask, like many other items of American oxygen equipment, was also used by the British Royal Air Force.

The Pressure Demand-Oxygen System

British and German experience during the first two years of World War II had shown the importance of military flying at very high altitude. The feasibility of operational flying above 40,000 feet was being discussed even before the United States entered the war, and development of the pressure cabin and pressure suit for aviators was already beyond the planning stage. After Pearl Harbor, an urgent military requirement existed for the development of equipment to enable aircrews to reach altitudes above those attainable with the demand-oxygen system, without recourse to pressure cabins or pressure suits, and to serve

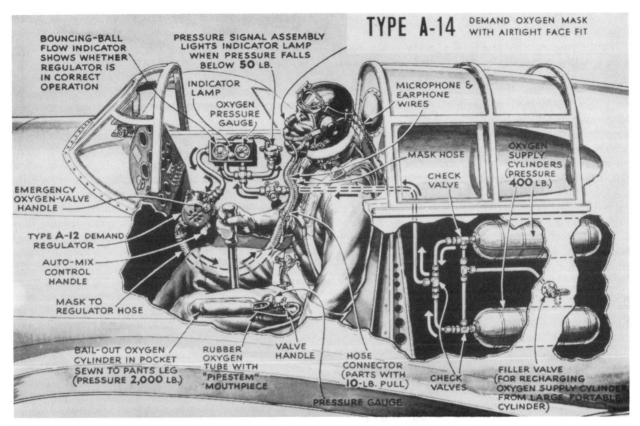

TYPE A-14 DEMAND OXYGEN MASK WITH AIRTIGHT FACE FIT

BOUNCING-BALL FLOW INDICATOR SHOWS WHETHER REGULATOR IS IN CORRECT OPERATION

PRESSURE SIGNAL ASSEMBLY LIGHTS INDICATOR LAMP WHEN PRESSURE FALLS BELOW 50 LB.

INDICATOR LAMP

OXYGEN PRESSURE GAUGE

MICROPHONE & EARPHONE WIRES

MASK HOSE

CHECK VALVE

OXYGEN SUPPLY CYLINDERS (PRESSURE 400 LB.)

EMERGENCY OXYGEN-VALVE HANDLE

TYPE A-12 DEMAND REGULATOR

AUTO-MIX CONTROL HANDLE

MASK TO REGULATOR HOSE

BAIL-OUT OXYGEN CYLINDER IN POCKET SEWN TO PANTS LEG (PRESSURE 2,000 LB.)

RUBBER OXYGEN TUBE WITH "PIPESTEM" MOUTHPIECE

VALVE HANDLE

HOSE CONNECTOR (PARTS WITH 10-LB. PULL)

PRESSURE GAUGE

CHECK VALVES

FILLER VALVE (FOR RECHARGING OXYGEN SUPPLY CYLINDER FROM LARGE PORTABLE CYLINDER)

Typical oxygen equipment used aboard a fighter during World War II, shown in an illustration reproduced from a 1943 instructional brochure distributed with the Type A-14 mask. The system includes the Type A-14 demand mask and the Type A-12 diluter-demand oxygen regulator. The regulator had an auto-mix switch, and when turned on, it automatically mixed the right amount of oxygen with the air for the altitude at which the plane was flying. When the red emergency-valve knob on the right side of the regulator was turned "on," the oxygen by-passed the demand mechanism, and entered the mask in a steady flow, regardless of breathing and altitude. The typical oxygen instrument panel, shown here mounted on the right side of the cockpit, included the Type A-1 flow indicator, a supply warning light, and the Type K-1 gauge that measured the oxygen cylinder pressure. The bailout oxygen bottle on the pilot's left thigh is the Type H-1. (Courtesy USAF)

as emergency equipment in pressure-cabin aircraft. It had been recognized for some time that even when breathing 100 percent pure oxygen, blood-oxygen saturation began to fall off at around 33,000 feet and reached a dangerously low level at 41,000 feet. Exertion made saturation fall more sharply, and this, together with possible mask leaks, also lowered the absolute ceiling. Oxygen administration, therefore, presented a serious drawback to very high-altitude operations, but also offered possibilities for favorable progress in a comparatively short period of time.

The most promising proposal considered by scientists at the Aero Medical Laboratory was a demand-type system, where oxygen under pressure was supplied continuously to the subject as required. Experiments in pressure-breathing techniques for the treatment of pulmonary edema had been made by Dr. Alvin L. Barach

of Columbia University in the early 1930s. This work came to the attention of Capt. A. Pharo Gagge of the Aero Medical Laboratory in 1941. It occurred to Captain Gagge that by employing even higher pressures than Barach had used, significant altitude gains might be made. He began experimentation that included the administering of pure oxygen, at simulated high altitudes in the low-pressure chamber, at pressures of 15 to 25 hectograms (8 to 12 inches of water pressure) above the ambient pressure. Gagge realized that the only way to maintain blood-oxygen saturation above 85 percent at altitudes above 41,000 feet was to increase the oxygen pressure in the lungs. Using himself as the subject, and experimental equipment of his own design, he successfully demonstrated pressure breathing at 50,000 feet in the low-pressure chamber to the Committee on Aviation

Medicine of the National Research Council, on December 12, 1941.[68]

Further studies soon resulted in a full-fledged research program that included the development of pressure-breathing oxygen equipment for service use. Simplification of Gagge's original equipment began, and a design for a spring-weighted A-12 demand regulator, especially for pressure breathing, was developed by the J. H. Emerson Company in June 1942. Experiments continued on both the regulator and mask, and, in October 1942, Capt. Francis E. Randall began the development of a pressure-breathing oxygen mask based on anthropometric facial measurements. The model was finally designated as the Type A-13, and samples of the mask were submitted to the Mine Safety Appliances Corporation for development as a production item. Meanwhile, Bradford Holmes of the Eclipse-Pioneer Instrument Division of Bendix was reworking the Emerson regulator, and in January of 1943 he brought out an improved pressure-demand regulator that was subsequently designated as the Type A-17.

The key to the success of pressure breathing was the compensated exhalation valve originally designed by Captain Gagge and Captain Randall. The first working sample was made by the Linde Air Products Company in their model shop in only one week. It included a small spring not in the original design, which insured the effective operation of the valve. The valve as made by Linde passed every test and was immediately accepted for production.[69]

In November 1942, Lt. Col. W. R. Lovelace of the Aero Medical Laboratory made the first aircraft flight with pressure-breathing equipment in a specially modified Boeing B-17E to an indicated altitude of 42,900 feet. The Emerson regulator was used with an experimental mask made in the laboratory by Captain Randall. In April 1943, Lovelace made another flight using this equipment in a two-place Lockheed P-38J to 44,980 feet. In this flight the special Holmes A-17 chest-type pressure-demand regulator was used, and the pilot and passenger exhaled through the mask-exhalation valve. Prototype equipment was tested in the field by the 28th Photographic Reconnaissance Squadron on October 26, 1943, and the pressure-breathing system was first adopted by the AAF for photoreconnaissance use in November 1943. Purchase was authorized for 4,000 sets of equipment, consisting of the Mine Safety–manufactured Type A-13 mask fitted with the compensated exhalation valve, and the new Aro Type A-14 pressure-demand regulator, which was still under development. The early sets of the A-14 equipment used the Holmes A-17 chest-mounted regulators with the Linde mask valve, and a reducing valve was used at the aircrew stations.

The first full operational mission against the enemy using pressure-breathing oxygen equipment was carried out in February 1944 by the 14th Photographic Reconnaissance Squadron, flying Spitfires, and in April this equipment was used for the first time over Berlin. By November 1944, all new F-5 and F-13 aircraft were equipped with Type A-14 regulators, and the pilots trained in pressure-breathing techniques at Will Rogers and Salina Fields. In the Pacific theater the 3rd and 28th Photographic Reconnaissance Squadrons (Very Heavy) were equipped with pressure-breathing equipment.[70]

The experimental Type A-13 pressure-breathing demand-oxygen mask as first produced was referred to as the XA-13, and it was used with the XA-16 portable oxygen-pressure demand regulator. The rubber in the early XA-13 masks was rather hard, and was soon changed to a softer rubber which proved to be much more satisfactory. The improved (soft) Type A-13 mask, for use with the A-14 regulator, was manufactured by the Mine Safety Appliances Corporation. It consisted of a medium-green rubber face piece with inhalation valves and pressure-compensated exhalation valve, and inside flaps that contacted the face around the nose and mouth area. It was designed to be sealed against positive pressure, and as the pressure built up the mask pressed tightly against the face. Despite this, many pilots claimed that the A-13 was more comfortable than the A-14 mask. Extra care was given to insure that the mask fit the airman's face exactly, because this was of vital importance in pressure breathing at high altitude. Cheek flaps were included for protection against extreme cold and flash burn. Connected to the bottom of the mask, and held in place by a clamp, was a pliable corrugated-rubber oxygen-delivery hose with a mask-to-regulator connector. Two rubber suspension lugs, incorporated on the front of the mask, supported a plastic nose piece and suspension harness composed of webbed straps. One side of the webbed strap was fitted with a metal helmet hook, and the other side with a double snap (stud) fastener. The nose strap of the A-13 mask was incorporated to aid in maintaining a leak-proof seal.

Above 30,000 feet, the mask was provided with oxygen at a pressure higher than that of the surrounding air. No effort was made to inhale, as oxygen was forced into the lungs. A slight effort was required to breathe out against the pressure in the mask. An integrally constructed microphone pocket was located just above the mouthpiece, and a bailout adapter was added in the mask-hose connection for use with the H-2 emergency-oxygen cylinder (bailout bottle). A limited procurement of the A-13 mask was made on January 24, 1944, because of urgent operational requirements, and the mask was finally designated as substitute standard on August 28, 1944, the date that the improved Type A-13A mask was standardized.

Reports from operational photoreconnaissance units described certain deficiencies in the A-13 mask. Among the problems encountered was the difficulty in conducting voice communication while engaged in pressure breath-

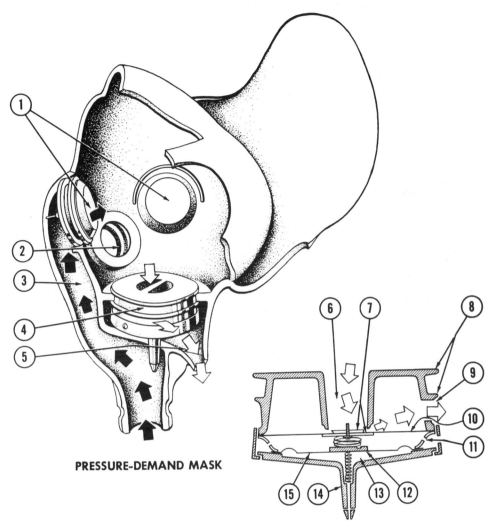

PRESSURE-DEMAND MASK

EXHALATION VALVE DETAILS

1. Inlet Valves
2. Recess for Microphone
3. Inlet Port to Mask
4. Exhalation Valve
5. Outlet for Exhaled Air

 OXYGEN

 **EXHALED AIR**

6. Exhaled air enter exhalation valve here
7. These plates stiffen the main diaphragm
8. Projections on valve housing which seat in mask
9. Exhaled air leaves the valve here
10. Main diaphragm
11. This port permits pressure between the two diaphragms to equalize with the outside atmosphere.

12. This cup holds hairspring in place between the two diaphragms
13. Oxygen supply pressure is exerted in this "compensating" chamber
14. This tube sticks down into the mask inlet
15. This "compensating diaphragm" responds to oxygen supply pressure by pressing up against the main diaphragm

Diagram showing operation of the Type A-13 pressure-demand oxygen mask and exhalation valve. Note the small spring between 7 and 12 in the illustration. This spring was the reason for the instant success of the Linde exhalation valve, which in turn was the key to the success of pressure breathing. The addition of the spring, which was not in the original drawing made by Captain Gagge and Captain Randall in the Aero Medical Laboratory, was a vital addition to the valve design. It was added by a brilliant but unknown engineer of the Linde Oxygen Company, who has never received credit for this outstanding accomplishment. (Reproduced from Lovelace, Gagge and Bray, Aviation Medicine and Psychology, Air Materiel Command, AAF, Wright Field, Ohio, 1946)

62

The Type A-13 oxygen mask, developed as part of the "pressure demand" system, protected AAF flyers against anoxia when flying at altitudes above 35,000 feet. This photo shows the mask integrated with a Type A-11 intermediate flying helmet and B-8 goggle to cover and protect the face from cold and flash burn. Note the "L"-shaped bailout adapter, attached at the oxygen-hose connection, for use with the Type H-2 emergency oxygen cylinder. The microphone cord is connected to the center of the mask. The cord on the wearer's right connects the ANB-H-1 earphones in the sound-insulated mountings of the helmet to the aircraft radio. (Courtesy USAF)

ing. Lt. Col. Donald S. Lopez, a World War II fighter pilot, described his experience with pressure-breathing oxygen equipment:

> When trying to talk while using a pressure-breathing mask, you sounded as though you were being choked with your mouth full of peanut butter. It was very hard to force the air out of your mouth to talk against the pressure and it was very difficult to understand anyone who was transmitting. I, and most of the pilots in the squadron, would switch off the pressure while transmitting. It was for such a short period that it was not dangerous.[71]

Comments from flyers in the field, and continued experiments at the Aero Medical Laboratory under the supervision of Lt. Col. Gagge, Chief, Biophysics Branch, resulted in the development of an improved mask. The modified mask was standardized as the Type A-13A on August 28, 1944. It functioned as either a demand or pressure-demand mask and was capable of holding eight inches of water pressure. The A-13A featured a rubber face piece resembling the A-13 but with inhalation valves and an interchangeable pressure-compensation or demand-type exhalation valve (for pressure-demand or demand usage of the mask, respectively). It was similar to the A-13 in most other aspects. The Type E-2 mask heater was available to provide heat to the face piece and exhalation channel, to prevent the formation of a serious amount of ice or frost in the inlet ports or the exhalation valve or channel. The Type A-13A mask was used with jet aircraft and remained in service for many years after the war. It was still the standard U.S. Navy mask until finally superseded in recent years.

Another type of pressure-breathing mask was developed during the last two years of the war. In October 1943, the Ohio Chemical and Manufacturing Company initiated development of a molded rubber pressure-breathing mask, based on a design submitted by Dr. A. H. Bulbulian of the Mayo Clinic. This model was designated as the Type A-15, but after service tests by the AAF Proving Ground Command, which began on November 14, 1944, it was not accepted by the Army Air Forces Board.[72] An improved version, the Type A-15A, entered service-test status on May 28, 1945. It resembled the A-13, but featured an adjustable system of braces for the nasal and cheek areas. The A-15A had inlet-cheek valves and a compensated exhalation valve, with oxygen pressure of eight inches of water at 40,000 feet. After installing an ordinary exhalation valve, it could be used as a demand mask. Tests by both the AAF and the U.S. Navy indicated that the A-15A did not represent a significant improvement over the A-13A and A-14A masks, and was inferior in certain respects. Development was discontinued after the end of the war. The A-15A was the last type-numbered oxygen mask developed up to the end of 1945.

By the spring of 1944, two models of the Type A-14 diluter-demand, pressure-breathing oxygen regulator were undergoing tests at the Aero Medical Laboratory. One design was produced by the Aro Equipment Corporation, and the other by the Pioneer Division of the Bendix Corporation. Defects were still found in both designs during operational use, particularly gasket leakage, and it was recommended in June, 1944, that only the Aro design be used because an exhalation blockage in the Pioneer design made it impossible to use that type regulator with the standard AAF oxygen-flow indicator system.

The revised Type A-14 pressure-demand regulator as finally standardized on November 1, 1944, was a modification of the Aro Type A-12 or AN-R-5, AN6004–1 demand

perience showed that the Type A-14 regulator, when used with the Type A-13A mask, was safe up to a maximum altitude of 42,000 feet.

Other regulators under development for many months included the Type A-15. It delivered an adequate mixture of air and oxygen, the richness of which was automatically

Prototype of the Type A-15 pressure-breathing demand mask during testing in late 1944. Like the A-13, it sealed against a positive pressure, and was intended for use with aircraft operating over 35,000 feet. The A-15 and the improved A-15A were not standardized for use by the AAF. No microphone was installed in the mask in this photo, and the aperture is sealed with a black plastic plug. The rubber ring located at the bottom of the mask, where it joins with the oxygen hose, was used to anchor the microphone cord. The helmet is the Type A-11 intermediate with ANB-H-1 earphones. (Courtesy USAF)

Type A-14 diluter-demand pressure-breathing oxygen regulator. This regulator was developed from the Aro Type A-12 diluter-demand regulator and standardized on November 1, 1944. It was similar to the A-12, but was equipped with a manually controlled, spring-loaded diaphragm, which maintained a positive pressure in the mask and mask hose, while operating on the demand principle. Below 30,000 feet, its function was identical to low-pressure diluter-demand regulators, automatically mixing physiologically appropriate quantities of air and oxygen. It incorporated the auto-mix feature, which permitted 100 percent oxygen at any altitude when set at the "normal oxygen" position. Above 30,000 feet, manual selection of the pressure required was made by rotating a knob to the position corresponding to flight altitude, permitting the regulator to supply oxygen at a higher pressure than that of the surrounding air. The A-14 went through a long period of development and modification. This photo from June 1944 is of an Aro A-14 model, considered superior to the Pioneer A-14 design. (Courtesy USAF)

regulator. It differed in having a manual dial added, to regulate delivery of positive pressure up to 12 inches of water over existing ambient pressure. A spring mechanism for depressing the diaphragm was geared to a knob calibrated in thousands of feet. The compensating exhalation valve built into the masks permitted the user to breathe against a positive pressure varying from 1 to 12 inches of water, depending upon the degree of depression of the regulator diaphragm. Oxygen did not flow during exhalation. The system operated as a conventional demand system apart from this positive-pressure feature (for example, when the diaphragm of the regulator was in its normal position). Ex-

controlled by prevailing barometric pressure. The A-15 was also standardized on November 1, 1944, for use with a walk-around assembly.

The Type A-16 was a low-pressure demand-oxygen regulator for use at extreme altitude. It was standardized on February 10, 1944, but proved to have a number of problems, and was declared obsolete on January 8, 1945. The successful standardization of the A-14 made further development of the A-16 unnecessary.

The last regulator in the "A" series that was under development during World War II was the experimental Type A-17 pressure-demand regulator, previously described.

The author inspected the Boeing B-29 *Enola Gay,* on January 30, 1986, at the National Air and Space Museum storage and restoration center at Silver Hill, Maryland. On August 6, 1945, this plane, piloted by Col. Paul W. Tibbets, Jr., dropped the first atomic bomb, destroying much of Hiroshima, Japan, and hastening the end of World War II. The original Type A-14 pressure-demand regulators remain installed at each crew position. This aircraft was equipped with pressure-breathing oxygen equipment as a backup system in case cabin pressurization was lost at high altitude. Type A-13A oxygen masks were sometimes worn by crewmen of regular B-29 units as a precaution while flying over enemy territory. The masks were usually kept in a cloth container at the crewman's side, or suspended on the flying helmet.

The development of pressure-breathing equipment during World War II for long-term high-altitude flight not only played an important part in the success of our military operations, but was also a necessary step in the program to introduce high-flying jet-propelled aircraft into active service in the postwar era.

Portable and Emergency Oxygen Equipment

Portable Oxygen Gear

Experience with large, multi-place aircraft during the late 1930s showed that it was frequently necessary for men to move about during flight at high altitude, beyond the limits of the flexible oxygen hose attached to the regulator at each crew station. It was, of course, very dangerous to move about without oxygen, even for a short period, at an altitude at which oxygen was necessary. Portable oxygen equipment was developed to meet this need and it was usually called the "walk-around bottle." This portable equipment was also available for use in the event of failure of the main oxygen supply or for providing oxygen to incapacitated or injured crewmen.

Technical Order no. 03-50-1, dated July 1, 1943, describes the following equipment as available for AAF use:

1. In transports, without oxygen for passengers and sometimes crew, high-pressure continuous-flow portable units consisted of the Type B-1 cylinder, A-8A regulator and canvas carrying sling. The B-1 cylinder, standardized on August 22, 1935, was the same as the Type A-1 except that it had a capacity of 295 cubic inches instead of 57 cubic inches.

2. In other airplanes, such as late model B-25s and B-26s in which oxygen equipment was not installed, low-pressure portable demand-oxygen units for ferry and special missions requiring flight at high altitudes consisted of the following: Type F-1 cylinder, standardized July 30, 1940, with a capacity of 1,000 cubic inches; Type A-12 regulator; pressure gauge; filler valve; and mask-to-regulator hose.

3. Heavy bombardment aircraft with low-pressure continuous-flow oxygen systems used the high-pressure continuous-flow portable Type A-2 cylinder, A-8A regulator, and canvas carrying sling. The Type A-2 cylinder, standardized on December 1, 1939, had a capacity of 96 cubic inches. An alternative could be made up using a D-2 cylinder, A-9A regulator, filler valve and canvas carrying sling. The low-pressure Type D-2 cylinder, standardized on May 23, 1941, had a capacity of 500 cubic inches.

4. Heavy bombardment aircraft with demand-oxygen systems used the Type A-4 low-pressure cylinder and Type A-13 regulator, which together formed the complete unit, AN6020. A unit was located at each crew position in a multi-place aircraft. No sling was required because this small assembly was attached to the clothing or parachute harness by a clip on the back of the regulator. The Type A-4 cylinder, standardized on November 12, 1941, had a capacity of 104 cubic inches. Attached to the Type A-13 demand regulator, it provided 100 percent pure oxygen for only about six to eight minutes, a duration that was found to be inadequate in combat. An alternative assembly, with a duration of 20 to 50 minutes, could be made up by using a Type D-2 cylinder and A-13 regulator, with a canvas carrying sling if necessary.[73]

The Type A-13 regulator was standardized on November 12, 1941, and placed in production early in 1942. It was changed to limited standard on February 2, 1943, when the Spec. AN-R-11, AN6022-1 regulator, of almost identical design, was officially standardized for both Army and Navy use. The A-13 was similar to the A-12 regulator but was intended for use only with portable oxygen cylinders, had no "auto-mix" feature, and dispensed only pure oxygen on demand. There was a cylinder pressure gauge on top, which showed how much oxygen was in the cyl-

The B-24 bomber crewman in this 1944 photo is inspecting a portable (walk-around) oxygen assembly, consisting of the Type A-13 regulator and A-4 cylinder. He is wearing a Type A-14 demand-oxygen mask, connected by standard, corrugated oxygen hose to a Type A-12 diluter-demand regulator mounted on the side of the fuselage. The instrument panel includes a Type A-1 oxygen-flow indicator (left), a supply-warning light, and a Type K-1 oxygen-cylinder pressure gauge (right). Clothing consists of sheep shearling winter flying jacket, trousers, and Type B-6 helmet, with Type B-7 goggle and A-12 gloves. Parachute is the Type B-8 back-type. (SI Photo 84–4401)

number of casualties due to anoxia were attributed to the limited duration of the A-4, which was sometimes sufficient only for four minutes when the user was engaged in strenuous activity. In 1944 this walk-around assembly was superseded by the Type A-15 regulator and Type A-6 280-cubic inch low-pressure cylinder, which gave approximately thirty minutes supply. This amount was sufficient to allow an aircraft to descend to a safe altitude if the main oxygen system failed.

The Type A-15 was an automatic, diluter-demand regulator with an auto-mix, a feature added to increase the duration of the oxygen supply at moderate altitudes. It unfortunately had the characteristic of being difficult to adjust easily at high altitudes where pure oxygen (as given by the emergency valve of the standard A-12 demand regulator) was needed. The more economical A-15 regulator was standardized on November 1, 1944, and when attached to an intermediate-size oxygen bottle, was used in the limited space occupied by ball-turret gunners. Like the A-13, it had an attaching clip on the back.

The most severe problem with the walk-around units, in addition to the limited duration of the cylinders, was the inadvertent separation of the quick-disconnect fitting. This seemingly simple item had no locking device, and many cases of anoxia in the Eighth Air Force in 1943 were caused by accidental disconnect of the mask-regulator connection. A positive lock was devised and, to speed up delivery, arrangements were made for it to be manufactured in England as well as the United States.

An interesting use of portable oxygen equipment was announced in 1944, when it was found that this gear could be used by personnel in escape from submerged aircraft. Tests conducted by the Aero Medical Laboratory confirmed that underwater evacuation of the crew from ditched and submerged aircraft could be successfully accomplished, using the portable walk-around oxygen equipment, provided that escape could be effected before exhaustion of the assembly's oxygen supply. The unit functioned normally, as a straight demand assembly, provided the regulator was maintained at the same water level as the face mask and hose, so that the oxygen pressure was the same as the surrounding water pressure. Use of the assembly at depths greater than 50 feet was also practical but not recommended, because of the duration of the oxygen supply and the possible adverse physiological effects of breathing pure oxygen under the increased pressure conditions. Standard portable equipment tested included demand-oxygen masks and the Type A-13 regulator with the A-4 cylinder, and with the larger D-2 cylinder, which had five times the volume of the A-4. The buoyancy of the Type D-2 cylinder was sufficient to keep an individual afloat when the water surface was reached.[74]

inder, and a trap-door oxygen outlet into which the hose end of a demand-type mask was inserted. On the side was a spout for refilling the oxygen cylinder from the walk-around recharger assembly at the oxygen station in the aircraft. There were two designs of the A-13 regulator: that made by the Aro Equipment Company and that made by the Scott Aviation Corporation. Both were also produced under contract by other manufacturers, and all models were used with the standard walk-around cylinders. The original intention was to supply a limited quantity of 100 percent oxygen for a short period of time while a crew member moved about, and it was considered that eight minutes would be ample. Combat experience proved that the capacity of the A-4 cylinder was inadequate. A

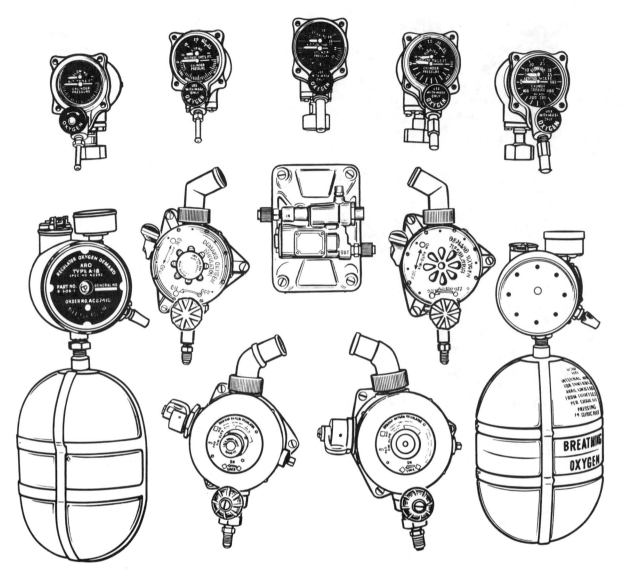

Examples of AAF oxygen regulators used during World War II. Oxygen regulators reduced the pressure of the compressed oxygen flowing from the storage cylinders to a usable pressure, and accurately controlled its flow to the mask. There were three general types in use by the AAF in World War II: continuous-flow, diluter-demand, and pressure-demand. From left to right, top row (all continuous-flow types): Type A-6, high-pressure; A-8, high-pressure; A-8A, high-pressure, with bayonet-type outlet nipple; A-9, low-pressure; A-9A, low-pressure. Middle row: Type A-13 demand-type, Aro design, with A-4 walk-around cylinder; A-12 low-pressure diluter-demand, Aro design, manufacturer's variation; A-11, low-pressure automatic continuous-flow; A-12, Aro (Airco) design, Aro Corp. manufacture; A-13, Scott Aviation Corp. design, with A-4 cylinder. The two diluter-demand regulators at bottom center are A-12s of Pioneer design, early model at left. (SI Photo 85–1933)

Emergency-Bailout Oxygen Gear

The first use of oxygen equipment by Army flyers for high-altitude parachute jumps occurred in the early 1920s. Capt. A. W. Stevens made a high-altitude test jump over McCook Field in 1922 using a small oxygen cylinder with manual regulator and tube strapped to his right thigh. There was little need for such equipment until the late 1930s when flying at high altitude became commonplace. With the beginning of the war in Europe, it was realized that many things could happen to an aircraft which could compel the flyer to abandon his plane at great height. Severe damage inflicted by enemy gunfire, structural failure, or fire, might make it necessary to bail out immediately, before the airplane could be taken to lower altitude. It was also desirable to have an emergency oxygen supply that could be used in case of the failure of the main oxygen system in fighter or other aircraft flying at very high altitude. It was originally intended to issue emergency-bailout equipment to photoreconnaissance, fighter and heavy bomber crewmen, however, in late 1944 it was announced that this equipment was not necessary for heavy-bomber personnel.[75]

An experimental emergency-bailout oxygen unit was designed, built, and tested in a low-pressure chamber during the spring of 1940 by Capt. Otis O. Benson of the Aero Medical Laboratory, in cooperation with Dr. Walter M. Boothby and Dr. W. Randolph Lovelace of the Mayo Clinic. This apparatus used a small commercial cylinder and valve and was tested with both the A-8 oxygen mask and the pipestem. It was demonstrated to Army officials, and described in the June 1940 issue of the *Journal of Aviation Medicine*. This assembly formed the basis for the development of the unit adopted for AAF use the following year.[76]

Two types of emergency-bailout oxygen assemblies were developed for use by AAF flyers during World War II. The first unit in general use consisted of the Type H-1 oxygen cylinder with high-pressure gauge, hand-operated valve, and rubber tubing with plastic pipestem mouthpiece. The pipestem was apparently adopted because the A-8 series masks, with the large rebreather bag, were unlikely to stay on the face during bailout. The Type H-1 emergency oxygen cylinder, usually called the "bailout bottle," was standardized on October 2, 1941, changed to limited standard on April 20, 1943, and declared obsolete on October 23, 1945. It was a high-pressure steel cylinder two inches in diameter and eight inches long, with an internal volume of twenty cubic inches. This was normally enough oxygen for up to ten minutes, depending on the temperature and the exertion of the user. Each bailout bottle was contained in a fabric sheath and was designed to be carried in a pocket on the flying suit, usually on the thigh. It was recommended that the sheath be sewn to the suit, for security during bailout. It could also be strapped to the thigh, when it was best to draw the upper strap on the sheath through the parachute harness which ran under the leg. The H-1 assembly was intended to be used by flyers who had to bail out above 30,000 feet. Frostbite is a constant hazard at high altitude, but the jumper using the H-1 could protect his face from cold, wind, and hailstones, by retaining his demand-oxygen mask and inserting the pipestem under the chin margin of the mask and into his mouth. This might also help prevent the jumper from losing the tube as a result of the opening shock of the parachute. Tests at the Aero Medical Laboratory and complaints from the field prompted the de-

velopment of an improved type of bailout assembly. The complaints revealed manufacturing defects in the H-1, and the initial oxygen-flow rate was considered too low.[77]

The Type H-2 bailout-cylinder assembly was an improved design made of shatterproof steel that would not explode if hit by a .50 caliber bullet. The H-2 directed the oxygen through a tube into the mask, so that the mask could remain firmly on the face when the emergency oxygen cylinder was used. It was standardized on April 20, 1943, and although similar to the H-1, contained ten percent more oxygen. A safe operating charge for both the H-1 and the H-2 cylinders was 1,800 psi, but a charge of 2,200 psi for the H-2 was allowed. The flow of oxygen from the H-2 was started with a ripcord-type of valve, by pulling on a round wooden knob usually called the "green apple." In the H-1 assembly, a screw valve was used to start the flow, and was often hard to operate in the cold, even when using both hands. The oxygen tube from the H-2 valve was connected before jumping to the special L-shaped bailout adapter attached to the oxygen-hose connection to the mask. Before bailout, the corrugated oxygen-mask hose with the quick-disconnect fitting was withdrawn from the regulator, or the extension hose was detached from the regulator, and a small metal flap fell over the inside of the disconnect-fitting aperture to resist the outward flow of air during breathing with the bottle, and thus conserve oxygen. The flap had a small one-eighth-inch-diameter hole in it so some air could get out.

The upper limit of safety, when parachuting with the H-2 cylinder during a difficult escape, was determined to be about 35,000 feet, if the temperature of the cylinder was −40 degrees C. (−40 degrees F.). If escape from the airplane involved very little work, the H-2 bottle was adequate for open-parachute descent from 40,000 feet. It was recommended for several reasons that emergency jumpers free-fall to about 15,000 feet before opening their parachutes, and to a lower altitude if in a combat zone where there was a danger of being strafed.[78]

Parachute jumps from high altitude were a major concern for the AAF in 1943. Lt. Col. W. Randolph Lovelace II of the Aero Medical Laboratory decided to demonstrate that it was possible to survive an open-parachute jump from very high altitude, by using the Type H-2 bailout bottle and other items of standard clothing and equipment. For this mission, he arranged to use a specially equipped B-17E bomber and crew from the Boeing Company that had been engaged in high-altitude flight testing. Support aircraft and personnel were provided from Ephrata Army Air Field, Washington, while equipment and instruction were furnished by specialists at Wright Field.

The flight began at Boeing Field, Seattle, on the morning of June 24, 1943, and during the climb experimental pressure-breathing oxygen masks and equipment were used. Before his jump, Lovelace disconnected his mask

AAF training chart dated September 5, 1942, described the use of the portable (walk-around), and the emergency-bailout oxygen equipment. The walk-around unit shown here consisted of the Type A-13 regulator attached to the top of the Type A-4 oxygen cylinder of 104-cubic inch capacity. This assembly could be used with any demand-oxygen mask. Larger portable oxygen cylinders were also available. The bailout equipment illustrated is the Type H-1 emergency oxygen cylinder assembly with a capacity of 40-liters, standardized on October 2, 1941. The flow of oxygen was turned on by a manually operated valve and delivered to the mouth through a pipestem. An improved version, the Type H-2, containing 10 percent more oxygen, was standardized on April 20, 1943. The flow of compressed oxygen in the H-2 was started by a ripcord and delivered directly to the mask. Both types were normally worn in a pocket on the thigh, or attached to the parachute harness. (Courtesy USAF)

from the regulator in the plane and attached the tube from the H-2 bailout bottle to his mask. At 12:33 p.m. Lovelace completed his check list and stepped out of the bomb bay at an altitude of 42,200 feet. This was Lovelace's first parachute jump and the highest altitude jump ever attempted up to that time. His Type T-5 back-type parachute with a 28-foot canopy was deployed immediately by means of a static line, and the violent shock knocked him unconscious and caused his gloves to fly off. Lovelace revived at about 30,000 feet and the rest of the jump was routine. Not only did the jump prove the efficiency of the bailout equipment, but other important discoveries were made. It was proven that the danger of shock from the opening of a parachute at an altitude in excess of 30,000

feet was far greater than from an opening made closer to the ground. To ease the jerk of the opening, AAF flyers were advised to fall free of the plane until their forward momentum was lost, before opening their parachutes.[79] The plucky doctor survived the 23-minute, 51-second jump with only a frostbitten hand, and he was appointed Chief of the Aero Medical Laboratory in September 1943.

Work began at the Aero Medical Laboratory in 1944 to develop an advanced pressure-breathing bailout assembly. This apparatus included a regulator and large-capacity cylinder that would provide a supply of oxygen under pressure, sufficient in duration and quantity for emergency open-parachute escape from jet aircraft flying at altitudes up to 50,000 feet.[80] Development was not completed

Operational suitability testing of the Type H-2 bailout oxygen assembly was conducted at the AAF Tactical Center, Orlando, Fla. In this photo from July 1944, an airman is shown in the doorway of an aircraft ready to jump, with the H-2 bailout bottle strapped to his right thigh and connected to the special attachment on his Type A-14 demand-oxygen mask by a rubber tube. The mask protected the jumper against frostbite during descent, and the increased capacity of the H-2 bottle allowed emergency jumps from greater heights, and more time to clear the plane interior. The jumper, with right hand on his ripcord handle, is wearing heavy shearling winter flying clothing, Type B-4 Mae West, first aid kit tied to parachute harness, and Type B-8 goggle. (Courtesy USAF)

before the end of the war, and the Type H-2 equipment continued in use for many years with the Army Air Forces and later the U.S. Air Force.

Oxygen Mask and Helmet Combinations

One of the most interesting developments during the war was a combination oxygen mask and helmet. The purpose was to provide complete protection for the head while

delivering oxygen, without wearing a mask or regular flying helmet and goggle. The idea was actually not new; an unsuccessful design designated as the Type A-2 was tested by the Engineering Division at McCook Field in the mid-1920s. The A-2 was one of many ideas investigated in the attempt to solve the problem of providing a practical oxygen mask. As mentioned previously in this chapter, several experimental mask-helmet combinations reached the testing stage during the early years of World War II, including the Type G-2, evaluated in the fall of 1942, and the Types A-11 and A-12 that were tested over many months and finally discontinued on November 10, 1943.

Earphones and microphones were built into the experimental mask-helmet combinations, which were fabricated of rubber and plastic. Most of the designs employed the demand-oxygen system; however, the continuous-flow oxygen system was also considered long before the war, and at least one mask-helmet of this type was built for test-

Experimental oxygen-mask-and-helmet combination utilizing the continuous-flow oxygen system. The design shown in this photo, taken at the Equipment Laboratory at Wright Field on May 12, 1942, used the same basic rubber and plastic helmet design as the G-2 demand type, but was modified to accommodate the rebreather bag and hose of the Type A-8B oxygen mask. (Courtesy USAF)

ing in the spring of 1942. It used the same style of full-head helmet intended for the demand-oxygen system, but was modified to accommodate the rebreather bag and hose as used on the Type A-8B oxygen mask.

The most successful of these experimental designs was the combination mask and helmet designated as the Type C-1. This was an unpressurized, full-head-cover helmet that was initially developed by the Equipment Laboratory of the Engineering Division, but responsibility was transferred in 1943 to the Aero Medical Laboratory. According to the Type Designation Sheets, the C-1 was standardized on December 31, 1942. A small quantity was procured under contract for service testing in late 1942, and an elaborate, illustrated booklet was distributed with it. The booklet stated that "The C-1 Combination Mask and Helmet for use with demand oxygen systems is sup-

This experimental plastic demand-oxygen mask-and-helmet combination is believed to be the Type A-11. It was intended to provide protection to the head from flash fire, wind, and cold, as well as to supply oxygen without wearing a demand mask. This photo was taken at Wright Field during comparison tests at the Equipment Laboratory on April 9, 1942. The sheep-shearling material was attached around the neck aperture to reduce leakage, without making the helmet opening too tight and uncomfortable. Other variations of this unsuccessful mask-helmet were produced during the same period. (Courtesy USAF)

plied for experimental tests and comments." Full instructions were provided for fitting and donning the helmet, a rather complicated task, and the booklet explained that it was intended to furnish flyers, maintenance crews, and ground crews protection and comfort in freezing temperatures. For flyers or ground crews it provided "complete protection for the eyes and face against gasoline flash and flame. Due to the double construction of the face piece, and the insulation of the lining and plastic material, the face is protected with the mask for ten to fifteen seconds." Radio receivers and a microphone could be installed in the C-1 helmet and a selection of detachable, antifogging visors in various colors was available, including a cobalt-blue visor for welding.[81]

After testing at the Aero Medical Laboratory and in Alaska during the winter of 1942–43, it was determined that the C-1 should not be adopted for use as a demand mask because of excessive leakage. It was also unsatisfactory because the visor could not be kept clear at temperatures of −20 degrees F. The mask-helmet was also very difficult to put on and required assistance to do the job. The wearer had to push the helmet together in the back, and another person zipped it shut. It was stated in an engineering report that a way should be devised to incorporate pressure-demand oxygen equipment in the item.[82]

Research and Development Projects

Hundreds of other research and development (R&D) projects dealing with the problems of flight at high altitude were initiated during World War II by the Aero Medical and Personal Equipment laboratories, and the School of Aviation Medicine. They received valuable assistance from the Mayo Clinic, U.S. National Bureau of Standards, and other organizations and manufacturing firms. Space limitations permit a discussion of only a few of these projects. Some were in the category of basic research; for example, it was confirmed that hypoxia was a contributing factor in frostbite among airmen, because deficient blood oxygenation rendered tissue particularly susceptible. Oxygen lack also played a role in combat fatigue, respiratory ailments, and similar problems encountered by flyers performing their grueling work at high altitude. Many of these problems were resolved or aided by wartime research. The development of the demand-oxygen system and later the pressure-breathing demand oxygen system, was of great benefit to airmen flying at very high altitudes and pressure-breathing equipment proved important for use with the new jet aircraft entering service at the end of the war.

Research and development projects, particularly those accomplished at Wright Field, helped provide greater flex-

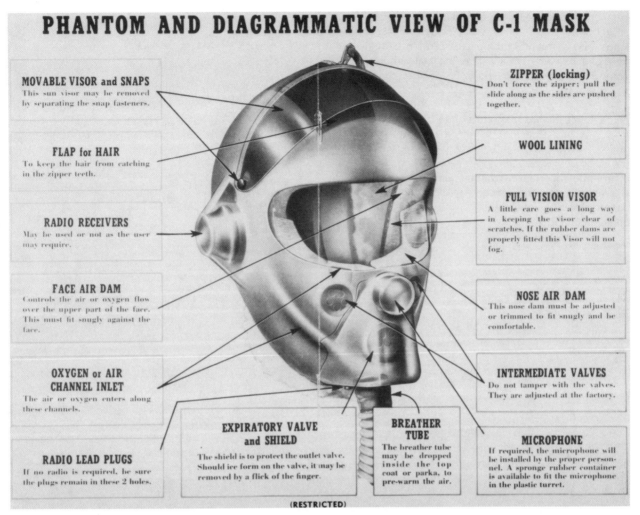

PHANTOM AND DIAGRAMMATIC VIEW OF C-1 MASK

MOVABLE VISOR and SNAPS
This sun visor may be removed by separating the snap fasteners.

FLAP for HAIR
To keep the hair from catching in the zipper teeth.

RADIO RECEIVERS
May be used or not as the user may require.

FACE AIR DAM
Controls the air or oxygen flow over the upper part of the face. This must fit snugly against the face.

OXYGEN or AIR CHANNEL INLET
The air or oxygen enters along these channels.

RADIO LEAD PLUGS
If no radio is required, be sure the plugs remain in these 2 holes.

ZIPPER (locking)
Don't force the zipper; pull the slide along as the sides are pushed together.

WOOL LINING

FULL VISION VISOR
A little care goes a long way in keeping the visor clear of scratches. If the rubber dams are properly fitted this Visor will not fog.

NOSE AIR DAM
This nose dam must be adjusted or trimmed to fit snugly and be comfortable.

INTERMEDIATE VALVES
Do not tamper with the valves. They are adjusted at the factory.

MICROPHONE
If required, the microphone will be installed by the proper personnel. A sponge rubber container is available to fit the microphone in the plastic turret.

EXPIRATORY VALVE and SHIELD
The shield is to protect the outlet valve. Should ice form on the valve, it may be removed by a flick of the finger.

BREATHER TUBE
The breather tube may be dropped inside the top coat or parka, to pre-warm the air.

(RESTRICTED)

The C-1 combination-oxygen-mask-and-helmet, as illustrated in the original booklet that accompanied the small number procured for testing in late 1942. This unpressurized helmet was intended to provide full protection to the head, while operating on the demand-oxygen system. It was not adopted for standard use because of excessive oxygen leakage, fogging of the visor, discomfort, and other deficiencies. (Author's Collection)

ibility, economy, and dependability in oxygen equipment. Wartime developments made it possible for combat crewmen to move about freely with portable equipment during long flights, and parachute safely from high altitudes with bailout bottles. Research during the development of oxygen devices established the desirability of using oxygen at all altitudes from the ground up on night flights.

Other associated equipment developed included a mobile oxygen-generating plant that could be mounted on a truck or trailer, and an efficient dryer to remove excess moisture from oxygen—a big help in preventing the formation of ice in the oxygen system. A pneumatic balance resuscitator was developed by Henry L. Burns of the Oxygen Branch of the Aero Medical Laboratory. The resuscitator was used for aiding flying personnel who were suffering from hypoxia and required artificial respiration.[83] The special oxygen masks for use with full pressure suits will be discussed in Chapter V.

Oxygen in Combat

The contributions made by aviation physiologists and personal equipment officers, with the support of flight surgeons and the aeromedical research agencies, in meeting the anoxia problem "may be judged," wrote the Air Sur-

72   geon, "from the thousands of missions flown at altitudes of 20,000 to 30,000 feet without incident."[84] A good example can be found in the anoxia accident statistics of the Eighth Air Force. The anoxia accident rate among heavy-bomber crews was reduced in a one-year period from 115.5 per 100,000 man-missions in November 1943, to 23.4 per 100,000 in November 1944, a decrease of 80 percent. Meanwhile, the fatality rate for anoxia dropped from 21.6 to 7.1 per 100,000 man-missions, a reduction of 68 percent.[85] These representative figures were a tribute to all of the personnel involved in flying safety, and even more important in wartime, they were indicative of the vital support that helped American airmen gain air supremacy in every theater of war in which they were engaged during World War II.

Military Parachutes

1st. Lt. Harold R. Harris, Chief of the Flight Test Branch at McCook Field, Ohio, had no idea on the morning of October 20, 1922, that he was going to set an historic precedent. He was scheduled that day for what he thought would be a routine test of the experimental ailerons installed on a Loening PW-2A monoplane. Army Type "A" parachutes were available at McCook Field, but were not always worn, despite an order from the commanding officer on March 29, directing that parachutes be worn by test pilots.[1] When Harris put on his parachute, he found that the harness was too tight because of a cushion that had been installed, and after trying another chute with an even smaller and more uncomfortable harness, almost left without one. He finally decided to wear the first chute after all, and took off to conduct maneuverability tests at about 2,500 feet with Lt. Muir Fairchild, who was flying a Thomas Morse MB-3. According to Harris:

> During a turn to the left at about 150 miles an hour, all hell broke loose! The whole airplane shook violently and the control stick began to oscillate rapidly, back and forth, beating against my legs. I tried to control the over-balanced ailerons by slowing the speed of the airplane but the vibrations soon caused the wing structure to be torn apart internally. I knew it was impossible to regain control of the airplane, and there was only one thing to do to save my life. The plane went into a dive and portions of the wing began to blow off, so I released my seat belt, climbed on top of the fuselage, and the tremendous wind pressure of probably 250 miles an hour, blew me clear of the plane. I did not feel any faintness or failure of my faculties, and pulled what I though was the ring on the ripcord. Nothing happened. I was spinning like a top, and three times I located what I thought was the release ring, but each time I was pulling on a leg strap. I finally pulled the right ring, felt something snap, and found I was looking down at the ground. I looked up at my parachute and could not understand how silk could be kept so white and clean around an airplane hanger. I landed in a grape arbor and the only damage I suffered, other than the terrific beating I received on the legs from the control stick, was a tear in the best pair of pants I owned.[2]

1st. Lt. Harold R. Harris, Chief of the Flight Test Branch, McCook Field, Dayton, Ohio, in 1920. Despite his many other accomplishments, Harris is perhaps best remembered as being the first U.S. Army pilot to make an emergency, free-fall parachute jump from an airplane. This was accomplished with a Type "A" parachute on October 20, 1922, when he was forced to bail out of a disabled Loening PW-2A monoplane he was testing. Harris set ten world and fifteen American records, for speed, distance, altitude, and duration, with various weights carried. He also made the first pressurized-cabin flight in a modified USD-9A aircraft on June 8, 1921. In this photo, taken in front of a Martin MB-1 bomber, he is wearing a heavy winter flying suit, developed for the Air Service during World War 1, and later designated as the Type B-1. (SI Photo 82–7295, Courtesy of Brig. Gen. Harold R. Harris, USAF [Ret.])

Lieutenant Harris' dramatic experience was not, of course, the first time a life had been saved by means of a parachute, and not the first jump from an airplane. However, his accident marked a milestone in American military aviation history, because he is credited with making the first emergency free-fall parachute jump from an airplane by a U.S. Army pilot.[3] The lesson learned from Harris' successful jump, and another by Lt. Frank B. Tyndall less than a month later, led Maj. Gen. Mason M. Patrick, then Chief of the Air Service, to decree the wearing of parachutes as mandatory for all Army aviators, and he issued a directive to that effect on January 15, 1923.[4]

THE AERONAUT AND THE PARACHUTE

The parachute is not a modern invention, and to better understand the history and development of military parachutes in the United States, it is necessary to look back several centuries. The word "parachute" derives from the Italian verb *parare* and the French noun *chute,* and translates "to shield or defend against a fall." Although the exact origin of the parachute is unknown, the principle is so simple that the idea must have occurred to persons throughout the ages. The parasol, in use in Assyria 2,800 years ago, is believed to have provided the inspiration for the parachute, because of the resistance it offered to the wind. Legends in China, Siam, India and elsewhere, mention experiments and demonstration descents with large umbrellas and similar devices, but the world's first actual parachute design was possibly a conical contraption drawn by an unnamed engineer, probably from Sienna, Italy, in the late 1470s or early 1480s. By that time, it was certainly understood that an umbrella-shaped device would retard the speed of a body descending through the air. The versatile Leonardo da Vinci sketched a pyramid-shaped parachute in 1495 and described its proposed use: escape from tall burning buildings. There is no proof that any of these or other early designs were ever tested, even in model form.

It was not until the invention of the balloon, by the Montgolfier brothers in France during the early 1780s, that the parachute found a practical application. André-Jacques Garnerin, a Frenchman, made the first confirmed manned parachute descent from a balloon, near Paris on October 22, 1797, from a height of about 3,000 feet. His parachute was shaped like a giant umbrella, had 32 ribbed segments of white fabric, and was 23 feet in projected diameter. He was suspended below the chute in a wicker basket. The parachute was quite unstable and swayed back and forth, causing Garnerin to become nauseated by the time he reached the ground. He made several other "jumps" from balloons, including the first in England, when he descended from a height of about 8,000 feet over London

André-Jacques Garnerin making the world's first parachute descent from a balloon. The descent was made from an altitude of about 3,000 feet near Paris on October 22, 1797, and is believed to be the first time a parachute was used by a man from anything higher than a building. The abandoned balloon can be seen to the left of the parachute. Early parachutes, like balloons, were equipped with a wicker basket. (SI Photo 42693)

on September 21, 1802. His wife, Jeanne-Geneviève, was the first woman to fly "solo" in a balloon, and the first woman to make a parachute descent from a balloon.

Garnerin experienced a very common and dangerous characteristic of early parachutes; excessive oscillation or swaying. References attribute the solution of the problem to various persons, but the French astronomer De Le-Lande, a contemporary of Garnerin, was probably the first to attempt to solve this major difficulty.[5] He believed that the air, entrapped and compressed beneath the canopy, spilled out, first on one side, then on the other, creating an accelerated rocking motion. He suggested that if some of this air were permitted to escape through an opening in the center of the canopy, the oscillation would be reduced. Garnerin is said to have tested this theory, but it was found that too large an aperture increased the speed of descent. Determining the optimum size of the hole took many years of experimentation, and also involved understanding the importance of the porosity of the canopy material.

The first emergency descent by parachute is reputed to have been made by Jordaki Kuparinto, a Polish aeronaut, on July 24, 1808, when his hot-air balloon caught fire at a considerable height over Warsaw. This incident was widely publicized, and some references list the date as 1804. According to the Aero club of Poland, Kuparinto's life was indeed saved, but not actually by a parachute. Unburned remnants of his balloon envelope billowed up within the balloon's netting, thus forming a life-saving "parachute" effect, which lowered Kuparinto to the ground.[6] Other balloonists, including Henry Coxwell of England, made safe descents with ruptured balloons, which spread out like parachutes within their nets. The American balloonist, John Wise, made at least two successful descents with deliberately collapsed gas-balloon envelopes acting as makeshift parachutes, including a well-known descent at Easton, Pennsylvania, on August 11, 1838.

Charles Guillé made the first parachute descent in America on August 2, 1819, when he cut away from a hydrogen balloon at an altitude of about 500 feet, landing in his wicker basket at Bushwick, Long Island, N.Y.

Robert Cocking built what he considered to be a much more stable parachute. The "canopy," weighing over 200 pounds, was a rigid structure resembling an inverted cone 34 feet in diameter, to which a basket was fastened. He ascended from London's Vauxhall Gardens on July 24, 1837, attached under the *Royal Nassau* balloon, and cut loose at about 5,000 feet. The parachute collapsed almost immediately, throwing Cocking to his death, and giving him the distinction of being the first known parachuting fatality. Cocking's tragic demise tended to dampen enthusiasm for parachuting for some time, and little was done to improve the design of the parachute during the next forty years.

Thrilling exhibition descents from balloons at fairs and carnivals increased in popularity in the United States and abroad, particularly during the late 1800s. Until this time, the typical parachute had been a bulky, inefficient, stiff-ribbed umbrella, impractical for use as an emergency life-saving device. However, the exhibition jumpers of that period introduced innovations in design.

One of the most popular American exhibition balloonist-parachutists of the 1880s was "Captain" Thomas S. Baldwin, who has been credited with the first actual use of the collapsible, frameless silk parachute. (Aeronauts and jumpers often used the title Captain or Professor.) Some historians think that P. A. Van Tassell and an Italian balloonist named Farini, who used chutes of this type at about the same time, were also instrumental in the development of the flexible parachute.[7] They correctly concluded that air pressure would not only support the canopy during descent but would "blow" it open as well. Baldwin also claimed to have introduced the use of the vent in the peak of the canopy to help reduce oscillation. He used a parachute harness strapped to his body, and his vented parachute canopy was hung down the side of the balloon, with the rigging lines terminating at the balloon basket. A trapeze was often included by daring jumpers to add excitement to the aerial show.

Most balloonists in the late nineteenth century used the "attached" type, consisting of a fabric canopy, with hemp suspension lines, folded into a pack that was attached to the side of the wicker balloon basket or hung in the rigging. A "life-line" was connected to the junction point of the suspension lines with the other end attached to the jumper's body harness or trapeze. The canopy was deployed from the pack or container by the weight of the jumper as he fell away from the balloon basket. Often called a "sail" by old-time parachutists, the typical canopy was nothing more than a large disk of cotton, linen, or silk, perfectly flat if laid out on the ground.

It is difficult to determine exactly who invented the first backpack parachute. Certainly Charles Broadwick, the famous balloonist and jumper, was one of the first to develop and use a pack-on-the-body parachute. In the early 1900s, he began to fold the vented silk canopy into a compact backpack fastened by straps to the body of the jumper. A static line was used to break open the pack and deploy the canopy as the jumper fell away from the balloon basket. He devised a better harness, and eventually integrated it in a vest-like canvas garment that he called the "coat-pack." Different models of Broadwick's custom-made parachutes were used by a number of other American exhibition jumpers, including his foster daughter, Georgia "Tiny" Broadwick, who made over 600 jumps from balloons and airplanes before retiring in 1916.[8]

THE PARACHUTE AND THE AIRPLANE

With the successful invention of the airplane by the Wright brothers in 1903, it was only a matter of a few years until aircraft of various types were making exhibition flights at airshows and fairs in the United States and Europe. Very few early airplane pilots carried parachutes. Despite many engine and structural failures, and numerous fatalities, most of the pioneer aviators preferred to take their chances with a disabled aircraft, and make an emergency landing on a road or cow pasture. Many pilots considered the parachute to be unreliable or suitable only for exhibition "stunts." They believed that it was safer to glide to earth in their planes and preferable to try to save an expensive investment. Many of the available parachutes were rather bulky and heavy, and jumping in an emergency from a wire-braced plane, when it was burning or out of control, would have been quite difficult. Other pilots disdained the use of a parachute as a lifesaving device, feeling that its use would reflect upon their faith in their plane and their ability to fly it. This attitude was not changed until after the beginning of air combat in World War I.

To be practical for use with an airplane as a life-saving device, a parachute had to be relatively lightweight, compact, strong and, preferably, opened by the jumper after he cleared the aircraft. Virtually all parachutes of that period were opened by a static line, a strong cord connecting the parachute with the aircraft. The static line opened the pack as the jumper fell away from the balloon basket or airplane, and this procedure is still employed by paratroopers to this day.

The first "official" parachute descent, from an airplane flying at normal speed, was made on March 1, 1912, when "Captain" Albert Berry jumped from a Benoist pusher biplane, piloted by Antony Jannus at an altitude of approximately 1,500 feet over Jefferson Barracks, Missouri. Berry was not an Army aviator as has so often been stated, but a civilian professional balloonist and parachutist. His

The world's first parachute jump from an airplane flying at normal speed was made by Albert Berry (right), on March 1, 1912. This historic event occurred when Berry jumped from the Benoist pusher biplane piloted by Antony Jannus (left), while flying at about 1,500 feet over Jefferson Barracks, Missouri. The parachute canopy was secured by rubber bands inside the cone-shaped tin container strapped to the framework of the aircraft. Upon reaching the desired location and altitude, Berry crawled down under the aircraft structure where he attached himself to the trapeze connected to the parachute-shroud lines, and deployed the canopy by the use of an ordinary snatch block. Berry fell about 300 feet before the canopy opened with a loud "pop," and lowered him to a safe landing just off the parade grounds. (SI Photo A4857)

parachute canopy of unbleached muslin was 36 feet in diameter, and attached by suspension lines to a trapeze-and-strap arrangement donned by Berry while in the air. The canopy was contained in a metal cone fastened to the airplane's framework. After positioning himself on a skid, Berry swung off and deployed the canopy at the appropriate moment by giving a jerk on a snatch block. According to a magazine account; "Berry made as easy a landing as usually experienced when leaping from a balloon."[9] The article went on to speculate about the possibility in wartime of dropping soldiers by parachute, from a fleet of 1,000 airplanes, at a distance of up to 100 miles behind enemy lines. Berry's historic jump greatly pleased the soldiers at the Army post, but despite wide publicity it did little to impress Army officials with the potential military uses of the parachute.

Charles Broadwick arranged a special demonstration for the military on February 23, 1914, when he exhibited his eight pound knapsack-type back parachute which he called a "life preserver for pilots." Broadwick made a successful jump, from a plane piloted by Glenn L. Martin at an altitude of 1,500 feet over the Army Signal Corps Aviation School at North Island, San Diego, California. The report of the Chief Signal Officer, dated July 1, 1914, described the jump and stated "It is believed that as a life-saving device this parachute pack has considerable merit and warrants its development for use in our service." There is no record of any further action being taken toward completing its development and adoption by the Army.[10]

"Tiny" Broadwick had made the first jump by a woman from an airplane on June 21, 1913, and she performed two other well-publicized descents in March 1915, for the benefit of the Army. On the first occasion, she jumped over North Island before a group of military pilots and Brig. Gen. George P. Scriven, the commanding officer of the Army Signal Corps, which at that time included the Aviation Section. A week later, she repeated her jump over North Island, before visiting congressmen and military officials. The short-sighted military saw little use for this "circus stuff." Shortly after the demonstrations, the U.S. Government purchased two of Broadwick's parachutes for use in aircraft, but they were apparently stored away and never used.[11]

Another well-known American aeronaut, balloon and parachute manufacturer, A. Leo Stevens, made significant advances in parachute development during the early years of this century. By 1912 he was producing his "Life Pack," which consisted of a spring-operated backpack resembling a Civil War knapsack. It was attached to the wearer with leather shoulder and waist belts, and opened by a static line.[12] Some accounts state that Stevens experimented with a type of "ripcord" to manually open his "free-fall" backpack parachute, but he apparently discontinued development in favor of the automatic, attached-type parachute using a static line connected to the balloon or airplane.[13]

There was intense activity in aircraft and parachute development in Europe, especially in France, during the years immediately preceeding World War I. The parachutes produced in small numbers in the United States and Europe demonstrated many original ideas and designs, some good and some impractical. Many featured unnecessary apparatus to force open the parachute pack and insure inflation of the canopy. These approaches included springs, compressed air, and in one case, gunpowder. Even Louis Blériot built a parachute in 1913, which he called a "life-buoy for aviators shipwrecked in air," and successfully demonstrated it with a dummy dropped in flight from his monoplane. A backpack parachute, developed by an Italian inventor named Joseph Pino, introduced the use of a small pilot parachute to assist in opening the main canopy. The pilot chute also lessened the opening shock on the canopy and jumper. The pilot chute, patented by Pino in 1911, was mounted on top of the wearer's cap and when he jumped, the small parachute jerked off his cap and at the same time released his main parachute, to which it was attached.[14]

Other imaginative inventions included a proposed parachute system designed by Capt. M. Couade, a French engineer, intended to lower an entire aircraft to the ground in case of emergency. This idea was to surface again in the United States during the 1920s, and the concept finally proved successful with the modular, encapsulated, crew compartments in modern B-58, F-111, and B-1A bombers.

On the eve of World War I, the most common parachute continued to be the proven "attached" type, fastened to the balloon basket or some part of the fuselage or wings of an airplane. Most pilots, however, still considered the parachute to be a dangerous novelty, for exhibition jumping, and quite unsuitable as a lifesaving device for aviators.

THE PARACHUTE IN WORLD WAR I

World War I began as a war of movement, but soon bogged down into positional or trench warfare on the Western Front. Parachutes were not carried by the handful of military pilots, but this omission did not seem very important during the first few hectic months because few airplanes were armed, and they were employed almost solely for reconnaissance.

Tethered kite balloons soon became of great importance to both the Allies and Central Powers, for directing artillery fire and observing and photographing the enemy on the other side of the lines. One, and occasionally two, observers were carried in the balloon basket, and a few balloons were fitted with two baskets. The giant hydrogen-

filled gasbags were made of rubberized fabric and raised on a cable from a truck-mounted windlass. On a clear day they could ascend to an altitude of 5,000 feet, and from this vantage point, the observers could view enemy dispositions and activities for up to five miles behind the lines. The introduction of airplanes armed with machine guns in the spring of 1915, soon made the captive "sausages" prime targets for offensive air patrols.

Parachutes for Balloonists

Both sides provided individual parachutes for the observers riding in balloon baskets. All of the parachutes were of the "attached" type, and were improved models of those used by the earlier balloon-exhibition jumpers. The use of this type of parachute was quite simple and automatic in operation. The parachute pack, or bag containing the canopy and suspension lines, was usually attached to the side of the wicker basket. The observer wore a body harness while aloft, and a "life-line" was attached to the confluence point of the suspension lines inside the pack. The other end of this line terminated in a snap, or was securely attached directly to the body harness. When the balloon was attacked and had to be abandoned, the observer leaped over the side of the basket, and his canopy was deployed from the pack as he fell away. The observer had to be prepared to jump without hesitation, because of the swiftness with which the hydrogen-filled balloon envelope could explode, especially if hit by incendiary machine-gun bullets.

The balloon parachutes employed during the war were all quite similar in appearance and operation. The German Army developed an attached type of balloon parachute in 1915, based on the design of the chute used by Kathe Paulus, a well-known German woman balloonist and jumper of the 1890s. Attached to the rigging above the basket, the chute featured an apex suspension line, which the jumper could manipulate to slightly change the descent characteristics of his parachute. German histories and wartime photographs show that attached parachutes were carried aboard at least some of the giant airships. According to General von Hoeppner, commanding general of the German Army Air Forces, parachutes were provided for morale purposes, but the airships burst into flame and were consumed so fast when hit that the crewmen were unable to use them.[15]

The English provided the Spencer and Calthrop "Guardian Angel" parachutes for their balloon observers, and the French employed the STA model, which was tested during jumps from the Eiffel Tower. U.S. Army balloon observers in France used the French type, equipped with a silk canopy. By the Armistice on November 11, 1918, six firms in the United States had produced a total of 256 balloon

1st. Lt. R. K. Patterson, Air Service observer assigned to the 2nd Balloon Company, First Army Corps, Montreuil, France, in the balloon basket preparing to ascend on July 8, 1918. He is studying a map with another officer, surrounded by the ground crew. Additional maps can be seen in the rack on the side of the basket. His attached-type parachute in its canvas container is fixed to the basket, on the left in this photo. Patterson is wearing his parachute harness over a flying suit, and a telephone mouthpiece is located on his chest. Lieutenant Patterson was credited with two emergency parachute jumps during 1918; one from a burning balloon, and another when his balloon was attacked by enemy aircraft. (Courtesy USAF)

parachutes. Only four of these were shipped to the port, and apparently arrived in France too late to be used in action before the end of the war.[16]

Thomas S. Baldwin, the famous "Captain Tom," balloonist and exhibition jumper of prewar days, was commissioned a major after the United States entered the war in April 1917. He was appointed chief inspector of all U.S. Army balloons and parachutes and, with his long and varied experience, contributed materially to the training and equipping of Army balloon units in the United States, prior to their embarkation for France.

The reliability of the individual parachute for balloon observers was proven hundreds of times during the course of the war. However, when an observation balloon was consumed by fire the maps, records, telephone, camera, and other valuable items of equipment in the basket were usually lost. To overcome this problem, French designers produced the basket parachute, which was adopted by the French Army, and also by the U.S. Army, during the summer of 1918. The German Army also adopted a basket parachute during the last year of the war. The basket parachute was considerably larger than the individual type, and to operate it in an emergency, the balloonist pulled a cord which cut the basket away from the balloon entirely. The parachute canopy then deployed and floated the basket, with the men and contents inside, safely and quickly to the ground.[17]

It is estimated that parachutes saved the lives of over 800 Allied balloonists during the course of the war.[18] The *Air Corps News Letter* dated August 29, 1928, published a list of 75 Americans, who were saved through emergency parachute jumps from U.S. Army observation balloons during 1917–18. Some men made more than one jump, and 1st. Lt. Glenn Phelps made no less than five. A grand total of 117 jumps was made from U.S. Army balloons attacked by enemy aircraft.[19] There were no fatalities from failure of the parachutes to open. The sole American jump fatality was 1st. Lt. C. J. Ross, who was killed when the burning balloon overtook his descending parachute.[20]

Without question, the successful use of parachutes by kite-balloon observers did much to change the perception of the parachute from exhibition novelty to aerial life preserver.

Parachutes for Aviators

As the war progressed, many airplane pilots must have seen observers floating safely to earth from their flaming balloons, and wondered why parachute protection was not available to them. Combat crewmen were all too frequently faced with the terrible choice of either burning up

Attached parachutes were used with observation balloons during and after World War I, and occasionally with airplanes during 1918–19. At left is a parachute made by A. Leo Stevens, with accompanying body harness and rope for attaching the parachute pack to the balloon basket. At right is the Air Service Type F-1 attached or fixed-station type of parachute, which was also made by Stevens. It is complete with body harness and attaching straps. (SI Photo A4841G)

as their flaming plane fell to earth or, like Maj. Raoul Luf-
bery, a World War I flying ace, jumping to certain death
without a parachute. There were technical problems in
adapting the rather bulky and heavy balloon parachutes
for use with airplanes. The main difficulty was where to
attach the parachute pack on, or in, the small pursuit planes,
without causing excessive drag, and allow the chute to
be deployed without snagging on the the tail surfaces or
skid. Some officials also put forth the argument that pilots
with parachutes would be tempted to jump out of their
airplanes prematurely, thus losing aircraft that might otherwise be saved![21] It was also claimed that many pilots
rejected the parachute, because of skepticism and the
belief that its use would reflect on their courage and flying
ability.

Reports that German flyers were using parachutes began to circulate in the spring of 1918, and the clamor for
similar equipment for Allied pilots grew louder. Newspa-
per editorials demanded an explanation, and well-known
airmen, such as Brig. Gen. "Billy" Mitchell and Capt. "Eddie" Rickenbacker, added their voices. The capture of a
parachute-equipped German airplane disclosed that the
airmen were being supplied with the Heinecke parachute,
manufactured by Schroeder and Company of Berlin. This
parachute was designed by Unteroffizier Otto Heinecke,
a junior NCO assigned to Army Aviation Detachment A,
Group 6, who tested it at Adlershof near Berlin on May
1, and again on May 6, 1917. A test of what was probably
a production model was made personally by Heinecke on
February 21, 1918, at the same field.[22] The Heinecke was
no engineering marvel, but more of a transition between
the bulky attached-type of balloon parachute, and the
modern, compact, on-the-body parachute for aviators introduced after the war. It had, however, the distinction of
being the first parachute used in quantity by airplane crewmen for lifesaving purposes.

The factory manual for the Heinecke shows that the
sack-like pack, for the canopy and suspension lines, could
be attached to the upper part of a body harness and worn
as a backpack, however, the pack was usually attached
by side cords and carried as a low-hanging seat pack. The
pack formed either a seat or back cushion in the aircraft.
The Heinecke had a central suspension line connected to
the harness, similar to that used on the Paulus balloon
parachute. The diameter of the cotton, 20-gore canopy
was 21.25 feet, and it, along with the shroud lines, was
contained in its pack by draw wires. A static line attached
to the airplane was connected to the pack's draw wires,
and the canopy vent was tied to the static line by a 50-
pound break-strength cord. The weight of the falling flyer
withdrew the wires from the pack and allowed it to open.
As the aviator continued to fall, his weight deployed the
canopy from the pack by means of the static line, and
upon reaching full stretch at the end of the line, the canopy

The German Heinecke parachute was the first used in quantity
for lifesaving purposes by airplane crewmen. The observer-gunner
of this Halberstadt C.L. IV escort-ground attack aircraft, built by
the Roland Company in 1918, is shown with the bulky parachute
attached to his body harness. The static line (Zugleine) can be
seen connected to the parachute pack-opening device and canopy, with the other end attached to the machine-gun ring mount.
The Heinecke is credited with saving many German flyers, including several prominent aces, during the last months of World
War I. (SI Photo 85–1526)

broke away from the break-cord and filled with air.[23] Although crude, the design was workable, and according to
a report from the U.S. Air Service Technical Section in
France; "There is no case in evidence where a German
parachute failed to open."[24] The lives of many German
airmen were saved by the use of the Heinecke parachute.
The first to use it in an emergency was probably Viza-
feldwebel Weimer of Jasta 56, who bailed out on April 1,
1918, when his Albatross D-Va pursuit was shot down
over the British lines. He descended safely and was taken
prisoner. Other more famous airmen included Germany's
second ranking ace, 1st. Lt. (later Col. Gen.) Ernst Udet,
who was forced to bail out when his Fokker D-VII pursuit
was set on fire during a dogfight on June 28, 1918.[25]
Because of the Heinecke, Udet lived to become one of
the organizers of the Luftwaffe and Director of the Technical Office, until his suicide on November 17, 1941.

Allied engineers studied the Heinecke, and realized
that attached-type balloon parachutes could be adapted
for use in airplanes. Experiments on several types began
in England and France, and the Technical Section of the
A.E.F. started testing various models. The English con-

centrated on installing their muffin-shaped Calthrop Guardian Angel parachute on airplanes. This was a bulky, but dependable, parachute that was being attached experimentally on or in RAF aircraft late in the war. Like all "automatic" chutes, it depended on the jumper's weight to deploy the canopy from the attached metal container. The silk canopy had 24 gores and was 27 feet, 9 inches in diameter. A lifeline extended from the suspension lines in the bottom of the pack, up and over the fuselage to the flyer's harness.[26]

In France, the Ors and Roberts parachutes were under development for aircraft use. The Roberts was tested by the Instrument and Testing Division of the U.S. Air Service, and was considered to be the best type available, but adoption of this bulky parachute would have required modification of the seats in all airplanes.[27] The Guardian Angel and other types were also tested with dummies, and in a wind tunnel at St. Cyr. Two designs, known as A.E.F. types "A" and "B," were developed by Air Service personnel in France who combined the best features of the various existing parachutes. The "A" model was made with a silk canopy, and the "B" model, which closely resembled the well-known S.T.A. balloon parachute, had a cotton canopy. A conference on parachutes was held in Paris in early November 1918, attended by representatives from France, England, Italy, and the United States. A.E.F. participants reported that England and France had placed parachutes in production after extensive tests and experiments, and a few had been sent to the front. American officials stated that "Some of the (new A.E.F.) parachutes had been sent to the front . . . and that large orders had been placed for production, but these had been cancelled after the signing of the Armistice."[28]

Parachutes did see extensive service for other purposes during the war. Countless small parachutes were used by both sides for signals and flares to light up the battlefield. These were usually fired from a grenade discharger such as the V-B, mounted on the muzzle of a rifle, or from a pyrotechnic pistol. Some were launched on rockets and other types were dropped from aircraft. Flares were occasionally dropped from planes at night to illuminate landing fields.

Some spies and saboteurs were dropped by parachute in rear areas. Parachutes were also employed on a limited basis for dropping supplies to troops on the ground, in isolated positions in Europe and the Middle East. The first recorded instance was in March 1916, when the British Royal Naval Air Service began air drops of supplies to the Army garrison at Kut-el-Amara in Mesopotamia during the Turkish siege.[29]

The most ambitious proposal of World War I involving the use of the parachute, was the plan by Brig. Gen. William "Billy" Mitchell for an airborne assault on the fortifications of Metz. This was important because it was the first serious suggestion for the use of the parachute in offensive warfare. Mitchell, then commander of the combined air service of the army group engaged in the Meuse-Argonne offensive, presented his plan to a less than enthusiastic Gen. John J. Pershing in October 1918. It called for men of the U.S. 1st Infantry Division to be trained as parachute troops, while a fleet of 1,200 giant Handley-Page 0/400 and V/1500 bombers was built to carry and drop the soldiers in heavily-armed 10-man squads behind the German lines. The airborne force, depending on surprise and close air support, would attack from the rear, while troops and tanks broke through the German front lines to join in a combined offensive. The war ended before any action was taken to implement the plan, and although Mitchell continued to advocate the use of parachute troops, and the concept of "vertical envelopment," few Army officials paid any attention until the German Air Force demonstrated the combat capabilities of airborne forces in the spring of 1940.

POSTWAR PARACHUTE DEVELOPMENT

Experiments with parachutes also began in 1918 at Wilbur Wright Field, at Fairfield, near Dayton, Ohio. A parachute section was established in the Technical Division and a small military and civilian staff assigned, after urging from Brigadier General Mitchell and others, who believed that a suitable lifesaving parachute should be developed for Army aviators as quickly as possible. Guy M. Ball joined the section as a civilian employee in September 1918, and his inventive genius contributed many technical refinements to the development of military parachutes. J. Floyd Smith began work in October, and brought with him a reputation as an engineer, jumper, and enthusiastic proponent of the free-type pack parachute. He had conceived the idea of a manually operated parachute pack as early as 1914, and made many successful parachute-design and engineering advances during the following years. Pvt. Rodman Law, expert prewar parachutist, was also detailed for temporary duty.

The study and testing of existing parachutes soon determined that "an automatic releasing device (attached or static line type) is not in any way necessary to a successful parachute, and the most promising parachute type is one which is worn on the pilot's back ("free" type), or merely set in the seat beside him . . ."[30] This conclusion was made tragically obvious on July 11, 1919, when Lt. R. A. Caldwell of England was killed, because the lifeline of the attached-type Guardian Angel parachute he was demonstrating at McCook Field caught on an external control rocker arm of the USD-9 airplane, causing the failure of his harness, and allowing him to fall 600 feet to the ground.[31] His death, which was witnessed by many spectators, caused renewed skepticism among pilots and encouraged critics who still said that parachutes were for the circus and not for aviators.

The conclusion reached through tests by the Air Service, both in France and at Wilbur Wright Field, that the attached-type of parachute was neither necessary nor desirable, was at variance with the views of most British and some American authorities. It was assumed by many at the time that an automatic opening device was required because a pilot bailing out of a disabled aircraft would become unconscious, or would not have the presence of mind to pull a ripcord and operate his parachute. The decision to concentrate on a free type of parachute was very important, because it marked the end of an era and the beginning of a period in which America would lead the world in parachute development. During the following four years, almost all of the basic principles were developed that influenced parachute design through World War II and for many years thereafter.

Parachute development was transferred in January 1919, from Wilbur Wright Field to McCook Field, Dayton, where better facilities were available. Maj. Edward L. Hoffman arrived at McCook for assignment as Chief of the Equipment Section of the Engineering Division, a position including active supervision of the new Parachute Branch. Hoffman was a pilot with a flare for engineering, and his assignment was to have a significant influence on the development of military parachutes and many other items of clothing and personal equipment. He managed to obtain sufficient funds to purchase the equipment and supplies necessary for a real parachute-development program, and assembled a small group of capable and enthusiastic "parachute engineers," including Floyd Smith and Guy Ball. James "Jimmy" Russell joined the dedicated staff in February 1919, and with his long experience in aircraft engineering, provided valuable assistance at an important period in parachute research and development. Among others assigned was Sgt. Ralph W. Bottriell, already a well-known parachutist with much practical experience gained while stationed at Kelly Field, Texas.

Major Hoffman accelerated the testing and examination of all American and foreign parachutes that could be obtained. It was clearly demonstrated that none of the existing parachutes were suitable for Air Service use. Some had good features, but most were either too bulky or too weak, with a few, including the Heinecke, failing at speeds of only 100 miles per hour when dropped with a 200-pound load. It was obvious that the attached types were dangerous in an emergency, especially if the plane was in a spin or on fire, and limited all-around operation. The free, or pack-on-the-aviator, type was not only more versatile and practical, allowing the airman greater freedom of movement within larger aircraft, but it also permitted delayed opening jumps, a safety factor that, to a large extent, eliminated the possibility of the chute becoming entangled in any part of the aircraft. The free type also allowed the flyer to jump from either side of the plane, which was vital if the aircraft were in a spin. Tests also showed that the "soaring" type of parachute, which pulled the aviator from the airplane, had little practical value, and required extensive modification of the aircraft.

One of the better pack-on-the-back parachutes tested was submitted by Floyd Smith, and was similar to the Type "A", soon developed for the Air Service. Another was designed by a young balloonist and parachute jumper named Leslie L. Irvin, but since it was static line-actuated, he had to redesign it as a manually operated pack parachute. He made several trips between McCook Field and Buffalo, N.Y., where he had formed a small company to manufacture parachutes, and provided several silk parachutes for testing. Irvin became a staunch advocate of manually operated parachutes, and offered ideas for the design of the optimum parachute as well as refinement of various components then under development by the Parachute Branch.

In early experiments at McCook, attention was largely focused upon strengthening the canopy, for it was obvious that the chute must stand up under severe strains and heavy loads. A 170-pound life-sized figure called Dummy Sam was used to simulate a live load during test drops. Although there was a lack of parachute engineering and scientific knowledge at the start of the program, and little practical parachute-test data, the staff was learning fast. Various sizes of canopies were tried; the length of shroud lines was tested; the harness and pack were closely studied; and ways of controlling oscillation, or swing, were examined. Many materials and manufacturing techniques were tried, and improvements tested in cooperation with the small parachute industry. Attention was also given to vents in the canopy, and variations were developed and first tested, along with other innovations, by Major Hoffman, Milton H. St. Clair, and other members of the staff.

The U.S. Airplane Type "A" Parachute

Floyd Smith, working closely with Guy Ball, performed the primary work of developing a pack-on-the-aviator parachute, worn with an improved body harness, and manually activated during free-fall by a ripcord. During the first four months of 1919, this parachute was designed, built, and tested successfully eleven times during drop tests with a dummy. By the latter part of April, progress seemed sufficient to justify a live jump with the prototype of the backpack, designated as the Type "A." Major Hoffman chose Leslie Irvin to make the first crucial jump because of his extensive experience as a parachutist, and on April 28, 1919, "Ski-Hi" Irvin took off in a USD-9 airplane piloted

Floyd Smith wearing the predecessor of the U.S. Airplane Type "A" parachute. This was the first modern, free-fall, manually operated parachute adopted by the U.S. Army Air Service, and it set the pattern for parachute development during the next two decades. Smith and Guy Ball were primarily responsible for the design and development of this outstanding parachute for aviators. This photo of Floyd Smith would have to have been taken prior to May 12, 1919, when Smith made the second live test jump with the new Type "A." The first live test jump was made by Leslie "Ski-Hi" Irvin on April 28, 1919. Note position of ripcord ring on upper right shoulder strap of harness. (SI Photo A4842J)

following months.[32] On May 19, 1919, Sgt. Ralph W. Bottriell made the first jump by an Army man with a manually operated free-type parachute Type "A."

While in the hospital, Irvin learned that a procurement contract was being written for the manufacture of the first batch of Type "A" parachutes, and decided that his company should be incorporated. He phoned George Waite, his partner in Buffalo, and while the incorporation papers were being prepared, a typist erroneously added a "g" to Irvin's name—an error that was never corrected—and the *Irving* Air Chute Company, Inc., was established.[33] A con-

Rear view of predecessor of the U.S. Airplane Type "A" parachute, worn by Floyd Smith in a photo taken prior to May 12, 1919. To use the manually operated parachute, the user jumped and fell freely under gravity until he was clear of the aircraft. He then pulled the ripcord, which released a small spring-loaded pilot parachute, which in turn pulled out the main canopy by its apex. The drag of the pilot parachute and the partly opened main canopy pulled the shroud lines out of the pack, and the canopy then developed fully. (Courtesy USAF)

by a disappointed Smith, who had hoped to make the initial jump with his brainchild. At 1,500 feet over McCook Field, the courageous Irvin jumped from the plane travelling at 80 miles per hour and yanked the ripcord. The parachute opened perfectly in 1.4 seconds, but upon landing Irvin broke his ankle when an unexpected gust of wind swung him into the ground. This minor mishap in no way reflected on the excellence of this outstanding development, and Smith, Hoffman, and others successfully made many additional test jumps with the Type "A" during the

Sgt. Ralph W. Bottriell (center) shown here preparing for a test jump, with the original version of the U.S. Airplane Type "A" parachute, developed at the Parachute Branch, McCook Field, Ohio. Called the first "modern" parachute, it was similar to the first 300 manufactured by Leslie L. Irvin (right) at his Irving Air Chute Company in Buffalo, N.Y. The man at left is the Curtiss JN-4D pilot, called Ray. Sergeant Bottriell made the first jump by an Army man with the prototype on May 19, 1919. Between January 1918 and January 1920, Bottriell made approximately 200 jumps from airplanes with various attached and free-type parachutes, including the Type "A." He became the premier parachute jumper of the Army Air Corps during his distinguished service career. For his pioneering work and fearless, untiring effort in connection with the parachute, Sgt. Bottriell, then a master sergeant in charge of the Parachute Section at Kelly Field, Texas, was awarded the Distinguished Flying Cross on March 18, 1932. (Courtesy USAF)

tract was signed with Irvin on June 20, 1919, for the construction of the first 300 Type "A" parachutes, the order to be completed within six months at a cost of $550 each.[34]

The U.S. Airplane Type "A" Parachute consisted of a flat circular canopy that became a perfect polygon when spread out. The prototype was 30 feet in diameter, with 40 panels or gores, but this was changed in the production parachute to a 28-foot Japanese Habutai silk (10 momme) or Chinese pongee (12 momme) canopy, of 60-pounds per inch tensile strength. A shock-absorbing feature was soon incorporated by the use of a 48-inch expanding vent, with a covering in the form of a chimney operated by rubber bands, to insure rapid deployment. The prime pur-

pose of a vent in a parachute is to reduce oscillation, and the careful design and testing of the Type "A," including the length of rigging, size and location of the vent, and density of the fabric, helped to minimize this problem. It was designed to allow reasonable latitude in steering by arranging for the forty shroud lines to terminate in four webs. The jumper could grasp these webs, and by hanging his weight on them, a portion of the parachute would be drawn into the center and cause a skid in the desired direction.[35]

The harness was another important feature of the Type "A." The adjustable harness was carefully designed to spread the opening shock over the entire body, and was a big improvement over other early parachute harnesses.

84

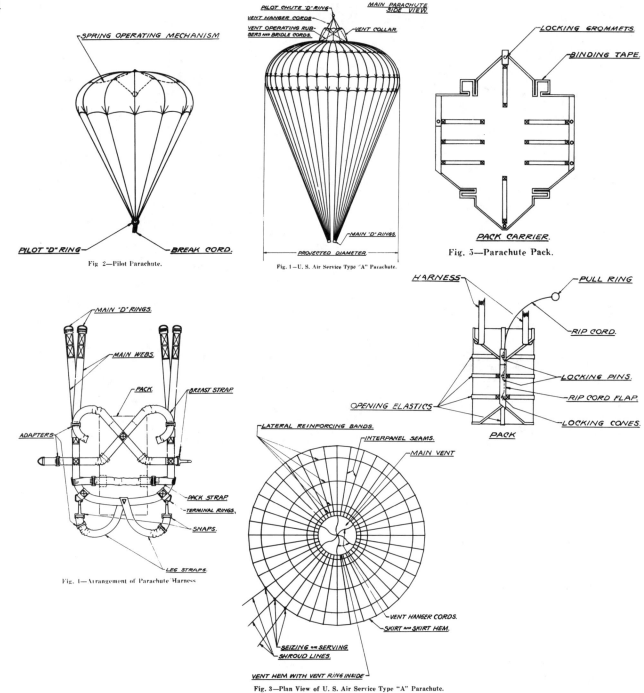

- SPRING OPERATING MECHANISM

- PILOT "D" RING
- BREAK CORD.

Fig 2—Pilot Parachute.

- PILOT CHUTE "D" RING
- VENT HANGER CORDS
- VENT OPERATING RUBBERS AND BRIDLE CORDS.
- MAIN PARACHUTE SIDE VIEW.
- VENT COLLAR.
- MAIN "D" RINGS.
- PROJECTED DIAMETER.

Fig. 1—U. S. Air Service Type "A" Parachute.

- LOCKING GROMMETS.
- BINDING TAPE.
- PACK CARRIER.

Fig. 5—Parachute Pack.

- MAIN "D" RINGS.
- MAIN WEBS.
- PACK.
- BREAST STRAP.
- ADAPTERS.
- PACK STRAP.
- TERMINAL RINGS.
- SNAPS.
- LEG STRAPS.

Fig. 4—Arrangement of Parachute Harness.

- HARNESS
- PULL RING
- RIP CORD.
- LOCKING PINS.
- RIP CORD FLAP.
- LOCKING CONES.
- OPENING ELASTICS
- PACK

- LATERAL REINFORCING BANDS.
- INTERPANEL SEAMS.
- MAIN VENT
- VENT HANGER CORDS.
- SKIRT AND SKIRT HEM.
- SEIZING AND SERVING.
- SHROUD LINES.
- VENT HEM WITH VENT RING INSIDE

Fig. 3—Plan View of U. S. Air Service Type "A" Parachute.

The component parts of the U.S. Airplane Type "A" parachute, adopted by the U.S. Army Air Service in 1919. These illustrations are reproduced from the first edition of the "Parachute Manual," prepared by the Parachute Branch at McCook Field, Dayton, Ohio, in October 1920. The Type A and all subsequent personnel-parachute assemblies, consist of three main parts; the harness, pack, and canopy with accessories. The harness consists of a series of straps, arranged to fit the body by means of sewn or metal connecting devices. The pack protects the canopy and accessories and holds them in place for orderly sequential release when the ripcord is pulled. The canopy is composed of panels of fabric called gores. The pilot chute is attached to the canopy apex, and accelerates its deployment from the pack. The suspension or shroud lines connect the canopy with the harness. (NASM Archives)

It did not bruise the jumper, as did most other types, and with minor modifications, it is the style still in use today.

Air Service Specification Number 40,990, as amended, specified all materials to be used in the construction of the Type "A." These included, in addition to the canopy fabric, 8-ounce khaki duck for the parachute pack, and shroud lines made of braided silk with twisted cores, having a breaking strength of not less than 250 pounds. Silk was found to be much more suitable and reliable than the cotton, linen, or hemp cordage used on other parachutes at that time. Elastics were used to draw back the pack flaps, and the vastly improved body harness was made with 3,000-pound test linen webbing, and high-grade steel fittings with a breaking strength of 2,500 pounds. A spring-loaded 3-foot pilot-chute was attached to the apex of the parachute canopy.[36]

The mode of operation was remarkably simple and positive; a yank on the ripcord freed the four pack flaps, the elastic bands drew them back, and the spring-loaded pilot-chute ejected itself into the airstream. Acting as an air anchor, it extracted the folded canopy and suspension lines from the carrier as the jumper fell away, and the parachute opened. The October 1920 edition, and subsequent editions, of the Air Service "Parachute Manual," gave detailed instructions for parachute jumping and the important tasks of packing, inspecting, testing and repairing the Type "A" and subsequent models of the service parachute. The manual mentions that the Type "A" was designed to withstand a drop with a weight of 300 pounds at 160 miles per hour.[37]

Floyd Smith left government service in September 1919, and opened his own parachute factory in Chicago, where the Floyd Smith Aerial Equipment Company was soon producing "Aerial Life Packs." Guy Ball then assumed technical direction of the Parachute Branch at McCook Field, under the supervision of Major Hoffman. Intense work to improve the bulky Type "A" continued, and the groundwork was laid for many innovations, including canopies featuring new gore configurations, novel vent designs, and annular slotted openings.

To meet the different requirements of various aircraft, the original Type "A" backpack parachute was modified in 1920, so that it could be worn as a seat pack. This redesign required the development of a modified harness. The pilot sat on the seat pack as on a cushion, which necessitated the lowering of the aircraft seat. This chute, which evolved into the Type "S," followed the general design of the Type "A," but was more comfortable, more compact, lighter in weight, and stronger in construction. Development also began on a lap pack for observers and a reserve parachute for wear on the chest during training and exhibition jumps. They were manufactured by the Irving Air Chute Company and became popularly known in the United States and abroad as the "Irvin Air Chute."

The successful tests of the new Type "A" parachutes did not immediately convince all of the skeptics at McCook Field and elsewhere that the parachute was a reliable, worthwhile, lifesaving device. Furthermore, most of the airplanes of the period were not designed with the parachute in mind, and seats, controls, and cockpits could not properly accommodate a pilot or crewman wearing one. With some small aircraft, including fighters, there was no practical way to modify them. Because of the limited appropriations for the Air Service, funds were not available to modify many of the aircraft, let alone purchase new airplanes with remodelled cockpits. In addition to the discomfort and difficulty of wearing a parachute under cramped conditions, there were still many pilots who felt that wearing one was cowardly or indicated a lack of confidence in their own flying ability. Parachutes had remained optional equipment in the Air Service, even for test pilots, but people's perception of the parachute was changing. On September 26, 1919, the Director of the Air Service in Washington, D.C., published the following order:[38]

> 1. Parachute jumps from heavier-than-air craft will not be made for exhibition, test, or in any case other than emergency, unless the person making the descent wears two parachutes and harnesses complete, at least one of which shall be a free type, manually operated, preferably the U.S. Airplane Type "A."
>
> 2. No live jumps will be made, except in an emergency, at an altitude of less than 1,500 feet.

This directive was no doubt a result of the death of Lt. R. A. Caldwell of England, who was killed during a demonstration jump on July 11, 1919, when the lifeline on his attached-type chute caught on the airplane. The untimely death of Lt. Frederick W. Niedermeyer, Jr. during a simulated combat flight on March 13, 1922, made a greater, though very different, impression on many aviators at McCook Field. He had taken off without a parachute because the seat in the Fokker V-40 pursuit was too high, resulting in his head and shoulders extending above the windshield, and into the slipstream. The plane broke up in the air during maneuvers and Niedermeyer was killed in the resulting crash. It was recognized that his life could have been saved had he been wearing a parachute, and on March 29, Maj. Thurman H. Bane, the commanding officer of McCook Field, ordered the wearing of parachutes by McCook Field pilots during test flights or combat practice.[39]

Major Hoffman made a trip to Washington, D.C. where he urged Maj. Gen. Mason M. Patrick, Chief of the Air Service, to issue a regulation requiring the use of parachutes by all Army flyers. Major General Patrick had been considering such an order for months, but its issuance was delayed because there were simply not enough par-

Guy Ball, in 1920, wearing the auxiliary, or reserve, parachute pack along with the Type "A" backpack parachute. Note position of ripcord ring on reserve pack and ring for ripcord of backpack located on the right shoulder-harness strap. Air Service Orders No. 44 were published in Washington on September 26, 1919, requiring that a reserve parachute be worn during exhibition and test jumps at Army installations. The aircraft in the background is a Curtiss JN-4H trainer. (Courtesy USAF)

achutes available for the entire Air Service. The successful emergency jump by Lieutenant Harris, on October 20, described at the beginning of this chapter, and another by Lieutenant Tyndall, on November 11, finally resulted in the publication of Circular No. 6 by the Chief of the Air Service on January 15, 1923, making the wearing of parachutes mandatory for all Army aviators.[40] Circular No. 6 required that: "Pilots and passengers in Army aircraft will be equipped with parachutes on all flights. Exceptions . . . authorized only where parachutes are not available or when the design of the aircraft is such as to render the use of a parachute inadvisable. . ."

The shortage of parachutes in the Air Service was not resolved overnight. Procurement was dependent on funding, and it took some time before new parachutes were supplied to every flying field in sufficient quantity to fulfill all requirements. Flying activities had to be adjusted accordingly during the interim period.

Shortly after Lieutenant Harris' remarkable experience, an informal organization called the "Caterpillar Club" was founded at McCook Field by Milton H. St. Clair of the Parachute Branch, together with Maurice Hutton and Verne Timmerman of the *Dayton Daily Herald*. The club was so named because of the association of the silk in a parachute with the caterpillar. The intention was to give recognition to those intrepid Army airmen whose lives were saved through the emergency use of the parachute. A small, gold lapel pin in the shape of a caterpillar was given to those who qualified by the Irving Air Chute Company. In time the club included thousands of military and civilian "members" around the world and became well known, although over the years it remained unofficial with no meetings, dues, or elected officers.[41]

The historic directive from Major General Patrick marked the close of the pioneering phase of parachute development, but certainly not the end of parachute research and progress. Just as the introduction of the back- and seat-pack parachutes required modifications to the airplanes, increases in speed and in altitude, and changes in tactics required corresponding changes in parachute design. Parachutes had to be strengthened and improved, and the original specifications were frequently revised. The Parachute Branch was well supplied with equipment to make suitable tests, and airplanes were available that had been specially fitted to hoist and handle dummies, weights, and various testing devices.

STANDARD ARMY AIR SERVICE PARACHUTES

By 1924, the Air Service had standardized three types of improved parachutes and had adopted a system of standard designations for parachutes and components. The old Type "A" backpack, after many successful training and practice jumps, and several emergency jumps, was virtually phased out of use because of its bulk and inconvenience in service aircraft. The Type "A" backpack was superseded for general use by the seat pack, the lap pack, and the training pack.

The seat pack was designed for pilots and other personnel who did not move around during flight. It contained a 24-foot diameter service-parachute canopy, with the warp of the fabric of the body placed at an angle of 45 degrees to the center line of each panel. This arrangement made for economy in cutting the cloth, and reduced the probability of the fabric tearing for any distance before being checked by a seam. A slightly slower rate of descent was also obtained because of a reduction of porosity of the fabric when pulled at an angle of 45 degrees. The weight, with improved harness, was about 18 pounds. The Air Service "S" type parachute was the model on which many

87

The lap-pack parachute for observers, being worn by Lt. "Jimmie" Doolittle (left), who eventually became one of America's most famous airmen. Lt. W. H. Brookley, at right, is wearing the pilot's "S" type seat-pack parachute with improved body harness. These chutes embodied the design principles of the original Type "A" backpack, but were more compact, more comfortable, lighter in weight, and stronger in construction. The seat pack set the pattern for parachutes for years to come. Note ripcord ring on top front of lap pack, and on the harness worn with the seat pack, under the flyer's left hand. The aircraft in this 1923 photo is a DH-4B with twin .30 caliber Lewis machine guns on a flexible ring mount in the observer's cockpit. (SI Photo A4844)

American and foreign parachutes were based during the next two decades.

The lap pack, with the 24-foot service canopy, was intended for use by observers and gunners, or where circumstances made use of another type of parachute inadvisable. Backpacks were considered dangerous for use by observers or gunners in an open cockpit, when the pack would be exposed to the slipstream, as the wearer might be dragged from the airplane. The lap pack evolved later into the quick-attachable chest pack.

The training outfit consisted of a harness with a double set of lift webs, one set being connected to a "TM" (Train-

ing Main), a 28-foot-diameter parachute carried in a backpack; the other set was connected to a Type "TR" (Training Reserve), a 22-foot-diameter parachute carried in a compact chest-type pack. All premeditated jumps had to be made with two parachutes, and this outfit conformed to the regulation. The Type "TR" was only used in emergency.

A standard backpack containing a 24-foot-diameter service parachute was supplied to Army lighter-than-air stations. Also under development in the early 1920s was a soft, flexible, backpack parachute. It was intended that all service needs would be filled with the one standard type

88 of parachute canopy, which would be placed in the types of packs best suited to the needs of the particular service where it was used.[42]

The designations of all parachutes, pack carriers, and harnesses authorized for use in 1924 are as follows:[43]

Parachutes

Type	Title
S	Service parachute, 24-feet in diameter.
TM	Training Main parachute, 28-feet in diameter.
TR	Training Reserve parachute, 22-feet in diameter.

Pack Carriers

SS	Seat Service pack carrier used with service parachute.
B	Back training pack carrier used with the training main parachute.
C	Chest (and lap) pack carrier used with the training reserve parachute.

Harness

S	Seat harness used with the seat pack carrier.
L	Lap harness used with the lap pack carrier.
D	Double harness used with the back training and chest pack carriers.

Travelling Bags

One type only. One type of travelling bag accomodated one service parachute, complete, packed in either the seat service pack carrier or lap pack carrier, together with harness, fully assembled.

Parachutes had originally been used exclusively in daylight. On June 18, 1924, 1st. Lt. John A. Macready, veteran Army test pilot, made what Air Service officials stated at the time was the first night parachute jump. According to the Associated Press, Macready was returning to McCook Field from a night flight when the engine of his DH-4B aircraft stopped, and could not be restarted. He then headed the plane away from Dayton towards open country, bailed out at an altitude of about 4,000 feet, and landed safely in a tree on the edge of a ravine 90-feet deep.

Major Hoffman established new objectives and methods for the Parachute Branch during this period, including the construction of a wind tunnel, in which scientific methods could be employed in studying and testing new designs. All sizes, shapes and types of parachutes underwent analysis, along with various materials, with some experiments carried out along radically new lines. Al-

though up to this time only circular parachute canopies had been considered, Major Hoffman began the first experiments with a canopy of a triangular shape, which he hoped would permit slower descent with a greater weight.

In February 1925, Major Hoffman was transferred to Grissard Field, Cincinnati, Ohio, for duty with an Air Service reserve unit, but his contributions did not go unrecognized. He was awarded the prestigious Collier Trophy in recognition of the outstanding part he had played in the development of the parachute.[44] Parachutes in the mid 1920s, were recognized by almost everyone in the military as being both reliable and necessary, but much remained to be done in applying formal engineering principles to parachute design.

ARMY AIR CORPS PARACHUTES

Obtaining sufficient funds for the development of new equipment such as parachutes was always a problem, and little significant improvement resulted from the five-

Maj. Edward L. Hoffman (right), receiving the Collier Trophy for 1926 from President Calvin Coolidge (left), during a ceremony at the White House on February 7, 1926. The trophy was awarded to Hoffman for his outstanding contributions to the development of the parachute, which resulted in the saving of many lives. (SI Photo A44109B)

year expansion and modernization program authorized by Congress as part of the Air Corps Act of 1926. When the Army Air Service was reorganized as the Army Air Corps, the Engineering Division at McCook Field became the Materiel Division and underwent its own reorganization. In 1927 the Parachute Unit, of what was now the Equipment Branch, moved with the rest of the organization from McCook Field to new and improved facilities at Wright Field, near Dayton.

Parachute development continued with emphasis on improvements in the personnel parachute. By the end of 1926, 1,200 test drops had been made by the Parachute Unit. Jimmy Russell left government service, and established a company that offered the beret-shaped Russell "Lobe" parachute of his design. Russell "Lobe" chutes were made without a pilot chute, and were remarkably stable with an absence of undesirable oscillations in descent. The type was not accepted by the Air Corps because of its comparatively greater weight and volume, and the lack of ability to "steer" it by slipping. Floyd Smith, who had become affiliated with Stanley Switlik, developed a soft and thin back parachute. The Switlik Parachute Company, established about 1929, introduced a series of quick-attachable parachutes of all pack types, which met with great success during the next few years.

During the summer of 1927, a quick-attachable type of free parachute was developed that was designed to give greater freedom of movement to observers, gunners and other members of combat crews. This chest chute, which was intended as a replacement for the lap pack, was of standard design and construction, and when not in use was attached to the back of the aircraft seat. When needed, it was attached to the chest harness by means of two sturdy clips. It had a varied reception from its users. Many felt that it was satisfactory, but others reported in questionnaires that they considered it dangerous, because a crew member might forget to attach the parachute before jumping during an emergency, or not have sufficient time to do so.[45] This chest pack was designated as the Type D-1 in 1928.

The procurement of parachutes by the Materiel Division during the period from 1925 to 1930 was at the rate of approximately 1,000 per year. The majority of the parachutes used during this period, by the U.S. Navy and the U.S. Air Mail Service, were also procured through the Air Corps. Major General Patrick stated in a letter to Mr. Davidson, Assistant Secretary of War, on June 21, 1927, that all service parachutes in use at that time had been procured from the Irving Air Chute Company, and that their functioning had always been satisfactory whenever they had been used at sufficient altitude.[46] Leslie Irvin also established a factory in England in 1925, and Irvin Air Chutes were used by dozens of military and civilian organizations and thousands of individuals all over the world.

New parachutes procured in 1928 from the Irving Air Chute Company cost $260.00.[47]

The useful life span of a parachute was originally thought to be two years, depending on the amount of wear. By the late 1920s, this had been increased to five years, with a maximum of two years for the harness. The dependability period for parachutes used in the tropics remained at two years. Parachutes not in active use were to be repacked once a month and drop-tested at least twice a year.

Changes in Air Corps parachute nomenclature occurred in 1928. Air Corps Training Manual No. 2170–72, "The Parachute Rigger," dated June 29, 1929, listed the new nomenclature and added additional parachute components as indicated:[48]

Type	Pack Carriers
S (seat)	Pack carrier.
L (lap)	Pack carrier.
BT (back)	Training pack carrier.
CT (chest)	Training reserve pack carrier.
B (back)	Service pack carrier.
	Harnesses
B	Back harness.
	Travelling Bags
	For carrying the parachute assembly when not in use. Bag is constructed of 12-ounce double-filled duck and reinforced with leather.

Parachutes were included during the late 1920s, in the new standardization system developed by the Materiel Division for all types of aeronautical equipment. All parachutes and component parts were eventually given type numbers and systematically recorded on Type Designation Sheets.[49] All parachutes in use were standardized by 1928 and new equipment was added as each item was developed; for example, the standard seat parachute was designated as the Type S-1, the back parachute, Type B-1, etc. The standard 24-foot-diameter service parachute canopy, which could be used with more than one type of chute, was also designated as the Type S-1.

According to the Type Designation Sheets, the earliest complete parachutes to be recorded and type designated under the new system were fixed station or attached types. The Type F-1 was a Stevens balloon parachute, procured around the end of World War I and classed as limited standard when originally received. It was declared obsolete on July 7, 1926. The Type F-2 was a Type S-1 parachute with fixed station harness attachments, standardized in November 1925, and declared obsolete on the same date as the F-1. No additional parachutes were classified in the "F" series.

The service backpack, Type B-1, consisted of the standard Type S-1 24-foot-diameter canopy, Type A-1 pilot parachute, Type B-1 pack and Type B-1 harness. This type of chute had been in use for some time, but was not standardized under the new system until May 11, 1928. After its status was changed to limited standard on July 19, 1932, it remained in service and was not officially declared obsolete until February 12, 1944.

The Type B-2 backpack parachute was similar to the B-1, except that it used the form-fitting Type B-2 pack. It was service-tested from January 10, 1929, until placed on inactive status on April 30, 1930, because of deficiencies in performance.

The Type L-1 lap-pack parachute, another type already in use, was officially standardized on May 11, 1928. It consisted of the Type S-1 canopy, Type A-1 pilot chute, Type L-2 pack, and Type L-1 harness. It was changed to limited standard on July 19, 1932, when the Type A-1 attachable type parachute was standardized, and finally declared obsolete on February 12, 1944, along with several other older models that were long out of stock.

Seat-type parachutes saw extensive service from the early 1920s until after the end of World War II. The Type S-1 had been in use for several years but was not standardized and designated under the new type designation system until May 11, 1928. It consisted of the standard Type S-1 canopy, Type A-1 pilot chute, Type S-2 pack, and Type S-1 (later Type S-3) harness. With its 24-foot-diameter canopy, the S-1 was recommended for use by personnel weighing under 180 pounds.

The Type S-2 seat parachute, standardized on June 19, 1929, was the same as the Type S-1, except for a slightly thicker pack (the Type S-3) to accomodate the Type TM-1 28-foot-diameter canopy. The Type S-2 was recommended for use by personnel weighing over 180 pounds.

The first "T" series training parachute assembly to be recorded under the type designation system was the Type T-1, which consisted of both back- and chest-type parachutes. The T-1 included the Types TM-1 28-foot-diameter main canopy carried in the Type BT-2 pack, and the TR-1 22-foot-diameter canopy carried in the CT-2 chest pack. Type A-1 pilot chutes and the Type D-1 harness completed the outfit. The Type T-1 was standardized on May 11, 1928, changed to limited standard on July 19, 1932, and finally declared obsolete on February 12, 1944.

The last parachute to be standardized in 1928 was the Type D-1 detachable-type parachute. It consisted of the Type S-1 canopy, Type A-1 pilot chute, Type G-1 pack and Type G-1 harness. The D-1 was standardized on August 21, 1928, changed to limited standard on August 30, 1930, and declared obsolete on February 5, 1936, after stock was exhausted. This chest-style of parachute was later referred to as the attachable type.

In reviewing the work of the Parachute Unit during the ten years following World War I, Maj. Leslie MacDill, then chief of the Experimental Engineering Section at Wright Field, stated that simplicity of construction, with a minimum of working parts had been the aim of the parachute designers. "The Air Corps' standard parachute," said MacDill, "has been adopted by nearly all of the military services of the world."[50]

Valuable work was also accomplished by commercial firms including the Irving Air Chute Company, Russell Parachute Company, and the Switlik Parachute and Equipment Company. From the late 1920s, until World War II refined commercial versions of seat, back, and chest parachutes similar to those used by the U.S. armed services were produced for the civilian market and for export.[51]

Parachute Fabrics

The four requisites of parachute-canopy cloth were weight, strength, tear resistance, and porosity. Weight had to be held within close limits so that the bulk of the cloth (approximately 65 square yards for a 24-foot canopy) would be correct for encasing in a standard container or pack. Tensile strength and tear resistance had to be adequate to provide the strength of assembly desired for safety. Porosity directly governed the performance characteristics, such as the time of opening and the rate of descent and oscillation of the parachute.

Silk remained the principal material for canopies and suspension lines in the 1920s and 1930s, because of its superiority over cotton in tensile strength and bulk, and because it was less flammable. Its elastic, fluffy properties also aided greatly in opening the canopy more quickly, especially after it had been packed for some time. Linen and cotton were used mainly in the ancillary parachute components.

Efforts were made during the 1920s to find a substitute for silk, which was imported mainly from Japan. Domestic silk had been used in a few Army parachutes as early as 1921 and had been found to be entirely satisfactory, but the supply was limited and the cost greater than imported silk. Domestic silk was standardized by the Air Corps for emergency use in 1930, in case the supply of foreign silk should be cut off. The financial restrictions experienced during the depression also prompted a renewed search for satisfactory substitute materials.

Synthetic fibers first came into the picture during tests conducted on rayon in 1929 and 1930. The attention which had been given to cotton as a substitute during the previous ten years, was now directed to this new fiber. The principal objections to cotton for use in canopies had been its bulk and slowness in opening. Rayon, while not having the strength and elasticity of silk, was found to be far superior to cotton in these respects, and was standardized in 1930 as a substitute if silk should become unavailable.[52] The invention of nylon in 1938 finally solved the problem of a substitute parachute material.

The Triangular Parachute

After an absence of three years, Maj. Edward L. Hoffman returned to Dayton and resumed his duties with the reorganized Materiel Division. As Chief of the Equipment Branch, formerly called the Equipment Section, he again became absorbed in parachute development, including a triangular personnel parachute, and a large plane-carrying parachute that would lower both an aircraft and passengers to the ground in case of an emergency. In order to allow him an opportunity to pursue the plane-carrying parachute project, the Air Corps assigned him to the U.S. Department of Commerce for a short time. This period of experimentation resulted in the development of a huge triangular parachute measuring 80 feet in diameter, which was tested at Fairfield, near Dayton, in mid-November 1930. The parachute, weighing only 125 pounds, was stowed in the center section of the fuselage of a primary training plane. Attached to the plane, weighing 2,500 pounds and carrying Major Hoffman as operator and Captain St. Clair Streett as pilot, the chute was released at an altitude of 5,000 feet when Streett cut the engine. The huge mass of silk billowed out and snapped into shape and, at the rate of only 12 feet per second, safely lowered the aircraft and crew to the ground.

During the late 1920s, giant Russell "valve" parachutes were also used in demonstrations, to lower freight as well as airplanes safely to earth. Although these demonstrations of aircraft parachutes were spectacular, they proved to be impractical for application to larger, heavier, military or commercial aircraft.

Experiments in the parachute deceleration of an airplane at the moment of landing were also conducted by Major Hoffman and his associates, but with less success. In the first trial, the release of a 24-foot parachute when the landing airplane was still 200 feet off the ground, produced startling results. The plane was effectively stopped, but torn to pieces by the opening shock. In the hope that fastening the chute to the tail rather than to the center of the aircraft might bring better results, a second trial-landing was made. When that attempt also proved to be unsatisfactory, the experiments were discontinued, and not seriously considered again until World War II.

Major Hoffman continued his work with personnel parachute development, especially his design for a triangular parachute. He became a member of the board of the Triangle Parachute Company, a firm established to manufacture the triangular parachutes of his design.[53] Hoffman had a deep personal conviction that the triangular type of parachute was superior to the conventional circular

or hemispherical designs. This type, sometimes called the "Hoffman parachute" because of his personal interest in its development, had some of the characteristics of a glider. All triangular parachute canopies were constructed on the flat, approximating an equilateral triangle when spread out. Two of the corners were slightly rounded, while the third corner was shaped like the small end of a funnel and functioned in much the same way. The escape of the entrapped air through this funnel-like exit, caused the gliding parachute to move forward and slightly to the right or left at the rate of about three miles per hour, depending on how it was guided into the wind. A small vent was provided at the apex of the canopy for the release of excessive pressure on high-speed openings. Hoffman claimed that the triangular type of parachute was more steerable, and had a slower rate of descent, reduced oscillation, safer fastening, and a stronger, more comfortable harness. In addition, it did not require springs to eject the pilot parachute from the pack as did the standard type.[54]

After several years of development and considerable controversy regarding the merits of this type, the triangular parachute entered service-test status on November 22, 1930, as the Type S-3 seat pack. It consisted of the Type S-2 24-foot triangular canopy, Type A-2 pilot chute, Type S-4 pack, and Type S-3 harness. The Type S-3 par-

Top view of the triangular parachute, designed by Maj. Edward L. Hoffman, during tests by the Air Corps in 1929. Note the vent and pilot chute, and method of sewing the sections of the canopy. Two of the corners of the canopy were slightly rounded, while the third corner was shaped to resemble the small end of a funnel, and to function somewhat like one. The escaping of the entrapped air through this funnel-like exit would cause the gliding parachute to move forward and slightly to the right or left, at the rate of about three miles per hour, depending on how it was guided into the wind. (SI Photo A4845A)

92

The Type S-3 seat-pack parachute, with 24-foot Type S-2 triangular canopy, standardized on July 27, 1932. This photo, taken during service testing in 1931, clearly shows the bayonet-type release on the straps, and the improved type of ripcord handle. (SI Photo A4846)

achute was standardized on July 27, 1932, for limited procurement, even though the majority of the service-test reports were unfavorable to this type of parachute. Mitchel Field reported before the end of 1931, that the chute was hard to pack and that it was not recommended over the conventional Type S-1 parachute, then in use. Chanute Field stated in their evaluation that the S-3 was hard to pack, difficult to adjust, the ripcord was hard to reach, it was slower to open than the S-1, and had a dangerous sideways drift.[55]

The triangular parachute was also more difficult to construct and, consequently, more expensive to produce. These objections, together with the unfamiliarity of the users with this new type of parachute, as well as the difficulties in maintenance, caused the cessation of the procurement of triangular parachutes by the spring of 1936. On July 24, 1936, the Office of the Chief of the Air Corps stated that "no future procurement of triangular parachutes of any type was desired." Those on hand were to be used for quick-attachable service and placed under

limited standard classification effective September 29, 1936.[56] The Type S-3 parachute was finally declared obsolete on February 12, 1944, along with several other older types of parachutes. However, the harness designed by Hoffman for the triangular parachutes, was retained and used for many years with the Air Corps standard-service flat-circular parachutes. His use of rubber bands to retain bighted suspension lines in a parachute container also became standard, and is still in use with some designs today.

Other types of triangular parachutes were used by the Air Corps in addition to the S-3. The Type S-4 was an experimental seat-type parachute which, like other seat packs, was intended for use by pilots and passengers who were not required to move about while flying. The S-4 also had a 24-foot triangular canopy, and it had heavy shoulder straps, adjustable on the harness for use with the Type T-2 back-type parachute. The advent of the low-wing monoplane revealed that difficulties resulting from the use of the seat pack warranted possible elimination of this type for general use by pilots and other crewmen. The S-4 was placed in inactive status on March 12, 1935.

The Type A-1 quick-attachable chest parachute was designed for use by observers, gunners, and photographers who required freedom of action. It consisted of a Type S-2 or S-3 triangular canopy, Type A-2 pilot chute, Type A-1 pack, and Type A-1 harness. It was service-tested beginning on April 2, 1931, and standardized for use on July 19, 1932. The A-1 was changed to limited standard on November 6, 1936, and finally declared obsolete on February 12, 1944.

The Type T-2 training parachute included a Type TM-2 28-foot triangular canopy and the Type A-2 pilot chute, with the Type BT-4 backpack. Combined with the Type S-3 parachute and Type D-2 harness, it made up the Type C-1 parachute-combination training outfit, which was standardized on July 19, 1932. The Type C-1 was changed to limited standard on November 30, 1936, and declared obsolete on February 12, 1944, along with other old triangular types.

The striking appearance of the triangular parachute and the enthusiasm of Major Hoffman attracted a good deal of attention for several years. Tests and demonstrations continued during the 1930s in England as well as the United States. The Triangle Parachute Company also produced seat, back, and chest parachutes of triangular design for commercial sale, but the difficulties in manufacture and packing, and the relatively high cost, discouraged use of these parachutes for general purposes.[57] They were, however, quite popular with exhibition and competition jumpers who valued the ability to steer this stable parachute to a degree not otherwise attainable at that time.

Major Hoffman was promoted to the rank of lieutenant colonel on March 11, 1935, and retired from active duty on May 31, 1937, because of disability in the line of duty.

His retirement brought to a close a remarkably dedicated and productive military career. His basic theory on how to make a parachute glide, influenced many later designers and was influential in the whole area of gliding parachute design.

The triangular parachute, however, was an idea that would not die! In the fall of 1941, interest was renewed in the triangular design for possible paratrooper equipment; and examples were included in a series of tests conducted at Camp MacKall, North Carolina, by the U.S. Army Airborne Board. Comparative tests with standard circular types as well as the experimental Hart and Derry parachutes showed no marked advantages, and studies at Camp MacKall and the Personal Equipment Laboratory

at Wright Field were finally discontinued when the war ended. The great increase in sport parachuting after World War II, led to the reemergence of the triangular type of steerable parachute for use by some exhibition jumpers.

Parachutes in Peacetime

Parachute development at Wright Field continued at a moderate level during the 1930s. Although Major Hoffman had made some progress in introducing sound engineering principles in the development of equipment, testing by the Parachute Unit was still to a large degree done by trial and error. American parachutes had, nevertheless,

Technical Order No. 13-5-1, dated May 17, 1934, summarized the triangular parachutes and components in use by the Air Corps:[58]

Parachutes

Type	Description	Canopy
A-1	Quick-attachable	S-2, 24-foot
C-1	Combination-seat-and-back	S-4, later S-3 seat and T-2 back with Type S-2 and TM-2 canopies
S-3	Seat-type	S-2, 24-foot
S-4	Seat-type	S-2, 24-foot
T-2	Back-type	TM-2, 28-foot

Canopies

Type	Article
TM-2	Back-type, 28-foot triangular
S-2	Seat-type, 24-foot triangular
S-3	Quick-Attachable Type, 21-foot triangular

Pack Assemblies

Type	Used with
A-1	A-1 Quick-attachable parachute
BT-4	T-2 Back-type parachute
S-4	S-3 Seat-type parachute

Harnesses

Type	Use
A-1	A-1 Quick-attachable parachute
D-3	S-4 Seat-type parachute
S-3	S-3 Seat-type parachute

Flyer's Kit Bag

For conveniently carrying and transporting the parachute when not being worn. Constructed of 12-ounce double-filled duck, reinforced with linen webbing. The webbing around the middle formed two loop handles at the top of the bag.

A summary of conventional circular type parachutes in use by the Air Corps is contained in Technical Order No. 13–5–2, dated June 15, 1933:[59]

Parachutes

Type	Description	Diameter in feet	Weight of wearer
S-1	Seat	24	under 180 pounds
S-2	Seat	28	over 180 pounds
B-1	Back	24	no limitation
L-1	Lap	24	no limitation
T-1	Double training	22 and 28	no limitation

Canopies

Type	Article	Diameter in feet	Rate of descent in feet per second	Used with packs, types
S-1	Service parachute S-1	24	16 to 24	S, L, or B
TM-1	Training main parachute and service parachute S-2	28	14 to 20	S or BT
TR-1	Training reserve parachute	22	17 to 26	CT

Pack Assemblies

Type	Used With
S-2	24-foot seat parachute
S-3	28-foot seat parachute
L-2	24-foot lap parachute
B-1	24-foot back parachute
BT-2	28-foot back training parachute
CT-2	22-foot chest training parachute

Harnesses

Type	Use
S-1	Seat type
L-1	Lap type
D-1	Double training type
B-1	Back type

Flyer's kit bag

The same type of flyer's kit bag was used with all parachutes. The bag was made of 12-ounce double-filled duck reinforced with linen webbing. The webbing straps around the center of the bag formed two loop handles at the top. Bags were marked: "U.S. Air Corps Parachute Traveling Bag 073760," on the body, and a patch sewed to the flap on top was marked: "U.S. Airplane Parachute," and the name of the manufacturer, e.g.: "Irving Air Chute Co., Inc., Buffalo, N.Y." The flap was secured by snap fasteners and a cord.

gained a well-deserved reputation for dependability, reliable performance, and unfailing precision when handled properly. As a result of experiments in parachuting technique, and live and dummy tests of new equipment, it was realized that the increase in performance of future combat aircraft would necessitate stronger and more versatile parachute designs.

The Parachute Unit acted promptly to replace the triangular parachutes, and standardized a new quick-attachable chest parachute on November 6, 1936, which

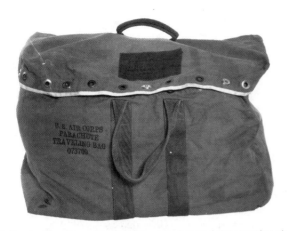

A flyer's kit or traveling bag, for carrying and transporting the parachute when it was not being worn or stored. The bag could also be used for clothing. The label on the flap was marked: "U.S. Airplane Parachute," and included the name of the manufacturer. Later models of similar design were closed with zippers. Designated Types A-1, A-2, and A-3, they were superseded during World War II by the AN6505–1 bag, which was almost identical to the A-3. (Courtesy USAF)

superseded the triangular Type A-1. Known as the Type A-2, the new chute assembly consisted of the standard Type S-1 24-foot circular canopy, Type A-1 pilot chute, Type A-2 pack, and an improved Type A-2 harness. The pack had a one-point steel coupling for attachment to the female base section on the harness. According to the Type Designation Sheets, "The changes were made to eliminate the triangular canopy as per instructions from the Chief of the Air Corps."[60] The A-2 remained standard for gunners and observers until officially superseded by the AN6513 chest chute in 1942, as part of the program to standardize similar equipment for use by the U.S. armed forces during World War II. The Type A-2 was not officially declared obsolete until September 29, 1944.

A new training outfit was also developed for Air Corps use to supersede the triangular Type C-1. The Type T-3, standardized on November 30, 1936, was an improved T-1 consisting of the Types TM-1 28-foot and TR-1 22-foot circular canopies, with Type A-1 pilot chute, the Types BT-2 back and CT-2 chest packs, and the improved Type D-4 harness. The Type T-3 was changed to limited standard on February 24, 1944, and declared obsolete on November 21, 1944. It not only saw long service with the Air Corps, but was also the first type used for training of the new U.S. Army parachute troops organized in 1940.

The development of an improved back-type parachute was renewed by the Parachute Unit in 1937. The introduction of the modern bomber with small machine-gun turrets and the capability for flying long combat missions, made the need for comfort and compactness paramount in parachute construction. Service-testing of a new Type

B-3 backpack parachute began on December 2, 1938, but this design did not prove entirely satisfactory. It consisted of the Type S-1 canopy and Type A-1 pilot chute, with a new Type B-3 pack and Type B-2 harness. The B-3 was declared obsolete on May 1, 1940, and the limited number procured for testing were reworked into Type B-6 parachutes.

The Type B-4 back-type parachute was an improved Type B-3. It was standardized on August 16, 1939, and consisted of the standard Type S-1 24-foot canopy and Type A-1 pilot chute, with a new Type B-4 pack and Type B-3 harness. It was changed to limited standard on March 15, 1940, and declared obsolete on February 12, 1944, after stock was exhausted. No new design features were incorporated in the B-4, except for the inclusion of a combined back and seat cushion attached to the pack and harness assembly. It was used mainly for passengers in cabin and transport aircraft already in service.

A back-type parachute similar to the B-4 was standardized as the Type B-5 on August 31, 1939. It used the same components as the B-4 except that a 28-foot canopy was employed for use by personnel weighing 180 pounds or more. It too was changed to limited standard on March 15, 1940, but was not declared obsolete before the end of the war, despite the fact that stock was exhausted on March 12, 1942, and no further procurement was made.

The Type B-6 back-type parachute was a radical modification of the Type B-3, and was an improvement over the Types B-4 and B-5. It was designed especially for use by gunners and observers in restricted positions in bombardment and attack airplanes. The B-6 utilized the conventional Type B-3 harness assembly and the Type S-1 canopy and A-1 pilot chute, contained in a new, soft, partially streamlined pack container, arranged to fit the wearer's back and reduce bulk to a minimum. Reduction in bulk was effected to prevent the parachute pack from catching on projections while the wearer was operating flexible guns or moving from one gun position to another in a bomber. It was recommended that the B-6 be used to supplement the Type A-2 quick-attachable parachute. The B-6 was standardized on March 15, 1940, changed to limited standard on October 10, 1940, after the Type B-7 was standardized, and declared obsolete on February 12, 1944, when stock was exhausted.

Development of back-type parachutes continued at a rapid pace, based on the results of laboratory experiments and the practical knowledge gained from the service use of back parachutes in modern aircraft. The Type B-7 back-type parachute was designed primarily so that gunners and non-stationary crew members would have a comfortable parachute, usable under combat conditions and attached to the wearer at all times. Thus it would overcome the feature considered objectionable in the Type A-2 quick-attachable parachute. Standardized on

October 1, 1940, the B-7 utilized the standard S-1 24-foot canopy and A-1 pilot chute as before, but featured a new Type B-7 pack and Type B-4 three-point release harness with waist band to hold the parachute close to the body. The chest and leg straps had bayonet-type fasteners but snap-fasteners were in use by 1943. The complete parachute assembly was eight pounds lighter than the standard S-1 seat parachute. Originally intended as a soft back-type parachute contributing to the comfort of the wearer, modifications were incorporated to prevent premature openings which resulted in a harder, more rigid pack, considered by many to be uncomfortable. Plans were made to correct this fault and, as a result, the Type B-8 back parachute was eventually adopted, and standardized in the fall of 1942. In the meantime, the B-7 was changed to limited standard on June 19, 1942, when the AN-A-P-121, AN6512 back parachute was standardized for use by both the U.S. Army and Navy. The AN6512 design was very similar to the Type B-7, and both remained in service until after the end of the war. The Type B-7 was finally declared obsolete for AAF use on November 9, 1945.

The lengthening of the flight time during which a parachute might have to be worn, made necessary the development of cushions and pads of various types. Some crewmen had been adding a cushion or padding to their parachute harness for years, and indeed Lt. Harold Harris had installed a cushion on his harness as early as 1922. A standard back pad which could be made a part of the parachute harness was developed by the Parachute Unit in 1936. A pneumatic cushion was also developed, but was not very durable, and was superseded in January 1939, by a cushion constructed of light sponge rubber. Because of the wartime rubber shortage, these cushions were in turn superseded in 1943 by cushions filled with curled hair.

Back pads were also developed, which could be used as emergency survival containers. They were attached to the parachute harness and used as a back pad or cushion, but the container was actually an emergency kit. These containers were often procured during the war without the components, and were assembled using appropriate items by the area Air Service Command units prior to issue.[61] They will be discussed in Chapter VI along with other items of survival equipment.

Nylon for Parachutes

The military situation in Europe during 1938 and 1939, and the increasing tension in American international relations, especially with Japan, stimulated interest in the utilization of synthetic substitute materials for military use. Nylon appeared as the answer to the growing concern about the supply of silk for parachutes. A synthetic material yielding fibers of great toughness, strength, and elasticity, nylon was developed by the E. I. du Pont de Nemours Company of Delaware, and placed in commercial production in 1939. Tests at the Materials Laboratory of the Engineering Section began immediately, and soon showed that nylon would not only serve as an acceptable substitute but also had several characteristics which made it superior to the best grade of silk. The Equipment Laboratory reported in June 1940, that tests conducted with standard-type parachutes constructed of nylon showed that they compared favorably with those made of silk. The nylon fabrics of that period were found to be somewhat stronger than silk, but more porous. The nylon was also bulkier when packed and tended to "pull" at the seams to a greater extent than silk.[62]

A continuous effort was made to improve the quality, and to increase the quantity, of nylon available for parachute material. One thousand all-nylon parachutes were procured during the autumn of 1941, and a survey of production facilities revealed that a maximum of 16,000 nylon parachutes per month could be produced at that time.[63] Even though all of the parachutes procured during the first few months after Pearl Harbor were made of silk, the Equipment and Materials Laboratories had proved the superiority of nylon. It had greater tensile strength and greater elasticity; it was not subject to mold; and it was not weakened by immersion in salt water. It actually absorbed little water and consequently dried very quickly, and though it would melt under intense heat, it was not flammable. The fiber could also be made uniform, to a predetermined size and length. Another major advantage of nylon was that the supply could be greatly increased to meet all wartime requirements.

Harness made from long-fiber cotton webbing with nylon filling was found to be superior to the standard harness of linen construction, and was standardized for use. In the case of suspension (or shroud) lines and harness webbing, nylon's elasticity was of prime importance, because it tended to absorb the opening shock load and minimize its transmission to the wearer. Studies on the impact and elasticity properties of nylon were continued through an agreement in 1943 between the Materials Laboratory at Wright Field and the Massachusetts Institute of Technology (MIT).

The use of nylon for parachutes was given priority during the first years of the war. One million pounds of nylon material was made available each month; thus there was a supply sufficient to produce one million parachutes annually. Fifteen thousand nylon parachutes were on procurement by March 1942. The last silk parachutes procured for the AAF were delivered during the spring of 1943, and during the fiscal year ending June 30, 1944, approximately 228,500 man-carrying nylon parachutes were on procurement.[64] Nylon was available when it was needed most, and it lived up to all expectations.

Parachutes for War

The acquisition of modern aircraft stimulated considerable discussion concerning the types of parachutes that should be developed for Air Corps use. The debate gained in importance after the German invasion of Poland, and in anticipation of an increase in Air Corps procurement of aircraft and equipment. Numerous differences of opinion existed, and on October 13, 1939, the Chief of the Materiel Division presented the problem to the Chief of the Air Corps over what type of parachute was to be used in the future. He included the recommendation that the pilot and copilot seats should provide for the standard seat-type parachute, and all other seats and crew positions should accommodate the standard seat-type or the current quick-attachable Type A-2 parachute.

Correspondence on the subject brought a diversity of opinions, and as a result, a board was appointed consisting of officers representing various bombardment, pursuit, attack, and observation units. Enlisted men from parachute-maintenance shops and crew chiefs were included. The board convened at Wright Field on November 18, 1939, and the results were formulated in a statement of policy that guided Air Corps parachute development for the next couple of years. According to Statement of Policy No. 189, dated May 11, 1940, the airplane seats for personnel occupying fixed positions such as pilots would accomodate either seat- or back-type parachutes. Personnel not in fixed positions would be provided with a seat, which would accomodate a back-type parachute. Future procurement of parachutes would consist of either seat or back-types, and quick-attachable parachutes would be ordered only as replacements in existing aircraft or those in current production.[65] Actual combat experience during the war required changes in this policy, especially concerning the types of parachutes that were to be developed and procured.

The beginning of World War II in Europe accelerated advances in parachute technology, as requirements for improved equipment became urgent and new roles for parachutes evolved. The modern aeronautical research and development facilities established in England and Germany began exploring basic aerodynamic and other performance criteria. The use of the vertical wind tunnel for testing parachutes originated in England where Professor A. V. Stephens built the first such structure in 1931. This made it possible to test any type of parachute without the use of airplanes.[66]

German experimenters appreciated the need for scientific investigations into the factors determining para-

chute performance, and German research was quite advanced at the beginning of the war. Notable work was accomplished by both Dr. Helmut G. Heinrich and Theodore Knacke, who continued their research in the United States after the war. Knacke, under the supervision of Dr. G. Madelung of the Graf Zeppelin Research Institute near Stuttgart, originated the concept of ribbon-construction gores for high-speed parachutes. The ribbon parachute, made of horizontal ribbons supported by vertical ribbons, resulted from his work. This type of parachute has been used for many years for the deceleration of high-speed jet aircraft. Heinrich conceived the guide-surface parachute, when an extremely stable, solid type of parachute was required for special retardation purposes. Both of these designs were developed to a high degree, based on thorough theoretical investigations coupled with scientific experiments, in Germany and later in the United States.[67]

AAF PARACHUTES IN WORLD WAR II

At Wright Field, the increase in technical and support personnel and the improvement of the facilities of the Materiel Division, including construction of a vertical wind tunnel during the war, permitted an acceleration in the research and development program. Engineers worked overtime to develop improved designs and Parachute Branch specialists cooperated closely with the technical personnel of the parachute industry. The great expansion of the Air Corps (from June 20, 1941, Army Air Forces [AAF]), created an urgent need for more parachutes, just as it did for all types of personal equipment.

The companies on the approved Air Corps procurement list manufacturing parachutes before the war were the Irving Air Chute Company, Switlik Parachute and Equipment Company, Pioneer Parachute Company, and the Eagle Parachute Corporation; but their capacity was not sufficient to meet the needs of the AAF after the outbreak of hostilities. The entry of the United States into the war, led to large production contracts being awarded to commercial firms for the manufacture of standard service parachutes, utilizing the new nylon material then available. Five sources for nylon parachutes were originally approved under the parachute-procurement policy. In addition to the Irving, Switlik, and Pioneer companies, there was the Standard Parachute Corporation and the Reliance Manufacturing Company. As demand grew and more factories were needed, the companies determined to be the most competent were active in the women's undergarment industry. By February 1943, twenty-three additional sources for manufacture had been approved, and a total of thirty-one companies fabricated parachutes for the AAF during World War II.

The following is a summary of the three basic types of personnel parachutes in use by the AAF when the United States entered the war on December 7, 1941:[68]

Chest type. This type was called the quick-attachable chest, or "QAC" parachute, because the pack was separate from the harness and could be attached quickly in an emergency. It was intended for use where it was impractical to wear the back-type parachute. The harness was worn during flight, and the pack was stowed in a location which permitted immediate access in case of need. If a crewman was required to perform his duties in a different part of the aircraft, it was recommended that an extra QAC pack be located at his alternate position. The Type A-2 was the standard parachute of this kind at the time of Pearl Harbor.

Back type. The back-type parachute was recommended for use by all flyers when it would not hamper them in performing their duties. The back-type parachute restricted the movement of the body somewhat, and therefore limited the view to the rear. In positions with limited head space, the back-pack was preferred to the seat pack. Back-type parachutes available in 1941 included the Types B-4, B-5, B-6, and B-7. The Type B-7 was the standard parachute normally issued to combat crewmen requiring a back-type chute.

Seat type. Flyers wearing the seat-type parachute could turn and flex in their seats more readily than those wearing the back-type, and therefore enjoyed greater visibility in all directions. Despite the many minor improvements that had been made in the seat-type parachutes since they were introduced in the early 1920s, they still caused difficulty when moving about inside an aircraft. Their awkward location caused them to catch easily on projections. It was also more difficult to bail out with a seat chute, and during the war, it was recommended that this type be used in action only when back- or chest-types could not be worn. Seat chutes continued to be used widely, especially in training planes by instructors and cadets. Seat-type parachutes available to combat crewmen at the time of the United States entry into the war, were the Type S-1, with a 24-foot canopy, and the Type S-2, with a 28-foot canopy, intended for flyers weighing over 180 pounds.

Training, troop, and cargo parachutes will be discussed later in this chapter.

Parachutes were carried in a kit bag when not being worn, and the bags could also be used for carrying clothing and personal items. The Types A-1 and A-2 were similar olive-drab duck bags with zipper tops, introduced before the war. They were replaced in production by the Type A-3, also of OD duck, which had a double-acting

Maj. Gen. Elwood R. Quesada, CG of the IX Tactical Air Command, is shown climbing into a P-51C fighter, in this 1945 photo. He is wearing a Type S-1 or AN6510 seat-type parachute with cushion. The ripcord handle is located under his left hand, and the snap fasteners for the three-point harness release can be seen, one on the chest and one on each leg strap. Other items of personal equipment include a Type B-4 or AN-V-18 life-preserver vest, early Type B-7 goggle with separate lens cushions, Type A-14 demand-oxygen mask, and a British RAF Type C flying helmet. Quesada appears to be wearing a U.S. Army tanker's lined field jacket. (Courtesy USAF)

zipper with padlock. The A-3 was superseded as standard in 1943 by the AN6505-1, a bag of similar design.

Much was accomplished by the Parachute Branch during World War II, and by the parachute industry, in the mass production of high-quality parachutes for the armed forces. Beginning in 1943, Lt. Col. Emry V. Stewart provided experienced leadership for the Parachute Branch. The Branch was transferred from the Equipment Laboratory to the new Personal Equipment Laboratory when it was established on April 13, 1944.

Wartime experience dictated many changes and challenges. For example, the problems encountered with the rather uncomfortable Type B-7 back-type parachute, and the AN6512 copy standardized on June 19, 1942, for use by both the Army and Navy, were at least partially resolved with the introduction of the Type B-8 back parachute.

The Type B-8, standardized for AAF use on October 16, 1942, was developed originally by the Pioneer Parachute Company as their Model B-3-B. It featured a semi-flexible soft pack, which was spread over a larger area than previous Air Corps backpacks, and was therefore less bulky. Because the pack was semi-flexible, it allowed greater freedom of movement; a very valuable feature during wartime. The longer, thinner, less rigid pack was also more comfortable than the Type B-7. A conventional circular canopy 24 feet in diameter was utilized, and opening was facilitated by a small pilot parachute, 36 inches in diameter, attached to the apex. It was actuated by a spring-operated, quick-opening device sewed within the canopy. The three-point release harness remained similar to that used with the Type B-7, but the waistband was eliminated. Snap fasteners were used during most of the war, but bayonet-type fasteners were introduced by 1945. The Type B-8 parachute continued in standard use until well after the end of the conflict.

Despite previous reservations concerning the safety of wearing only the harness and attaching the pack when needed in an emergency, the quick-attachable chest parachute was found to be very convenient and practical for many crewmen of multi-place aircraft. The production of quick-attachable chutes increased greatly during the course of the war, because of their extensive use by bomber crewmen.

A new quick-attachable chest-type parachute was also adopted for AAF use during 1942, as a result of requests from American flyers in England for a parachute harness which, during suspension, would place the pack above and out of the way of the wearer, and also have the points of suspension across the shoulders. Designated as the Type A-3, the chute was developed originally by the Naval Aircraft Factory, for Navy and Marine Corps use. Drawings and specifications were obtained from the Navy, which allowed the manufacture and release of the parachute to AAF combat groups in a relatively short period of time. The Type A-3 included a redesign of the Type D-2 "D" rings attached to the new barrel-type pack. The snap fasteners for the pack were a part of the harness. The harness used three-point release fasteners of the bayonet type. The canopy and pilot chute were standard designs similar to those used on the Type A-2. The Type A-3 was changed to substitute standard on February 17, 1944, and continued in service through the end of the war.

Camouflage of Parachutes

Parachute canopies had traditionally been white in color, however, during 1942 and 1943 the question of camouflaging parachutes became one of considerable importance. The original investigation had been initiated at the request of AAF pilots in the Pacific theater of operations who believed that a suitable color would make perception of personnel more difficult, and thus result in a measure of protection from enemy gunfire during descent. The problem was extensively investigated by the Materiel Command, partly in response to inquiries from the Airborne Command at Fort Benning, Georgia. Tests were performed in collaboration with the AAF Proving Ground at Eglin Field, Florida, the Las Vegas Army Gunnery School, Nevada, and at Camp Indio, California.

Tests included the dummy-drop testing of parachutes and observation from higher altitudes. White, olive-drab, foliage and sand-colored canopies were tested. After all factors were considered, including the evasion of the enemy and the location and rescue of American flyers forced down over various terrain, the Director of Military Requirements issued a policy regarding color in November 1942. Since parachutes for use by AAF flyers were desired primarily to save the lives of aircrew members forced to abandon disabled aircraft in flight, AAF procurement should continue to be 100 percent white. However, the Airborne Command had indicated its desire for parachutes on the basis of 50 percent camouflaged and 50 percent white, so these percentages of the two colors should apply to the Army Ground Forces.

The policy of procuring all-white parachutes for the AAF, was in conflict with the recommendations made by the Equipment Laboratory at Wright Field in a report on the utility of camouflage of parachutes for flying personnel. After testing several colors, their unanimous conclusion was that the AAF emergency type parachutes should be a dark, dull, solid olive-drab color, and a green and brown foliage pattern should be adopted for the parachute troops.

The foliage pattern of camouflage was eventually employed for all parts of the parachutes procured for combat use by paratroopers, but the majority of parachutes used by AAF flyers remained white. The exceptions were the AN6510 and AN6511 series seat-type parachutes for Army and Navy use, similar to the AAF Types S-1 and S-2, respectively. The canopies of the AN6510-1 and AN6511-1 were white, and the canopies of the AN6510-2 and AN6511-2 had alternating panels of red and white. It is believed that the red and white canopies were intended to make it easier to locate flyers downed in the sea, or on snow and ice.[69]

Army-Navy "AN" Parachutes

The U.S. Army and Navy standardized a number of different types of ordnance, equipment, and supplies for joint use during World War II in an effort to speed up production and distribution. An agreement was reached early in 1942, for the standardization of parachutes of similar type for mutual use, and these parachutes, identified by their "AN" (Army-Navy) numbers, were placed in production. Although agreements for the joint production and use of many items, including guns and bombs, were successfully carried out during the war, it appears that only the Army Air Forces and not the Navy actually procured the "AN" parachutes.

The Type A-2 quick-attachable chest-type parachute was superseded in 1942 by the AN6513 quick-attachable chest (QAC) parachute, and shortly thereafter by the AN6513-1 QAC. Both had square packs, bayonet fasteners on chest and leg straps, and D-rings for attachment of the pack. By 1944 the AN6513-1A QAC, with a barrel-type pack, was in use by the AAF. Unlike the previous types, the AN6513-1A harness had snap fasteners on the chest and leg straps, but retained the D-rings for attachment of the pack. All "AN" QAC packs included snaps for attachment. The AAF eventually converted most AN6513-1 and AN6513-1A QAC parachutes to the Type A-3.

The Type B-7 back-type parachute was restandardized as the AN6512 on June 19, 1942, and continued in production. By 1943, the slightly modified AN6512-1 was in use, followed in 1944 by the improved AN6512-1A.

The Type S-1 seat-type parachute, with its 24-foot diameter canopy, was officially superseded by the AN-A-P-121, AN6510 seat parachute on June 19, 1942. The AN6510 was almost identical to the S-1, with some minor differences in the type of fastener, chest-strap guards, and cushions. The AN6510-1 was produced with a white canopy, and the AN6510-2 was made with a red and white canopy. Both were placed on substitute-standard status on December 29, 1943, when the Type S-5 with the Irving quick-release seat-type harness was standardized for AAF use. They were changed to limited standard on August 23, 1944. The Type S-2 seat-type parachute with a 28-foot diameter canopy was officially replaced by the AN6511 on June 19, 1942. It was produced as the AN6511-1, with a white canopy and AN6511-2, with a red and white canopy. Both were declared limited standard on January 9, 1945.[70]

Other types of AAF parachutes, including later chest, back, and seat models, were not standardized under the Army-Navy "AN" system and retained their AAF nomenclature. Troop-type parachutes were also not standardized for joint use. By 1945 the parachutes used by the AAF reverted back to their original Army nomenclature and designation system.[71]

Before discussing further wartime developments in parachutes, the subject of the quick-release mechanism must be considered because of its influence on subsequent designs.

Quick-release Mechanisms

Considerable controversy arose during World War II concerning the advisability of using some form of instantaneous or quick-release device on the parachute harness worn by aviators and parachute troops. Several other countries had introduced quick-release mechanisms, including Great Britain, Japan, Italy, and Germany. The Italian device was extremely complicated and difficult to fasten. Germany employed a device similar to the Irving design.

British experience with such a device went back to 1918, when the Calthrop "Guardian Angel" parachute incorporated a "lever-operated central-instantaneous release buckle," as part of the harness.[72] The British quick-release device used in World War II was developed in 1929 by two Englishmen; Frank S. Wigley and Leonard F. Austing. The British patent rights were assigned to the Irving Air Chute Company, which also secured an American patent on the same device in February 1933.[73]

The Irving single-point quick-release device, in its fully developed form, consisted of a small, metal box containing four spring-activated pins. When the harness was donned, perforated metal tips on the ends of the two chest and two thigh bands were held in place by these pins. When the harness was to be released, a metal disk on the front of the box, which was positioned on the chest, was rotated 90° and depressed with a sharp blow. This operation released the four straps or bands and instantly freed the harness from the wearer.

The Royal Air Force (RAF) adopted the Irving quick-release device in 1931. Because RAF personnel flew over water extensively, there was always a greater interest in a quick-release mechanism for the parachute harness in Britain than in the United States. The British considered the quick release a necessary safety factor in case of landing in water, and American flying personnel arriving in England and North Africa in 1942 were favorably impressed with the RAF quick-release device.

The standard three-point release, which had been developed at McCook Field in the 1920s and was standard in the Air Corps and AAF, held the harness in place by the use of three harness snaps attached to one chest strap and two leg straps. Bayonet-type fasteners were also used at various times. They gave a broader and smoother under surface than the snap type, and were favored by Major Hoffman. In March 1931, the Irving Air Chute Company of Buffalo, New York, submitted photographs and a description of a parachute harness with the quick-release mechanism to the Materiel Division. Several other designs were also studied over the years but all were either too complex, too fragile, or lacked the security so essential in a device of this type. Tests were eventually performed on the Irving device by the Parachute Unit, and service tests were conducted at several Air Corps flying

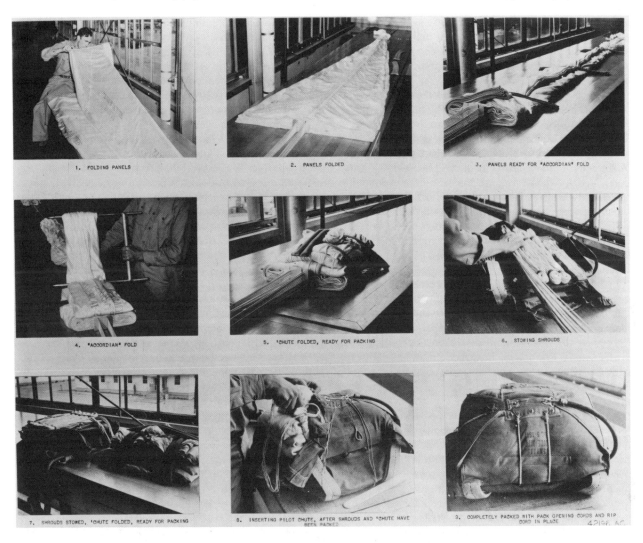

1. FOLDING PANELS 2. PANELS FOLDED 3. PANELS READY FOR "ACCORDIAN" FOLD

4. "ACCORDIAN" FOLD 5. 'CHUTE FOLDED, READY FOR PACKING 6. STOWING SHROUDS

7. SHROUDS STOWED, 'CHUTE FOLDED, READY FOR PACKING 8. INSERTING PILOT CHUTE, AFTER SHROUDS AND 'CHUTE HAVE BEEN PACKED 9. COMPLETELY PACKED WITH PACK OPENING CORDS AND RIP CORD IN PLACE

Steps in packing a Type S-1 or AN6510–1 seat parachute during World War II. These photos were made at the parachute loft, Fort Devens Army Air Base, Mass., on May 4, 1943. Parachute riggers had and have an important responsibility for the safety of the aviators who use their equipment. They must be experts on the packing and maintenance of parachutes and related equipment. Canopies left packed for extended periods tend to develop permanent wrinkles and possible weak areas in their folds. Parachutes stored or unused, must therefore be periodically hung up, inspected, and thoroughly aired for at least twenty-four hours before repacking. (Courtesy USAF)

fields during 1936 and 1937. According to the reports issued at the time, the concept of the quick-release mechanism was very desirable, but the English harness to which it was attached had been found unsatisfactory.[74] Six Type S-4 harnesses with the Irving device were service-tested for six months, beginning in September 1936, but they were not adopted because of certain defects. The Irving device was also considered expensive when compared with the simple three-point release. The Irving commercial parachute with quick-release device was also tested by

the U.S. Navy during this period. The latest Irving quick-release harness was considered an improvement, but testing disclosed sufficient faults to pronounce the harness unsuitable for Navy use.

Most Army Air Corps flights in peacetime were over land, and interest in quick-release mechanisms was negligible during the years before the war. In November 1940, the Parachute Branch purchased two improved Irving devices with the new pin-type lock. After a period of extensive drop testing at Wright Field, three experimental quick release-type parachute harnesses were sent to Fort Benning, Georgia, for live-jump testing by the Provisional Parachute Group. Tests were completed, and adoption of the Irving device was recommended. In the spring of 1941, the Irving device with pin-type lock was finally adopted and incorporated into the harness of the new Type T-5 parachute assembly, designed for use by parachute troops. However, during one of the test jumps that summer at Fort Benning, a premature release had occurred in one of the quick-release boxes, and it was felt by those in charge of the tests that paratroopers at the post had lost confidence in the Irving device, and that no other type of quick-release mechanism was considered satisfactory. It was recommended that the quick-release type be replaced with the snap-type harness for all current production.[75] In the meantime, the Materiel Division reiterated that the development of a satisfactory quick-release box should continue.

In late 1942, the U.S. VIII Bomber Command stationed in England requested a quick-release harness similar to that used by the British. A conference was held at Wright Field on April 5–6, 1943, between officers of the Bomber Command and representatives of the Engineering Division, Materiel Command. They recommended that a satisfactory quick-release type harness be developed as soon as possible, and that changes be made in the American attachable chest parachute. In the meantime, flying personnel of the VIII Bomber Command (from February 22, 1944, Eighth Air Force) used 2,500 Irving quick-attachable, quick-release parachutes which had been loaned to them by the RAF. These were much preferred over the AAF Type A-3 and AN6513 Army-Navy standard quick-attachable chest-type parachutes.[76]

Tests of the Irving quick-connector-quick-release parachute by the Parachute Branch at Wright Field disclosed specific deficiencies in the mechanism. A detailed report rendered on April 29, 1943, stated that it was disapproved for use because of the following reasons:

1. The possibility of serious facial injuries at the time of opening resulting from the heavy harness hardware.

2. This type was not simple in construction and would cause more maintenance difficulties than the present standard type. (The box had to be taken apart each time a complete inspection was made).

3. The Irving model required more hardware and harness and, therefore, would be approximately twice as expensive as the present type.[77]

Later tests also indicated that difficulty was sometimes encountered by the wearer when trying to open the box under water. The water tended to cushion the force of the blow needed to open the box, thus delaying release of the wearer from the parachute harness.

The quick-release problem was again brought to the attention of the Materiel Command by the report of Col. John Hargraves, MC, on his observations in North Africa and England in the summer of 1943. He stated that "In both theaters of action a large amount of flying is over water and the quick release of the British harness is far superior to ours. Wherever available, they (the American crews) use the British harness . . ."[78]

Development work continued at Wright Field where a conference held on September 9, 1943, indicated that two other firms, the Lion Manufacturing Company and the Airchox Company, both of Chicago, had developed quick-release devices. Plans were made for the AAF Board to test these along with the latest Irving box. Further field tests were conducted at Camp MacKall, North Carolina, and Eglin Field, Florida, resulting in the recommendations by the Airborne Command at Camp MacKall and the AAF Equipment Board at Orlando, Florida, that the Irving quick-release box be used on all parachute harnesses.[79] Immediate action was taken by the Materiel Command on these recommendations, and 2,500 sets were ordered from the Irving Company during November 1943.

A safety key or fork was to be used in the boxes. This simple device had been copied from those used on captured German parachutes, and while it remained inserted under the depression disk of the release box, it prevented its accidental depression. According to the Engineering Division, the Irving box was secure when equipped with the safety key.

Unfortunately, the changeover was delayed by patent problems, availability of drawings, and the actual production of the hardware. Technical Instruction No. 1560 directed that wherever possible, all parachute harness on contract be converted to the quick-release type, and by March 1944, 125,000 quick-release boxes had been placed on procurement. These were produced by thirteen manufacturers, and incorporated into the British-type harness, used with a QAC parachute designated as the Type A-4, standardized on December 14, 1944. It was intended to give the Eighth Air Force priority on delivery of the new harnesses, but a study of photos of combat crews indicates that few were used in action before the end of the war in Europe.

As soon as the Irving type of quick-release mechanism (sometimes called the bang box), was adopted for use with AAF parachutes, attention was turned to the modification of the harness previously used with the Irving release. The Parachute Branch developed a semi-quick release type of harness, which made use of the Irving release box but not the uncomfortable British-type harness design. This new harness distributed the opening impact more uniformly over the wearer's body. A wide belt or band of the harness around the thighs, could be used like the seat of a swing to support the wearer's

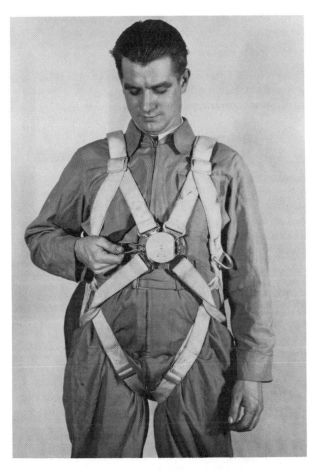

The Irving quick-release mechanism or box allowed the wearer to free himself from his parachute harness without delay. This photo clearly shows the safety key or fork, copied from German parachutes, which was added to the Irving quick-release box. While the key remained inserted under the depression disk of the release box, it prevented its accidental depression, and premature release of the parachute harness. When the harness was to be released, the safety key was withdrawn from the so-called "bang box," and the disk on the front of the box was rotated a quarter of a circle and depressed with a sharp blow. This harness is believed to be an experimental type developed by the Parachute Branch, for use with the T-7 troop parachute used by paratroopers. (SI Photo A4848A)

weight during a jump, and lift webs or risers with their heavy hardware were placed further apart at the shoulders, thus reducing the possibility of injury to the head. This harness design also enabled the wearer to open the quick-release device at any time before landing while still remaining seated, as in a swing. When landing on any surface, all that remained necessary was the straightening of the legs and lifting of the arms, and the wearer's body would slide out of the harness. Greater strength was also secured without added weight, through better integration

in the arrangement of the webbing. This design was standardized in the Type A-5 chest-type, and Type B-10 back-type parachutes, and supplanted the British type of harness, on equipment produced beginning in early 1945.[80] The Type T-7 troop parachute with improved quick-release harness was standardized for paratroopers in March 1944.

Despite all of the effort involved in adopting the Irving quick-release box, it is interesting to note that after the end of the war it was phased out for use with aircrew parachutes and replaced by new quick-release hooks. The bang box, however, continued in use with troop-type parachutes for paratroopers.

Wartime Progress in Parachutes

The simultaneous use of several models of the QAC type parachutes and harnesses during the war led to some confusion, and a potentially hazardous situation, because not all of the chute packs and harnesses were interchangable. By late 1942, the Type A-3, the AN6513, and AN6513-1 QACs, were the principal parachutes of this type in use by the AAF. The square packs of the AN6513 and AN6513-1 could not be attached to the harness of the Type A-3, and conversely, the barrel pack of the Type A-3 could not be attached to the harness used with the AN6513 QAC types. In order to prevent mix-ups in the issue of incompatible aircrew parachutes and harnesses, causing disaster in an emergency, the QAC parachutes were divided into two groups: Group 1, "Red," and Group 2, "Yellow." The packs and harnesses were color coded in the webbing and ripcord protector flaps, and it was emphasized that the pilot was responsible for the prevention of mismatching of quick-attachable chest chutes in his airplane. Technical Order No. 13–5–39 directed that the pilot inspect all QAC parachutes before each flight, and actually snap each pack to its harness to make certain it matched. This was reiterated in the instructions contained in the "Pilot's Information File," which also provided instructions on how to bail out of the various AAF aircraft, and included useful information on parachuting.[81]

By late 1942, American airmen were being forced to bail out frequently over the English Channel, North Sea, Mediterranean, and Pacific areas, and lives were being lost, presumably because the men had difficulty releasing themselves from the Type A-3 (Group 2, Yellow) and AN6513 (Group 1, Red) QAC parachutes, with their three points of release.

The Type A-4 quick-attachable chest-type parachute, (Group 2, Yellow), was developed and sent overseas by the AAF, in response to the urgent demand for a quick-release harness of the British type. The pack and canopy of the Type A-4 were virtually identical with the A-3, but the assembly included a back pad, which enclosed the back harness webbing as a protection against snagging on projections within the aircraft. Unsatisfactory reports were received almost immediately, especially from the Eighth Air Force. Release of the box under suspension was said to be difficult, cases of discomfort during descent were reported, and injuries to the face and head were caused by the position of the riser adapters at the time of the opening shock. Although the Type A-4 was finally standardized on December 14, 1944, action was underway to modify the harness. Instructions on how to adjust the harness for maximum comfort and safety were revised, and the Irving bang box itself was altered so that the force necessary to effect release was decreased. Modification kits were developed, and personnel of the Parachute Branch at Wright Field were of the opinion that once the kits reached the theaters and the changes were made, the Types A-4 and B-9 parachutes would be much improved.

The Type A-5 quick-attachable chest parachute (Group 2, Yellow), was developed on a priority basis and placed in immediate production. The Type A-5, standardized on January 5, 1945, consisted of the Type A-3 canopy and pack with an improved harness that included the quick-release box. The harness of the Type A-5, as previously described, eliminated the objectionable features encountered in the British-type harness of the Type A-4 chute, and proved very satisfactory. During 1945, the Irving quick-release box, with safety key, was further developed and modified for easier release.

Quick-attachable chest-type parachutes used by the AAF during World War II included the British RAF QAC and the following AAF types:

Type A-2. The pack and harness of the Type A-2 are not believed to have been interchangeable with the components from Groups 1 and 2.

Group 1, Red

Type QAC AN6513
Type QAC AN6513-1
Type QAC AN6513-1A

On "AN" QAC parachute assemblies, the snaps were on the pack and the D-rings were on the harness. The same harness could be used with any of the "AN" QAC packs.

Group 2, Yellow

Type A-3
Type A-4
Type A-5

On these parachute assemblies, the rings were on the pack and the snaps were on the harness. The packs in Group 2 could be used with any of the har-

nesses in Group 2. Parachutes in Group 1, Red, were *not* interchangeable with parachutes in Group 2, Yellow.

One difficulty arose with the quick-attachable chest parachutes that had not been considered when their extensive use by bomber crewmen was directed. They could not be fully attached to the harness and worn during combat at the same time that the new "flak vest" was worn. When the aircraft received a fatal hit and broke up right away, or burst into flame, necessitating an immediate bailout, there was often no time or opportunity for a crewman to reach his chest pack and attach it to his harness. To overcome this, airmen began pulling the flak vest aside and attaching the chest pack by one ring, usually on the left side. This was very awkward, especially for gunners, but it was the only way that both the parachute chest-pack and the armored vest could be worn at the same time.

The development of back-type parachutes during the war continued concurrently with that of the quick-attachable chest parachutes. Beginning in late 1942, reports received from the combat theaters stressed the advantages of the British-type parachute harness with a quick-release mechanism, which allowed a man to free himself from his parachute without delay. In response, the Parachute Branch developed a new back parachute, which used the canopy and pack of the Type B-8, combined with a harness that duplicated the British type fitted with the Irving quick-release box. The new back parachute was designated as the Type B-9, and was standardized for use on January 4, 1944. As was the case with the Type A-4, unsatisfactory reports were received almost as soon as the B-9 chutes reached the combat areas. The complaints stated that the quick-release box would not function if the weight of the wearer was still suspended in the harness. Injuries to the groin during the opening shock were also experienced because of the position of the risers at the time of opening. These deficiencies required corrective action, and the Parachute Branch began development of an improved quick-release harness.

The Type B-10 back-type parachute was developed during 1944 and standardized on January 5, 1945. It incorporated the use of the same canopy as the Types B-8 and B-9, and the pack was also the same, except for slight modification to the side wing assemblies required for adaptation to the new quick-release harness. The improved harness, as previously described, incorporated the Irving quick-release box used with the Type B-9, as well as the proper shock distribution of the Types B-7 and B-8 harnesses. The load was more evenly distributed and did not bind the quick-release box under any circumstances. The Type B-10 was considered to be the most desirable parachute available to the Army Air Forces.[82] A Type B-10A parachute was developed and introduced just after the end of the war. It had the standard pack of the B-10 but the cotton harness webbing was replaced with nylon webbing. The new nylon webbing was stronger, lighter, and more flexible, and was mildew-proof. It is believed that the same change was made in the harnesses for the A-5 chest- and S-6 seat-type parachutes and their nomenclature was changed to Type A-5A and S-6A, respectively, as shown in AAF Technical Order No. 00–30–41, "Kit, Flyer's Clothing and Equipment," dated October 20, 1945.

Seat-type parachutes were also improved during the war years. The Types S-1 and S-2 were changed to limited standard on June 19, 1942, with the introduction of the virtually identical AN6510 Army-Navy seat-type parachute, but all continued in service through the end of the war. Concurrent with the development of the chest- and back-type parachutes using the British-type quick-release harness, the Type S-5 seat-type parachute was produced for AAF use. The Type S-5 was standardized on December 29, 1943, to satisfy demands from overseas combat areas, and consisted of the pack and canopy of the AN6510, combined with the British Irving-style seat harness with quick-release box. Ten thousand S-1 chutes were ordered, modified to the S-5 quick-release configuration. Problems with the harness of the Type S-5 were soon reported that were similar to those experienced with the Types A-4 and B-9. Work began to make the necessary improvements and a new seat-type parachute was developed, the Type S-6. It retained the pack and canopy used with the S-5, but employed a harness similar to the ones developed for the Types A-5 and B-10. Reports indicated that the performance of the Type S-6 parachute and harness was very satisfactory, but the war ended before it was officially adopted. According to the Type Designation Sheets, the Type S-6 was finally standardized on July 25, 1946.

TROOP-TYPE PARACHUTES

The idea of airborne troops was described by Benjamin Franklin in 1784, shortly after he observed the ascension of the Charles hydrogen-filled balloon at Paris. He wrote: ". . . ten thousand men descending from the clouds might not in many places do an infinite deal of mischief before a force could be brought together to repel them."[83] Proposals to use balloons for an aerial invasion of England were discussed during the Napoleonic Wars, and by imaginative fiction writers over the ensuing years, but the first serious, though unfulfilled, plan for actually flying combat troops and supplies behind enemy lines was made by Brig. Gen. "Billy" Mitchell in October 1918.

Although the U.S. Army took the lead in the development of the parachute, little interest was shown in airborne or parachute troops during the years between the wars. Other nations, notably the Soviet Union, gave serious consideration to the concept of airborne warfare and began experiments with parachute troops and the aircraft to carry them. By the mid-1930s, large numbers of troops were being dropped by parachute during Red Army maneuvers, but little use was made of parachute troops by the Russians after 1939. Italy, France, Poland, and even Spain also began experimenting with organized parachute units; however, it was Germany that brought the use of parachute and airborne forces to a high level of efficiency during the late 1930s. German parachute troops, organized as part of the German Air Force, were used with success in several important combat operations during the first two years of World War II, including the invasions of Norway, the low countries, Greece, and the island of Crete. Japanese parachute troops were also employed with good results in a few actions in the Pacific theater in 1942.[84]

Both Great Britain and the United States studied the well-publicized German parachute operations, and began organizing and training parachute and airborne forces in 1940. The U.S. Army set up its paratroop training program at Lawson Field, Fort Benning, Georgia, in May 1940, with the establishment of a volunteer test platoon. The first parachute battalion was formed in October of that year.[85] Maj. (later Maj. Gen.) William C. Lee was selected to head the new "air infantry" project, and because of his dedicated efforts in developing the parachute and glider-borne troop programs, he became known as the "father" of Army airborne forces. Beginning in November 1942, U.S. Army parachute and glider troops were used in ever increasing numbers, particularly in the Mediterranean area and in other parts of Europe. They spearheaded several invasions and offensives, including Sicily, Italy, Normandy, Southern France, Holland, the Battle of the Bulge, and Germany. American airborne forces also fought in the Pacific, where they were heavily engaged in the Philippines, including the reconquest of the island of Corregidor in Manila Bay.

Although parachute troops belonged to the U.S. Army Ground Forces, the development of parachutes was the responsibility of the Army Air Forces. The AAF also provided cargo parachutes and transport aircraft in support of airborne operations during the war. By August 1942, the general policy of equipping all cargo airplanes for parachute troop use had been established.[86] In fact, the availability of suitable transport aircraft made large-scale airborne and air-supply operations possible. The workhorse was the excellent twin-engine Douglas C-47, affectionately known as the "Gooney Bird." The C-47, along with the Curtiss C-46 and the four-engine Douglas C-54, were the best transport aircraft employed by any nation during World War II.

Troop-type parachutes used by the U.S. Army were developed from the training outfits used by the Army Air Corps.[87] Unlike the emergency parachute, the troop parachute had to be capable not merely of saving life, but of lowering a soldier trained in jumping, complete with equipment, so that he was ready to fight immediately upon landing. A low descent rate was therefore desired, so a larger canopy than that used with the emergency type had to be employed. Further, a paratrooper's parachute had to be used frequently in training jumps, and so must be able to withstand hard wear and tear.

The main parachute, worn on the paratrooper's back, was opened automatically by a static line. The readoption of the static line was part of the development of the tactics for parachute-troop operations. One end of the static line was attached to the pack carrier and the other end was hooked inside the aircraft. The static line and pack carrier remained with the plane when a man jumped. The static line, which served as a ripcord, assured uniform opening and spacing of the parachutes in the air. Paratroopers were usually heavily laden with arms and equipment, and the transport planes from which they jumped often flew at a relatively low altitude, so the opening of the parachute had to occur within a few seconds after clearing the aircraft. The static line developed during the war allowed for a drop of fifteen feet before opening the pack. The other parachute worn in the assembly was similar to the QAC parachute. It was hooked on the front of the harness and was opened with a conventional ripcord. This pack was called the reserve, and was used only if the main canopy was damaged or a malfunction occurred. As a matter of interest, the Soviets were the only other nation whose troops normally carried a reserve parachute during World War II.

The first type of parachute assembly used by the new Army parachute troops in 1940 was the manually operated Type T-3, with back and chest packs, standardized for Air Corps training in 1936. This outfit was soon replaced by the new Type T-4, especially designed for training parachute troops. The T-4 also featured back- and chest-type parachutes, but the backpack was operated by a static line. The large backpack was fastened to the fully adjustable harness by three hooks. The flat, circular main canopy was 28 feet in diameter, while a 22-foot diameter canopy was fitted in the manually operated chest or reserve pack. The pack opened to release the canopy within seconds of the jumper clearing the door, when the static line broke a light line laced through the flaps of the pack's cover panel. Another breakable tie released the apex of the canopy from the cover, which remained attached to the static line connected inside the aircraft. During the opening sequence, the canopy deployed before the rigging lines, which was the reverse of the procedure for the British "X" type parachute. Although the American procedure gave the jumper more of a jolt, the canopies in the "T" series opened quickly, and this was a valuable advantage during drops from low altitude. Oscillation and drift during descent were controlled to a limited extent by the manipulation of the risers. The Type T-4 was standardized on September 16, 1940, but was changed to limited standard on June 13, 1941, when the improved Type T-5 was standardized. The T-4 was declared obsolete on February 12, 1944, after stock was exhausted.

The Type T-5 parachute assembly was developed rapidly as a result of the experience gained in the parachute training program. The T-5, consisting of back and chest parachutes, was standardized for operational use by par-

U.S. Army paratroopers of the 82nd Airborne Division, in front of the jump door of a Douglas C-47 transport during preparations for the drop at Salerno, Italy, in September 1943. The parachute assembly is the Troop Type T-5, with static line-operated main backpack and ripcord-operated reserve chest pack. A first-aid pouch can be seen on the right shoulder of the corporal (left), armed with a Colt .45 pistol. The American flag identification patch is being worn on the sleeve of the private first class (right), who has an old style non-folding entrenching shovel on his left thigh. Both are wearing the special M1C steel helmet assembly for paratroopers and the Type B-3 pneumatic life preserver. (Courtesy USAF)

achute troops on June 13, 1941. Improved packs were incorporated in the T-5 assembly, which permitted more uniform withdrawal of the canopy. The flap-type backpack included a waistband, and a soft-type detachable chest pack was worn on the front of the harness. The backpack contained the 28-foot diameter olive-drab canopy and was operated by a static line, while the manually operated chest (reserve) pack employed a 22-foot diameter canopy.

The new harness was the improved type designed for parachute troops, incorporating the Irving quick-release, box but as recounted earlier, dissatisfaction materialized because of the possibility of premature harness release. As a result, the parachute harness with snap fasteners was also used until after the introduction of the improved Type T-7 troop parachute assembly. The standardization of the quick-release harness for paratroop use was requested by the commanding general of the Army Ground Forces on December 13, 1943. When the scheduled deliveries had been completed, it was planned to change over the (then) current Type T-5 design to the Type T-7 configuration, which incorporated the quick-release box. The T-7 used the same 28-foot canopy as the T-3, but was made of camouflaged nylon, and the pack was attached to the harness by three hooks. It was firmly secured to the wearer's back by a wide body band. As was the case with the AAF Types A-5 and B-10 aircrew parachutes, the new quick-release harness proved to be comfortable and efficient for paratroop use, and the Type T-7 was standardized on March 13, 1944. At that time the Type T-5 was changed to substitute standard.

The only other troop-type parachute assembly in the "T" series to receive serious consideration by the Materiel Command during the war, was the Type T-6. This was an experimental troop-training assembly, with a backpack containing the usual 28-foot diameter canopy. However, the attachable reserve parachute was a sheet pack with a 24-foot diameter canopy. Both parachutes were attached to a two-point connection harness. Although the Type T-6 was tested, it was not standardized for service use.

One final style of parachute was developed and used in connection with the paratroop training program. This was the jump-tower type of parachute, used when jumping from the huge metal towers constructed for the basic jump training of recruits. Fort Benning, home of the Army Parachute School, originally had no static training facilities other than 34-foot jump towers built in 1941. Two 250-foot-high jumping towers were erected in New Jersey, based on the "parachute tower" built for entertainment at the New York World's Fair of 1939–40. The parachute descent from the training towers was controlled by wires, and specially designed commercial parachutes were procured for this purpose. Four 250-foot-high steel jump towers were constructed during the war at Fort Benning, and

improved parachutes were developed for both free-fall and controlled fall training from towers.

The Type J-1 was especially designed for the training of paratroops on free-fall jump towers. Standardized on December 20, 1943, the J-1 had a canopy 32 feet in diameter and was made of nylon fabric with silk suspension lines. The canopy was provided with metal rings for quick attachment to the lifting mechanism of the tower, and also included an automatic release device.

The Type J-2, standardized on February 10, 1944, was similar to the J-1 except that it was constructed for controlled fall. The canopy was the same size, but it was fabricated of cotton cloth. A suspension cable for hoisting the parachute to the top of the tower was attached to the center vent. Guide wires to insure vertical descent, regardless of ground wind, were run through metal rings fastened to the edge of the canopy. Neither type of jump-tower parachute was provided with a pack.

Free-fall training for paratroopers from a 250-foot jump tower at Fort Benning, Ga., during World War II. The trainees are using the Type J-1 free-fall training parachute, with a nylon canopy 32 feet in diameter. The student jumpers at right and lower center of photo are being hoisted to the top of the tower, with their canopies attached to parachute rings. The jumper at top of photo has just been released from the top of the tower, and is descending freely to earth. (SI Photo A4848H)

Paratroopers were specially trained, armed, and equipped, and were considered to be among the finest troops fielded by the warring powers. American airborne operations, particularly in Sicily, Normandy, and central Europe, were conducted on a grand scale, and helped speed the Allied victory in Europe during World War II.

AERIAL DELIVERY AND CARGO PARACHUTES

Aerial delivery and cargo parachutes and containers were developed for use in dropping military equipment and supplies to the armed forces, and their value was proven during World War II. Landing fields for transport aircraft were often unavailable in front-line areas and there was frequently no time to bring up needed supplies over land. In some locations, a lack of roads also made ground transport extremely difficult. When aerial deliveries were undertaken, it was invariably a matter of the utmost urgency that the materials quickly reach their destination in good condition. Every precaution was therefore exercised in handling, stowing, and maintaining aerial equipment to insure proper performance and low maintenance.

The U.S. Army made a few experiments in dropping supplies by parachute as early as World War I, but the first important trials were made in 1932. The original type of aerial delivery container consisted of a metal box attached by suspension or shroud lines to a cotton parachute canopy. The Types A-1 and A-2 turned out to be unsatisfactory because they were not sufficiently sturdy. The Type A-3 was soon developed, and this model included a parachute made from the silk fabric salvaged from discarded man-carrying parachutes. The chute was attached to a cylindrical-shaped bag constructed of duck fabric, which originally contained a five-gallon commercial milk can. This assembly was, of course, of limited capacity. The Type A-3 was launched from wing bomb racks on tactical aircraft or from cargo-plane doorways by means of a static line.[88]

The parachute canopies developed in the early 1940s for use with the aerial delivery containers were constructed of rayon, and were classified as "aerial delivery" and "cargo" on the basis of size. During 1942, 108,000 aerial delivery and cargo parachutes were on procurement, and this number was increased to 277,000 for the fiscal year starting July 1, 1943.[89]

Acetate-rayon fabrics were tested and accepted as substitute materials for the construction of aerial delivery parachutes, and nylon was eventually substituted for rayon in the larger cargo types, with the intent of reducing their excessive bulk. The suspension or shroud lines of the larger cargo types were made of nylon tube webbing of 3,000 pounds tensile strength. Cargo parachutes of paper were tested in 1943 and 1944, but were found to be unsatisfactory because they were too weak to support their loads. If reinforced with fabric strips, they were almost as expensive to produce as the regular fabric parachutes.

Both aerial delivery and cargo parachutes were constructed of fabrics dyed a variety of colors, for identification of the materials dropped and for camouflage. All of these parachutes were of the static-line type.

Aerial delivery parachutes were utilized for dropping loads weighing up to 300 pounds, at air speeds not exceeding 150 miles per hour. The weight and shock-absorbing characteristics of the load to be dropped determined the size of the parachute which would be used. The first of the new series of parachutes of this type to be developed was the Type G-1, standardized on December 7, 1942. It was used with various containers such as cartons, packs, slings, and nets carrying a load up to a maximum weight of 300 pounds. The canopy, 24 feet in diameter, was constructed of four-ounce rayon. It constituted the lifting surface of the parachute assembly, and incorporated the framework of cords or lines, known as suspension lines, by which the load on the parachute was suspended.[90]

The next model in the "G" series to be developed and standardized was the Type G-2, a cargo parachute designed to handle loads up to 3,000 pounds dropped at a speed of up to 125 mph. The 24-foot diameter canopy was constructed out of eight-ounce rayon. The Type G-3 was similar to the G-2, except that the canopy was 28 feet in diameter. The Types G-4 and G-5, also with a maximum capacity of 3,000 pounds, were of similar design but featured canopies of four-ounce nylon, 36 and 48 feet in diameter, respectively. The number of shroud lines for parachutes G-2 through G-5 was the same as the canopy diameter in feet, twenty-four lines for a twenty-four foot canopy, etc. According to the Type Designation Sheets, the Types G-2 through G-5 cargo parachutes could be dropped at speeds of up to 125 mph. All were standardized on December 7, 1942.

The Type G-6 was a parachute very similar to the Type G-1 in design, except that the pack was redesigned for dropping the landing gear of the Waco CG-4A glider. It was standardized on February 5, 1943, but actually remained in an experimental status until declared obsolete on November 9, 1944.

The Type G-7 was an aerial delivery parachute, similar in design to the Type G-1, which utilized a small canopy 12 feet in diameter. The G-7 was standardized on May 19, 1943, and used by the AAF Antisubmarine Command to drop emergency-sustenance kits. The Type G-8, with an 8-foot canopy, was similar to the G-7, and was used for dropping the Types E-9 and E-16 emergency kits up to 50 pounds in weight, at speeds up to 150 mph.

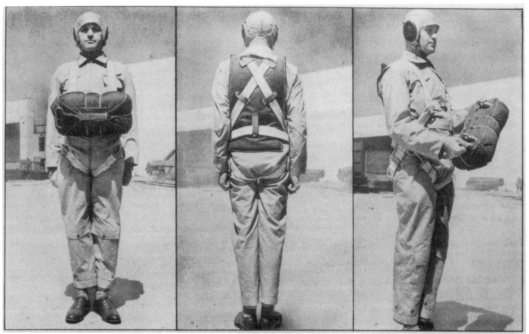

Type QAC

Type A-3

Front, rear, and side views of the principal parachutes in use in 1945. The Type QAC quick-attachable chest-type parachute is the AN6513–1A. The Type A-3 was an improved type of quick-attachable chest-type parachute, introduced in 1942. (These and subsequent three-view photos are reproduced from the "Reference Manual for Personal Equipment Officers," AAF Manual No. 55–0–1, published by Headquarters, Army Air Forces, Washington, D.C., June 1, 1945)

Type A-4

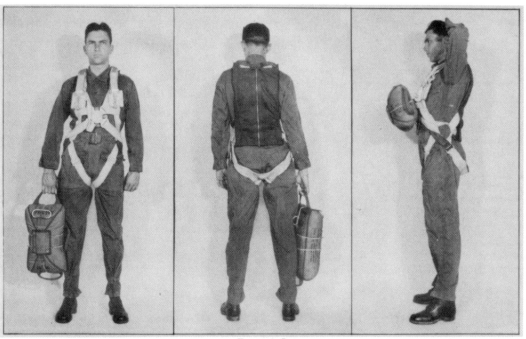

Type A-5

The Type A-4 quick-attachable chest-type parachute used the harness copied from the British RAF Irving-type with quick-release device. The Type A-5 featured the improved harness developed by the Parachute Branch at Wright Field, which incorporated the Irving quick-release box. (From AAF Manual 55–0–1)

Type B-7

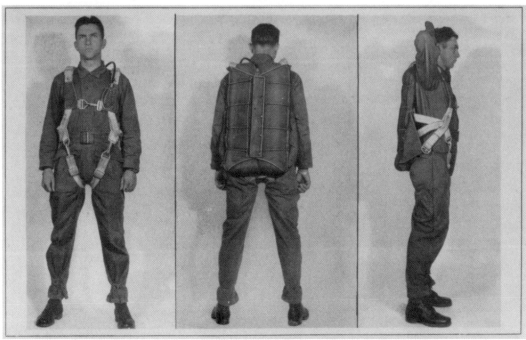

Type B-8

On the Type B-7 back-type parachute, the chest and leg straps had bayonet or snap fasteners. Note that the parachute belt was worn outside the harness to hold webbing in place. The Type B-8 had a flexible backpack and no waist belt. Older B-8 parachutes had snap fasteners on chest and leg straps, while those produced later had bayonet-type fasteners. Both the B-7 and B-8 parachutes utilized the standard three-point harness release in use since the 1920s. (From AAF Manual 55–0–1)

112

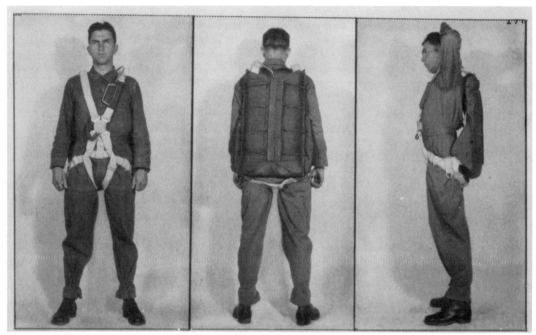

Type B-9

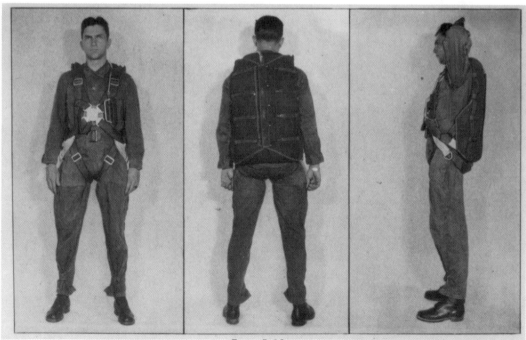

Type B-10

The Type B-9 back-type parachute showing the troublesome British-type Irving harness with quick-release device. The Type B-10 back-type parachute, developed by the Parachute Branch, was similar to the Type B-9 but featured an improved harness incorporating the Irving quick-release box. The B-10 was considered to be the most desirable parachute available to the AAF and was recommended for use whenever possible. (From AAF Manual 55–0–1)

Type S-1

Type S-5

Type S-6

The Type S-1 seat-type parachute, which saw service with some modification from the 1920s through World War II. The Type S-5 was introduced in 1943, to provide a seat-type parachute with the British-style Irving harness with quick-release device. The Type S-6 seat-type parachute was developed to eliminate the deficiencies found in the British RAF harness, while retaining the Irving quick-release box. After service tests, it was standardized in 1946. (From AAF Manual 55–0–1)

114

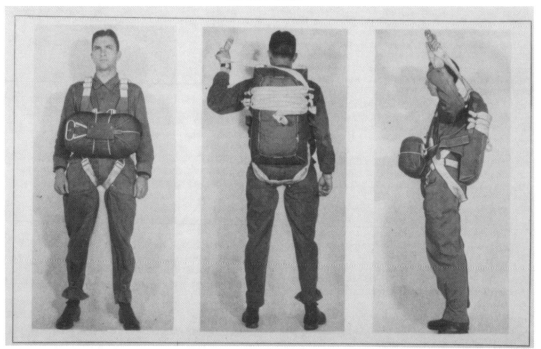

Type T-5

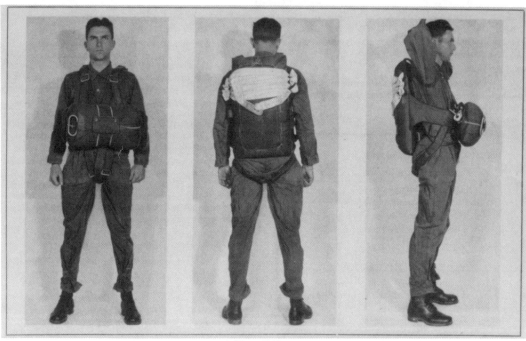

Type T-7

Troop-type parachute assemblies that saw extensive service with paratroopers during World War II included the Types T-5 and T-7. The Type T-5 is shown with the three-point snap fasteners for the harness, and the Type T-7 has the improved harness incorporating the single-point Irving quick-release device. Note the carrying position of the static line for the main back parachute before it is connected to the wire inside the aircraft. (From AAF Manual 55–0–1)

The Type G-1 aerial delivery parachute with a 24-foot rayon canopy, as used with the Type A-10 net-type container. Note static line on top of fabric parachute pack. (SI Photo A4850B)

The last chute in the "G" series to be introduced during World War II was the Type G-9, an aerial delivery type standardized on March 10, 1945. It had a canopy 18 feet in diameter and could carry a 200-pound load dropped at a speed of 150 mph. The G-9 was already on procurement in March, for use in the rugged terrain of the China-Burma-India theater.

Aerial delivery containers used with these parachutes were constructed in various forms. The type of container selected depended on the size, weight, and fragility of the material to be dropped. During the period 1940–42, rubber containers for liquids, and collapsible containers of fiberboard for rations, medicine, and supplies, and nets for heavy munitions were developed and tested in co-operation with interested manufacturers. Pallets of various materials were also designed for use in dropping certain items of equipment, such as generators and artillery pieces.[91]

The Type A-3 container, in its developed form, consisted of a five-gallon metal can, with a metal covering, which extended beyond the top of the can to form a holder for the canopy and beyond the bottom of the can to provide a pocket for a pad to absorb landing shock. A pack cover was provided, which fitted over the parachute pack and a rope static line attached to the cover. The bottom of the canvas was weighted with a five-pound sandbag. A weighted rope uncoiled during the drop, but remained attached to the bottom of the unit, and was used to retrieve the unit in the event of it landing in a tree. The A-3

was the only one of the A-series not used with the standard G-1 parachute.

The Type A-4 delivery container consisted of an adjustable canvas cover, approximately 12 × 24 × 30 inches when fully extended, with a suspension harness of webbing which was sewed to the canvas body. One end was open for loading, and was closed by means of flaps laced together with cord, the other end being equipped with sets of tapes for tying up excess fabric after the container was loaded. The top was equipped with webbing straps and V-rings for attachment to the parachute. The A-4 was suitable for miscellaneous supplies such as food, clothing, tents, water containers, medical supplies, and related equipment.

Aerial delivery container Type A-5 was composed of a sheet of heavy canvas, 15-feet long and 56-inches wide, with a pad of felt 40-inches wide running down the center. The canvas edges folded in over the load and the unit was rolled up to form a roll about 18 inches in diameter, over which removeable end caps were fitted. The A-5 was developed for the aerial delivery of rifles and other similar items of equipment and supplies.

The Type A-6 was composed of three parts; a corrugated fiber carton into which the cargo was packed, protected by a canvas cover; a parachute assembly; and a shock-absorbing pad which was attached to the bottom of the completed unit. The carton measured approximately 12 × 12 × 30 inches. The assembly was used for the delivery of miscellaneous supplies and equipment.

The Type A-7 consisted of an adjustable webbing sling, developed specifically for use in delivering .30, .45, and .50-caliber and 37mm ammunition. However, since the sling was adjustable, it was readily adaptable for the delivery of other equipment and supplies, including standard cans for water and other liquids.

The Type A-8 was a rigid, octagonal-shaped, collapsible container constructed of reinforced fiberboard, about 50x18 inches in size. It was intended for the delivery of rifles and other supplies and equipment of a similar nature.

Aerial container Type A-9 consisted of an adjustable webbing sling. It was developed for the delivery by air of cases containing ammunition up to 81mm.

Early in 1943 a heavy, cord cargo net, 9x9 feet, was standardized as aerial container Type A-10. This square netting was used in the aerial delivery of clothing, food, shovels and other sturdy items of miscellaneous equipment. Improvised aerial delivery containers were also produced and used by units in the various theaters of operation.

An ingenious arrangement of clustering parachutes, developed by the Materiel Command, was successfully used for dropping heavy equipment and munitions in excess of 3,000 pounds. Tractor-like cargo carriers, air-sea rescue boats, and radio transmitters were lowered by using three, four, or more 48-foot diameter parachutes.

Four 48-foot G-5 parachutes lowered cargo weighing up to 4,000 pounds with a rate of descent of thirty feet per second. Parachute clusters proved to be very stable during descent. Using several smaller parachutes in a cluster also made packing and handling much easier than would have been the case if one extremely large parachute had been employed.

PARACHUTES FOR OTHER USES

The first real military use of non-man carrying parachutes was probably the employment of small parachutes for delaying the descent of magnesium flares and signal lights during World War I. The Mark I Airplane Flare was used chiefly for illuminating targets for night bombing and artillery work, for dazzling the eyes of enemy antiaircraft and searchlight crews, and for lighting up landing fields for night landing.[92] The Parachute Branch at McCook Field cooperated with the Army Ordnance Department in the development of parachutes for flares, and by 1923 magnesium flares weighing 25 pounds were available. These were suspended from wing bomb racks and released by the pilot for the purpose of landing-field illumination or to expose "enemy" troop movement during maneuvers. By 1928, parachutes 16 feet in diameter were being used to drop flares from an altitude of 4,000 feet, which burned for as long as three minutes and illuminated a large area. In 1933 triangular parachutes made from salvaged material were produced because it was thought that this particular shape would add to the speed of launching and materially reduce the degree of oscillation.[93]

Flares of approximately one million candlepower were available by 1940, and were used principally from photo-reconnaissance aircraft. These parachute flares would illuminate an area approximately one mile square. The Flare, Aircraft, Parachute, AN-M26, was a typical wartime example. It weighed 52.5 pounds and burned for 3 to 3.5 minutes, with a yellowish light of 800,000 candlepower. Flares and pyrotechnic signals with parachutes attached could also be launched from the ground; thus a pre-arranged message could be transmitted simultaneously to a large number of widely dispersed troops. Parachutes were also used to drop colored signal lights and smoke bombs. During the war, parachutes were provided for aerial mines, fragmentation bombs, and bomb-cluster adapters. The parachutes served to retard their descent when released at low level, allowing time for the aircraft to escape safely from the blast area.[94]

Various experiments were made from time to time in the use of parachutes as air brakes to reduce a plane's landing speed, and even to lower an entire aircraft to the ground, but the results were never very satisfactory. Some of these tests are described in this chapter in connection with the development of the triangular parachute in the early 1930s. The concept of parachutes to lower planes and to retard their landing speed was revived during World War II, for use with small radio-controlled target planes and troop-carrying gliders. Standard 24-foot parachutes of nylon and rayon were used successfully since 1941, to lower target drones weighing 130 pounds and traveling at a speed of 150 mph. The parachute was contained within a compartment located in the top of the fuselage. When the engine was stopped by variation of the radio signal, the door to the compartment opened automatically and the parachute was ejected by means of springs. Tests were also made with 32-foot parachutes attached to 260-pound target planes capable of a speed of 200 mph.[95]

During the summer of 1943, the Parachute Branch at Wright Field developed a special strength ten-foot nylon glider-drag parachute. When attached to the tail of a transport glider, this parachute materially reduced the required length of the landing strip required.

An unusual and imaginative use of the parachute occurred in connection with the invasion of Normandy early on June 6, 1944. During the airborne assault, paratrooper mannequins, about one-fourth life-size, were dropped in the dark by the AAF in selected locations in Northern France to divert and confuse the German defenders concerning the size of the operation and the actual paratroop landing areas. The dummies, dressed in OD "uniforms," looked quite realistic during descent, and some were reportedly booby trapped to further harass the German forces. The example of this mannequin at the U.S. Army Ordnance Museum, Aberdeen Proving Ground, Maryland, is still equipped with its original light-blue parachute.

Shortly after the end of the war, the Parachute Branch began testing ribbon parachutes, originally developed by the Germans for high-speed bailout, for use in reducing a jet plane's landing speed and the length of runway necessary during landing. Improved parachutes of this type were successfully developed for use with American jet aircraft.

EXPERIMENTAL PARACHUTES AND ACCESSORIES

Numerous experimental parachutes and related devices were tested by the Parachute Branch, including designs originated by the staff and those obtained from private individuals, civilian organizations, and the parachute industry. Captured enemy parachutes, and equipment used by Allied and other foreign nations, were also examined and tested. In fact, testing all available American and foreign parachutes was the first major project undertaken at the end of World War I. Some design features proved to be worthy of adoption for service use, while many others turned out to be either unsound or of no advantage over standard equipment. The Pioneer Model B-3-B, for example, was a good design that was adopted for use by the AAF in 1942 as the Type B-8 back parachute.

Among the many experimental designs tested by the Parachute Branch was the Frieder "Baseball" parachute, an unusual configuration submitted in 1941 by the General Textile Mills. The Frieder parachute canopy was a developed spherical surface that formed, according to the company, a "perfect hemisphere," and consisted of sections of material cut in the form of a baseball cover, resulting in the elimination of oscillation. After a long series of tests during the war it was finally judged to be unsatisfactory, because of long and varied opening times at moderate speeds.

Another interesting design was produced by Richard H. Hart, who first submitted his parachute for testing in January 1937. It featured a complicated sliding backpack, and suspension lines arranged in the form of a net, which was intended to prevent fouling. The Hart parachute was rejected, because it was structurally weak and the automatic release feature was considered highly impractical. Modified designs were submitted by Mr. Hart, and later by the Eagle Parachute Company, who manufactured test models of his improved "steerable, low-jumping" parachute intended for use by paratroopers. After many trials at Wright Field, by the Parachute School at Fort Benning, and the Airborne Center at Camp MacKall, experiments with the Hart designs were finally discontinued after the war.[96]

Experiments were conducted during the war to develop a parachute especially for use by women. A smaller size backpack parachute, very similar to the Type B-8 was made by the Hayes Manufacturing Company, and tested by the Parachute Branch during September and October 1944. It featured a 24-foot diameter nylon canopy and had a three-point release harness with bayonet-type fasteners. It is presumed that the development of this parachute was discontinued as a result of the termination of the Women's Airforce Service Pilot (WASP) program in December 1944, which eliminated most of the potential users.

Research and development cannot be carried out without risk. Individuals volunteering their services were heroes of the same caliber as those who willingly faced enemy action, and they lived daily with danger. The testing of parachutes was often accomplished through the use of dummies dropped from airplanes, but live jumps under controlled conditions were also made. A noted example was the successful high-altitude research jump from 40,200 feet made by Lt. Col. W. R. Lovelace II, recounted in Chapter II. His record-breaking jump also provided the first in-flight data on the serious danger of opening shock when parachuting at altitudes in excess of 30,000 feet. Lieutenant Colonel Lovelace lived to tell his story, but another researcher, Lt. Col. Melbourne W. Boynton, MC, did not.

Lieutenant Colonel Boynton, Chief of the Medical Division, Office of Flying Safety, was intensely interested in the problem of parachute landings. In connection with his research, he undertook what he considered to be a continuation of the Lovelace experiments in high-altitude parachuting. Boynton intended to make a delayed-opening free-fall descent from above 40,000 feet, opening his parachute at 5,000 feet, where opening shock is easily tolerable. His jump would establish the aerodynamic characteristics of free-fall, and determine the optimum point for opening. He hoped to develop better procedures for aircrew personnel bailing out at high altitudes.

At 1:13 p.m. on August 19, 1944, Boynton dropped through the bomb bay of a Boeing B-17, which had taken off from Wright Field, while it flew at 43,000 feet over Clinton County Army Air Field near Wilmington, Ohio. Two minutes and fifteen seconds later, he struck the ground in a cornfield at the edge of the base. Apparently he had made no attempt to open either his Type B-8 back parachute or AN6513-1A reserve chest parachute. All items of equipment were believed to have been in perfect operating condition, and prior to the jump, he had been trained in the use of his bailout oxygen equipment while fully clothed in the Aero Medical Laboratory's Altitude Chamber, and during preliminary flights in the B-17 to 25,000 feet. When ground personnel reached the body, they found the Type H-2 oxygen bottle still "hissing". It appeared that this tragic accident resulted from some unknown condition which caused human failure.[97]

Automatic opening devices, as a safety feature for parachutes, were suggested and tested from time to time. The Daronin brothers, in Russia, developed an automatic time-controlled opener in 1938, which could be set to operate at any time within a period of 5 to 180 seconds. The Aero Medical and Aircraft Laboratories at Wright Field conducted experiments on an automatic atmospheric pressure-opening mechanism. This was officially called "An Aneroid-activated Combustion Powered Automatic Pressure Device for Pulling Ripcords.[98] When the jumper fell to a pre-determined altitude, the increased air pressure activated the mechanism, which pulled the ripcord. The aneroid unit closed an electric circuit at a desired altitude pressure, firing a small explosive charge in a piston-cylinder arrangement. Piston motion within the cylinder pulled the parachute ripcord with an auxiliary cable. Maj. George A. Hallenbeck and 1st. Lt. Ernest E. Martin of the Aero Medical Laboratory are credited with developing the mechanism in 1944.

The device was intended as an additional safety factor, to overcome any inability on the part of a parachutist to manually operate the ripcord in the usual manner. Limited

118

Among the many dedicated men who willingly accepted the risks and sacrifices in the interest of research was Lt. Col. Melbourne W. Boynton, MC, who hoped to develop better procedures for aircrew personnel bailing out at high altitudes. He died on August 19, 1944, while making an experimental free-fall parachute jump from 43,000 feet. His equipment was found to be in working order, but for reasons unknown, he made no apparent attempt to deploy either his back or reserve parachutes. This photo shows Boynton, just prior to boarding a B-17 at Wright Field, for the flight over Clinton County Army Air Field, near Wilmington, Ohio. (Left to right) Lt. Col. A. Pharo Gagge, Chief, Biophysics Branch, Aero Medical Laboratory; Lieutenant Colonel Boynton; Lt. Col. Emry V. Stewart, Chief, Parachute Branch, Personal Equipment Laboratory (on crutches from an unrelated minor accident); and probably Maj. Oscar C. Olson, a flight surgeon. A camera is strapped to Boynton's right thigh. For the jump he wore a Type B-15 jacket and modified A-11 trousers, over standard clothing, an AN-H-16 winter flying helmet, Type B-8 goggle, Type A-13 oxygen mask with Type H-2 bailout bottle, and Type B-8 back and AN6513-1A QAC parachutes with special harness. His trousers were modified to incorporate "chaff," narrow metallic strips used to assist tracking of his descent by truck-mounted ground radar. (Courtesy USAF)

tests made in the summer of 1944 indicated that the principle was sound, but additional tests in 1945 turned up unexpected difficulties. It was found that the various positions of the jumper's body affected the accuracy of the aneroid, requiring compensation in the aneroid setting for body-induced altitude errors and existing terrain features. During the tests, it was also determined that the terminal velocities of man in free-fall at sea level (standard atmosphere) vary from 84 mph to 132 mph according to his position in space.[99] Development and testing of the device continued after the war both by the laboratories at Wright Field and by the U.S. Navy. A barometric sensor device for automatically opening a parachute was perfected and eventually entered service use.

According to Col. A. P. Gagge, a chest chute with an automatic opening device was demonstrated to Lieutenant Colonel Boynton on the day before his jump, but he refused to wear it for the jump which resulted in his tragic death.[100]

Parachute testing was conducted for many years in wind tunnels including the large aircraft wind tunnel at Langley Field, Virginia. Construction began during the war on a vertical wind tunnel at Wright Field, and even though it was not entirely completed, numerous tests with parachute models were made there during 1944. Use of the vertical wind tunnel accelerated the testing of parachutes by decreasing the need for dummy-drop testing from aircraft and potentially dangerous live jumps with prototype parachutes and accessories.

Another problem that required immediate attention had emerged by the latter part of World War II. It had become obvious that the speeds attained by fighter aircraft had made escape by conventional bailout almost impossible. The escape-fatality rate increased significantly, and collision with aircraft structures on bailout was responsible for a number of deaths and injuries. Escape from the new jet aircraft coming into service was even more difficult, because of increased wind blast and immobilization by G forces. The Germans had anticipated the need for a positive means of escape from jet aircraft, which would overcome these forces, and began installing special ejection seats in fighters in 1944. In an emergency, the pilot and his seat were ejected from the plane as a unit, and after clearing the tail, the pilot separated from the seat and deployed his parachute. British development of an ejection-seat system proceeded rapidly after 1944, in the form of the Martin-Baker seat, and the United States made use of both British and German research in developing ejection seats for high-performance aircraft. In the postwar years, improved parachutes and survival kits were eventually built into automatic ejection seats for maximum efficiency and protection.

Many peacetime activities also profited materially from the multitude of experiments in parachute technology conducted for military purposes. Modern parachutes have many applications, including slowing down jet aircraft during landing, recovering manned and unmanned space vehicles, dropping emergency supplies, fighting forest fires, lowering weather instruments to earth, slowing down race cars, delivering weapons, equipment, and troops, and the increasingly popular sport of skydiving.

The most important use of the parachute, of course, is still lifesaving, a function performed with increasing safety and certainty since World War I. The lives of thousands of airmen have been saved through emergency parachute jumps in both peace and war. Those saved include such famous flyers as Douglas Bader, Pappy Boyington, Jimmy Doolittle, Adolf Galland, Erich Hartmann, Charles Lindbergh, William H. Rankin, Peter Townsend, Ernest Udet and Chuck Yeager, to name just a few. Without the parachute, today's world would be a very different place.

Parachute testing was conducted in the new vertical wind tunnel at Wright Field, beginning in 1944. This photo was taken in August 1945, during testing of the aneroid-activated parachute-opening device, which can be seen attached to the right side of a chest parachute. The full-scale plastic mannequin used for this test was dressed in standard flying clothing, and was rigidly secured to a 14-foot length of pipe installed across the 12-foot wind-tunnel test section. (Courtesy USAF)

# IV *Armor for Aviators*

S/Sgt. Albert J. Riley of the 392nd Bombardment Group, Eighth Air Force, was completing his 25th combat mission out of Wendling, England, when he had an experience he will never forget. In his post-mission interrogation report, he recounted the incident:

> While flying as right waist gunner on a B-24H on 22 April 1944, I was hit directly over the heart by two large pieces of flak. The blow knocked me backwards into the left waist gun position but I received no injuries beyond mild bruises. I advise everyone to wear flak suits. I'd be in pretty bad shape now if I hadn't had mine on.

The flight surgeon who examined Sergeant Riley stated that his body armor had saved him from a severe chest wound and probably death.[1] He was just one of hundreds of American combat airmen, who were struck by antiaircraft or aircraft cannon-shell fragments during World War II, and lived to tell about it, thanks to the protection afforded by flyer's armor. Helmets and body armor were highly successful in decreasing the total number of wounds, and especially the number of lethal wounds, received by American airmen on combat missions. But before discussing the World War II innovations, it is useful to place the subject of individual armor in perspective by briefly tracing its history over the centuries.

THE DEVELOPMENT OF ARMOR

Man has protected his body with garments and devices of one form or another since the dawn of history. Early man utilized heavy skins or furs as protection from the elements and to provide a defense against attack by animals, as well as the blows and missiles of his human enemies. Helmets, body armor, and shields were eventually developed, utilizing a great variety of materials. A record dating from about 1015 B.C. may be found in the Old Testament, I. Samuel 17:38, "And Saul armed David with his armour, and he put a helmet of brass upon his head; also he armed him with a coat of mail."

The Assyrians were well known for their armor, and the forms were further improved in classical Greece and Rome. The typical armor worn by men of the Roman legions was a hammered bronze or iron helmet with neck guard and earflaps, and a cuirass easily fabricated of long strips of metal, attached in overlapping rows on a jerkin or harness of leather or fabric. Scale and mail armor was also worn and leg armor and shields were used for added protection.[2]

Mail was worn extensively during the period from about 600 to 1250 A.D., and was eventually reinforced with bands and plates of metal at vital points. By the early 15th century, complete suits of steel plate armor were being worn on the battlefields of Europe by medieval knights and others who could afford them. The common foot soldier often had no armor, and considered himself fortunate if he acquired an iron helmet, worn over a padded liner, and a stuffed and quilted fabric or leather coat called a gambeson or aketon. The jack and brigandine were other types of simple armor, used by foot soldiers, consisting of jackets made of canvas or leather with small plates of metal stitched inside.[3]

It is generally believed that the advent of gunpowder and the introduction of portable or hand guns brought an end to the use of armor. This is not really correct, because of the long period of time that elapsed before the crude black powder small arms became accurate enough, and had sufficient range and penetrating power, to defeat plate armor. A bolt from a crossbow, and an arrow fired from a long bow or a bow such as those used by the Mongols, could penetrate even the finest armor of the 14th century.[4] Bows could also be fired much faster than the early guns, and worked even in the rain. As firearms improved, the armorer was forced to increase the thickness and improve the quality of the armor, thereby adding considerably to its weight and expense. Armorers also discovered that increased strength and rigidity could be obtained without adding to the weight by fluting the metal and providing a rounded or "glancing" surface to deflect blows and missiles. By the 16th century, armor was actually tested with bullets, and the dent caused by the proof shot can still be seen on many surviving specimens.

The weight of armor eventually became extreme and the maneuverability and endurance of the soldier was critically restricted; and, accordingly, armor was gradually abandoned as outmoded during the 16th and 17th centuries.[5] However, protective armor never disappeared completely, and metal helmets and cuirasses continued in use, mainly by heavy cavalry, until World War I. Even today, such equipment is worn for ceremonial purposes by the Papal guards and some European mounted units.

Armor was brought to America by the Pilgrims and other colonists in the early 17th century, but was soon discarded as impractical in fighting the illusive Indians.[6] Partial armor was used to some extent in the French and Indian War of 1755–63, and on rare instances during the American Revolution of 1775–83.[7] During the American Civil War of 1861–65, no armor was issued, but commercially made body armor of several different types was purchased and worn by some officers. An example of a "vest" of steel plates attached by leather straps, which was usually worn under the coat, is in the collection of the Fort Ward Museum in Alexandria, Virginia. Armor of this type was found to be fairly effective in providing protection against lead musket balls, but it proved heavy and awkward for wear during extended battles in the field, and was best suited for use in siege or positional warfare.

The French also used several kinds of body armor to a limited degree during the Franco-German War of 1870–71. An armored waistcoat manufactured in Paris during the siege was made of many small, rectangular plates of low-carbon steel riveted to canvas. Weighing only about five pounds, it could be worn with a reasonable degree of comfort, but tests showed that it provided little protection except against spent bullets or shell splinters.[8]

A Russian inventor named Casimir Zeglin, working in New York and Chicago, produced a heavy silk vest covered with khaki drill, which could be worn in conjunction with a thin breast plate of ballistic chrome-nickel steel. Some of these vests were reportedly used by the Russian Army during the Russo-Japanese War of 1904–05. Zeglin vests failed to pass the firing tests conducted by the U.S. Army Ordnance Department in 1899, 1904 and 1914.[9] Many other experimental protective vests, constructed of various materials, were tested during this period, but the introduction of the magazine rifle and machine gun chambered for high-velocity smokeless powder ammunition, made the design of effective, light-weight body armor extremely difficult.

WORLD WAR I

When the conflict in Europe began in August 1914, the only armor in use was the thin steel cuirass and helmet worn by some cavalry regiments. Cavalry soon ceased to play a role on the Western Front as the war of movement ground to a halt, and positional warfare developed along a line that stretched from Switzerland to the North Sea. Military leaders failed to appreciate the fact that modern firepower, especially the machine gun, favored the defender rather than the attacker. Although German and Al-

lied troops dug in for protection against the devastating effects of small arms and artillery fire, both sides suffered appalling casualties during the repeated frontal assaults intended to break the stalemate.

In trench warfare, the head and shoulders were exposed most often, and wounds to the upper body from shrapnel balls and shell fragments increased alarmingly. Head and neck wounds accounted for approximately 20 percent of all wound cases receiving hospitalization during World War I.[10] Protective helmets were urgently needed and the warring powers began developing steel helmets and experimenting with body armor and shields. Considerable difficulty was experienced in trying to mass-produce helmets of ballistic steel by the stamping process. By 1916 all the major powers had introduced steel helmets, for standard use at the front. Before the adoption of the protective helmet, about one head wound in four proved fatal; after introduction, the fatalities were often decreased to one in seven.[11]

The success of the steel helmet in reducing the number of deaths and serious wounds stimulated interest in developing protective devices for other parts of the body. The designers of modern armor encountered the same basic problems however, as the armorers of the 17th century. Armor was developed for the torso and the extremities, but the excessive weight and reduction in mobility, or lack of adequate protection, restricted its general use in combat. Some form of body armor was seen on all fronts from 1915 through 1918, but only on an experimental basis, and it was never in general use. The most successful use of armor was by sentinels, stationary machine-gun crews, and members of patrols.[12] Despite the relatively low troop acceptability, because of the weight and discomfort, some types of body armor, produced officially or made and sold commercially, did offer useful protection against low-velocity missiles. These included shrapnel balls and shell and grenade fragments, which caused the majority of wounds during the war.[13]

Body armor in World War I included "hard" armor, composed of steel plates, usually covered with canvas, "soft" armor, generally made of layers of silk and resembling the medieval gambeson, and composite types featuring small metal plates attached to fabric, similar in design to the ancient brigandine jackets. Body armor composed of steel plates was intended to stop or deflect a missile by its hardness while the soft or flexible types were designed to slow down the projectile and stop it through the cohesive properties of the fabric.

Flyer's Armor

The Russians were the first to experiment with individual armor for aviators in World War I. The armor was designed for crewmen of the giant four-engined Il'ya Muromets, engaged in bombing and long-range reconnaissance operations in early 1915. A Russian account only recently translated into English states:[14]

> The Putilov factory sent armor made of beautiful well-hardened two millimeter steel for testing as modern-day knights' armor on our airplanes. Clad in this armor, a crew member could hardly move. One can understand how cannons installed on the Il'ya Muromets and personal armor dramatically increased the weight of each flying ship, thereby reducing the useful load available for combat operations.

The suits of armor were quickly discarded as impractical, and at this early stage of the war, unnecessary. There were few antiaircraft guns on the Eastern Front in 1915, and it was many months before German and Austro-Hungarian pursuit aircraft armed with machine guns were available in any numbers, for air defense against the few Russian bombing raids. In fact, only one Russian Il'ya Muromets was shot down by a fighter plane during the entire war.

The situation was quite different on the Western Front, where flying became increasingly dangerous as the war progressed into its second year. Antiaircraft fire intensified and became more accurate, and almost every aircraft was eventually armed with at least one machine gun. Armor plate was installed on a few types of airplanes later in the war, to protect vital areas of the engine and cockpit, and armored seats were tried experimentally. German ground-attack aircraft, introduced in 1917–18, were well equipped with defensive armor, however, weight considerations prevented its use on pursuit and most other types of combat airplanes.

The French and British also experimented with individual body armor for aviators. An official French military armament catalog dated February 1917, illustrated and described a steel breast shield, designed especially for use by flyers. According to the catalog, the "Jointed Shield S.T. Aé. was made in 7mm special steel as protection for gunner and pilot against aeroplane bullets. This shield is attached by two straps, crossing in the back. The stomach shield is held in position by a belt."[15] No photos have been found showing this body armor in use by aviators, and it is believed that it was actually experimental and not a standard item of issue. Although obviously awkward to wear, body armor of this type would have provided useful protection, particularly for gunners.

Steel Helmets for Flyers

The successful use of the steel helmet by ground troops made it clear that many fragments and projectiles, even

French S.T. Aé. breast shield for flyers, c. 1916–17. Made of 7-mm special steel, it was attached by two straps crossing at the back, while the jointed stomach section was held in position by a belt. The shield was curved to conform to the contour of the body, to reduce air resistance, and to help deflect bullets and shell fragments. A special edge or "lip" was riveted to the top to prevent bullet "splash" from striking the face of the wearer. This is the only known photo of this body armor, and it is reproduced from an official French aeronautical catalog dated February 1917. This armor is believed to have been experimental and was not in operational use. (SI Photo 82–11907)

those of rather high velocity, would be deflected by a relatively light helmet of alloy steel. Aviators at that time wore either a soft leather or fabric helmet, or a stiff crash helmet usually of leather, padded with rubber or cork. They provided little ballistic protection and, unfortunately, the shape of the British and French steel helmets made them impractical for wear in flight, because of their resistance to the air. The deeper design of the German steel helmet allowed it to be worn aloft in an open cockpit, and it was used for protection by some German combat flyers, particularly those involved in ground attack or low-level operations.

The U.S. Army adopted the British steel helmet for the use of ground troops after America's entry into the war, and designated the first steel helmet the M1917. During 1918 the Engineering Section of the U.S. Army Ordnance Department, with the assistance of the armor workshop of the Metropolitan Museum of Art in New York City, developed several experimental models of a steel helmet for aviators. The test models were provided with linings of different types, some cushioned on the three-pad system, and some with a soft lining in the form of the regular winter flying helmet. All were close-fitting and streamlined, and proved comfortable and well balanced. The total weight of these helmets, made of steel .036 inch in thickness, was from 1 pound, 10 ounces to 2 pounds. In each case, the ear section of the helmet was hinged so that it could be worn with headphones. The chin strap was attached to the lower edge of each ear plate, and the hinge of the latter was fastened above by a single rivet. Tightening the chin strap would therefore cause each earflap to conform to the natural contour of the wearer's face.[16]

The three most promising designs were Aviator's Helmet numbers 14, 14A, and 15. Dr. Bashford Dean, Curator of Armor at the Metropolitan Museum of Art, and commissioned a major in the Ordnance Department during the war, considered helmet no. 15 to be the best design.[17] It fit closer to the head than the other designs, and had an intervening space of only 0.5 to 0.75 of inch. When made of Baker's nickel-manganese steel, it was light in weight, but insured great rigidity and minimum indentation when struck. This helmet was well balanced and provided with a continuously cushioned lining to prevent air from entering under the edge.

These aviator's steel helmets were prepared too late to be tested at the front in France. Official tests of the prototypes were held at Bolling Field, Washington, D.C., and helmet no. 14A received an especially favorable report. The Armistice on November 11, 1918, brought an end to the development of steel helmets for aviators and none were procured for Air Service use.

WORLD WAR II

During the period between 1918 and the onset of World War II, experimentation in body armor materials and design was maintained at a very low level. The beginning of the war in Europe in 1939, brought a resurgence in military planning and expenditures in the United States, including renewed interest in developing an improved steel helmet that would provide better protection for the head and neck. Designers took advantage of the advances in steel-alloy manufacture, liner materials, and mass-production methods, and a new helmet with a separate, adjustable liner containing the suspension was produced and standardized as the Helmet, Steel, M1, on April 30, 1941.

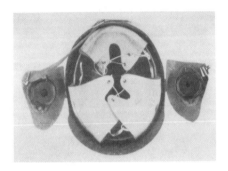

American aviator's helmet, Model No. 14. This experimental helmet was designed especially for aviators in 1918 by the U.S. Army Ordnance Department. It was made of ballistic steel, and allowed a space for indentation of about one inch around the cranium. This compact helmet was cushioned on the three-pad system, and earphones were installed inside each hinged earflap. It could also be worn over a regular soft flying helmet. The Model No. 14 was not placed in production. (Courtesy U.S. Army)

The U.S. Army Ordnance Department conducted many experiments during World War II, but body armor for use by the ground forces was not adopted until the Armor, Vest, M12, was standardized in August 1945. The long period of time required for development was basically due to the same problems that had been encountered in World War I and earlier, namely, the weight and discomfort of the armor balanced against the degree of actual protection provided the wearer. Fortunately, the development of armor for aviators, who had different requirements and circumstances, was much more successful.

Body Armor for Flyers

The initial impetus in the development of body armor for American combat flyers was due to the research and field testing which the British were performing during 1941

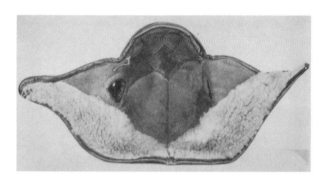

Aviator's Helmet, Model No. 14A. Similar in construction to the Model No. 14, this experimental steel helmet was closer-fitting, and featured a recessed area in both hinged earflaps to allow room for earphones. The lining was a soft flying helmet, which prevented air from entering under the edge. The Model No. 14A received an especially favorable report during testing, but the war ended before it was placed in production. (Courtesy U.S. Army)

and 1942, in an attempt to provide some form of personal armor for their ground troops fighting in North Africa. The results of the studies were furnished to American forces and proved of interest to some AAF officers stationed in England at Headquarters, U.S. Eighth Air force. Experience showed that contrary to popular belief, few men were killed by direct hits. The great majority of the casualties among both air and ground personnel were caused by small fragments of high-explosive shells travelling at comparatively low velocities. As AAF bomber aircraft in England and North Africa began entering action in the fall of 1942, an analysis of wounds incurred revealed that approximately 70 percent were due to relatively low-velocity missiles. Surveys of American casualties conducted before the adoption of body armor, found that shell fragments (flak) from German antiaircraft guns were responsible for 38 percent of the wounds; 20mm aircraft-cannon shell fragments, 39 percent; machine-gun bullets,

15 percent; and secondary missiles, 8 percent.[18] The studies indicated that protection provided to the chest and abdomen would bring about the greatest reduction in aircrew casualties.

It appeared to Col. Malcolm C. Grow, then surgeon of the U.S. Eighth Air Force, that some kind of individual body armor might serve to protect flyers against small, low-velocity fragments and save a considerable number of lives. He realized that although additional armor for the aircraft itself was impractical because of the weight factor,

Aviator's Helmet, Model No. 15. Another of the experimental protective helmets for flyers developed during 1918, the M15 was a well-balanced helmet, more closely modelled to the head, having an intervening space of only 0.5 to 0.75 inch. It therefore afforded excellent upward visibility. When made of Baker's nickel-manganese steel, it offered great rigidity and minimum indentation. This design included a continuously cushioned type of lining to prevent the entry of air under the edge in flight. The chin strap was attached to the hinged earflaps and insured that they remained close to the head. The Model No. 15, like the other special designs, was developed too late for production before the end of World War I. (Courtesy U.S. Army)

aircrewmen could wear heavier personal armor than could be tolerated by ground troops, because they did not have to move around much inside the plane.

Colonel Grow, in association with the Wilkinson Sword Company of London, a firm with long experience in the manufacture of armor, designed a flexible armored vest, capable of being mass-produced. It was made of overlapping 2-inch square plates of 1mm-thick Hadfield manganese steel, secured in pockets and sewed to a backing of flax canvas. The vest was covered with tan canvas, and a sporran or apron of the same construction was attached to the front at the lower edge. The weight of the full vest and apron was just over 22 pounds. The design was actually quite similar to experimental armored vests developed in World War I, and generally resembled armored jackets in use centuries earlier.

Preliminary testing of the armor was so favorable that Lt. Gen. Carl Spaatz, commanding general of the Eighth Air Force, approved the procurement of ten suits for experimental testing on October 15, 1942. In the year 1943, the air offensive against Germany increased in tempo and strategic bombing became a grim reality. This resulted in a proportional increase in the American casualty rate. The initial order for ten suits was followed promptly by a request for sufficient armor for the crews of twelve B-17 bombers, which was received about March 1, 1943. Lt. Gen. Ira C. Eaker, who had assumed command of the Eighth Air Force, studied the encouraging results and directed that sufficient armor be procured to equip all operational heavy bombers in England. He also recommended that armor suits be provided for all heavy-bomber units destined for the Eighth Air Force.[19] It was also intended that vests would be used by crewmen of medium bombers, such as the B-26.

The Original Flak Vests

The body armor made by the Wilkinson Company and commonly referred to as a "flak vest" or "flak suit," provided protection for the chest and abdomen, and also the back of the flyer's torso when required. When entering action, the vest was placed across the shoulder, over all other flying equipment, and fastened over the other shoulder. The sporran or apron section was worn suspended from the vest by hook fasteners. It provided protection for the lower abdomen, groin, and part of the lower extremities.

Two different vests and sporrans were produced for wear by various crew members, depending upon their position and function in the aircraft. The parts were marked, to indicate which was intended for wear by specific crewmen.

The Type "A" was a full vest weighing 16 pounds, with an armored front and back to protect crewmen who had to move around inside the aircraft. It was intended for wear by the bombardier, navigator, two waist gunners, tail gunner and radio operator-gunner of B-17 aircraft. Abroad B-24 bombers, the Type "A" was worn by crewmen flying in the same positions and also by the belly gunner and tunnel gunner. The bombardier, navigator, radio gunner, top turret gunner and tail gunner of B-26 aircraft also wore this vest. The Type "D" full sporran was normally worn with the Type "A" Vest.

The Type "B" half vest was worn by pilots and copilots who were protected from the rear by armor, such as by an armored seat. The half vest weighed 7 pounds, was armored only in the front, and had a fabric back.

The Type "C" sporran or apron, weighing 4.5 pounds, and tapered toward the bottom, was designed for use with the type "B" vest. It was worn by the pilot, copilot and bombardier of B-17 aircraft, who occupied a sitting position in flight, and also by the same crewmen and the navigator of a B-24. This apron was also worn by the crewmen aboard B-26 bombers, including the radio gunner and the top turret gunner.

The Type "D" full apron, for use with the Type "A" vest, weighed 6.5 pounds, and was recommended for wear aboard the B-17 by the bombardier, navigator, two waist gunners, and the radio gunner. It could also be worn by the navigator, two waist gunners and radio gunner assigned to B-24 bombers, but was not intended for use aboard B-26 aircraft.

An important feature of the armor was the ease with which it could be jettisoned, in the event an emergency bailout or water landing was necessary. The flak suit could be discarded by the flyer by jerking a red-colored strap connected by web tapes and thongs to the fasteners holding the parts of the vest together. One pull released the fasteners, and the front and rear sections of armor fell away instantly.

Leg protective pads, made of the same material as the armored suits, were worn by a few navagators, bombardiers, pilots, and copilots on short missions during the late spring and early summer of 1943. They were seldom used on long missions because of their weight and encumbrance, and should be considered as experimental.

Armor Produced in the United States

Flyer's armor was initially produced solely by the Wilkinson Sword Company in England. However, it soon became apparent that production would be slow and that the British should not be the sole source of supply for the critically needed manganese steel. It was also desired that AAF bombardment units in other theaters be equipped with flyer's armor as soon as possible and this would require greatly increased production. A total of only 600 suits were made in England, and samples were forwarded

The original British-made flyers' body armor or "flak suits," being worn by B-17 crewmen from VIII Bomber Command, in this photo taken on June 26, 1943. Flyers' armor was intended mainly as a protection against low-velocity shell fragments. Lt. J. B. Wilkinson (left) is wearing the Type "B" half-vest and Type "C" sporran or apron, designed for pilots and crewmen with armored seats. T/Sgt. Wilbur E. Kloth is wearing the Type "A" full vest, which protected both the front and back of the torso, and the Type "D" full apron, intended for wear by bombardiers, gunners, and other crewmen who had to move around inside the plane. Both men are carrying the standard Army M1 steel helmet and T/Sgt. Kloth also has a parachute slung over his right shoulder. Flyer's armor was normally worn in combat over the back-type parachute, life vest, and all other flying clothing and equipment, but could be discarded quickly in an emergency by pulling one strap. (Courtesy USAF)

to the United States in July 1943. The U.S. Army Ordnance Department took over the task of quantity production and improvement in design, and from that date until the end of the war, the Ordnance Department and various civilian institutions were responsible for developing approximately 23 types of flyer's armor.

The AAF Materiel Command at Wright Field, Ohio, had also been interested in development and production of flyer's armor, but this function was turned over to the Army Ordnance Department.

The armor workshop of the Metropolitan Museum of Art in New York City became the main design research laboratory for the development of armor, just as it had in World War I. The workshop was uniquely equipped and manned by skilled armorers with a wealth of knowledge and experience in the design and fabrication of armor. Prototypes of body armour and helmets were made by hand in the museum workshop, usually in soft metal. When desired, experimental models in ballistic metal were usually produced later, by or through the Ordnance De-

Brig. Gen. Malcolm C. Grow (left), and Brig. Gen. Leon W. Johnson, inspect a modified armored vest being worn by S/Sgt. Ambrous T. Hansen, B-24 gunner. Staff Sergeant Hansen is also wearing the original type of M4 armored helmet, called the "Grow helmet," over a standard soft flying helmet equipped with earphones. General Grow received the Legion of Merit for his outstanding accomplishments, while surgeon of the Eighth Air Force, in the design and development of the individual protective armor, credited with saving the lives of hundreds of American combat flyers during World War II. A flak suit saved the life of Brig. Gen. (then Col.) Johnson, who was awarded the Medal of Honor for gallantry while leading a B-24 formation, during the mission to bomb the vital oil refineries and tanks at Ploesti, Rumania, on August 1, 1943. (Courtesy USAF)

partment. Development or experimental items were given a "T" designation by the Ordnance Department, and major modifications were assigned an "E" number, for example, T1E1. When the item was adopted as standard by the Ordnance Technical Committee, it was given an "M" designation, such as M1, M2, etc. Standard items that received a major change were given an "A" number, such as M1A1, M1A2, etc.

An intensive program was conducted during the war by the Army Ordnance Technical Division to improve the armor and provide additional protective devices, including special helmets. A wide variety of materials were tested and evaluated, and realistic firing and fragmentation tests were conducted at Aberdeen Proving Ground and Edgewood Arsenal, Maryland, and Wright Field, Ohio. Live sheep were sometimes used in firing and fragmentation tests of armor. These included the 20mm triangular fragmentation test.

The armor first produced in the United States was based entirely on the designs which had been developed by Colonel Grow and his British advisers. Ballistic protection was provided by Hadfield manganese-steel plates of the same composition as that used in the U.S. M1 helmet. These plates were sewn into cloth pockets and fastened to an olive-drab cotton duck backing, because linen of the type used by the Wilkinson Company was not available in the United States. However, by the end of 1943, an olive-drab nylon duck cloth was substituted for the cotton material, after nylon was found to have ballistic properties similar to silk and actually increased the protection limits of the vest. The hard steel plates were intended to deflect, or shatter and slow up shell fragments or pieces of aircraft debris, and the multiple layers of nylon behind the plates would catch those fragments that penetrated through the metal.

The production and distribution of armor did not proceed as rapidly as desired. The Wilkinson Company did not fulfill its contract before the latter part of August 1943, and it was requested that production in the United States be expedited. Flak suits from the limited supply were not issued to flyers as an item of individual equipment, but were requisitioned from Personal Equipment Officers just prior to each flight. This method of distribution permitted full usage of the armor, inasmuch as the same suit would be in use more or less continuously, during any given period of sustained attacks upon the enemy. The supply situation improved somewhat during the autumn, and by January 1, 1944, it was reported that approximately 13,500 suits had been produced for the Eighth and Ninth Air Forces. This was sufficient to enable every combat flyer in all heavy-bomber groups to wear a flak suit.[20] Deliveries of armor to the Twelfth and Fifteenth Air Forces began early in 1944, and by May of that year flak suits were in general use by bomber crewmen in the Mediterranean area.

Armor also became available to combat crewmen of the Fifth and Thirteenth Air Forces in the Pacific in January 1944. The Fifth Air Force never required the use of armor by combat crews of medium or heavy bombers. It was felt that the protection afforded by the equipment was not sufficiently great to outweigh the added load, which in some instances would reduce the payload of the plane, particularly on long missions. In the Thirteenth Air Force, the wearing of flak suits was not mandatory, though their use was strongly advocated, but almost all members of medium- and heavy-bombardment crews wore them after they became available. The total extra weight added to the load of the plane was met by a more careful balancing of the equipment, to provide for more efficient operation of the aircraft.

The first vests to be standardized and manufactured in the United States, were quite similar to the armor originally produced by the Wilkinson Sword Company in the United Kingdom. However, certain minor modifications were made, including the use of nylon fabric and quick-release "lift-a-dot" fasteners. In April 1944, a web-loop attachment called an oxygen tab was added to the M1 and M2 vests at the request of the AAF, in order to facilitate the use of a new oxygen mask and portable bottle.

The Armor, Flyer's Vest, M1, was copied from the Type "A" vest, and was designated by the Ordnance Department as the T1 during development. It was adopted as standard on October 5, 1943, and the classification was changed to limited standard on July 1, 1945, when the M6 vest was standardized. The M1 was a full vest, consisting of front and back armor sections, fastened together at the shoulders by quick-release dot fasteners. The vest

Back section of the M1 armored vest, with fabric covering removed to show damage by shell fragments. The front and back of the M1 vest were constructed of overlapping 2-inch square Hadfield manganese steel plates, 1-mm thick, secured in pockets attached to nylon fabric backing. Several other items of armor were of similar construction, including the front of the M2 vest, the M3 and M4 aprons, M5 groin armor, and T44 neck armor. (Courtesy U.S. Army)

was constructed of overlapping 2-inch squares of 0.045-inch (20-gauge) Hadfield manganese steel, secured in pockets attached to nylon canvas backing. The M1, like the Type "A," was intended for use by gunners, navigators, bombardiers, and radio operators, whose combat duties might require them to stand or move about, so that they were equally exposed to injury in front and behind. The vest weighed 17 pounds, 6 ounces, and provided a protective covering of 3.82 square feet.[21] Although the aprons were interchangeable, the M4 apron was intended for wear with the M1 vest.

The M2 vest was similar to the Type "B" vest, and was designed for use by pilots and other personnel whose duties permitted them to sit in a seat with an armored back that would provide protection from the rear. Initially designated as the T2, the M2 was standardized along with the M1 on October 5, 1943, and changed to limited standard on July 1, 1945, when the M7 vest was standardized. The M2 vest had a front section constructed of the same materials as the M1, but had an unarmored nylon back. It fastened at the shoulders and, like the M1, was attached with quick-release fasteners. The M2 vest weighed 7 pounds, 13 ounces, and provided a protective area of 1.45 square feet. The M3 apron was normally worn with the M2 vest.

The armored flyers' aprons M3 and M4 had the same construction as the M1 vest. The Armor, Flyer's Apron, M3, was initially designated as Flyer's Apron, T3, during

Waist gunner manning a .50 caliber Browning M2 machine gun aboard a Boeing B-17 bomber. He is wearing the standard American-made M1 full armored vest, M4 apron, and M3 steel helmet. The M1 vest protected both the front and back of the body and, along with the M4 full apron, was intended for use by crewmen who had to move around inside the aircraft. The airman in this photo is also wearing the popular B-15 intermediate jacket and A-11 trouser combination, A-6A flying shoes, and A-14 demand-oxygen mask. (Courtesy USAF)

testing by the Ordnance Department. It was triangular-shaped like the Type "C" apron, and was intended for use by pilots and certain crew members, such as turret gunners, whose space was limited. The M3 attached to the front of either the M1 or M2 vest with three quick-release fasteners, weighed 4 pounds, 14 ounces, and provided protective coverage of 1.15 square feet.

The M4 apron was based on the Type "D" apron and was originally designated as the T4. The M4 was a rectangular-shaped full-apron, and was intended for use by waist gunners and personnel with similar duties. It could also be attached to either the M1 or M2 vest by three quick-release fasteners. The M4 apron weighed 7 pounds, 2 ounces, and provided protective coverage of 1.66 square feet.

The Flyer's Armor Vest M2, and Armor Apron M3, were intended for wear by pilots and other combat crewmen whose duties allowed them to sit in an armored seat. The M2 vest had an armored front section similar to the M1 vest, but the backpiece was unarmored. Like the M1 vest, it fastened at the shoulders and was provided with a quick-detaching device. The staff sergeant in this picture is wearing the M4 armored helmet over a shearling winter flying helmet. (Courtesy USAF)

The vests and aprons were worn over other flying equipment, and all parts were attached to each other by quick-release fasteners. Tapes ran between each section, and connected the fasteners to a red "ripcord" located at the wearer's waist. Jerking this strap in an emergency allowed the armor sections to separate and fall away instantly.

It was determined through experience that additional protection should be provided to the groin, abdomen, and thighs of combat personnel who remained seated. The first item designed to provide this protection was the Groin Armor, T12, produced in December 1943.[22] It consisted of ten steel plates, which were shaped and hinged to give better protection than could be provided by either the M3 or M4 aprons. The T12 weighed approximately 8 pounds and gave an area of protection of 235 square inches. A hand-made example of groin armor, designated as the T13, was received from the Eighth Air Force in January 1944, and after examination, 4,000 were ordered for extended service tests. The T13 was made of three sections of overlapping steel plates, and was similar in construction to the M1 vest. The T13 weighed approximately 14 pounds, and provided an area of protection similar to that of the T12. The T13 was modified in March 1944, and standardized as Armor, Flyer's, Groin, M5.

The M5 groin armor was made in three sections, so that the central area could be drawn up between the legs and sat upon. The side sections lay over the thighs and provided protection to the upper portion of the legs. The entire piece could be attached by three dot fasteners to the M2 vest usually worn by pilots, copilots, and others who remained seated. The M5 weighed 15 pounds, 4 ounces, and provided an area protection of 3.72 square feet. Like the other forms of standardized armor, it was equipped, with quick-release dot fasteners, and tapes and thongs connected by a ripcord, for rapid jettisoning of the armor by the wearer. The T1 belt, designed to redistribute the weight of the groin and apron armor suspended from the wearer's shoulders, was approved and designated as a required item to be provided with each new M5 groin armor.

The introduction of body armor, in the spring of 1943, did not result in universal willingness on the part of the crews to wear and use it for the purpose intended. Even when its effectiveness had been amply proven, not all commanders were cooperative at first, and many flyers thought that armor, on top of all of the other items of personal equipment, would hinder the performance of their duties. To overcome the initial inertia and skepticism, a program of indoctrination was initiated that included visits to combat units by a specially trained officer, who gave lectures and demonstrations on the use and practical benefits of body armor. A motion picture was prepared later, which proved quite effective. While the crews were

The Flyer's Groin Armor, M5, was designed for pilots and other crewmen who remained seated, but because of space limitations it could not be worn by top-turret and ball-turret gunners. It was usually worn with the M2 vest in place of the flyer's apron, and provided maximum protection to the abdomen, groin area, and thighs. The components of the M5, as shown, consisted of an armored skirt for each thigh and a center extension piece upon which the wearer sat. The man walking from the B-17 in this AAF photo dated June 19, 1944, is also wearing an M3 steel helmet over a regular flying helmet, a Type A-14 demand-oxygen mask, B-15 jacket, A-11 trousers, A-9 gloves and A-6A flying shoes. (Courtesy USAF)

The well-equipped B-29 pilot in this photograph, dated June 8, 1945, is wearing an M5 steel helmet over a standard flying helmet, and an M2 armored vest with attached M5 groin armor. This combination, in conjunction with his armored aircraft seat, provided him maximum protection against shell fragments, while his multilayer winter suit, electrically heated flying clothing, B-8 goggle, and A-13 oxygen mask guarded against the hazards of frostbite and anoxia. (Courtesy USAF)

it was reported that approximately 4,000 flak pads had been manufactured in England, and padding material produced in the United States had arrived, ready to be cut into pads. Time and circumstances, however, made it impossible to complete their fabrication in England before the end of the war.[24]

The flak curtain was another device developed to provide additional protection for the body. Based on experience gained with the broader combat use of body armor, the flak curtain was a portable, semi-flexible section of light armor, introduced for use as a shield against flak fragments entering the plane near crew stations. Two types were produced, each similar to the flak suit in consisting of overlapping plates of .044-inch Hadfield steel in individual cloth pockets. In one type, the plates were 2 x 2 inches, as in the M1 vest, with sufficient overlap to produce an average thickness of two plates. In the other type, the plates were 4 x 8 inches, but the proportion of overlap was relatively small. Interposed between the bursting point of a projectile and the flak vest, the curtain reduced perforations of the body armor and the number of small fragments which sprayed the vicinity of the wearer.[25]

Several hundred AAF bomber and fighter aircraft in the European theater were equipped with the curtains. Tests and combat experience indicated that the curtains would be more effective if stronger binding material and larger plates were employed. Plates measuring 6 x 12 or 8 x 16 inches were recommended as preferable. It was also found that protection against 20mm-explosive aircraft cannon fire was improved, by allowing as much space as possible between the curtain and that part of the fuselage wall that it was especially desired to cover.[26]

Research on armored vests and other devices, continued after the M1 and M2 vests were standardized and entered quantity production. Activity was directed primarily at securing a more complete coverage and reducing total weight, without sacrificing protection. Fragmentation testing of different materials indicated that a combination of aluminum and nylon could be used to replace the manganese steel in body armor, with no loss in protection, and with a reduction in the weight of protective materials from 63 to 43 ounces per square foot. The Army Air Forces approved the Ordnance Department recommendation of December 1944, that aluminum and nylon be used in the construction of body armor, and development proceeded at a rapid pace. The T40 front or breast armor and T41 back armor were developed, fashioned of heat-treated aluminum-alloy plates with nylon back padding, and 1,000 of each, along with 1,000 aprons, were constructed using the improved E5 design of plate lay-out.

The combination of T40E5 and T41E5 armor sections was designated as Armor, Vest, T46, and approved for limited procurement. The T46 weighed 14 pounds, 8

never under any illusions that the flak suit could provide complete protection against machine-gun bullets, the indoctrination successfully convinced most of the men that the suit afforded valuable protection against flak. The demand for armor became universal and persistent, and the effect on morale was pronounced.[23] Groin armor, in particular, was considered especially important and desirable by many young, virile, combat airmen.

Not all of the erroneous conceptions concerning the armor were dispelled by lectures and movies, for example, many airmen believed that placing the vests on the floor of the plane to intercept missiles from below provided better protection than actually wearing them on the body. Despite efforts to encourage crewmen to wear body armor correctly, some remained unconvinced. To resolve the problem, armor pads and screens were designed for use aboard bombers, transports and gliders. On April 3, 1945,

View of the experimental flyer's back armor, T41E3, with fabric covering partially removed. This photo was taken at Aberdeen Proving Ground on February 2, 1945, during firing tests to determine protection against 20-mm aircraft cannon projectile fragments. The overlapping of the special heat-treated aluminum alloy plates with nylon backing, provided flexibility and additional protection. This type of construction was incorporated into the M6 and M7 vests and M8 and M9 aprons, standardized for AAF use in the summer of 1945. Only a few were procured before the end of World War II. (Courtesy U.S. Army)

ounces, and had an area of protection of 4.09 square feet. Because of satisfactory results from combat tests and the proven effectiveness of aluminum, standardization was recommended in June 1945.

On July 1, 1945, the T46 vest was standardized as Armor, Flyer's Vests, M6 and M7. The M6 and M7 vests resembled the M1 and M2 vests, and were intended to better fulfill the same functions. Components of the M6 were interchangeable with those of the M7. Production was withheld pending establishment of AAF requirements for the air war in the Pacific, and only 1,075 of the M6 vests were produced before the end of the war.

The Flyer's Vest, M6 was constructed of 0.102-inch 24 ST heat-treated aluminum plates with 7-ply 19-ounce nylon-duck back padding, and provided protective coverage of the front and back of the torso. It weighed 14 pounds, 8 ounces (2 pounds, 14 ounces less than the M1), and provided total coverage of 4.09 square feet (0.27 square feet more than the M1).

The Flyer's Vest, M7, was of the same construction as the M6, but provided protective coverage only in front, as did the M2 vest. It weighed 7 pounds, 13 ounces, with an area protection of 1.82 square feet. Only a few of the M7 vests were produced for testing, and the item was not placed in quantity production to replace the M2 before the war ended.

Because of the greatly increased use of the backpack parachutes in the Pacific areas during 1945, the armor designs were modified to fit over the back parachutes, resulting in two modified models, the M6A1 and M7A1. Improved materials were incorporated into the designs in the summer of 1945, consisting of 0.102-inch 75 ST aluminum plates and 6-ply, 13-ounce nylon duck. The M6A1 vest weighed 16 pounds, 15 ounces, and provided an area protection of 5.88 square feet. The M7A1 vest weighed 7 pounds, 12 ounces, and provided an area protection of 2.08 square feet. The M6 and M7 vests were changed to limited standard when the M6A1 and M7A1 vests were standardized, but only a few were made for testing before the end of the war.

The aprons designed for use with the T46 vest (standardized as the M6 and M7 vests), were constructed of the same combination of aluminum plates and nylon-duck pads. These aprons, initially designated as the T55 and T56, were standardized in July 1945 as the M8 and M9 aprons, respectively.

The Armor, Flyer's Apron, M8, was a tapered design similar in shape to the M3 apron. It was intended for use with the M7 vest, but could also be worn with the M6. The M8 weighed 4 pounds, 11 ounces, and had an area of protection of 1.23 square feet.

The M9 apron resembled the M4 apron in shape, and was designed for use with the M6 vest. It weighed 6 pounds, 8 ounces, and had an area of protection of 1.89 square feet.

The improved materials in the Armor Vests, M6A1 and M7A1, were incorporated in the design of the M8 and M9 aprons, which were designated as the M8E1 and M9E1. These aprons were soon standardized as the M8A1 and M9A1, and the M8 and M9 were changed to limited standard. The war ended before any were produced for service use. The M8A1 apron weighed 4 pounds, 4 ounces, and had an area of protection of 1.23 square feet. The M9A1 apron weighed 5 pounds, 12 ounces, and the area of protection was 1.89 square feet.

The replacement of the Hadfield steel plates in the vests and aprons by aluminum and nylon, led to a similar change in groin armor. The T57 groin armor was similar in construction to the T46 vest, and the materials used were a combination of aluminum-alloy plates and nylon-duck pads. Seven test models were constructed and in June, 1945, the Ordnance Committee recommended a limited procurement of 400 items. The T57 was standardized in July 1945, as the M10. The Armor, Flyer's, Groin, M10, weighed 13 pounds, 11 ounces, and was comparable in size to the groin armor, M5. Intended for use with the M7 vest, it offered an area of protection of 3.62 square feet.

The improved materials used in the armor vests M6A1 and M7A1 were also incorporated in the design of the

M10 groin armor, which became the M10E1, then finally the M10A1 groin armor. The M10A1 weighed 12 pounds, 5 ounces, and had an area of protection of 3.62 square feet. Only a few test models are believed to have been fabricated before the end of World War II.

Combat reports and Ordnance Department research, indicated a need for additional protection for the neck area that was exposed between the armored vest and helmet. A T44 series of experimental neck armor was therefore, developed, including a one-piece leather-covered model with an almost square front edge, resembling a tall collar. It rested on the shoulders and fastened at the lower front with a dot fastener. The upper front corners had small straps that were attached by dot fasteners to the sides

The T44 neck armor was intended to surround and protect the neck, between the areas covered by body armor and helmet. The construction was of 2 x 2-inch steel plates and nylon, similar to that of the M1 and M2 vests. The 4.5-pound T44 rested on the shoulders, was fastened in front by a dot fastener, and the upper forward corners were stabilized by the strap connections provided for attachment to the M4 series of helmets. Over 10,000 T44 neck armors were produced during 1945. Although it provided considerable additional protection, the T44 tended to restrict the movement of the head and reduce the field of vision. The airman in this 1945 photo is probably wearing a Type B-5 winter flying helmet with chamois-lined chin strap with cup, visible in the photo, under his M4A2 armored helmet. (SI Photo 82–11903)

of the leather-covered M4 armored helmet. This device was followed by another leather-covered design, with a curved front edge allowing better lateral vision. It was also attached by small straps to the sides of the M4 helmet. The latter design was more practical, and from this evolved a fabric-covered one-piece neckpiece called the ''Queen Anne'' type, which rested more comfortably on the shoulders and also attached to the M4 series of helmets.

The final version of the T44 was fastened in front by a dot fastener and, like the earlier models, the upper forward corners were stabilized by the strap connections provided for attachment to the M4A2 helmet. The construction was comparable to the M1 vest and consisted of 2-inch square Hadfield steel plates 0.045-inch thick, attached to an olive-drab fabric covering. The T44 weighed 4 pounds, 5 ounces, and provided an area of protection of 0.98 square feet. Although the Armor, Neck, T44, as it was officially known, was never actually standardized, over 10,000 were manufactured during 1945 and many sent to the war zones. Development was terminated in June, when a shift was made to aluminum and nylon as the best ballistic materials.

Experience with the T44 neck armor led to the development of the T59 series, which integrated with the M5 steel helmet and the T46 vest, thus providing as nearly complete coverage of the upper torso, head, neck, and collar bone as was possible without limiting freedom of movement. The T59 neck armor consisted of aluminum plates and nylon-duck backing pads curved to fit the contours of the shoulder and neck of the average man. It was made in two fabric-covered pieces, with dot fasteners for attachment to the armored vest T46 (later M6 and M7), of similar construction. The T59 could also be used with the M1 and M2 vests. Because of insufficient clearance in the T59 for the demand-oxygen mask, it was modified, and the new model was designated as Armor, Neck, T59E1. One hundred of the slightly modified T59E1 neck protectors were produced for field tests.

The T59E1 was followed by an improved experimental model, designated as the T59E2, which incorporated the new materials used in the M6A1 and M7A1 vests. The T59E2 was standardized as the M13 in September 1945, but production plans were cancelled when the war ended. The Armor, Flyer's Neck, M13, weighed 3 pounds, 13 ounces, and provided an area of protection of 1.33 square feet. The M13 was so made that it was released along with the vest, when the ripcord of the vest was pulled.

Experimental Flyer's Armor

Many interesting items of experimental body armor were developed during the last two years of World War II. New concepts were evaluated and new devices produced as

The Armor, Neck, T59E1 and helmet, M5. The T59E1 was an advanced two-piece design, made of aluminum plates and nylon, as used in the T46 (later M6 and M7) vests. When worn with an armor vest and M5 steel helmet, it provided as nearly complete protection of the upper torso, head, neck, and collarbone as was possible without limiting freedom of movement. One hundred of the 4.8-pound T59E1 neck protectors were produced in 1945, before being superseded by the T59E2, a slight modification incorporating the new, lighter materials used in the M6A1 and M7A1 vests. The T59E2 was standardized as the M13 neck armor in September 1945, but the war ended before it entered mass production. (SI Photo 82–11915)

three large steel main plates secured together, to allow for expansion to the wearer's size. The T7 breast armor was tested in conjunction with the T8 back armor and the T9 apron.

Experiments were also conducted involving the application of larger aluminum plates than those used in the M6 and M7 flyers' vests. A number of modifications of the T40 front and T41 back armor were produced, in order to achieve a reduction in multiple layers or overlapping areas, without loss of flexibility. None of these designs resulted in a standardized item for use by AAF flyers.

In April 1944, Headquarters, Army Air Forces, expressed a need for armor that would provide additional protection for an airman's thighs and buttocks. Designs were submitted by the Ordnance Department, and samples were delivered in May for inspection and testing by the AAF. The Armor, Flyer's Seat, T15, was constructed in the same manner as the standard M1 and M2 vests,

Prototype large-plate body armor, during testing by the Army Ordnance Department in 1944. The experimental armor of the T5 series featured large steel plates, flexibly mounted, and was not unlike the segmented armor worn by knights in the fifteenth century. This photo shows the unpainted armor being worn over a shearling winter flying suit. The steel helmet is probably the T6E4, worn over a winter flying helmet with B-8 goggle. (Courtesy U.S. Army)

a result of combat experience. In this connection, the Eighth Air Force was constantly at the forefront of armor design, testing, and evaluation. As a result of extensive testing of various materials, the development of steel body armor was discontinued by 1945, in favor of armor constructed of aluminum and nylon.

Hadfield manganese steel plates were used in the fabrication of a number of different components before 1945, including experimental vests of the T5 series, which featured larger, lighter front plates of improved shape. Elastic webbing was utilized to hold the flexibly mounted plates firmly in position, against the body. In February 1944, the T5E1 front and the T8 back armor were used together, in the continuing effort to reduce weight and increase the area covered. The T10 series of back armor was also designed for use with the T5 front armor, and featured

but because of the excessive weight, it was recommended in June that no further work on the T15 be conducted.

The T16 and T17 were designs for crotch armor, developed in mid-1944 at the request of AAF headquarters. The T16 was intended for attachment to the T15 seat armor and to the lower edge of either the M1 or M2 vests. Resembling the M4 apron in shape, it would have permitted the adjustment of the T15 to the wearer. After tests, it was decided that it was not advisable to add the extra weight to the existing armor. The T17 was designed in May 1944, and followed the general principles used in the standard metallic athletic supporters. Although this smaller design was agreed to informally by the Air Surgeon's Office in England, no further action was taken on the sample forwarded to Wright Field for examination in September 1944.

Armor was designed in the summer of 1944, to provide additional protection in the areas above the collar bone and on the sides of the torso not covered by the standard M1 and M2 vests. These prototypes, made of manganese steel, included the Body Armor, Chest, T18, the Armor, Back, T32 and T33, and Armor, Side Extension, T25, T26 and T27. The side-extension armor was intended to provide greater protection under the arms. Development of these items was terminated in the fall of 1944.

Another experimental armor combination was developed in the late spring of 1944, for the purpose of providing more comprehensive protection for the thorax and abdomen. The T19 front armor and T20 back armor furnished more area coverage around the shoulders and under the arms. The T19 and T20 were constructed of steel plates similar to the M1 vest, and they were intended for use with the T21 shoulder cape armor, T23 neck armor, and M4A2 helmet. Development was discontinued in the summer of 1944, because of the excessive weight of the armor pieces when used with the standard M4 apron.

The Armor, Flyer's shoulder Cape, T21 and T22, were experimental designs developed in June 1944, that were also similar in construction to the M1 and M2 vests. The T21 was intended to be worn under the armored vest to provide additional protection to the shoulders. It featured "wings" or projections that extended out to the left and right side of the shoulders and upper arms. Development work on the T21 and T22 shoulder capes was stopped when the AAF decided that there was no requirement for this type of armor.

Two additional types of neck armor, the T23 and T24, were developed, and a sample of each was submitted to the AAF for examination on June 3, 1944. The T23 was constructed of ten curved, overlapping metal plates, sewed in flexible pockets, and covered with nylon fabric. The whole assembly was secured to the M4E2 helmet by snap buttons or loops. Neck Armor, T24, was similar to the T23,

but was not fastened to the helmet and, therefore, allowed maximum freedom of the head. Development was discontinued in June, in favor of more promising designs then on the drawing boards, such as the T44.

The use of nonmetallic ballistic material for body armor was explored by both the U.S. Army and Navy, because of the need to reduce the overall weight of armor and find a substitute for the metals that were then in critical supply. Research was conducted by both the Army Quartermaster Corps and the Ordnance Department, with the latter responsible for all ballistic evaluation tests. The Naval Research Laboratory was also involved in research pertaining to lightweight body armor, for use by U.S. Marine Corps ground forces and certain shipboard personnel. One of the materials considered was made by the Dow Chemical Company, and consisted of layers of fiberglass filaments bonded together with an ethyl cellulose resin under high pressure. This material was called "doron," in honor of Col. (later Brig. Gen.) Georges F. Doriot, then director of the Military Planning Division, Office of the Quartermaster General.

The Ordnance Department developed the T37 and T38 series of front armor, to test the feasibility of using doron instead of Hadfield steel. The T37 closely followed the construction of the M1 vest, but with flat 0.130-inch thick doron plates, 2 inches square, substituted for the steel. Curved and dished shapes of doron of different thicknesses, were also tested and evaluated. While doron showed slightly better resistance to fragmentation than manganese steel, it proved to be inferior to the combination of aluminum and nylon as used in the M6 and M7 flyers' vests. No further work was done on doron by the Army Ordnance Department, after the favorable results of fragmentation tests on the aluminum and nylon combination were received in November 1944.[27]

The U.S. Navy, however, felt that doron was a most promising material, and prepared approximately 1,000 jackets armored with doron plates for combat testing by the U.S. Marine Corps in the spring of 1945.[28] The Navy maintained its interest and confidence in doron armor, and improved vests using this material were developed and worn by Marine Corps troops during the Korean and Vietnam conflicts.

Steel Helmets for Aviators

It became increasingly obvious, by the autumn of 1942, that American combat airmen required ballistic protection for the head, as well as for other parts of the body. Little thought had been given to protective helmets since World War I, but the considerable number of head injuries and deaths sustained by airmen wearing soft flying helmets of leather and cloth was a serious problem. Some flyers began wearing the M1 steel infantry helmet and liner over a flying helmet, for protection against shell fragments and the debris caused by missiles striking the aircraft. However, most crewmen soon found the M1 to be impractical, because of the discomfort experienced when the helmet was worn over earphones. The tight fit also decreased circulation in the ears, which could contribute to frostbite.

In January 1943, personnel of the 306th Bombardment Group in England developed a modification to the M1, which made it much more comfortable to wear over a flying helmet or headset. The procedure involved spreading the Hadfield steel shell at the sides in the area of the ears by the use of a screw-jack. Sections were cut from the plastic-impregnated fabric liner to accomodate earphones. The inner headband of the liner was then adjusted to receive a fabric or leather flying helmet and snap fasteners installed to hold it in place. This field modification was subsequently adopted by units in various theaters,

The M1 steel helmet designed for ground troops was the only ballistic headgear available to American airmen for protection against flak, during the first two years of their participation in World War II. However, few flyers wore the M1 over their soft flying helmet, because of the discomfort caused by pressure on the earphones. A modification for the M1 was developed, during 1943, which partially solved the problem. The steel shell was first spread at the sides by use of a screwjack. Sections were then cut from the hard liner to accommodate earphones, and the inner head-band was adjusted to receive a leather flying helmet. Lastly, the leather helmet and earphones were placed in the liner and snap fasteners fixed to hold it in place. The M1 helmet, with this field modification, was reasonably comfortable and stable, and provided the crewman with the additional protection required. (SI Photo 8316AC)

until the M3 steel helmet for flyers came into general use early in 1944.

The M1 helmet was also used for duties not originally anticipated by Army officials. Former Capt. Carl R. Thompson flew as a copilot and pilot with the 306th Bombardment Group from October 1943 until April 1944, and recently described the use of the M1 during his thirty combat missions over Europe:

> We wore steel Army helmets reshaped to make room for earphones. This was done by a GI at our bicycle shop. They were used as flak helmets when the going got rough. Their other duty was as portable latrines, which we would use and then sit on the floor of the cockpit to freeze. When we got the plane back on the hardstand we would dump the cake of ice out, kick it out on the grass, and store our helmet back in our flight bag until needed again.[29]

Standardized Flyer's Helmets

On August 9, 1943, a meeting was held at Wright Field to initiate design of a satisfactory protective helmet for aviators. The Air Ordnance Officer, and representatives from the Ordnance Department, the Aero Medical Laboratory, and the Clothing Branch, determined the necessary characteristics of size and shape for an improved helmet, by studying the positions in the aircraft normally taken by crew members. The seven precisely sculptured plaster heads prepared by the Aero Medical Laboratory in 1942 after a survey of 1,871 airmen, were also used in the development of this and later helmets. The Ordnance Department then made clay models and sketches of various designs, and submitted them to the Army Air Forces for consideration. The helmet design selected during this study was designated as the Helmet, Steel, T2. At the next meeting, the T2 prototype was judged satisfactory for use in a large number of positions in combat airplanes, but unsatisfactory in certain extremely cramped positions in which nothing except a skullcap-type of helmet could be worn. Members of the Clothing Branch involved in the design of the T2, and later the T3, were Maj. John W. Schenck, Dr. J. L. Clark, and Mr. William Moore.

The T2 helmet was a direct modification of the M1, which considerably expedited the development process. The main difference between the two helmets was that the T2 had no separate liner, as the adjustable head suspension was attached directly to the steel shell. The body of the helmet was cut away to allow clearance for earphones, and hinged steel ear plates were provided to cover the earphones and prevent possible injury from their fragmentation. The hinged earflaps were welded to the helmet shell and had a round felt pad glued inside. A web chin strap was attached to the lower edge of the earflaps, and held them in place over the ears. The T2 was more comfortable and provided increased protection to the crewman's head, forehead, neck, and ears than the M1 helmet.

After accelerated service-testing, the T2 was adopted and standardized in December 1943 as the Helmet, M3. The production M3 was made of Hadfield manganese steel, weighed 3 pounds, 3 ounces, and was painted olive drab. A coating of flock, similar to cotton lint, was applied to the metal to prevent the flyer's bare skin from freezing to it in the extremely low temperatures at high altitude. Between December 1943 and April 1945, 213,543 M3 helmets were produced. The M3 was designated as lim-

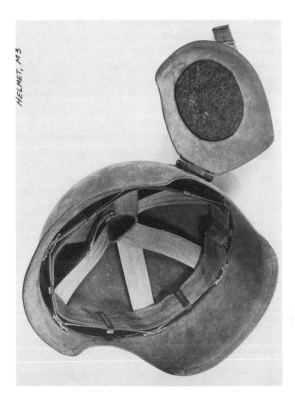

Interior view of Flyer's Helmet, M3, showing the adjustable head suspension and hinged earflaps. Made of Hadfield manganese steel and weighing 3 pounds, 3 ounces, the M3 was worn for protection over the standard flying helmet by thousands of airmen during 1944 and 1945. (Courtesy U.S. Army)

The Flyer's Helmet, M3, was a modified M1 helmet without a separate liner. An adjustable suspension system was attached directly to the steel shell, which was cut away on each side to provide clearance for the earphones. Hinged steel flaps provided protection over the earphones installed in the regulation leather or fabric flying helmet. This photograph, dated February 1944, shows how the M3 integrated with the flying helmet, Type A-14 demand-oxygen mask, and rubber-framed B-8 goggle. (Courtesy USAF)

ited standard when the M5 helmet was standardized in January 1945.[30]

While working on the development and manufacture of body armor, Col. Malcolm Grow, Surgeon of the Eighth Air Force in England, also recognized the requirement for an improved ballistic helmet for aviators. There had been a high number of injuries from fragments and facial burns suffered by airmen on raids against cities with heavily concentrated antiaircraft fire. The most pressing requirement was for a compact helmet for turret gunners and radio operators, who could not wear the M1 helmet because of its bulk. During the summer of 1943, Grow designed a skullcap-type, quick-release helmet from the Hadfield steel and fabric foundation used in the construction of body armor. The several unjoined, overlapping steel strips gave it some flexibility and the entire helmet weighed less than 2 pounds, 2 ounces, as compared to the M1 helmet weighing 3 pounds, 2 ounces. The "Grow helmet," as it came to be known, was cut out over the ears to allow free use of the intercommunication and radio headsets and, thus, could be worn over the standard summer or winter flying helmets and oxygen mask. No separate suspension was employed because the soft flying helmet provided adequate padding. The helmet was tightly covered with dark brown leather, and had a chamois-skin lining. Brown leather straps encircled the ears, and the chin strap had a buckle on one side and a dot fastener on the other.

After successful combat tests of the prototype, the resourceful Colonel Grow arranged through the commanding general of the Eighth Air Force, who sponsored the research and testing of armor, for the manufacture of 19,000 helmets in England by the Wilkinson Sword Company. Production, as in the case of body armor, was slow in the United Kingdom, and samples of the new helmet, with full information, were sent to the Ordnance Department with an urgent request for manufacture in the United States.

In September 1943, the "Grow helmet," initially designated by the Ordnance Department as the T3, was submitted for testing at Wright Field in conjunction with the T2 helmet. It was felt that the T3 afforded less protection than the T2, but tests confirmed that it could be worn in certain aircraft turrets where the larger M1 and T2 helmets could not be used. A decision was made to procure 2,500 of the T3 helmets for extended service tests and, on December 2, 1943, it was standardized as the Helmet, M4.

The first T3 and M4 helmets manufactured in the United States were very similar to the original "Grow helmet."

The Flyer's Helmet, M4, shown in this February 1944 photo being worn over a regulation leather flying helmet, Type A-14 demand-oxygen mask, and B-8 goggle. The close-fitting M4 weighed only 2 pounds, 1 ounce, and could be worn in gun turrets and other crew positions in combat aircraft where space was at a premium. (Courtesy USAF)

The T3 helmet, standardized as the M4 in December 1943, and placed in production in the United States. This helmet was copied from the original "Grow helmet," designed by Col. Malcolm C. Grow, Surgeon of the U.S. Eighth Air Force in England. This photo shows the Hadfield manganese steel plates that were inclosed inside the leather-and-fabric-covered skullcap. No suspension was utilized, as all helmets in the M4 series were worn directly over a soft flying helmet. (SI Photo 80–20848)

They had a dark-brown leather covering over Hadfield steel plates, and the same style of brown leather chin strap and buckle were employed. The M4 weighed 2 pounds, 1 ounce. The M4 design was modified during the next few months to slightly increase its length, for better fit over the thick shearling winter flying helmets. An olive-drab fabric covering and lining were substituted for leather, but the leather chin strap with buckle was retained. Slight variations of the M4 were produced by different manufacturing companies during this transition period.

It soon became obvious that armored ear plates or flaps were required, and an experimental model, the T3E1, was developed. The T3E1 was similar to the T3, but had an olive-drab canvas covering and steel earflaps, in pockets, to cover the headphones. Models T3E2 and T3E3 evolved during further experiments, and the latter was adopted in April 1944 as "required type, adopted type, standard article," and designated as Helmet, M4A1. At that time, the

M4A1 superceded the M4 in production, and the M4 was declared limited standard.

The M4A1 was slightly longer than the M4, and was equipped with Hadfield steel earflaps sewed quite rigidly in pockets. It had a nylon lining and weighed 2 pounds, 12 ounces. The leather chin strap was attached to the earflap covers, and used a catch similar to the one used on the Type A-11 flying helmet. Two web straps with snaps, and an additional strap secured at the top and bottom to form a permanent loop, were attached to the back of the cloth helmet cover. These keepers could be used for holding the goggle strap, but the main purpose was for securing the top edge of the T23 neck armor.

At the request of Headquarters, Army Air Forces, a method was devised for adding earflaps to the M4 helmets already produced, which involved furnishing a prefabricated cloth cover or hood to fit the M4 helmet body, the hood having the steel ear plates sewed in attached pockets. In this model, the earflaps were flexibly attached through the use of a webbing hinge. The M4E1, as this modified M4 helmet was originally designated, was actually a field-service modification of existing M4 helmets and was later also designated as Helmet, M4A1.

Experiments continued, and an improved method of attaching the earflaps on the helmet was found. In this modification, designated as the M4E2, the same ear plates

139

The M4E2 helmet, standardized for mass production as the Flyer's Helmet, M4A2, in June 1944. Similar in design and construction to the M4A1, it was made about 0.25 inch longer in order to fit all head sizes, and had improved clearance for goggles. Production M4A2 helmets had a hinge made as a part of the earflap cover, instead of using a separate web hinge as shown on this prototype. The M4A2 weighed 2 pounds, 12 ounces, and proved very effective for protection against flak fragments and other low-velocity missiles. (Courtesy U.S. Army)

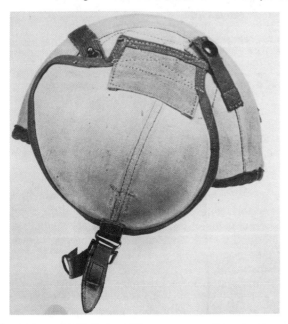

The Helmet, M4A1, was similar in design to the M4 helmet, except that protective steel plates were attached to cover the ears, and the chin strap was fastened to the earflaps. Many of the M4 helmets were converted to the M4A1 configuration in the spring of 1944 by the use of a prefabricated cloth cover, which included the ear plates in hinged pockets. (SI Photo 80–20844)

were used as in the M4A1, but the helmet was more compatible with other flying gear. It featured greater ease of manufacture, improved clearance for goggles, and greater ease of donning and removing the helmet from the head, with no increase in weight. The M4E2 was standardized as the Helmet, M4A2 in June 1944, and because it quickly replaced the earlier model in production, few M4A1 helmets were manufactured. About 86,000 M4 and M4A2 helmets were produced during 1944 and 1945.[31] All of the cloth-covered M4 series variations with earflaps looked very similar and proved serviceable, but most were replaced by the new M5 helmet during 1945.

Even before the M3 and M4 helmets were standardized, work was initiated by the Ordnance Department to develop an all-purpose steel helmet for aviators. Because of fabrication difficulties with the overlapping steel plates in the M4 series helmets, the emphasis was on developing a one-piece closely fitting helmet bowl, with protective plates attached over the ears. After a great amount of research and testing of the T6 series of experimental helmets, a new design emerged, designated as the Helmet, Steel, T8. The T8 was based on the design of the T6E4, but included many improvements as a result of data submitted by the Aero Medical Laboratory at Wright Field. In view of the progress in the development of the T8, work on all other models was discontinued.

The T8 had a one-piece steel bowl and long hinged cheek plates (earflaps), which followed the contour of the leather flyer's helmet and were riveted to the helmet body. The cheek plates were embossed for the earphones, and also for clearance for goggle straps, when the goggle was to be worn on the brow. The head suspension provided was fully adjustable, to fit the smallest or largest wearer. A webbing strap at the nape, functioning as a stabilizer, held the helmet against the forehead where it would not interfere with upward vision.

A T8 prototype helmet was submitted to the Air Ordnance Officer at Wright Field, for forwarding to Army Air Forces officials for approval as a possible substitute for both the M3 and M4A2 helmets. The T8 was evaluated by the AAF Proving Ground Command at Eglin Field, Florida, and adoption was recommended for use in most crew positions, with certain minor stipulations. The report recommended that the lower rear edge be rolled, to minimize danger to the neck in case of crash landings, and that the earflaps be welded to the helmet body, instead of being riveted as on the T8. The AAF Board at Orlando, Florida, concurred in the conclusions of the study on September 5, 1944, and forwarded it through channels for final approval.[32]

In January 1945, the modified T8 was adopted as standard and designated as Helmet, M5. As indicated in the test report, the helmet was intended for use in all combat-aircraft crew positions except the Martin upper turret of the Douglas A-20 and the ring-sight gunner station of the B-29. The M4A2 helmet remained standard for those two positions. The M5 helmet was also adopted as standard for the pilot, copilot, navigator, radio operator, and flight engineer on troop-carrier aircraft, and for the pilot and copilot of glider aircraft. The M5 helmet was made of Hadfield manganese steel, weighed 2 pounds, 12 ounces, and had the same type of olive-drab flock coating as the M3 helmet. Between February and August 1945, 93,495 helmets of this type were produced.[33]

Experimental Armored Helmets

A number of experimental armored helmets for flyers were developed during the period from 1943 to 1945. Some were intended as improvements on existing models and others were made to test new concepts or materials. The main effort, however, was devoted to producing a universal helmet for aviators with extended area coverage, increased protective ballistic limits, wearer acceptability, and compatibility with associated flying helmets, headphones, and goggles. A number of metallic and a few nonmetallic materials were considered, and for a time aluminum seemed to provide the promising combination of comparable ballistic protection at a somewhat lower

The M3 helmet equipped with experimental ballistic nylon earflaps, to provide a larger area of protection for the sides of the head and neck. The man in this 1943 photo is wearing an AN-J-4 shearling flying jacket, Type A-14 demand-oxygen mask, and B-8 goggle. (SI Photo A4861B)

weight. However, during World War II, Hadfield manganese steel continued to be the principal ballistic material for helmets.

Among the helmets reaching the prototype stage were the T4, T4E1, and T5, three modifications of the T3 concerned with different methods of mounting the overlapping steel strips or plates in the skullcap, by the use of rubber and plastic. Development was dropped because of the progress being made on helmets of other construction.

The T7 was a leather-covered helmet similar in design to the T3E1, except that the crown was made from one piece of steel instead of steel strips, which would have simplified production, but work was discontinued when rapid progress was made in the development of the T6E4 helmet.

Yet another experimental version of the T3E1, or perhaps of the M4E2 or M4A2 helmet, was produced in 1944 by the I. Miller Parachute Division of the Fox Chase Knit-

HELMET, T7

The experimental Helmet, T7, was similar to the T3E1 and M4A1 helmets, but the crown was made from one piece of steel instead of steel strips, to simplify mass production. The steel earflaps of the leather-covered T7 were also more rounded, and although flexible, they were not hinged as in the M4A1 and M4A2 designs. Work on the T7 was discontinued in favor of the promising T6E4 helmet, then under development. (SI Photo 80–20836)

ting Mills. This well-made helmet was very similar in configuration to the M4A2, but was covered with brown leather and had a large yellow leather star sewn on top. The label on the chamois lining was marked: "Helmet, Flying, Anti-Flack, Project H-28-C1, Property, U.S. Army, Air Forces."[34]

Development work on helmets in the T6 series was initiated in November 1943, at the same time as work was progressing on helmets T3, T3E1, T4 and T5. The purpose of the whole T6 project was to develop an all-purpose flyer's protective helmet. The original T6 was a close-fitting steel helmet that afforded excellent protection. The one-piece bowl was deeper than the M1 but the forehead region was not sufficiently sloped for use in gun turrets. It had simple hinged earflaps, but it was believed that manufacture of the T6 from Hadfield ballistic steel would be somewhat difficult.

The T6E1 helmet was an altered T6, in which the forehead sloped so as to enable the wearer to manipulate the

turret guns. The T6E2 was a shallower model, shaped to fit the skull but allowing a moderate amount of space between the head and the helmet. It had larger earflaps, which gave more protection than the T6 and T6E1 models. The T6E3 helmet was similar in design to the T6E2, but had a larger bowl, which allowed more space between the head and the helmet.

The T6E4 model was entirely different from the other helmets of the T6 series, in that it fitted very closely to the head, somewhat resembling a skullcap. The hinged earflaps of this model gave more coverage than those of the T3E1. This design originally had no suspension, and weighed 1 pound, 12 ounces. It was considered to be a practical design, and work was continued to increase the coverage of the earflaps and to adapt the helmet for possible use with face armor of the T6 type. Work on the earlier models was suspended and effort was concentrated on developing this design.

During a conference at Wright Field between the Air Ordnance Officer and representatives of the Ordnance Department and the Aero Medical Laboratory, the T6E4 helmet with large earflaps, and the T6E5 variation, were demonstrated in various turrets and crew positions. Several recommendations were made, and the modified helmet that resulted was designated as the Helmet, T6E6. In the meantime, however, the T6E4 helmet had already been utilized by the Ordnance Department as the basis for development of a new and greatly improved all-purpose helmet, the T8, and it was this model that eventually evolved into the helmet, M5, standardized for AAF use in January 1945.

The Helmet, T18, was a design intended to provide an improved head suspension for the Helmet, M3. The new suspension would allow a snugger fit to the head, through the use of special clips to enable the rigid fixing of the adjustable headband. Work on the T18 was halted in November 1944, when it was proposed that the Helmet, T8 be standardized as Helmet, M5, and the M3 be made limited standard.

The promising ballistic experiments with aluminum and nylon for body armor in the fall of 1944, also prompted an interest in the use of aluminum for helmets. To determine if aluminum afforded a sufficient saving in weight, two sets of segments made to the pattern of the steel segments used in the M4A2 helmet were fabricated and made up into two helmets designated M4A2E1. One example was subjected to 20mm fragmentation shell tests, and for comparison another aluminum model was produced, designated as Helmet, M4A2E2. The M4A2E2 was identical with the M4A2E1 except that the weight of aluminum used was comparable to the weight of Hadfield manganese steel in the standard M4A2 helmet. In November 1944, further development of these helmets was halted pending additional ballistic tests of aluminum.[35]

Experimental flak hood designed by Lt. Col. I. Louis Hoffman, MC, Headquarters, Fifteenth Air Force. The hood or helmet was draped over the shoulders, and was intended to be worn over a regular flying helmet, oxygen mask, and goggle. According to the original photo caption dated March 7, 1944, "It is made up of many small steel squares as used in the flak suit and is lined with sponge rubber to reduce shock and concussion. It overlaps the flak vest and provides additional protection to the head and neck of aerial gunners. Analysis having shown that 25 percent of air casualties suffer from head or neck wounds, this helmet would materially reduce the number so wounded." The design was not adopted for standard use by the AAF. The machine gun is a Browning .50 caliber M2 on an E-17 adapter mount, with a B-11 iron ring sight and A-5 post. (Courtesy USAF)

The T6E1 experimental face armor was made of two steel sections hinged to the sides of the M3 helmet. The overlapping front seam was held together by a simple web strap with dot fastener. The aperture at the bottom was for the demand-oxygen mask hose. (Courtesy U.S. Army)

Face Armor

A project was initated in October 1943, to develop armor for protection of the lower part of an airman's face and neck. The armor would cover a demand-oxygen mask and be worn in conjunction with a steel helmet and body armor. The initial model produced, designated as the T6, consisted of a single steel plate, which was attached for testing to the experimental steel helmets T6E2, T6E3, and T5E4. The plate weighed 14 ounces, and had a small pivoting plate in the neck region to permit movement of the head. This armor proved to be ungainly and several subsequent models were developed simultaneously with helmets of various types.

The next type of face armor to be developed was the T6E1, a modified version of the original T6, made of two steel sections hinged to the sides of an M3 helmet. The two sections joined in the front in an overlapping seam, held together by a web strap with a dot fastener. This model, in effect, replaced the regular steel earflaps on the M3 helmet. A small aperture for the demand-oxygen mask hose was located in the lower front.

The T6E2 face armor was of three-piece construction and consisted of a center or front section, and two side pieces, hinged to the bowl of the M3 helmet in place of the regular earflaps. The center section was attached to the side pieces, by web straps. Like its predecessors, the T6E2 fully covered the nose area and oxygen mask, and integrated with the Type B-8 goggle.

Several more variations in the T6 series followed, including the T6E3 model of three-piece construction, quite similar in design to the T6E2. It was also tested in conjunction with the M3 helmet. The T6E4 was another similar model but this armor was tested with the T6E5 experimental steel helmet, as was the next variation, the T6E5 face armor. The T6E6 and T6E7 were face-armor designs with minor changes, and both were tested in conjunction with the T6E6 experimental helmet. All of the above were hinged to the sides of the helmet shell like large earflaps. The last model of face armor in the T6

The T6E2 face armor, developed for flyers early in 1944. The T6E2 was typical of several experimental models of three-piece steel construction. The front section was attached by web straps to the two side sections, which were hinged to the bowl of the M3 helmet. This photo, taken about February 1944, shows how the face armor integrated with the B-8 goggle and covered the demand-oxygen mask, flying helmet, and earphones. Although face armor provided valuable additional protection to the head and neck, all designs were heavy and awkward, and proved impractical for general use. (SI Photo 82–11910)

series was the T6E8, a design that was tested with the T3E4 helmet. These models of a steel face shield included a heat-retaining lining, to fit over an electrically heated "overcoat" for the demand-oxygen mask. Yet another completely different design was tested, with fragment-resisting fabric, providing defense to the face, nape, and collarbone.

Both metallic and nonmetallic materials were tested. All types appear to have restricted the peripheral vision of the wearer. Testing indicated that face armor was too cumbersome, awkward, and restricting when worn with a steel helmet, leather flying helmet with earphones, goggle, and oxygen mask with microphone. None came close to attaining that all important requirement in equipment design—user acceptability. Development work was sus-

Production Figures for Flyers' Armor and Helmets, 1943–45[37]

Type of Armor	Total Produced
Flyer's Vest	
Types A and B	600
M1	338,780
M2	95,919
M6	1,075
Flyer's Apron	
Types C and D	
600	
M3	142,814
M4	209,144
Flyer's Groin Armor, M5	109,901
Flyer's Neck Armor	
T44	10,969
T59E1	100
Flyer's Helmet	
M3	213,543
M4 and M4A2	86,000
M5	93,495

The Effectiveness of Flyer's Armor

The efficiency of armor in World War II was measured in the comparative results of studies made on the fatality rate, the location of wounds, and the trend of the casualty rate among armored and unarmored combat crews. An Eighth Air Force study, for example, disclosed that the number of wounds received by crew members of heavy bombers wearing armor, declined by 61 percent during the period from November 1943 to May 1944, compared to the previous seven-month period when little or no armor was worn. However, it was also found that there was an 18 percent decrease in aircraft battle-damage during the period, so although it appeared that the 61 percent reduction in wounds during the periods compared was not due entirely to combat conditions, it was, to a great extent, due to the use of body armor.[38] A later study indicated that body armor prevented approximately 74 percent of wounds in covered areas.[39]

When all factors, including more effective methods of combat on the part of the AAF and decreased enemy action were considered, flyers' armor in World War II was deemed responsible for a reduction of 58 percent in per-

H.Q. USSTAF.—OFFICE OF THE DIRECTOR OF MEDICAL SERVICES
RESULT TO PERSONNEL = INDIVIDUALS STRUCK BY ENEMY MISSILES
ARMORED — UNARMORED

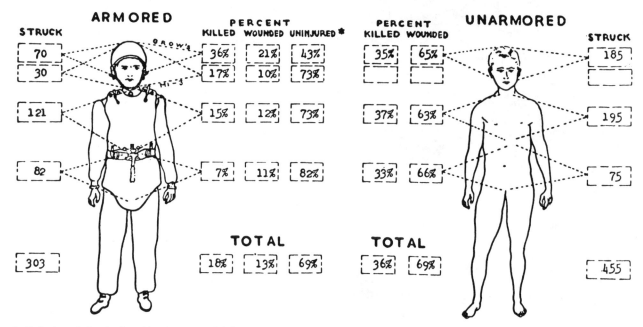

● Uninjured includes those very slightly injured.

This diagram on wound comparison was prepared by Headquarters, U.S. Strategic Air Force, and was originally published in the "Record of Army Ordnance Research and Development, Helmets and Body Armor," Vol. 2, Book 1, Section 3, Office of the Chief of Ordnance, Washington, D.C., Jan. 1946.

sons wounded and a reduction of 60 percent in the total number of wounds sustained per 1,000 crewmen on missions.[40] All wartime surveys agreed that armor for combat crewmen was a highly successful and valuable adjunct in decreasing the total number of wounds and the number of lethal wounds.[41] The effectiveness of protective helmets and body armor also helped sustain the morale of crew members during the long, stressful months of combat in the skys over Europe and the Pacific.

The pioneering efforts of the Army Ordnance Department, the Army Air Forces, the Office of the Surgeon General, and private industry, in developing and producing efficient armor for aviators during World War II, laid the groundwork for the development of the advanced individual protective systems in use today by the U.S. armed forces.

V. Anti-G Garments and Pressure Suits

ANTI-G GARMENTS

Brig. Gen. Charles E. "Chuck" Yeager, USAF (Ret.), gained fame as a record-setting test pilot in advanced supersonic aircraft, such as the Bell X-1 and X-1A. He made world history on October 14, 1947, when he became the first man to fly faster than the speed of sound in level flight. During World War II, however, he was a successful fighter pilot, scoring thirteen aerial victories while flying a P-51 Mustang with the Eighth Air Force in England. During a talk at the National Air and Space Museum, Brigadier General Yeager recalled his experiences with "G-forces," and the new anti-G garments developed during the war, in an effort to give Allied fighter pilots an advantage in aerial combat by protecting them against the effects of acceleration.[1]

One of the favorite tricks both we and the Germans used in dog fights, was using "high-G" in a very tight spiral, going straight down to keep up the air speed. Consequently, what happened to the pilot physiologically is the same thing that happens today; you sitting in the audience have one unit of gravity on you and we call it 1 "G." When you turn an airplane, you experience centrifugal force and you measure that force in units of gravity; if you pull 2 Gs, you have twice the pull of the one which you have on you now. What happens to the body when you get up to 4 Gs, is that the blood gets so heavy that the blood vessels expand in the lower extremities of your legs, your stomach, and body. It takes the blood away from your heart and it can't pump it up to your head and, consequently, the first thing you lose at about 4 to 4 1/2 Gs is your peripheral vision, because you are not getting enough oxygen to the brain. If you hold, say, about 4 1/2 Gs for another ten seconds, you see nothing; you can still feel but you can't see. If an enemy gets on your tail, you start in a very tight spiral, pulling about 4 1/4 Gs, and when you can't see anymore you know he can't see either, so you reverse your turn and head out the other way and hope the guy won't let up on it. We not only used this technique, but the Germans did too, and this led to a real funny system.

We were equipped with anti-G-suits after the invasion, about July 1944. If we could control the amount of expansion of the blood vessels under high Gs, we could keep the blood from pooling in the lower extremities of the body. The Canadians brought us a water-filled G-suit and we tried it along with our Army Air Forces G-suit from Wright Field. The American-built suit worked on a compressed air principle. The suit was almost like wearing a pair of pants, except that it had a bladder over your stomach and bladders over the thighs and calves of your legs. When we pulled Gs while wearing this tight-fitting fabric suit, compressed air bled into a valve and that inflated the bladders which squeezed you tightly. This held the blood up to your heart so you could get up to 5 1/2 or close to 6 Gs before you "grayed out" or "blacked out."

That system came along just a little bit later than the Canadian system, which worked on the water principle. In this system if you could immerse the pilot in water, the water having the same specific gravity as blood, then as you pulled Gs the water would get heavy and keep your blood vessels from expanding. The theory was really pretty good, and they gave us this long smoke about how if you landed in the sea you would have fresh water to drink, so we said 'O.K., we'll give it a go.' The suit was shaped like the chest waders that fishermen wear, except it was double walled and made out of rubberized cotton. You put the thing on—it had a couple of zippers on the sides—and got it zipped and laced up real tight around you, and then you put on your flying suit, leather jacket, scarf, Mae West, and parachute, and went out and got in the airplane. The crew chief then brought a bag of water and fitted it on the filler nipple on top, and gurgled about five gallons of water down in the double-walled suit. The first time he brought cold water, and that was the last time too!

Once you got capped off, you fired up and went on your mission. Because the suit was made of rubberized cotton, the fabric began to stretch a little bit, and after about an hour and a half, especially if you pulled a few Gs, all the water was down around the calves of your legs and great big bubbles of water were around your ankles. Everytime you kicked a rudder or moved your leg, you sounded like a couple of active people in a water bed with a lot of sloshing going on.

Needless to say, this system was a total failure, but it was fun at the end of the mission. When you ended up back on your hardstand and parked, the crew chief would come up to help you unbuckle, and your armorer was there with the other guys, usually including an intelligence officer to debrief you. You would lift your leg up over the edge of the cockpit and step out, and kind of waddle out to the leading edge of the wing. The G-suit had a drain valve down on your ankles, and you'd stand there with two streams of water flying off the edge of the wing. And since it had been about seven hours, and you drank a lot of coffee, you sort of entered into the spirit of the thing. As I like to say, the British gals that walked the perimeter of the field thought we were pretty talented pilots!

Basic Principles Involved in Acceleration

The effective maneuverability of a modern fighter plane is limited, as General Yeager indicated, by the tolerance of its pilot to acceleration. The pilot who can withstand higher G-forces, with clear vision and brain, than his adversary, has the advantage in aerial combat. The effects of G-forces encountered by fighter and dive-bomber pilots, became more pronounced as aircraft performance increased. It took years of research before a full understanding of these forces made possible the development of effective anti-G garments. The anti-G suits produced during World War II, were designed to reduce the effects of acceleration upon the crewman, and to raise his ability to withstand high positive-G maneuvers.

Acceleration is a change in a state of motion (direction, speed, or both) and is divided into three categories: linear, radial, and angular, which are explained below.[2]

  a. Linear acceleration: a change in speed, with direction remaining constant; for example, a rocket or catapult takeoff.
  b. Radial acceleration: a change of direction, with speed remaining constant; for example, a coordinated turn at a constant speed.
  c. Angular acceleration: a change of both speed and direction; for example: loops, lazy eights, chandelles, and so forth.

The gravity, or G-force, that is exerted against the body of a crewman results in the feeling of increased weight, and this is called "pulling Gs." The letter "G" represents the force of gravity which affects all objects. The weight of the body, as increased in proportion to the rate of change of acceleration, is expressed as "Gs." One unit of G is the force in pounds created by the earth's gravity on the mass of the body. All G-force is a result of acceleration, and tolerance to this force depends upon the amount of the force applied, duration of the application, the area over which the force is applied, and direction of application of the force to the body. Crewmen experience positive G, negative G, and transverse G during certain maneuvers.

The Effects of High G-Forces

The effects of high positive acceleration vary with the individual. Exposure to high positive acceleration or positive G in the upright position during a tight turn or pullout causes a series of symptoms, which in a normal man develop in definite order within a specific range of Gs.

Average values after ten seconds of application:
1 G - normal.
2 G - feeling of being pressed in seat.
3 G - impossible to get out of seat and difficult to move arms.
3 to 4 Gs - "grayout" (dimming of vision and loss of side vision).
4 and 5 Gs - "blackout" (loss of vision)
5 to 6 Gs - unconsciousness.

These symptoms develop as the flow of blood to the eyes and brain slows down and almost stops. The force of the acceleration creates a pressure upon the blood that becomes greater than the blood pressure itself, reducing the flow of blood.

Prolonged G-forces from ten to thirty or more seconds cause increased venous blood pooling in the lower part of the body. This results in a displacement of blood from the chest. Less blood will then fill the heart with each beat, and the blood pressure will drop. This too will prevent blood from reaching the eyes and brain. However, if the acceleration lasts only a few seconds, no symptoms will occur because there is sufficient oxygen held in the tissues to keep the brain cells going for that brief period. Sustained G was the particular enemy of the fighter pilot in World War II. Fear of blacking out often hampered his flight maneuvers so drastically that he lost a sure kill. Sustained G, even when it did not "black out" a pilot, fatigued both body and mind.

Other symptoms are experienced as a result of the effects of negative acceleration or negative G during pushover maneuvers, inverted flight, and outside turns, because centrifugal force acts in a direction upward from

Anti-G suits of World War II. Left to right: Franks Flying Suit (FFS), a water suit tested extensively by the RCAF, RAF, Fleet Air Arm, and USAAF. It was the first anti-G garment to see combat; Type G-1 pilot's pneumatic suit, a gradient pressure suit (GPS), the first type in limited use by the AAF (a similar GPS or ''Moeller-Carson Suit'' was tested in combat by the U.S. Navy); Arterial Occlusion Suit (AOS) or ''Clark-Wood Suit,'' was U.S. experimental garment that tightened against blood vessels to keep blood out of extremities; Type G-3A anti-G suit, AAF cutaway GPS, most advanced model adopted and used in combat by 1945, and continued in use long after 1945. (Courtesy USAF)

the flyer's hips toward his head. The crewman feels as though he is being lifted out of his seat. The resulting pressures are very unpleasant, and cause a sensation of fullness and a throbbing pain in the head and eyes.

Transverse G is defined as a force acting perpendicularly to the longitudinal axis of the body, and is caused by linear acceleration, such as the force on a seated flyer on takeoff or during a sudden stop.

The anti-G garment increased the pilot's tolerance of sustained G. A pilot wearing one of the latest models developed during World War II could pull 6.5 Gs for as long as thirty seconds without graying out or blacking out. Without a G-suit, no pilot could pull that many Gs for more than a second or two without losing consciousness. The G-suit also reduced fatigue and increased combat efficiency. The anti-G suit was (and is) a practical piece of equipment. It did not make the pilot a superman, but it did make him a better "G man" when properly indoctrinated and trained in its use.

Confronting the G-Problem

The first flyers to experience some limited effects of acceleration were probably fighter pilots engaged in aerial combat during the last year of World War I. The effects on the pilots were minimal, and few members of the medical profession were even aware of the phenomenon. One of the first pioneers was Dr. Paul Garsaux of France, mentioned in Chapter II in connection with his wartime work with oxygen equipment. He was also very active in the 1930s, during development of a full pressure suit. In July 1918, Dr. Garsaux began perhaps the first scientific experiments in acceleration, by strapping dogs to a wheel and subjecting them to high centrifugal forces. The reports of his findings were generally overlooked, because of the many more urgent problems at that time associated with the conduct of the air war.

During the early 1920s, a Naval aviator practising for an air race confided to Dr. John R. Poppen, a Navy medical officer, that on rounding the pylons that marked the course, he often experienced a sensation as if the amount of light in his visual field was suddenly reduced. It disappeared upon regaining straight and level flight. So far as is known this is the first actual reference by a pilot to a symptom which, in the course of a few years, was generally recognized and known as "blacking out."[3] The U.S. Navy began conducting flight experiments in 1921, to determine aircraft load factors, using an accelerometer mounted in the cockpit of a Curtiss JN-4H "Jenny," and other aircraft. The tests also produced a method of correlating an airman's reaction to specific G forces, and this was probably the beginning of scientific study of acceleration in the United States.

1st. Lt. Russell L. Maughan of the Army Air Service, the winner of the 1922 Pulitzer Trophy Race, reported that he became unconscious when making the sharp turns around the pylons in a Curtiss R-6 at high speed. "Graying out," and even "blacking out," was experienced by other racing pilots, including Navy Lt. Al Williams, winner of the 1923 Pulitzer Race, who stated to Dr. Poppen that graying out on the turns affected his sight and coordination.

Another famous aviator who experienced G-forces in the early 1920s, was James H. "Jimmy" Doolittle, then a first lieutenant in the Army Air Service. One of the first studies of acceleration was undertaken by Doolittle in 1924, as part of his master of science degree at Massachusetts Institute of Technology. He performed flight tests at McCook Field in a speedy Fokker PW-7 pursuit airplane, including a variety of radical maneuvers that eventually caused damage to the veneer covering of the upper wing. Doolittle experienced grayouts and blackouts as a result of pulling Gs, and during two flight tests, 5.3 to 5.5 G was maintained for several seconds, resulting in his complete loss of sight during the maneuvers. He stated that "The sensation is that of having a tight band around the forehead and a feeling that the eyeballs are about a half inch too low in their sockets." After considering the effects upon the pilot of the accelerations encountered in these tests, Doolittle wrote: "It is apparent that serious physical disorders do not result from extremely high accelerations of very short duration, but accelerations of the order of 4.5 G continued for any length of time result in complete loss of faculties."[4]

It was not until the late 1920s that new dive bombers and fighters achieved sufficient regular performance to intensify the radial acceleration problem. The subject had not been studied with any degree of continuity, and there was then only a general realization of the cause and effect of acceleration.

By the early 1930s, the Navy Bureau of Aeronautics had become concerned about the possible harmful effects resulting from accleration in their new and more powerful aircraft. In 1932 Lt. Comdr. John R. Poppen, MC, USN, undertook studies on acceleration effects and protective measures for overcoming G forces in flight. Contracts were let with the Fatigue Laboratory of the Harvard School of Public Health, under the administration of Dr. Cecil K. Drinker, and experiments were subsequently continued at the Naval Aircraft Factory in Philadelphia. Dogs were initially used for laboratory purposes and flight experiments were eventually conducted. A pneumatic compression belt, inflated by a hand pump, was developed, to provide support to the abdominal area as a means of helping to overcome blood pooling in the abdomen and legs. It was determined that the acceleration belt, which provided counterpressure, should be inflated in advance of an expected episode of increased G. This was the first known protective device against positive G. While it somewhat alleviated the effects of high acceleration, the belt tended to restrict breathing and could not be considered successful at that stage of development. It was also found that tensing the abdominal muscles during maneuvers delayed or minimized the effects of G-forces. Further research was recommended. The report on the study was submitted on February 14, 1934; but it remained classified until after the end of World War II.[5]

The most comprehensive study before World War II on the effects of acceleration was initiated in 1936 by Capt. Harry G. Armstrong, MC, and Dr. John W. Heim, of the Air Corps Physiological Research Laboratory at Wright Field. The study of G-forces was facilitated by the use of the first human centrifuge to be built in the United States, which was installed in the old balloon hanger. Animals were subjected to accelerations of more than 16 Gs for as long as thirty seconds. The 20-foot long centrifuge, constructed for these experiments, permitted the subject to either sit on an adjustable seat, or lie head inward to the center of the centrifuge, outward, or transversely to the direction of rotation. Flight tests were also conducted in a specially instumented PT-13 trainer aircraft.

The first human centrifuge in the United States was built in 1936, in the balloon hanger at Wright Field, Ohio. Designed by Capt. Harry G. Armstrong, MC, (left), Director of the Materiel Division's Physiological Research Laboratory, it allowed the first comprehensive study to be made of the effects of acceleration on the living organism. This photo shows Sgt. Lloyd Stevens of the laboratory, strapped on his side at the end of the boom, and the electric motor and belt, close to the floor, which powered the whirling machine at speeds up to 80 rpm. At that speed, a force of twenty times the pull of gravity was developed. Members of the staff acted as experimental subjects up to 8 Gs, and goats were often used for the higher forces, which might produce permanent or fatal injuries. (Courtesy USAF)

Armstrong and Heim found that three main factors influenced an airman's resistance to high G-forces: the natural tolerance of the individual, the physical and mental state of the individual, and the duration of the acceleration. They determined that rapidly repeated accelerations decreased the individual's tolerance to G-forces, while daily exposure increased the tolerance. Their tests confirmed that tensing or straining of the abdominal and leg muscles increased the flyer's endurance, and that a belt with an inflatable abdominal section was useful for increasing the tolerance of a flyer for positive accelerations by 2 to 3 Gs.[6] A crude experimental belt inflated by a carbon dioxide (CO_2) cylinder was developed at the laboratory in 1937. Armstrong and Heim's study also emphasized the dangers of exposure to negative accelerations of 3 to 5 Gs, and recommended that regulations be published prohibiting such maneuvers.

Great strides were made in aircraft performance during the two decades following World War I. The speed of fighter aircraft increased from about 135 mph in 1918 to over 350 mph by 1939. Although there was a growing awareness of the effects of high accelerations on both the aircraft and crewman, the United States had no comprehensive program of research into the subject of acceleration and methods of protecting the flyer against high G-forces. Captain Armstrong was in contact with Navy Lieutenant Commander Poppen, Dr. Drinker of Harvard, and Dr. E. H. Wood of the Mayo Clinic and Foundation in Rochester, Minnesota, but two major factors delayed the implementation of a full-fledged research program until after the beginning of World War II. First, the economic restrictions during the depression made it necessary to channel limited research funds into the most pressing projects. The second consideration was peacetime flying itself, which normally did not require wringing the last bit of performance from military aircraft and the men that flew them. This situation was to change drastically after the beginning of the conflict, when it became obvious that air superiority between two relatively equal opponents could depend on the ability of a pilot to withstand a tighter turn or more acute pullout from a dive than the man on his tail.

The development of high-performance aircraft during the 1930s prompted acceleration experiments in other countries. The Japanese built a large centrifuge in 1938 and began to study G-forces. They developed noninflatable belly bands and abdominal belts with solid pads, for use by the pilots of their dive bombers and very maneuverable fighter aircraft. Reports were received at Wright Field during the war, that Japanese fighter pilots were sometimes tightly taped to increase their tolerance to centrifugal force. The effectiveness of taping the body with a large "Ace" bandage was investigated, using the Aero Medical Laboratory centrifuge in 1943, and was found to offer so little benefit that use of this time-consuming procedure by the AAF was not recommended.[7]

It appeared from researches carried out in Great Britain, that centrifugal force caused the blood to flow from head to feet, resulting in increased volume of the lower limbs. A British expert observed that "Head and heart are drained of much blood and this reduces the blood pressure in the central artery of the retina, which blacks out vision until the return of normal blood pressure."[8] British researchers determined that the endurance of a flyer could be raised above 5 Gs, by straining the abdominal muscles, which caused resistance to the flow of blood to the lower torso and legs during positive Gs. This technique was suggested as early as August 1934, when Wing Comdr. G. S. Marshall of the RAF, in a speech before the Royal Aeronautical Society, recommended bracing of the entire abdomen, either by natural means, or the use of a broad, flexible corset that would operate automatically.

Germany began acceleration experiments using a human centrifuge constructed in 1934. The growing emphasis on dive bombing in the new Luftwaffe, led to a recommendation that the pilot be placed in an adjustable or tilting seat, and even in a prone position in combat aircraft, to transfer the G-forces encountered from a longitudinal to a transverse axis of the body. This idea was also considered in the United States but was not adopted during the war for practical reasons. The concept is still being considered for high-performance jet aircraft of the future.

The Germans designed a water-filled anti-G suit somewhat similar to the Canadian Franks Flying Suit, but discontinued development of the heavy outfit, perhaps in favor of projects considered more crucial to the war effort. Some dive-bomber, and possibly, fighter aircraft, were equipped with an alternate set of rudder pedals above the standard ones. This allowed a pilot entering a dive to raise his legs, almost parallel to the line of thrust of the airplane. This position was believed to offer greater resistance to the flow of blood from the head and torso. Despite the advanced state of German research on acceleration, no anti-G garment was produced for the German Air Force during the war. German pilots were instructed to use the "crouch and strain" method, which was apparently considered an adequate preventive measure by most German Air Force leaders. During a visit to the National Air and Space Museum in 1981, Lt. Gen. Adolf Galland, well-known fighter ace and chief of German fighter aviation in World War II, was asked why no anti-G garment was developed for Luftwaffe flyers. He replied: "I did not feel that they were worth bothering with."[9]

The most frequently recommended technique among flyers of all air forces called for the straining of the abdominal muscles to increase G tolerance during tight maneuvers and pullouts from dives. Crouching shortened the

vertical distance over which the G-force acted from heart to brain, and straining the abdominal muscles limited to some extent the flow of blood into the abdominal vessels. Yelling during maneuvers was also suggested, as this produced the same effect, contracting the muscles of the abdominal wall and raising the diaphragm, thus lessening the fall of blood pressure. The importance of physical fitness was emphasized, and a British researcher stated that this was the most simple and effective means of lessening the effects of high G.[10] One important drawback to crouching was that while bending over, in some cockpits, the pilot could not always look out or sight his guns. Nevertheless, the "crouch and strain" method eventually became standard procedure for combat-fighter and dive-bomber crewmen of all air forces during World War II.

Anti-G Suits in World War II

Allied Developments

When the war began, there was no anti-G suit available for use by any of the warring powers. Combat experience soon indicated a need for protecting the flyer against the effects of G-forces, and research programs were established on a priority basis in several countries. A variety of different approaches were explored, but it soon became evident that there was no easy or quick solution to the complex problems involved. Allied efforts were directed towards developing a workable anti-G garment, and the first to be used in combat was the Canadian Franks Flying Suit or "FFS."

The experimental Canadian anti-G suit tested by Chuck Yeager in 1944 was the Franks Flying Suit. The "water suit" operated on the hydrodynamic principle developed by Dr. (later Group Captain, RCAF) Wilbur R. Franks, a professor of medical research at the Banting Institute of the University of Toronto. Dr. Franks, like so many early pioneers, had determined independently that counterpressure applied to a pilot's body during high-G maneuvers would help prevent the flow of blood from the head. The full-body, double-walled suit produced by Franks contained rubber bladders that incased the pilot in water. The tight-fitting suit automatically provided pressure, by hydrostatic force on the lower torso and legs, to offset the tendency to gray out or black out when subjected to high-G forces. It was simple in operation because it had no valves or mechanical devices, and the first model FFS was ready for flight testing by Franks in May 1940. It was followed by a series of improved suits that covered less of the body, but a shortage of high-speed aircraft in the Royal Canadian Air Force (RCAF) delayed the development program until a human centrifuge was completed at Toronto in the late summer of 1941.

Flight tests of the latest Frank suit were made in a Curtiss P-40 at Wright Field during 1941, where experiments on a hydrostatic suit were also being made by the Aero Medical Laboratory. According to a Materiel Division status report written in September 1941, "Numerous objections to a hydrostatic suit as a means of overcoming the deleterious effect of high centrifugal forces can now be raised, but further investigation of this development is indicated."[11] Research on an American water-suit design continued into 1942. Flight tests were also conducted in England during the summer of 1941, from which it was stated in Air Ministry Report No. 301 that a force of 6 G acting for twelve seconds was tolerated without impairment of vision. Despite this claim, there was considerable skepticism on the part of Royal Air Force pilots, and the British decided to order 300 Mark II FFS outfits for more extensive evaluation. Dr. Franks continued his experiments on the new Canadian centrifuge, while his Mark II FFS was being produced under contract by the Dunlop Rubber Company. The suits were delivered to the British early in 1942, for testing by both the Royal Air Force and the Fleet Air Arm.

The first use of an anti-G suit in combat occurred in November 1942, when fighter pilots of the British Navy Fleet Air Arm used the Mark II FFS in action over Oran, Algeria. There were enthusiastic reports about the efficiency of the Mark II FFS, worn by carrier pilots during the invasion of North Africa. Less favorable comments concerning the all-around practicality of the water-filled suit were received from the Royal Air Force, who were evaluating the Mark III FFS. This was the type that was flight tested in 1944 by the U.S. Army Air Forces in England. The Franks suits were never adopted for general use or placed in mass production. Although the FFS was entirely automatic, required no complicated installation in the aircraft, and it performed the function for which it was designed, it failed to obtain general acceptance by pilots because of its weight, bulk, warmth, and restriction of movement.[12] In addition, it required expert fitting to function properly.

Dr. Franks and his associates also developed an anti-G suit, using a combination of air and water pressure; air pressure being furnished when a large bellows, with a battery on top, was compressed by the increase in weight during change of G-forces. This combination was designated as the "AB/BG System." By this time, however, the encouraging progress being made on pneumatic anti-G garments in the United States lessened interest in developing suits operating on other principles. Pneumatic anti-G suits had been developed by 1945, both at the RCAF Acceleration Laboratory at Toronto, Canada, and at the RAF Laboratory at Farnborough, England.

Another early anti-G suit considered by the Aero Medical Laboratory was developed by Dr. Frank S. Cotton,

professor of physiology at the University of Sydney. Dr. Cotton was one of the pioneers engaging in acceleration studies, and his active program in this specialized field is surprising, considering the small size of the Royal Australian Air Force (RAAF) in the early days of World War II. Working on a specially built human centrifuge, Cotton developed an air-inflated, gradient pressure anti-G outfit he called a "Pneumodynamic Suit," but which was usually referred to as the "Cotton Aerodynamic Anti-G" suit or "C.A.A.G." suit.

By the fall of 1941 Cotton had achieved promising results with an early model of the C.A.A.G. suit. He personally withstood 9 G for about thirty seconds on the centrifuge without losing consciousness. He also supervised flight tests made in conjunction with the RAAF using a Hawker Hurricane. Dr. Cotton departed for England in late November with a sample of his Mark 1 suit and stopped en route at Dayton, Ohio, where he conferred with Maj. Otis O. Benson, director of the Aero Medical Laboratory, Lt. Comdr. Leon D. Carson, U.S. Navy, Dr. W. M. Boothby of the Mayo Clinic and Foundation, and representatives of the Lockheed Aircraft Company.

The C.A.A.G. suit was described in a report prepared by Maj. Bruce Dill of the Aero Medical Laboratory.[13] According to Dill, the suit extended from the lower ribs to the feet, and consisted of an outer covering of inelastic moleskin and an inner rubber suit built in sections. Each unit was an overlapping air-filled bag, and the pressure in it was atmospheric except when under positive acceleration. Air was then forced in by a hydrostatic reservoir, the pressure being proportional to the accelerative force experienced. The pressure from the water reservoir, caused by acceleration, forced air into the bladders in contact with the flyer's body. The air pressure depended on a constant flow of air through five sets of cylinders and pistons, rigidly supported in the direction of the accelerative force. At 1 G the weight of the piston prevented any air from entering the suit. Increasing G caused the piston in No. 1 cylinder to depress enough to open a valve and admit some air to the boots. Further increase in G caused the other ducts to open. The entire mechanism weighed only about 4 pounds, and the suit weighed less than the water-filled anti-G suit developed by Dr. Franks. Dr. Cotton offered to work with Wright Field to perfect his design, but there is no record of further development of the C.A.A.G. suit in the United States.

Development of the C.A.A.G. suit continued in Australia during the war. The chief discomfort of the C.A.A.G. Mark 1 resulted from the lack of heat control, because of the continuous covering of rubber over the lower part of the body. This was a particular problem in tropical climates. During testing of the suit, wearers found that resistance to blackout increased, and the fatigue and lassitude commonly experienced after a number of high-G

152

maneuvers was diminished. However, the C.A.A.G. anti-G suits remained too heavy, bulky, uncomfortable and complex for regular service use.[14]

Efforts to lighten and simplify the C.A.A.G. suit led by 1944 to the development of the "Kelly One-Piece" suit or "K.O.P.," models I and II. Made by the Dunlop Rubber Company of Australia, these gradient pneumatic anti-G suits covered the body from the waist to the feet. Model I featured five different pressures, and included pressurization of the feet. Model II had only three different pressures, and the feet were unpressurized. Although the K.O.P. suits were an improvement, they lacked flexibility and still had most of the disadvantages of the C.A.A.G. suits. Capt. Clarence A. Maaske of the Aero Medical Laboratory interviewed Dr. Cotton and examined the suits during a visit to Australia in October 1944. After considerable testing by the RAAF the suits were not adopted for general service use because of their excessive weight, bulk, and complexity.[15]

Anti-G Suit Experiments in the United States

In 1939 the U.S. Navy produced and flight-tested another version of the Poppen pneumatic acceleration belt, which was later featured in the movie *Dive Bomber*. During 1940 both the Army Air Corps and Navy established more active programs to perform fundamental research on acceleration physiology. The Materiel Division included this experimental work, along with full pressure suit research, under classified Project MX-117, until that program was terminated in October 1943. Anti-G garment development was then continued under Project MX-389.

The Aero Medical Research Unit (from 1942, Aero Medical Laboratory or AML), at Wright Field, cooperated with the U.S. Navy and other scientists and organizations including Dr. Earl H. Wood of the Acceleration Laboratory, Aero Medical Unit, Mayo Clinic and Foundation, in Rochester, Minnesota. The second man-rated centrifuge built in the United States was also in operation at the Mayo Unit. Another, more sophisticated, human centrifuge was constructed at the AML, and became fully operational in May 1943. It was supervised during the war by Capt. George L. Maison, MC, Chief of the Acceleration Unit under the Physiological Branch. The AML and Mayo facilities established the unprotected and protected human tolerance to long-term acceleration, and gathered other vital data, using volunteers who underwent life-threatening experiments while exposed to acceleration forces.

The data from these experiments indicated that it was possible to design and produce a practical anti-G suit to protect the combat flyer. This information was integrated with the pioneering work of Capt. John R. Poppen of the U.S. Navy to establish the basis for achieving workable

anti-G garments. Parallel development of several different types of anti-G suits was soon underway in the United States and foreign countries. While most of the projects involved the cooperation of the Aero Medical Laboratory at Wright Field, some were conducted concurrently, and it is therefore rather difficult to describe the development of the various anti-G suits in chronological order.

The limited amount of research on acceleration performed in the United States and abroad before the war was conducted almost entirely by the military services and scientists working at universities and foundations. As the need for anti-G devices became more obvious in light of wartime experience in Europe, commercial manufacturers became interested in developing protective anti-G equipment. The United States Rubber Company of Mishawaka, Indiana, was already working by 1940 on an anti-G suit for the Materiel Division. Called the Type G, this rubberized-fabric suit proved unsatisfactory. Two of the most successful firms to become involved in G-suit development were the Berger Brothers Company of New Haven, Connecticut, a manufacturer of ladies' foundation garments and surgical devices, and the David Clark Company of Worcester, Massachusetts, a producer of underclothing.

The Acceleration Laboratory of the Mayo Unit, utilizing their human centrifuge, performed a great amount of important basic research and practical testing under the direction of Drs. E. H. Wood and E. J. Baldes. In accordance with an agreement concluded in 1941 with the David Clark Company, the Mayo Unit began centrifuge testing of a pneumatic anti-G suit made by David Clark. Clark possessed practical experience concerning the materials, construction techniques, and details of fitting an anti-G garment to the human body, while the Mayo Unit had the physiological expertise and the equipment for testing.

Preliminary tests began by 1942 on a new model suit incorporating suggestions by Dr. Wood. The Clark suit, as modified by Wood, consisted of inflatable cuffs around the thighs and arms, and an abdominal bladder. This suit worked on the principle of a tourniquet. It was based on the idea that inflation of arm and leg cuffs, to pressures high enough to occulude the principal arteries in those regions, would cause cessation of blood flow to distal parts, thus limiting the volume of the peripheral vascular bed, increasing blood pressure in the remainder of the body, and improving blood flow through the head during increased positive G. This idea was a departure at that time, because it changed the emphasis from supporting return of venous blood from the lower parts of the body, to stopping of blood flow through less critical areas in order to augment flow through more vital ones.[16]

This prototype suit became known as the "Arterial Occlusion Suit" (AOS) or the Clark-Wood Suit. It was further refined, so that it consisted of one pneumatic cuff around

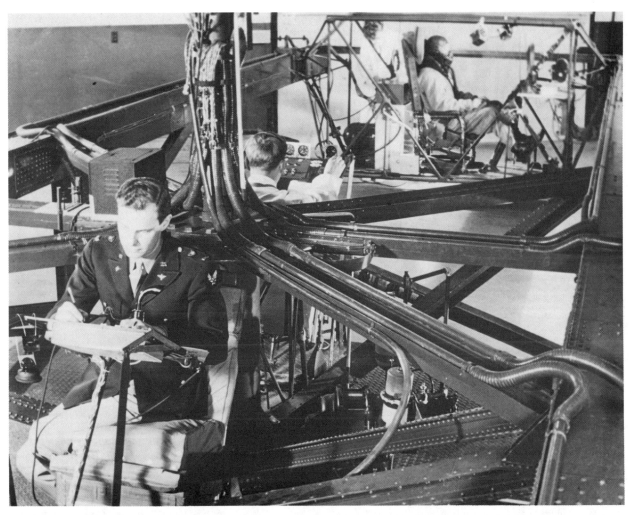

The new human centrifuge in the Aero Medical Laboratory became fully operational in Building 55, Wright Field, in May 1943. It was a much larger and more sophisticated tool for the study of acceleration and other aero-medical problems than its predecessor, and was especially useful during development and testing of anti-G garments. This photo, taken on February 19, 1944, shows 1st Lt. (later Capt.) Clarence A. Maaske, Assistant Chief of the Acceleration Unit, preparing to begin an experiment. A volunteer in full flying gear can be seen sitting in the cab in the background, on the end of the centrifuge boom, about to be whirled to the point of blackout or unconsciousness. (Courtesy USAF)

each limb close to the trunk, and a rubber abdominal bladder. The bladders were fitted into a zippered, fabric, one-piece suit, which resembled a regular summer flying suit. Air entered at the left side, and reached the right side of the suit through tubes that passed across the back. Outward expansion of the bladders was limited by cuffs of inelastic cloth, supported by metal stays, which were fastened taut around the bladder groups and secured by zippers. The AOS was inflated to three separate pressures in different parts of the suit, and afforded a high degree of protection against the effects of increased positive G. Data from the Mayo Unit indicated an average visual protection of 2.6 G. Several improved and simplified models followed, including one without cuffs. The AOS Model 9 was reduced to an abbreviated garment that reached from the chest to just above the knees.

After testing on the Mayo and Aero Medical Laboratory centrifuges, the Arterial Occlusion Suit and the Gradient Pressure Suit (GPS), were given competitive flight tests at the AAF Proving Ground Command at Eglin Field, Florida, during September and October 1943. The G protection offered by the AOS was found to be higher, but the suit was finally rejected in favor of the GPS, on two major points. First, the pilots found inflation to the high pressures very uncomfortable, and secondly, they complained that inflation of the arm and thigh cuffs to the arterio-occlusive pressures, produced tingling and numbness of the extremities in maneuvers of moderate duration, and pain during prolonged exposures to positive G. These trials led to the Clark-Wood Arterial Occlusion Suit being abandoned, as an impractical suit for military use. It was, however, a useful tool in the study of the effects of pressurizing various parts of the body for G protection.[17]

Following up the acceleration research of Captain Poppen, the U.S. Navy began development of an anti-G garment in association with the Berger Brothers Company and the National Research Council. Frederick Moeller and Irving Versey of Berger Brothers made impressive progress during 1941, in designing an experimental single-pressure, pneumatic torso belt with stockings and sleeves. It supplied pressure to bladders on the lower and upper arms, and the back of the calves and thighs, but the pressurization of the arms was soon determined to be unnecessary. Late in 1941 Lt. Comdr. Leon D. Carson and Lt. Comdr. T. J. Ferwerda began working with the Berger Brothers Company to develop two types of anti-G suits for possible service use.

The first type to be developed was a pulsating air-pressure suit with a G-activated valve for pressure regulation. Called the "Ferwerda Pulsatile Suit," it was constructed of a heavy open-weave material with seven bladders positioned crosswise in each leg. An automatic valve provided pressure that varied according to the G-load encountered. The pressure pulsated in a wave, travelling from the ankles to the thighs, creating a "milking effect" in the legs. The Ferwerda suit was tested by a Navy training squadron at Cecil Field, Florida in November 1942. Because of the great weight and complexity of the pulsating suit and valve assembly, and the fact that it was shown on the RCAF centrifuge and in the field trials to give essentially the same protection as the simpler gradient pressure suit, the Ferwerda suit was abandoned.[18]

The gradient pressure suit or "GPS" was also developed during roughly the same time period as the Ferwerda pulsatile and arterial occlusion suits. Like the Ferwerda, the GPS was initially sponsored by the U.S. Navy in cooperation with the Berger Brothers Company. It was also known as the "Moeller-Carson Suit," from the names of Fred Moeller of Berger Brothers and Lt. Comdr. Leon D. Carson of the U.S. Navy, who were active in its development.

The GPS resembled a pair of fitted overalls ensheathing groups of rubber air bladders. Rubber tubing conveyed air under pressure to the bladders, which in turn applied pressure to the rear of the wearer's calves, the front of the thighs, and to the abdomen. The crown-shaped abdominal bladder was incorporated into a corset-like belt stiffened with seven steel stays. Zippers, laces, and internal straps provided access and adjustment of the four sizes of suit to insure proper fitting to the individual. The suit was supported by shoulder straps and could be worn over or under other clothing. Air pressure was supplied automatically by the positive pressure side of an aircraft vacuum-instrument pump, and was metered to the suit through tubes by the G-1 valve. High pressure was provided to the two bladders over the ankle area, intermediate pressure to the two calf bladders and abdominal bladder, and low pressure to the four thigh bladders in each leg. The air was admitted through a valve, actuated by the same centrifugal force that causes the G-force to be exerted on the flyer. The inflation started at 2 to 2.5 Gs. Pressure increased in proportion to the increase in G-force, and was relieved by reverse action of the valve as the Gs reduced.

Development of the multiple pressure, pneumatic, gradient pressure suit presented an extremely complex challenge. Testing to determine the efficacy of the suit in lessening or postponing the symptoms resulting from exposure to radial acceleration, continued on the Mayo human centrifuge and, after May 1943, on the new 48-foot diameter centrifuge at the Aero Medical Laboratory at Wright Field. Flight tests of the GPS were carried out by the U.S. Navy at Cecil Field, Florida, in November 1942, and some prototype units of the equipment were delivered to Navy combat-fighter squadrons, for testing in the spring and summer of 1943. Flight service trials of the GPS, and the AOS, were carried out by the Army Air Forces at the Proving Ground Command, Eglin Field, Florida, in September and October 1943. Results of these tests confirmed the centrifuge data, which indicated that the GPS adequately protected the wearer against the effects of increased positive G, and was a more promising design than the AOS. The AAF Proving Ground Command and the AAF Board concluded that the GPS was effective, was operationally reliable, and should be given combat trials.[19]

Standardized Anti-G Suits

The Army Air Forces proceeded with the development of the three-pressure GPS under classified Project MX-389, and after minor changes in the suit were made as a result of testing, it was designated as the Suit, Pilot's Pneumatic, Type G-1.

Twenty-two of the Berger Brothers prototype GPS outfits, along with equipment for the aircraft, were taken to the Eighth and Ninth Air Forces in England in December 1943, by Capt. George L. Maison, MC, Chief of the Acceleration Unit of the Aero Medical Laboratory. Maison, who was the first person to ride the new AML human centrifuge, had been in charge of the GPS tests at Eglin Field. The Type G-1 "zoot suit," as it was sometimes

vantage provided by the anti-blackout suit during dives and tight turns. Not all of the Navy pilots were convinced, however, of the effectiveness or even the need for an anti-G suit, especially in this early form. Lt. Comdr. Harry Schroeder, USN, made recommendations to the Naval Air Crew Equipment Laboratory in Philadelphia, concerning simplification of the suit and air-supply system, and making it more comfortable for wear in tropical climates. This information was also conveyed to the Aero Medical Laboratory at Wright Field.

Although anti-G suits were urgently needed by combat units of the Army Air Forces and the U.S. Navy, it was realized that much effort was still required to resolve the defects in the gradient pressure suit. With a weight of 10 pounds, the Type G-1 was considered too heavy and bulky, and it was also very hot and uncomfortable for regular use. It restricted movement excessively and, with its complicated valve and oil separator, imposed more weight penalty on the aircraft than was desirable. It was obvious to both services that simplification was necessary.[20]

Experiments on the Mayo and Wright Field centrifuges produced evidence that the three-pressure system, as used in the Type G-1 suit, was an unnecessary encumbrance. A design for a single-pressure system was produced as the next step in simplification of the G-1 suit, and the Berger Brothers Company was requested to make samples for testing. This suit became the AAF Type G-2 anti-G suit.[21]

Made of ventilated cloth, the Type G-2 suit was similar to the Type G-1 suit in general outward appearance, sizing, lacing adjustment, and method of donning. The bladder system in the legs differed from that in the G-1, in that there were long rectangular bladders lying lengthwise, one over each thigh and one ever each calf. The abdominal bladder was the small type, similar to that of the G-1 suit, but the abdominal belt was simplified by making it a part of the outer garment, rather than a separate unit. All bladders were inflated to the same pressure; 1 pound per square inch (psi) per G, in maneuvers exceeding 2 G. Thus the number of bladders was reduced from 17 to five, and much rubber tubing was eliminated. These changes simplified the suit and valve, and reduced the weight of the suit to 4.5 pounds and the valve to 4 pounds.

On the Mayo centrifuge, with suit pressures of 1.25 psi per G, average visual protection was 1.4 G. On the Aero Medical Laboratory centrifuge with suit pressures of 1 psi per G, average visual protection was also 1.4 G. This was similar to the protection provided by the G-1 suit. The Type G-2 suit was given service trials at Eglin Field in February 1944, and was approved to replace the G-1 suit by the AAF Proving Ground Command and subsequently by the AAF Board. It was officially standardized for AAF use on June 19, 1944, but because of the fast-moving developments in G-suit design and testing, the G-

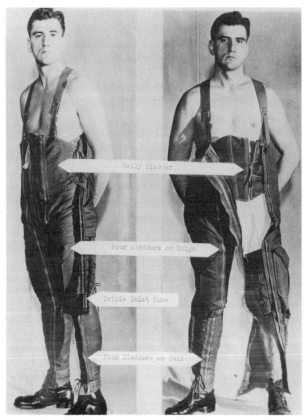

The Type G-1 anti-G suit, the first type of anti-blackout suit used by the AAF in the summer of 1944. It was a wrap-around, overalls style, three-pressure design, and proved to be too heavy, bulky, and uncomfortable. Its accessories were also too complicated for regular service use. Photo at right shows the wide inner "belt" that applied pressure to the abdomen under G-forces. (Courtesy USAF)

called, was worn over regulation clothing, and its wrap-around style was especially apropos, because the wearer's feet were frequently very muddy, and a step-through design would have made it essential for AAF pilots to remove their boots if clothing was to be kept reasonably clean. When the nonoperational tests were completed, the Eighth Air Force ordered 1,000 G-1 suits for combat use. Five hundred were delivered, before the G-1 suit and accessories were replaced by the simpler Type G-2 suit and valve in the summer of 1944.

The U.S. Navy Bureau of Aeronautics, after rejecting the Ferwerda Pulsatile Suit, concentrated on development of the GPS, or Moeller-Carson Suit. After some modifications, the Navy GPS was used with success by VF-8, flying F6F-3 fighters from the carrier "Bunker Hill," in the Pacific during late March 1944. Several victories over Japanese "Zeke" fighters, were attributed solely to the ad-

156

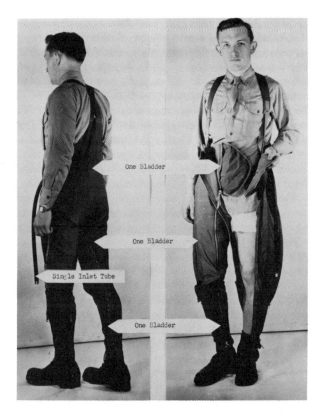

The Type G-2 anti-G suit, a simplified and much improved single-pressure design, standardized on June 19, 1944. As in its predecessor, the bladders in the G-2 suit were inflated automatically, when centrifugal force during maneuvers raised the flyer's weight to 2.5 times the normal pull of gravity. Pressure against the abdomen, thighs, and calves was regulated to keep blood from pooling in the lower extremities, helping the heart maintain circulation of blood to the brain during pullouts and turns. (Courtesy USAF)

2 was changed to substitute standard on August 14, 1944, when the improved Type G-3 suit was standardized. The G-2 suit was declared limited standard on May 21, 1945, and obsolete on April 10, 1946. The Type G-1 suit was declared obsolete on May 21, 1945.[22]

Some 3,500 Type G-2 suits were sent to the Eighth and Ninth Air Forces and saw combat use over Europe. Four suits and valves were furnished to the RAF in the summer of 1944, for tests at the Royal Aircraft Establishment, Farnborough, and one outfit was sent to the Fleet Air Arm of the Royal Navy. The G-2 suit, though an improvement over the Type G-1, remained hotter, bulkier, and heavier than was desirable. Other complaints were that the fly was too small and that there were no pockets. Further attention to simplicity, coolness, and weight was clearly required.[23]

In January 1944, David Clark of the David Clark Company, and Dr. E. H. Wood of the Mayo Aero Medical Unit, introduced the use of a single-piece bladder system, made of vinylite-coated nylon cloth, to replace the older system of five separate bladders of rubber or synthetic rubber joined by rubber tubing. Development of this single-piece bladder system with spring inserts, proved to be an important advance in the construction of anti-G suits, and was subsequently adopted for all G-suits to be used by the Army Air Forces and the U.S. Navy, whether the bladders were made of coated cloth or rubber substitutes.

Twelve initial models of the single-piece nylon bladder system, single pressure suit, were made, differing in minor details for comparative testing. Average visual protection as measured in centrifuge tests at the Mayo Unit was 1.9 G. This type of Clark nylon-bladder suit, was the lineal antecedent of the coverall type of suit used later by the U.S. Navy.[24]

Simplification, lighter weight, and coolness were the most pressing needs in G-suit development. The Mayo group had pointed out that the simple, single-unit, pneumatic bladder system, first made by Clark, if incorporated into any supporting garment providing reasonable fit and relative inelasticity, might offer adequate G protection. Two types of G-suits evolved, in which the functional parts of the G-2 suit were incorporated. One was a skeleton, or cutaway, suit consisting only of the supporting elements required by the bladder system, and the other was a coverall patterned after the standard summer flying suit. The cutaway suit was designed for wear with other clothing, and the coverall was to be used alone as a flying suit. They ultimately led to the standardization by the AAF of two types of anti-G suits, which were designated as the Types G-3 and G-4, respectively. All previous experience in the Eighth and Ninth Air Forces had shown that Army pilots preferred to fly combat missions in standard uniforms and flying clothing, which would be adequate and comfortable in case of long periods of imprisonment. This preference led to the Type G-3 cutaway suit, which was designed for use with other clothing, being selected for routine AAF use.

The AAF Type G-3 was a wrap-around, cutaway, single-pressure garment. It was waist to ankle in length, and pressurized the same areas of the body as the Type G-2 suit, but covered only those regions that were actually pressurized: abdomen, thighs, and calves. The crotch and the knee areas were cut away, and pockets were provided just above the ankles. The G-3 suit overcame practically all of the complaints about discomfort registered against the G-2 suit. The first model of the G-3 to go into production, was made by the Berger Brothers Company using rubber bladders. The David Clark Company model used vinylite-coated nylon. Both models were similarly effec-

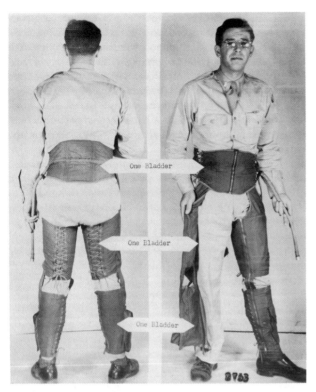

The Type G-3 anti-G suit was a cutaway, single-pressure garment that was much cooler and lighter than the G-2 suit. It used the functional parts of the G-2 and pressurized the same areas of the body, but covered only those regions actually pressurized. Like other G-suits, it was worn over uniform trousers and under flying clothing, or next to the skin under a summer flying suit. Lacings were adjusted to fit, and the suit zipped on and off. (Courtesy USAF)

tive, used the G-2 quick-disconnect developed by the Berger Brothers Company, had lacing adjustments for fitting, and were made in four sizes. The airplane-installation components were the same as used with the G-2 suit, and completely interchangeable.

An evaluation by the AAF Proving Ground Command during June and July 1944, determined that the Clark suit, with minor revisions, was superior to the Berger Brothers' suit, and recommended that the Clark suit be produced and the Berger Brothers' type discontinued.[25]

The Type G-3 suit was standardized on August 14, 1944, changed to substitute standard on March 10, 1945, and limited standard on May 21, 1945. During the second half of 1944, 4,100 G-3 suits were delivered to the Eighth, Ninth, and Twelfth Air Forces. The first production G-3 suits arrived in the Eighth Air Force in mid-October.

In November 1944, the anti-G suit was officially accepted for use throughout the Army Air Forces as standard

equipment, to be issued on the basis of one suit for each fighter pilot.[26]

Combat reports concerning the use of the G-suits were carefully evaluated, and development of the AAF cutaway anti-G suit continued. An improved model was quickly introduced, which differed in some details from the earlier Type G-3 suits. Designated as the Type G-3A, it was essentially a modification of the Clark G-3 suit, in that it utilized a single-piece neoprene bladder system with spring insert, had no tubing across the back, and carried the zipper that closed the abdominal belt section on the right side. The bladders were removable and interchangeable with other types, and a different quick-disconnect was employed. The use of airplane cloth, a closely woven fabric, in G-suit construction had resulted in a few instances of tearing in ordinary usage. In the Type G-3A suit, olive-drab basket-weave nylon cloth was used to form the outer garment, whereas oxford-weave cloth, chosen because it had less tendency for slippage at the seams, was used for the envelope immediately surrounding the bladder system.

Centrifuge tests at the Aero Medical Laboratory involving radial acceleration, where the suit was pressurized at 1.0 psi per G on a scale that assumed pressure rise to begin at 0 G, indicated that the average visual protection was 1.1 G. The corresponding figure from the Mayo centrifuge tests was 1.2 G.

The Type G-3A suit, like its predecessors, was made in four sizes: large long, large short, small long, and small short. Laces over the calves, thighs, and flanks provided further adjustment of size. The complete G-3A suit weighed 3.25 pounds, compared to 2.75 pounds for the Berger G-3 suit and 2.25 pounds for the Clark G-3 suit. The suit was eventually provided with a rubber plug and mouth inflation-valve device, which was attached by a cord to the clamp at the male disconnect fitting. This allowed a pilot forced down over water to use the anti-G suit as an aid to the "Mae West" life vest for flotation.[27]

The Type G-3A anti-G suit was officially standardized on March 10, 1945, and was mass-produced. It was used with success for several years after the end of World War II.

The U.S. Navy chose the one-piece coverall type of anti-G suit, and standardized a model made by the David Clark Company as the Type Z-1. It had to be cool to wear for operations in tropical areas, but protection against sunburn and insect bites was also necessary. This suit was also adopted for limited use by the Army Air Forces as the Type G-4.[28]

The Type G-4 (Navy Z-1) suit was a step-through coverall of light, inelastic, porous rayon, closed by one abdominal and two leg zippers. It was patterned after the regular summer flying suit and provided full coverage of

158 the arms, trunk, and legs. The legs, which had to fit more closely than those of an ordinary flying suit, were closed by zippers when the suit was donned. The abdominal and leg sections incorporated a single-piece vinylite-coated nylon bladder system, of the type used in the Clark Type G-3 suit. The suits were furnished in nine sizes, and, for reasons of simplicity and appearance, no lacing adjustments were provided.[29] Because of the lack of lacing, the G-4 suit had to be reevaluated by the AAF, even though the functional parts were identical to those of the G-3 suit. Testing was conducted under contract during 1944 and 1945 on both the Mayo centrifuge, under the supervision of Dr. E. H. Lambert, and the centrifuge of the Aeromed-

ical Laboratories of the University of Southern California at Los Angeles, under the direction of Dr. James P. Henry.[30]

The Type G-4 suit was largely satisfactory, but provided slightly less protection than the G-3A, because of the lack of interlacing adjustments. Improved models were developed after the war, and designated as the Types G-4A and G-4B.[31] Both were used by the U.S. Air Force during the Korean War. The U.S. Navy developed the improved Z-2 coverall suit in the spring of 1945, as well as a cutaway version similar to the AAF Type G-3A, which was designated as the Type Z-3. The Z-3 suit entered service with the Navy and Marine Corps in the summer of 1945, and both the Z-2 and Z-3 suits saw many years of service.

One final type of anti-G garment must be mentioned: the Lamport Pneumatic Lever Suit. This unique design was developed by Dr. Harold Lamport, MD, in cooperation with Drs. E. C. Hoff and L. P. Herrington at the John B. Pierce Foundation, Yale University, in conjunction with the Pioneer Products Division of the General Electric Company. It differed from the other pneumodynamic anti-G suits in that the air cells, instead of being contained in the fabric covering the parts of the body to be pressurized, were contained in separate envelopes laid next to these parts. Inflation of these bladders applied no direct pressure to the body, but pressurized the contiguous parts by tightening the surrounding suit fabric. The tightening was accomplished by the use of interlocking tapes connecting the bladder envelopes to the main part of the suit. During inflation of the bladders, tension in these tapes was transmitted to the main suit by the capstan principle, causing the suit to tighten around the body. The latest design of this type, the Model L-12, developed late in the war, offered slightly higher protection than the Types G-3 and Z-2 suits. However, the L-12 suit needed higher pressures to operate than other types of G-suits and would have required more powerful vacuum-instrument pumps to be installed in all aircraft.

The Lamport Pneumatic Lever Suit was tested but not adopted for use by the Army Air Forces. It is important, nevertheless, because the pneumatic lever principles was utilized by Dr. James P. Henry and his associates at the University of Southern California in developing the partial pressure suit, which was so vital to the postwar U.S. Air Force and Navy for use in jet and rocket-powered aircraft flying at very high altitudes.[32]

Sources of Air Pressure for Pneumatic Anti-G Garments

Air stored under pressure in tanks was often used to pressurize anti-G garments during experimental testing on centrifuges. This method was not practical for routine usage in service aircraft because tanks required space for installation, added weight to the airplane, and required a

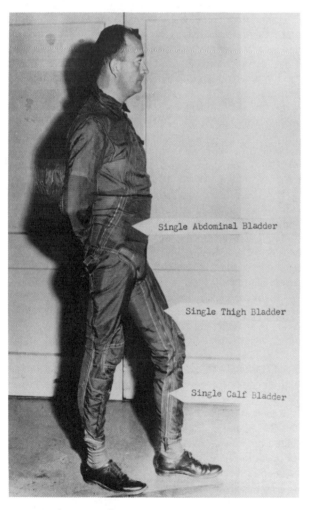

Single Abdominal Bladder

Single Thigh Bladder

Single Calf Bladder

The Type G-4 anti-G suit was actually a lightweight, one-piece summer flying suit, incorporating encased bladders of the type used in the Clark Type G-3 suit. It was supplied to the AAF late in World War II for use in tropical areas. The G-4 was almost identical to the U.S. Navy Type Z-1 suit, and improved models of both saw service during the Korean War. (Courtesy USAF)

leak-proof valve. The vacuum-instrument pump was used by both the AAF and Navy, as the standard source of air supply for anti-G suits in conventional fighters and dive bombers. Two types were used in fighter aircraft; the smaller type was the AAF Type B-11 (Navy B-2), and the larger was the Type B-12 (Navy B-3).

A three-pressure valve known as the G-1 was designed by the Berger Brothers Company for control of the three-pressure Type G-1 anti-G suit. It weighed 6.25 pounds, was 11 inches long, and quite complicated. The discovery that single-pressure suits were as effective as suits with multiple pressures rendered the G-1 valve and its accouterments obsolete.

Early in 1944, when the AAF changed from the triple-pressure Type G-1 suit to the single-pressure G-2 suit, a valve was needed to pressurize the anti-G suit at a single pressure of one psi per G, and adequately pressurize the aircraft auxiliary fuel tanks as well. The G-2 valve, which consisted of two connecting valve units, the control valve and the pressure-regulating valve, was designed quickly by the Berger Brothers Company to serve these purposes. It was slightly modified and standardized as the AAF Type M-2 valve.

Pressurization of the G-suit was controlled by the M-2 valve, which was itself activated by positive G. The valve caused no inflation in level flight, but at 2.75 G it began to supply air to the suit. To use the anti-G suit, the pilot needed only to plug in the tube attached to his suit to its mate in the aircraft cockpit. Operation was then automatic.

The pressure source was the positive side of the vacuum instrument pump, designed primarily to provide suction to power the gyroscopic flight instruments. Originally its output was waste, but this source was utilized to run deicer boots in aircraft other than fighters, to pressurize jettisonable fuel tanks on P-47 and P-51 aircraft, to prevent vapor lock, and also to operate the anti-G suits. The pressure output was metered to the suit in accordance with the amount of force applied, at a rate between 0.5 and 1.0 pound per G. This meant that at 5 G the suit was pressurized to the extent of 2.5 to 5.0 pounds. The broad range may be surprising; it was based on the fact that the exact pressure required to obtain adequate protection was not critical. The valve which metered the pressure (Type M-2) was entirely mechanical, weighed only 1.5 pounds, and had a special port for pressurizing jettisonable gasoline tanks, if needed. All the material added to the aircraft weighed less than 5 pounds, and once installed, the system required virtually no maintenance.[33] A new valve, the Type M-4, utilizing the compressor discharge of the jet engine, was produced for use with the Lockheed P-80 fighter.

Another valve used to a limited extent by the AAF was the Clark-Cornelius, which became the standard type used by the U.S. Navy. The CC-1 valve was designed by Richard

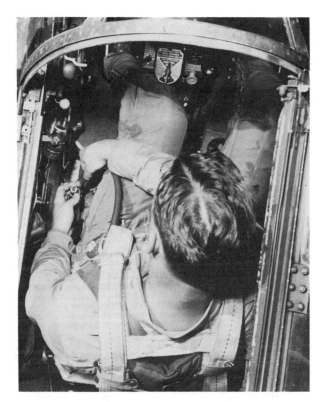

An AAF fighter pilot in the cockpit of a P-51C, attaching the hose from the Type G-2 anti-G suit to the vacuum-instrument pump exhaust outlet. Air was metered to the suit by the M-2 valve, at a pressure rate of approximately 1 psi per G. Once plugged in, all operation was automatic. Air was forced in and let out of the suit bladders by valve action, as G-forces varied during maneuvers. The G-2 suit allowed freedom of movement and did not interfere with the parachute (here the Type S-1 or AN6510 seat type). The suit weighed only 4.5 pounds, and could be worn inside or outside clothing. (Courtesy USAF)

Cornelius of the Cornelius Company, Minneapolis, Minnesota, and modified and manufactured by the David Clark Company. Like other valves, it was designed to receive air from a pump, to pressurize the G-suit during increased positive G, and to pressurize the auxiliary fuel-tank system when this function was required. The Clark-Cornelius valve was also modified for use with jet aircraft.

The Effectiveness of Anti-G Garments

Several studies were made late in the war of the performance of the anti-G suit to determine if its use encouraged pilots to overstress the aircraft. It was sometimes stated that the onset of visual symptoms caused by positive G served as a warning that dangerously high

A P-51C fighter pilot, inspecting the M-2 valve and fittings for inflating the Type G-2 anti-G suit by pressure supplied by the positive pressure side of the vacuum-instrument pump. Weighted valves automatically pressurized the suit bladders under G, at the rate of 0.5 to 1.0 pound per G. (Courtesy USAF)

G-levels were being reached. It was believed that prevention of these symptoms would remove the warning signal, and might increase the likelihood of overloading and structural failure.

In practice, it was found that some pilots considered increasing G-suit pressure itself a useful warning signal of high G-levels. Although the results of the studies varied, the general conclusions indicated that fighter pilots in combat, both with and without G-suits, occasionally exposed themselves and their airplanes to 8 or 9 Gs, values above permissible limits for some aircraft. However, because of its immense value in combat, few questioned the G-suit's usefulness. The increase in the magnitude of relatively prolonged positive G pilots could tolerate with clear vision and mental processes, and the reduction in that type of fatigue resulting from frequent exposures to positive G, was amply demonstrated. The anti-G suit offered a worthwhile safeguard on any combat mission; however, evidence indicated that its greatest usefulness was on missions in which encounters with enemy aircraft occurred, with consequent aerobatics.[34] This was especially true of fighter units of the Eighth and Ninth Air Forces flying over Germany. 1st Lt. William Krauss, a member of a successful P-51 fighter group, was interviewed after a mission during which he destroyed two German aircraft. He was quoted as saying: "I'm damned if I would fly without my G-suit. I had to go through a lot of turns that once would have blacked hell out of me, but the G-suit kept my head clear all the way."[35]

The Twelfth and Fifteenth Air Forces were in the Mediterranean theater of operations (MTO) in the fall of 1944, where there was little contact with enemy aircraft and anti-G equipment was not so essential. It was still desired for fighter pilots, especially for long-range missions.[36]

The Far East Air Force (FEAF), as well as the Southwest Pacific Area (SWPA) forces, reported that there was ". . . no present need for anti-G suits because . . . fighter pilots do not engage the enemy in 'dog fights,' but rely on numerical superiority (when feasible) and one 'pass and run.' Low level strafing and dive bombing missions are frequent, but as practiced in FEAF, do not involve G maneuvers of sufficient magnitude to cause undesirable symptoms."[37] A few pilots of the VII Fighter Command wore the Type G-3 anti-G suit, while flying P-51D aircraft from Iwo Jima on long escort missions over Japan. Pilots were concerned about heavy aircraft loading while over the target area, and refrained from engaging in dogfights. Personnel of this organization had not heard of the reports from pilots in other areas that activation of the G-suit reduced the fatigue, numbness, and discomfort of the lower extremities experienced on long escort missions. It was recommended that increased emphasis should be placed by the Air Technical Service Command on improving and demonstrating the anti-fatigue qualities of the anti-G suit, and it was suggested by the VII Fighter Command that the G-valve be modified so that it could be manually activated.[38]

The air forces of all major powers began using pneumatic anti-G garments as standard equipment soon after the end of the war. Fighter pilots of the Soviet Air Force used an almost exact copy of the AAF Type G-3A garment for many years.

Development of effective anti-G garments during wartime required the combined efforts of members of the U.S. Army Air Forces, U.S. Navy, British Royal Air Force, Royal Canadian Air Force, and Royal Australian Air Force. Technical specialists and scientists from several government agencies, universities, medical institutions, and private industry also contributed to the successful introduction of these important items of personal flying equipment.

The evolution of anti-G equipment from a heavy, restricting suit to a light, practical garment, together with development of associated pressure-regulating valves and accessories, posed a formidable challenge. The anti-G equipment finally mass-produced, enhanced the efficiency of combat airmen and played a role in the admirable record achieved by American air forces in World War II and subsequent conflicts.

PRESSURE SUITS

Running concurrently with the development of the G-suit was a classified project to develop an aeronautical full pressure suit to provide protection at extremely high altitudes. The pressure-suit program did not result in the production of a practical suit by 1945; however, the extensive knowledge gained from wartime research on this equipment formed the basis for the successful postwar development of the full pressure suit, and eventually the space suit. The immediate requirements for high-altitude protection were satisfied by the introduction of the emergency partial pressure suit, also based on wartime research.

The impetus behind the Army Air Forces pressure-suit program was the realization, early in the war, that the crews of the new jet and rocket-propelled aircraft, then on the drawing boards, would require either pressurized cabins or pressure suits to sustain life at the great altitudes these planes would be capable of achieving. A pressure suit was considered necessary for use in a high-altitude aircraft without a pressurized cabin, and as a backup system in a pressurized plane, in case of the loss of cabin pressure above 43,000 feet resulting in "explosive decompression." The full pressure suit itself was essentially a small, flexible, form-fitting pressurized enclosure. It would allow an airman to survive on the fringe of space by taking along his own artificial environment. The suit was internally pressurized by air, to achieve a higher pressure upon the body than that present at high altitude, effectively simulating for the wearer conditions at lower altitude.

Adequate protection against anoxia was afforded by conventional oxygen equipment between 10,000 and about 38,000 feet. Protection up to, and somewhat over, 40,000 feet could be provided by pressure-breathing oxygen equipment. At altitudes above 50,000 feet, however, where the air pressure is only 11 percent of that at sea level, the amount of pressure needed to "push" oxygen into the lungs became so great that circulation through the lungs and heart was impeded, and forcing breath out against the pressure was extremely tiring. While performing research on aeroembolism during the 1930s, Capt. Harry G. Armstrong of the Aero Medical Laboratory at Wright Field, discovered that unless body fluids are adequately protected in a sealed, pressurized suit or cabin, they will vaporize at 63,000 feet.[39] This altitude became known as the "Armstrong Line." He learned that in the near-vacuum found at 63,000 feet and above, the normal temperature of a man's body was high enough to cause water to boil, and since the human body was approximately 70 percent water, blood would soon vaporize or "boil." The body gases, responding to the low pressure outside the body, would produce large bubbles which would block circulation, the body would swell, and in ten seconds the pilot would be dead.[40]

Airmen and engineers were not suddenly and unexpectedly confronted by these altitude barriers. The problems of high-altitude flight, and the concept of the protective pressure suit and pressure cabin, had been discussed for many years before World War II, but the

development of appropriate equipment was hindered by a lack of funds and the technological state of the art.

Early Experimental Pressure Suits

It is difficult to determine exactly who was the first person to originate the idea of the aeronautical pressure suit. Fred M. Sample, an American inventor, was granted what is probably the first United States patent for a full pressure suit on July 16, 1918. His patent, number 1,272,537, covers a "suit for aviators" made of fabric and pressurized through the metal helmet by a hose connected to an air compressor. Under the outer coveralls was an inflatable bladder to be worn around the wearer's waist for counterpressure against acceleration effects. As far as is known, this very imaginative but impractical design was never constructed or tested.

One of the first people to seriously consider the pressure suit was Professor John Scott Haldane, an English respiratory physiologist, who developed a method of staged decompression in 1907, which made it possible for deep-sea divers to rise safely to the surface. In 1911, he led an expedition to Pikes Peak, Colorado, where he studied the effects of low barometric pressure, and it was at about this time that Haldane proposed the use of an oxygen-pressure suit for ascent to high altitudes in a balloon. At the beginning of World War I, he became fully occupied with the development of oxygen equipment, including an improved oxygen mask. Haldane clearly described his proposed "stratosphere flying suit" in 1920, and refined the concept in conjunction with Dr. J. G. Priestley in 1922. However, it was not until 1933 that construction began on an actual suit.

Professor Haldane and the British diving suit specialist, Sir Robert H. Davis, collaborated in designing a pressure suit, actually a modified diving suit, for Mark Ridge, an American balloonist. Ridge wanted the suit so that he could ascend to a record altitude in an open balloon basket, but his plans for a balloon flight into the stratosphere never materialized. The suit was fabricated in England by the firm of Siebe, Gorman and Company, manufacturers of diving suits, oxygen apparatus, and other technical equipment. Ridge wore the bulky suit during several tests in a low-pressure chamber and in the last test, on November 29, 1933, he attained a simulated altitude of 86,000 feet (17 mm of mercury) for 30 minutes.[41] These were the world's first tests in which a human was successfully protected in a pressure suit at a simulated low barometric pressure, and the experiments stimulated the interest of Group Captain G. Struan Marshall and other Royal Air Force altitude experts.

Other inventors and researchers were considering designs for pressurized suits, which would permit flyers to ascend to the great altitudes possible with the new aircraft powered by supercharged engines. A "stratosphere flying suit" was designed by Cecil F. De Lasaux of Milwaukee, Wisconsin, who filed a United States patent application on November 28, 1932. Patent number 1,991,601 was granted on February 19, 1935, covering the suit, its unique fastening devices, and the compressor and air-supply system.[42] There is no record of this primitive pressure suit ever being built or tested.

Also during the early 1930s, Wiley Post, famed American round-the-world flyer, was planning the design of a pressure suit for high-altitude flying in his Lockheed Vega, the *Winnie Mae.* He wanted to enter the MacRobertson England-to-Australia air race, to be held in October 1934, in the aging *Winnie Mae,* and believed that the use of such a suit would afford him the advantages of flying at very high altitudes. The suit would also be used during a planned attempt to break the world-altitude record. Post knew that it was impossible to pressurize the *Winnie Mae* because of the plywood construction, and complications attendant on building a pressurized cockpit were so great that it made that idea impractical. Post proposed instead to pressurize himself through the use of a special suit, an objective that would open the way to a new realm of high-speed flight above the inclement weather, and thus be of great benefit to future military and commercial operations.[43]

There is still some question as to whether Post conceived the idea of a high-altitude pressure suit independently. It is possible that Wiley or one of his many friends read about the Haldane-Davis pressure suit experiments in a British aeronautical magazine. When Ernest H. Shultz, Post's mechanic on the *Winnie Mae,* was recently questioned on this point, he stated:

> I do not believe that Wiley Post knew of any other pressure suit when he was planning his. He originally based his idea on that of the deep-sea diving suit. No electrical or other type of heating was used in the air-tight suit. Wiley found that his own body produced enough heat inside the suit to keep him warm.[44]

A similar reply was received from Russell S. Colley, retired B. F. Goodrich Company engineer, who built the second and third full pressure suits for Wiley Post:

> I can say positively that he (Post) never mentioned the English suit to me at any time during our very close relationship at my home or at the Goodrich plant. I am sure it was his idea to pressurize the entire body.[45]

After preparing the initial design for his pressurized suit, Post visited the Pacific branch of the B. F. Goodrich Company in Los Angeles on April 6, 1934, and requested the firm to build it. Under the supervision of William R. Hucks, project engineer, and John A. Diehl, his assistant, a two-piece pressure suit of double-ply rubberized parachute fabric was constructed, with built-in pigskin gloves and rubber boots. The cost was estimated at $75. The aluminum helmet included earphones and a double-layer plastic visor, to reduce the chance of faceplate fogging in the low temperatures at high altitude. The suit would be pressurized in flight by the aircraft-accessory supercharger, and oxygen would be obtained from a liquid oxygen vaporizer. After successful static tests with an air compressor at the factory, Post went to Wright Field, Ohio, in June 1934, and arranged for testing in the low-pressure and temperature chamber at the Engineering Section of the Air Corps Materiel Division. The empty suit ballooned and failed to hold pressure during initial chamber tests when pressurized to a differential of 2 pounds psi.[46]

A new two-piece suit was immediately constructed at the Goodrich factory in Akron, Ohio, under the supervision of Post and Russell S. Colley, the Goodrich project manager. The original helmet was used, with modifications, and the new suit incorporated several important improvements; it was less rigid when inflated, and included newly conceived elbow- and knee-ring joints to allow better limb movement. Post, who had gained a few pounds since being measured, tried on the tight-fitting suit on a hot, humid July day, and became firmly stuck in it. He finally had to be cut out and the suit was ruined in the process.

Much had already been learned about pressure-suit design and it was decided, after consultation with the Materiel Division engineers at Wright Field, that an entirely new suit and helmet should be produced. Post and Colley fabricated a new suit, intended for use in the sitting position, with arms fashioned so that the wearer could reach the stick and throttle when the suit was pressurized. Movable joints were not incorporated, although limited leg movement for rudder-pedal operation was obtained by bunching the material between metal ring joints, located above and below the knees. The suit was pressurized by using oxygen from a 5-liter, high-pressure liquid oxygen vaporizer carried in the cockpit. The vaporizer was provided by the Materiel Division at Wright Field.

This third pressure suit, completed late in August, consisted of an inner rubber "bag" that would contain the gaseous oxygen under pressure, and an outer, three-ply cloth suit, made to resist stretching and to hold the rubber suit to Post's body contours. The suit was designed to be entered feet-first through a large neck opening, instead of at the waist. It was planned to have a capability of holding an internal pressure of 7 psi, which was 2 pounds more than the previous two suits. An outlet just below the left knee was attached to a regulator and pressure gauge, to allow control of the oxygen outflow from the suit and also permit control of the suit pressure.

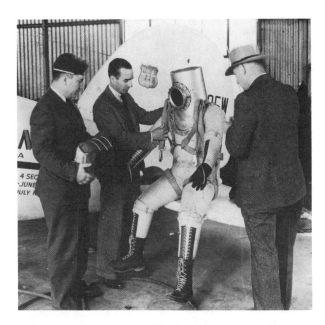

Wiley Post (left), holding his chest parachute during examination of the third pressure suit, the first to be used in actual flight. This photo from December 1934 shows William Parker, close friend and aviation director for Post's sponsor, the Phillips Petroleum Company, adjusting the parachute straps on the inflated suit. Man at right is believed to be a technical representative from the B. F. Goodrich Company, builders of the suit. The air hose used to inflate the suit can be seen on the floor, and plugs are seen in the oxygen-intake tube by the left side of the faceplate and in the left-leg outlet just below the knee of the suit. (SI Photo A47509)

The new aluminum helmet, which was the second to be constructed, was bolted in place with wing nuts after Post entered the suit. It had a removable, round, safety-glass visor that was relatively small since Post had sight in only one eye. Oxygen was directed across the window, to prevent fogging by breath moisture that might collect on the glass. Earphones were installed and a throat microphone could be accommodated. This second helmet had a tendency to rise, as did the first helmet, because of increasing internal gas pressure in the suit as the outside pressure fell. Helmet tie-down was effected by bandolier-type cords looped around the helmet and attached to a semi-rigid eight-inch wide belt upon which Post sat. Without the tie-down, the helmet rose and gave Post the sensation of "going down in the sewer."[47]

Following static tests and some additional refinements, the suit was taken from the Goodrich factory to Wright Field, where Post donned it over long-john underwear and, on August 27, 1934, made the first altitude-chamber test of an aeronautical pressure suit in the United States.[48]

The results of the low-pressure chamber tests were kept confidential by the Air Corps at the request of Wiley Post.[49] Great publicity was given to the pressure suits and their use in high-altitude flight, but the role played by the engineers at Wright Field was not made public until after the test reports were finally declassified on March 14, 1956. The long-forgotten reports were discovered by T. W. Walker of the Thermix Corporation, while he was researching at Wright-Patterson Air Force Base for an article on early pressure-suit development.[50]

As soon as the low-pressure chamber tests were completed, Post took the suit to the Akron Municipal Airport and made a test flight in the *Winnie Mae.* This flight at the end of August is believed to be the first time anyone had ever flown in an airplane while wearing a pressure suit.[51] He reported on September 5 that he had achieved an altitude of 40,000 feet over Chicago, and on a later flight, he set a record from Burbank to Cleveland while flying in the jet stream.

During the next few months, Post made at least ten documented flights in this third and final model of his pressure suit. He attempted unsuccessfully on several occasions to break the official world-altitude record of 47,360 feet, set by Commendatore Renato Donati of the Italian Air Force on April 11, 1934, while breathing only pure oxygen. Post was credited by the press with establishing a new world altitude record of 50,000 feet on December 7, 1935, but this could not be confirmed by the U.S. National Bureau of Standards, because of a malfunction of one of the two required National Aeronautic Association barographs. He was also unable to enter the London-to-Melbourne air race in the *Winnie Mae,* because of damage to the Wasp engine's supercharger and the need for modifications to the aircraft. Despite these disappointments, Post proved not only that the pressure suit concept was practical, but also that airspeed could be greatly increased by flying at high altitude.

Wiley Post was killed, along with Will Rogers, in the tragic crash of his new airplane while taking off near Point Barrow, Alaska, on August 15, 1935.

Wiley Post's death ended pressure-suit development in the United States for the next four years. No further experimental work on pressure suits was conducted by the Air Corps at that time, despite the interest shown at the Materiel Division in the innovative suit and its potential for use in high-altitude flying.[52] Work did continue on the development of the pressurized aircraft cabin. The Engineering Section of the Materiel Division at Wright Field was just in the process of establishing the Physiological Research Laboratory in 1935, and no funds were available for research on any flying equipment not considered absolutely essential. In view of the many deficiencies in equipment, disclosed as a result of the Air Corps deplorable performance while flying the airmail the previous

164

year, the limited resources of the Equipment Branch were directed toward the development of improved winter flying clothing, efficient oxygen equipment, and other badly needed items of flight materiel.

The course of action followed by the major European governments was in direct contrast to that of the United States. Despite the depression, England, France, and Italy engaged in a spirited competition between 1932 and 1938 to set world-altitude records. In addition to the prestige and propaganda value to be gained by establishing new records, the work involved gave a boost to the aviation industry, as well as having potential benefits for each nation's rearmament program. Pilots achieved new altitude records, initially while using conventional oxygen equipment. However, it was obvious by 1934 that flying at altitudes well over 40,000 feet stretched man's physiological performance beyond safe limits, and some innovative equipment or techniques would be required if significant progress was to be made. To accomplish this, several countries established programs to overcome the technical problems and develop improved aircraft, a pressurized aircraft cabin, or a high-altitude pressure suit.

The full pressure suits developed in Europe during the 1930s, reached about the same level of technical efficiency as the final Goodrich suit worn by Wiley Post. All encountered the same frustrating difficulties; they tended to balloon when pressurized, suffered from joint leakage and inflexibility, and were exhausting and uncomfortable to wear. In spite of their shortcomings, experimental pressure suits were worn by British and Italian flyers to set new altitude records almost every year.

The British regained the altitude record from Italy in 1936, when Sq. Ldr. F. R. D. Swain of the RAF reached 49,968 feet, while wearing a full pressure suit in a supercharged Bristol 138A monoplane.[53] His suit was an improved version of the Haldane-Davis outfit built for Mark Ridge in 1933, but rigidity and helmet fogging during descent almost resulted in a crash.

Lt. Col. Mario Pezzi of the Italian Air Force wore an experimental pressure suit during his record flight to 51,361 feet in 1937. The complicated suit obviously proved unsatisfactory, because his Caproni Ca 161 *bis* was modified to incorporate a crude pressurized cabin for his amazing climb to 56,032 feet on October 22, 1938. This official altitude record for piston-engine aircraft has never been broken.[54]

The French program to develop a full pressure suit and a pressurized aircraft cabin was backed by the Potez Airplane Company. Several suits were designed by Dr. M. Rosenstiel, with the assistance of the famous Dr. Paul Garsaux, but neither the suits, nor the pressurized cabin, were successful before the war ended all experiments.[55] Germany launched an ambitious research and development program in 1934, in order to make the Third Reich supreme in the air. The Germans forged ahead in many areas of advanced technology, including the successful development of the pressurized aircraft cabin. Despite years of effort by the Draegerwerke, however, they were unsuccessful in perfecting a practical pressure suit for use by the German Air Force.[56] The Soviet Union also initiated a secret program in late 1934, to produce a full pressure suit for wear in planned high-altitude aircraft. It appears that the Russians were unable to solve problems in suit design and efforts were discontinued during the war. The U.S.S.R. initiated a new program of high-altitude research and development, including the exploitation of foreign technology, in 1946.[57]

Army Air Forces Full Pressure Suit Program

The Materiel Division at Wright Field began research on pressure suits on October 10, 1939, in anticipation of the need for crew protection during flight at very high altitude.[58] The Aero Medical Laboratory, with its low-pressure (altitude) chamber and growing staff of specialists, became the focal point of research, within the Experimental Engineering Section, on the requirements for survival at great altitude. In addition to the full pressure suit-development project, the AML continued to assist in the refinement of the pressurized aircraft cabin. This work proceeded concurrently with projects to develop an anti-G garment, improved oxygen equipment, and many other items of personal equipment. Pressure suits and anti-G garments were originally included in the same program but followed separate lines of development during World War II.

Pressure-suit research and testing were supervised from September 1941 by Capt. (later Maj.) John G. Kearby of the Equipment Laboratory, and the classified program was given the code designation of Project MX-117. Three commercial companies were initially interested in working on high-altitude and anti-G suits: the United States Rubber Company of Mishawaka, Indiana, the Goodyear Tire and Rubber Company, and B. F. Goodrich Company of Akron, Ohio. Goodrich had made the pressure suits for Wiley Post in 1934, and was the only firm with any actual experience in building this type of equipment.[59]

On December 2, 1940, Maj. M. E. Gross, the Materiel Division Executive Officer, wrote to Dr. Vannever Bush, Chairman of the National Advisory Committee for Aeronautics (NACA), that "If the high altitude suit and the G-suit proved practicable, both types would be combined into one suit."[60] In his reply, Dr. Bush suggested appropriate action to promote a pressure suit-development program and offered the cooperation of NACA. The development of both types of protective devices increased in importance as a result of British air combat experience, gained in Europe during 1940 and 1941. The urgency was underlined by Maj. Gen. Henry H. Arnold, then Acting Deputy Chief of Staff, Air, in a memorandum of May 3, 1941, to Lt. Gen. George H. Brett, Chief of the Air Corps, in which Arnold stated that "It was absolutely essential that the United States be prepared to have engines and pilots ready and trained to go up to 37,000 feet without supercharged cabins until supercharged cabins or pressure suits were available."[61] Arnold attached a copy of a survey of high-altitude operations in England prepared by Maj. Harry Armstrong, then an American observer with the RAF.

The first full pressure suits were ordered from the U.S. Rubber Company and the B. F. Goodrich Company in November 1940. The suit made by the U.S. Rubber Company for only $500 was designed by Wright Field engineers. Testing in the AML altitude chamber disclosed numerous deficiencies, including excessive expansion, leakage, and discomfort. The most important problem encountered, and the one most difficult to correct, was the tendency of the suit to become rigid when pressurized, almost completely immobilizing the wearer. The tests of the Goodrich suit were more encouraging, but it was obvious that it too would require much improvement before it would approach even minimum performance requirements.

The optimistic expectations of the personnel of the Materiel Division and the contractors at that time are indicative of the lack of fundamental knowledge and understanding of the complexity and tremendous difficulty involved in developing a practical full pressure suit and anti-G garment.

As the center for pressure-suit testing, the Aero Medical Laboratory tried, as always, to identify the best features of each design and combine them to achieve a higher quality end product. Evaluating the feasibility of new concepts during that period involved considerable trial and error. After laboratory study and testing, including simulated flights to high altitude in the low-pressure chamber, promising designs were flight tested, mainly at the AAF Proving Ground at Eglin Field, Florida. Chamber testing was supervised during the war by Maj. Bruce Dill. The U.S. Navy had no immediate requirement for high-altitude suits, but was interested generally in their development. The Navy Bureau of Aeronautics sponsored research on full pressure suits and tested several during 1942 and 1943, including models supplied by the Army Air Forces, such as the Type XH-3, built by the Goodyear Tire and Rubber Company. In February 1942, the Materiel Division furnished an experimental full pressure suit and associated equipment to the RAF, for evaluation at the Royal Aircraft Establishment at Farnborough, England.

By the fall of 1941, several aircraft companies had joined the rubber companies in indicating an interest in developing pressure suits or components. The Bell Aircraft Corporation proposed developing a suit of their own design on contract, while the Boeing Aircraft Company suggested that a suit be produced, with the cost included in an existing B-17 bomber contract. These offers were accepted by the Materiel Division, and additional contracts were soon awarded for suits to be constructed by the U.S. Rubber Company, the B. F. Goodrich Company, and the Goodyear Tire and Rubber Company.

The year 1942 was a time of intense activity in full pressure suit design. Several contractors, universities, scientific foundations, and government agencies became involved in developing and testing suits, in conjunction with the work of the Materiel Center's Experimental Engineering Section and Aero Medical Laboratory. Many technical problems proved extremely difficult to resolve, but some were overcome. It was found, for example, that a pressure suit experienced excessive leakage if a zipper was used, because an ordinary zipper was not airtight and allowed the air, under pressure, to dissipate. Ward T. Van Orman, a Goodyear Company scientist, solved the problem in 1942 by inventing an airtight zipper.

Efforts were made by the Materiel Center to share development information among several industrial contractors and university research organizations striving to solve pressure-suit problems, but this cooperation never proved completely successful. Developments in rubber and fabric chemistry and their applications, as well as other work on pressure suit components, were often guarded jealously and protected from competitors under the cloak of proprietary interest. Military secrecy further restricted and delayed access to innovations. It is interesting to ponder the effects these restrictions and protectionist attitudes had on the development of pressure suits and the war effort in general.

A confidential report by the Engineering Division, covering research and development projects up to July 1, 1942, stated that eight types of experimental pressure suits had been procured and tested since October 1940. Five suits proved unsatisfactory, and work was continuing on the other three. It was still desired, at that time, to combine the features of the full pressure suit and the anti-G suit to provide a fighter pilot with full protection.

The report provided the following general description of the suits:

> The pressure suits are tight fitting crew suits of strong inelastic cloth which completely cover the aviator. Each suit is surmounted by a spherical headpiece of transparent plastic. A cloth helmet and a small oxygen mask are worn inside the plastic dome. These suits are designed to operate under a pressure of approximately 3.5 psi above ambient pressure which permits the wearer to fly at altitudes exceeding 35,000 feet.[62]

In other words, the AAF pressure suits were supposed to provide pressure upon the body so that respiratory and circulatory functions could continue normally, or nearly so, under the low-pressure conditions at high altitude.

The use of air instead of oxygen for suit pressurization proved to be not only more economical because of leakage around joints, but there was also less of a fire hazard. The administration of breathing oxygen through a mask was unnecessary during testing of a suit at ground level; however, oxygen and a mask were required when the suit was tested at low pressure in a chamber or in high-altitude flight.

Several types of experimental oxygen masks and regulators were produced for use with full pressure suits. The main types were oronasal demand-type masks which covered the nose and mouth, but nasal demand masks were also used with some suits. A clear plastic oronasal mask referred to as the A-6 is shown in a photo dated April 2, 1942, being worn by a man in a Goodrich Type 8-A suit. These special masks were reduced in size as much as possible so that they could be worn conveniently inside the Plexiglas "fishbowl" headpiece.

Testing and modification continued, but by the end of 1942, most of the experimental suits had proved inadequate. Development was then concentrated on improving the suits produced by Goodrich, Goodyear, and the U.S. Rubber Company. A series of high-altitude test flights were made by personnel of the Materiel Center and the AAF Proving Ground Command between October 1942 and

The Type MX-117 nasal-demand oxygen mask, being worn inside the Plexiglas dome of the Goodyear Type XH-3A full pressure suit. The compact design of the mask was intended to facilitate vision and movement of the head inside the dome. Use of oxygen and a mask was unnecessary during preliminary pressure testing of the suits at ground level, but was required when suits were tested at simulated or actual high altitudes. This photo was taken during flight testing of the XH-3A aboard a P-47 fighter at the AAF Proving Ground, Eglin Field, Florida, on December 23, 1942. (Courtesy USAF)

An oronasal demand-oxygen mask, designed specifically for wear inside the Plexiglas helmet of a full pressure suit. This photo dated September 2, 1943, shows the mask being worn with the Goodrich Type XH-5 suit prior to testing in the altitude chamber at the Aero Medical Laboratory. Note location of the oxygen hose on left side of mask. (Courtesy USAF)

February 1943. Most flights were made from Eglin Field, Florida, aboard B-17E and B17F bombers, with the airmen wearing pressure suits at various crew stations. Flights were also made in P-39 and P-47 fighter aircraft, to determine suit capabilities. The outfits tested were the Types XH-1, XH-2, XH-3, XH-3A, and X6-B.

The detailed test reports indicated that the suits were too heavy and restrictive when pressurized; a flyer's balance was affected so that movements were awkward and slow; and pilots found that the suits made them lose the "feel" of their aircraft. They were also uncomfortable to wear when pressurized and caused excessive fatigue. Ventilation was a vexing problem. The full pressure suit sealed in the wearer's body heat and moisture, often causing fogging of the Plexiglas helmet and extreme discomfort when the suit was worn for any length of time. The reports concluded that the suits were not satisfactory as presently designed, and further development was recommended.[63]

Description of the experimental full pressure suits produced by the various companies under wartime secrecy is difficult because of the number of types involved, and the fact that most models were modified several times in efforts to correct the deficiencies encountered during testing. Some of the suits encompassed rather novel approaches, which for various reasons proved unsatisfactory. Unfortunately, few of the suits and classified development and test reports have survived to document the program. The following pages summarize the main types of pressure suits produced by the principal firms involved during World War II.

United States Rubber Company

This well-known company fabricated the first of the several types and variations of experimental full pressure suits to reach the testing stage at the Aero Medical Laboratory. The first suit was designed by engineers of the Equipment Laboratory of the Materiel Division.[64] It was referred to as the Type A suit when ordered by the Materiel Division on November 20, 1940, at a cost of only $500. A Type G suit of similar design, but including a device intended to prevent blackout, was also ordered from the firm at a cost of $142. Delivery was estimated at thirty days and the suits arrived early in January 1941.

The Type A suit, later designated by the Materiel Division as the Type 1, was made of rubberized fabric with a lace-up front closure. It had a large Plexiglas helmet, weighed 80 pounds, and three men were required to dress the wearer in the suit. The suit was well-made and featured elaborate rubber accordian bellows at the elbows and knees to provide flexibility. It was apparently very difficult to move the fingers of the gloved hands when the suit was pressurized, so pressurized mittens and a claw-like steel, manipulating device were provided for alternate use during testing. The manipulating device with its movable clamp was a unique feature, but proved useless, because at 3 psi the suit became so rigid that the wearer could barely move. (3.5 psi were considered necessary to sustain human life at very high altitude.)[65]

The Type 1 (Type A) suit was deemed unsatisfactory because of its bulkiness, excessive leakage, and weight, as well as its rigidity when pressurized even at low levels. The Type G suit proved even less successful as an anti-G garment. Nevertheless, a purchase order in the amount of $4,352 was issued to the U.S. Rubber Company on February 18, 1941, to cover the cost of two modified high-altitude suits, designated as the Type 1-A. One Type 1-G acceleration suit was also ordered, but it again proved unsatisfactory and was discarded. When the Type 1-A suit was subjected to high pressure, the mid-section adjustment strap tore under load, and by August 1941, development was discontinued in favor of the new type of pressure suit designed and built by the B. F. Goodrich Company.

The U.S. Rubber Company continued pressure-suit development and produced improved suits, including the Type 2, which was similar to the Type 1-A. The main

The first AAF full pressure suit, during testing in the Aero Medical Laboratory on February 3, 1941. The Type 1, originally called the Type A, was designed by engineers of the Materiel Division's Equipment Laboratory and built by the U.S. Rubber Company. It was unique in having an optional manipulating device, which could be attached to the left forearm in place of the glove. Note the accordion-like bellows sections, built into the arms and legs to provide mobility. The entire suit became rigid when pressurized to 3 psi, and virtually immobilized the wearer. Rigidity remained the most intractable problem encountered with all subsequent full pressure suits, and was never fully resolved during World War II. (Courtesy USAF)

external differences were a zipper front closure and the use of rubber gloves on the Type 2, which utilized the same plastic dome-type helmet as the Types 1 and 1-A. These suits were also much too rigid when pressurized, and development was discontinued.

The Type 4 was a new kind of suit, produced late in 1941. It was an entirely different, and much less compli-

168

Full pressure suits in storage, after completion of testing at the Aero Medical Laboratory, Wright Field. This photograph, dated February 27, 1942, shows the Type 2 suit (left), with accordion-like bellows arm and leg sections, built by the U.S. Rubber Company. The suit has no helmet with it, and apparently used the same one as the original Type 1. The Goodrich Type 3 suit (center) was the first produced by that company for the AAF, and featured unique articulated-metal elbow joints. The Type 4 suit (right) was also built by the U.S. Rubber Company. (Courtesy USAF)

others, but utilized a larger Plexiglas helmet. It had detachable rubber gloves, and the lower legs and integral boots were removable at ring joints just above the knees. The pressurization air hose from the compressor attached to the left side of the abdomen in the usual manner. As with other suits, the hose conduit also contained the oxygen line and the wires for electricity and communication.

The Type XH-2 was among the improved suits flight-tested by Major Kearby and others aboard a B-17E at the

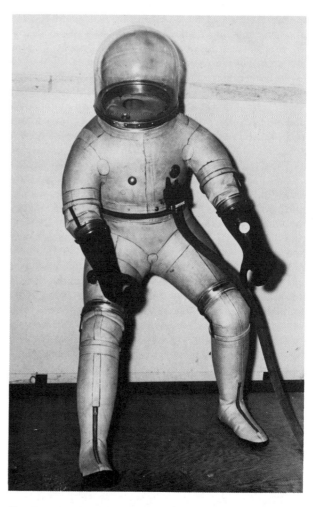

The Type XH-2 full pressure suit on October 1, 1942, during preliminary pressure testing of the empty suit at the Aero Medical Laboratory. The pressurization hose, oxygen tube, and communication wires were included in a single conduit, which attached to the left side of the abdomen with a quick-release device. An air-pressure gauge can be seen on the left wrist. This suit was the most advanced model produced by the U.S. Rubber Company, and was tested in flight by Maj. John G. Kearby aboard a B-17E at the AAF Proving Ground, Eglin Field, Florida. Like previous suits, the XH-2 proved to be too rigid and stiff when pressurized, and had inadequte ventilation. (SI Photo A4696)

cated, two-piece suit made of dark, rubberized fabric with an integral helmet of the same material built into the upper torso. This suit also failed to meet test objectives, and a promising modification, the Type 4-A, was soon introduced. Ten of the redesigned Type 4-A suits were ordered by the Materiel Division on January 20, 1942, at a cost of $25,000. After thorough evaluation by personnel of the Experimental Engineering Section and the Aero Medical Laboratory, development of this model was also terminated.

As a result of knowledge gained during the development program, a new two-piece model was produced, which was intended to overcome the shortcomings of the previous suits. Designated the Type XH-2, it was a considerable improvement over the earlier type built by U.S. Rubber. The XH-2 was made of rubberized fabric like the

AAF Proving Ground, Eglin Field, Florida, during October 1942.[66] Unfortunately, the suit was still too rigid and offered inadequate ventilation. This was the final type of suit produced by the U.S. Rubber Company, and although efforts to improve performance continued for a time, development was finally cancelled.

Boeing Aircraft Company

Several experimental one- and two-piece full pressure suits were designed, built, and tested for the Boeing Company by Prof. John D. Akerman of the University of Minnesota, based on his U.S. patent number 2,390,233, filed December 17, 1941. Drs. Walter M. Boothby, Arthur H. Bulbulian, and William R. Lovelace II were listed as co-inventors.[67] The work was financed by funds included in a B-17 bomber contract.

The first model was a lightweight, moderate pressure suit; the second was a two-piece garment made of Goodyear rubberized fabric with a double-layer jacket; while the third suit was built in one piece of single-layer material. The fourth and most advanced model was a two-piece, double-layer, close-fitting outfit, designed for a pressure differential of 1.5 psi. Professor Ackerman stressed the safety feature of the double-layer, which assured the continued functioning of one layer in case either the inner or outer layer ripped accidentally.[68] The Akerman-designed suits featured a tight-fitting fabric helmet and special oxygen mask with a breathing apparatus of complex design, utilizing either ". . . direct continuous flow or intermittent demand type flow."[69]

Several high-altitude and cold-chamber tests were conducted on these suits, and although each had some good features, none proved satisfactory. Experiments on the fourth type of suit continued, but after months of laboratory and flight testing, and numerous modifications, development was discontinued because of the familiar problems of rigidity and leakage, and the fact that the suit could not be pressurized to 3.5 psi.

Professor Akerman continued to design full pressure suits, while providing assistance to other manufacturers. He filed a patent, number 2,404,020, on another suit of his own design, on March 10, 1943. This patent covered a two-piece, two-ply suit with a large, cylindrical plastic helmet, utilizing a special oxygen mask designed by Dr. Walter M. Boothby.[70]

Bell Aircraft Corporation

Bell received a $12,695 contract from the Materiel Division on February 7, 1942, for the fabrication of one lightweight, two-piece, full pressure suit, for use in conjunction with the turbosupercharged Bell P-39D fighter. The suit was to be made of pressure-resistant material, and would be automatically regulated to maintain a pressure differ-

ential of approximately 1.25 psi between the atmosphere and the inside of the suit. The headgear would be an airtight, close-fitting helmet with built-in earphones, microphone, and oxygen mask. As originally designed, a "breathing bag" was incorporated in a light metal container, suspended from the helmet by means of two breathing tubes.

After considerable difficulty and delay, Bell engaged Prof. John D. Akerman, who had designed the Boeing suits, to assist the company in producing its outfit. The experimental Bell suit was referred to as the "BABM Type." The designation "BABM" may have been formed from the initials of the persons involved in the design of the Akerman suits and accessories: Boothby, Akerman and Bulbulian. The Type BABM-9 suit was eventually completed and subjected to altitude-chamber tests. The 18-pound suit was then flight-tested aboard a B-17 at the Boeing plant in Seattle, during July 1942, after which it was returned to Bell for a series of modifications. The BABM-9 suit was finally delivered to the Materiel Center in January 1943, at which time Bell, in an unusual move, voluntarily reduced the cost to $7,051.76.[71] After testing in the low-pressure chamber at the Aero Medical Laboratory disclosed serious inadequacies, development of the Bell suit was discontinued.

National Carbon Company

This firm, with a factory in Cleveland, Ohio, began working on an experimental full pressure suit during the months before Pearl Harbor. Although the company had no previous experience in pressure-garment design, a suit of multilayer, plastic-fabric construction was built under the direction of Dr. Walter M. Boothby of the Mayo Clinic, and the ubiquitous Prof. John D. Akerman of the University of Minnesota. The inner layer of this suit consisted of an airtight vinylite bladder, which was to be worn over full-length cotton underwear. A tight-fitting, one-piece fabric outer suit was worn over the vinylite to provide the necessary pressure-resisting strength, with the entire outfit weighing about 15 pounds.

Capt. John G. Kearby visited the National Carbon Company plant, on behalf of the Materiel Division, in February 1942, and examined the suit while it was being demonstrated by an employee. It appeared to be reasonably flexible when pressurized to 1.5 psi, and he recommended that the Equipment Laboratory investigate further the design characteristics of this suit, to determine its adaptability for use in flight operations between 35,000 and 50,000 feet, in airplanes having pilot compartments of small dimensions. The suit was judged to be of sufficient merit to be designated as the AAF Type 7. Kearby again visited the National Carbon Company in April to discuss improvements in the design of the vinylite undergarment of the experimental Type 7 suit.[72] The modifications were apparently unsuccessful, because no contract for development was awarded, and no further record of this suit can be found.

Goodyear Tire and Rubber Company

Goodyear researchers, headed by Ward T. Van Orman, began studying the problems involved in protecting the flyer at high altitude in 1940, and started building a full pressure suit early in 1942. A two-piece suit was handmade of unique rubberized fabric, which promised definite advantages over others tested. It was claimed that the fabric would stretch at proper joint locations, yet exhibit no tendency to ''balloon'' at operating pressures up to 4 psi. Four of the suits, designated as the Type 9, were procured by the Materiel Center on July 16, for testing at the Aero Medical Laboratory. An improved model, the Type 9-A, was examined at the factory in Akron in early August by Maj. John G. Kearby, and Maj. Joseph A. Resch of the Aero Medical Laboratory. According to Kearby, who donned the suit to determine flexibility and fit, it weighed only about 8 pounds and would operate comfortably at 4 psi.[73] Work on this suit continued, in an effort to resolve some of the same frustrating difficulties encountered by all of the firms engaged in full pressure suit development. One of the problems, leakage of pressurized air through a zipper, was solved by Van Orman in 1942 when he invented an airtight zipper, with overlapping, interlocking rubber strips. A patent application for this device was filed by Van Orman on February 9, 1943, and U.S. patent number 2,371,776 was granted on March 20, 1945.

An improved suit design was prepared in the fall of 1942, and designated as the ''Type XH-3 Pilot High Altitude Suit,'' under the new pressure-suit designation system introduced by the Materiel Center. It was designed to operate under pressure as high as 3 psi. The Goodyear XH-3 consisted of a tight-fitting, one-piece suit of the special, black rubberized material, weighing 12.25 pounds with a detachable plastic dome. It opened in front, utilizing Van Orman's airtight zipper. The laced gloves were not detachable, and the boots were built as an integral part of the legs. The pressurization-hose assembly also contained the oxygen tube and communication wires, and attached to a connection on the left side of the abdomen. The XH-3 was flight-tested at Eglin Field, Florida, in a B-17E during October 1942, and although a promising design, it still required much modification. According to Major Kearby, it was one of the lightest suits, and one of the easiest to don and doff.

An improved version of this suit was also tested by the U.S. Navy in July 1943, and was found to be unsatisfactory for a number of reasons; for example, it was extremely difficult to remove without the aid of an assis-

Pressure test of Goodyear Type XH-3 full pressure suit. This lightweight, one-piece suit was tested in the high-altitude chamber at the Aero Medical Laboratory, and flight-tested aboard a B-17E at Eglin Field, Florida, in October 1942. It was also tested by the U.S. Navy, when it again showed serious deficiencies requiring modification. Note nasal-demand oxygen mask, and the wearer's difficulty in trying to stand upright in the suit when pressurized to 2.5 psi. The knob on the upper left chest is the oxygen-regulator emergency-flow valve. The hose for air, oxygen, and communication wires attached to the left abdomen, and an air-pressure gauge was located on the left wrist. A pressure-control valve was located above each knee, and the automatic pressure-control valve was positioned on the lower right side of the abdomen. (Courtesy U.S. Navy)

tant. Among the serious defects encountered during pressure testing was the impossibility of standing up from a sitting position without help. The wearer could also not assume a normal standing position with the suit inflated to 2.5 psi, and the excessive effort required to bend or move caused great fatigue. At 2.5 psi the shoulders and dome of the suit were raised so high that only forward and upward vision was possible. (This was one of the problems Wiley Post experienced in 1934.) Ventilation was also unsatisfactory, causing the wearer to perspire excessively.

A modified suit, the Type XH-3A, was ready in late December for flight tests aboard an AAF B-17F, at altitudes up to 40,000 feet. The arms on this suit could be detached at ring joints above the elbows, and the legs could be removed just above the knees, to facilitate donning and permit sizing to the individual. The gloves were made a part of the lower arms and the suit retained the same round plastic headpiece. The main objection disclosed during testing of the XH-3A was that too much contraction occurred in the arms at the 90 degree bend of the elbow, and this necessitated additional modifications.[74]

Other experimental models, including suits with external wire bracing, were produced for testing in the Goodyear Research Laboratory. The final Goodyear suit procured by the Materiel Command was the Type XH-3B, ordered on April 7, 1943. The Type XH-3B resembled its predecessor and along with the Goodrich Types XH-1 and XH-5, came closest to meeting the minimum AAF operational requirements for a full pressure suit. Van Orman applied for a U.S. patent for this suit on October 6, 1943, and patent number 2,401,990 was granted on June 11, 1946. Experiments with the XH-3B and other suits were finally halted when development of all types of full pressure suits was discontinued by the AAF in October 1943.

Strato Equipment Company

This firm commenced development of a full pressure suit at their Minneapolis, Minnesota, plant in 1942. The rubberized fabric suit was identified as the Type BABM, which may indicate that Prof. John D. Akerman was involved in the design. No connection has been found, however, between it and the Type BABM-9 suit developed by the Bell Aircraft Corporation. The Strato BABM suit was tested by 1st Lt. Waring L. Dawbarn in the low-pressure chamber at the Aero Medical Laboratory on March 25, 1943, in a simulated flight to 30,000 feet. During the one-hour test, the suit was subjected to a pressure of 1.5 psi above ambient pressures. A number of deficiencies were recognized during the test and the suit was judged unsatisfactory for use in military aircraft, primarily because the rigidity of the arms prevented proper manipulation of all controls of the airplane and its accessories.[75]

B. F. Goodrich Company

Goodrich was probably the most capable all-around firm for the design and manufacture of full pressure suits. Russell S. Colley, who had constructed the second and

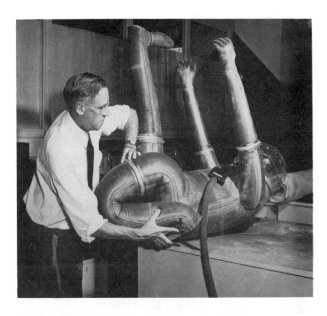

Ward T. Van Orman, Goodyear scientist, engineer, inventor, and balloonist, demonstrated the improved flexibility of the Type XH-3B full pressure suit, during testing at the Goodyear Laboratory in Akron, Ohio, on August 26, 1943. This was the most advanced suit produced by Van Orman in the Goodyear Research Department, and featured detachable arms and legs, to facilitate donning and permit sizing. An air-pressure gauge can be seen on the left wrist. The neck ring was improved to include a quick-release, for easy removal of the plastic dome by the wearer. Development of the Type XH-3B was halted when the full pressure suit program was terminated by the AAF in October 1943. (Courtesy Mrs. R. C. Dunn, via Richard Morris)

third pressure suits for Wiley Post, worked with determination through the war in an effort to produce a suit that would meet all AAF requirements.

The first Goodrich full pressure suit was ordered by the Materiel Division on November 29, 1940, at a cost of $6,100, but it was not delivered for testing at the Aero Medical Laboratory until the spring of 1941. It was a two-piece design, constructed of rubberized fabric, and had a rounded headpiece of transparent Plexiglas of a style that was used on most of the later models. It resembled a fishbowl and provided excellent all-around visibility. Unlike later suits, this suit was pressurized with oxygen, and an oxygen mask was therefore not required. The pressurization hose attached, rather inconveniently, to the helmet ring at the front of the suit. The tight-fitting suit had metal arms that attached below the shoulders, and used articulated-metal elbow joints that resembled those of a medieval suit of armor. This type of complex joint was not used on later suits.

The outfit was called a "Strato Suit" by Goodrich, and was originally designated as the Model 1-E, and later the

172 Type 3 by the Materiel Division. (Model 1-E may have been a factory designation.) During testing it was worn for approximately ten minutes at ground level, with the suit pressurized to about 2.5 psi. Results of the tests showed that comfort and freedom of motion were fair, but the complicated neck joint, difficulty of getting in and out of the heavy suit, and several other defects remained to be corrected.[76]

Action was taken on September 25, to procure two redesigned suit variations from Goodrich, at a total cost of $14,000. These were designated as AAF Types 5 and

6. The pressurization hose and electrical wires attached to the left side of the abdomen on the Type 5 suit. There was a steel brace across the chest, which opened in the middle and attached to the shoulder-ring joints for the arms. This was a characteristic feature of most later Goodrich suits, including the Type 6, and was intended to prevent ballooning. Both the Type 5 and 6 suits were made of rubberized fabric and had fabric bellows-type elbow joints, braced with thin steel rods to prevent excessive expansion.

Ten Goodrich suits were ordered by the Materiel Division on January 20, 1942, at a cost of $34,000. These are believed to have been Type 6 suits. This action was followed on February 17, by a purchase order for six examples of a modified version, the Type 6-A. Both the Type 6 and 6-A suits had the pressurization hose and electrical and communication wires attached at the center of the

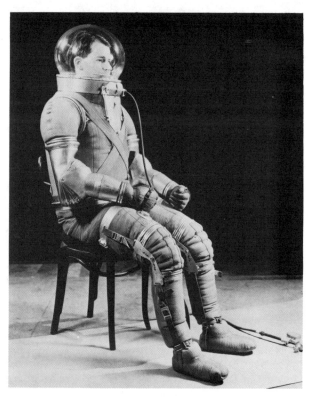

The AAF Type 3 was the first of several full pressure suit models built by the B. F. Goodrich Company during World War II. Don Shook, a Goodrich engineer, is wearing the ''Strato Suit'' in this photo, dated July 22, 1941. The detachable steel arms can be seen, with their unique elbow joints, patterned after the type used on medieval suits of armor. According to Russell S. Colley, project engineer, the joints did not leak during pressurization. Straps and braces on the torso and legs were intended to prevent ballooning. The characteristic Plexiglas fishbowl dome or helmet was detachable from the suit, by means of a complicated neck-ring mechanism. The metal device below the neck ring was part of the suit closure, and also included the connection for the oxygen pressure hose. This suit, unlike others, was pressurized with pure oxygen, so an oxygen mask was unnecessary. The pressure-control valve can be seen on the right leg above the knee. Although well-made, the suit was unsatisfactory because it was very stiff when pressurized, complicated, heavy, and difficult to put on and remove. (SI Photo 84–10722)

Fogging of the Plexiglas dome, because of inadequate ventilation, was one of the problems encountered during testing of the Goodrich Type 6-A full pressure suit at cold temperatures in the altitude chamber on February 6, 1942. The pressurization hose, oxygen tube, and electrical and communication wires were attached to the center of the abdomen on the Type 6 and 6-A suits. Standard AAF Type A-9 gloves and A-6 flying shoes were also worn for protection during the tests at sub-freezing temperatures. (Courtesy USAF)

abdomen. A further modification, the Type 6-B, was made in an effort to improve ventilation. In this model, the pressurization hose, oxygen tube, and electrical and communication wires were contained in a single conduit, which was moved to the left side of the abdomen, where it remained on later models. The conduit could be disconnected by one quick movement, should the aviator have to bail out. The Type 6-B suit was tested in flight at Eglin Field in October, aboard a B-17E, but was still found to have expansion problems, especially in the limbs.

Yet another variation, the Type 8, was designed and built, but it was quickly superseded by a modification, the Type 8-A. The Type 8-A was completed by April 1942, and tested in the altitude chamber at the Aero Medical Laboratory. Although performance had improved, it still did not meet minimum specifications.

At a conference held at the Goodrich factory in April 1942, it was observed that the improved material used in the altitude suits was practically snag-proof and almost self-sealing against gunfire of .50 caliber or less. In fact, a report stated that ''. . . it was anticipated that if the suit and its occupant [were] struck with a 20mm shell, or larger, the occupant [would] have no further need for the pressurization.''[77]

Experience gained with these experimental suits contributed to the design of the Goodrich Type XH-1 pilot suit, introduced in the fall of 1942. The XH-1 was one of the most promising types of full pressure suits developed during World War II. Made of brown rubberized fabric, of special Goodrich design, it included bellows at the elbows and knees supported by thin steel rods attached to rings. The chest brace connected to the shoulder-ring joints, and other wires from the waist ring to rings above the knees, provided additional support to minimize expansion during pressurization. A clear Plexiglas headpiece was attached to the neck ring and, as usual, a soft flying helmet with earphones and a special demand-oxygen mask were worn during tests.

The XH-1 suit was subjected to extensive altitude-chamber and flight-testing, including five flights aboard a B-17E at Eglin Field during October 1942. The tests disclosed that the XH-1, like other contemporary suits, still suffered from excessive bulkiness, poor mobility when pressurized, and inadequate ventilation. These deficiencies resulted in several modifications during the following months, and eventually the development of two improved Goodrich models: the Type XH-1C, soon redesignated as the Type XH-5, and the Type XH-6.

The prototype of the Type XH-6 pilot-altitude suit was delivered to the Materiel Command, as it was then called, in April 1943, three months before the Type XH-5. The XH-6 resembled the XH-5, except for the detachable arms and legs, which were of normal Goodrich design. The chest brace used with previous models was also discon-

The Goodrich Type XH-1 pilot-altitude suit, after completion of a simulated flight to 58,200 feet in the refrigerated altitude chamber, on November 5, 1942. Note the small demand-oxygen mask of special design, and the steel wires attached to the waist, arm- and leg-separation rings, in order to try and control excessive expansion of the suit during pressurization. Standard Type A-6 shearling flying shoes are being worn over the suit's built-in feet. The Type XH-1 was a further refinement of the Type 8-A suit, and was one of the most promising full pressure suits developed during the war. It was extensively tested in flight aboard a B-17E, but was found to be too bulky and rigid when pressurized. (Courtesy USAF)

tinued in favor of a flexible wire that ran from the groin area to encircle the neck. During testing in the altitude chamber at the Aero Medical Laboratory, this suit too proved to be stiff and tiring to wear when pressurized. The Type XH-6 was discarded, and all effort was concentrated on the Type XH-5 suit, of more unconventional design.

The Goodrich Type XH-6 was a variation that eliminated the familiar chest-restraining brace in favor of a flexible wire, which extended from the groin area across the chest and around the back of the neck. Capt. Waring L. "Pete" Dawbarn of the Equipment Laboratory is shown during a preliminary pressurization test in this photo, dated April 19, 1943. The XH-6 was discontinued because stiffness of the arms and legs when pressurized caused excessive hindrance and fatigue to the wearer. (Courtesy USAF)

The Goodrich Type XH-5 is considered to be the most advanced of all the full pressure suits developed during the war. It was designed by Russell S. Colley in the spring of 1943, and featured large, rounded bellows that formed the arms and legs in an attempt to improve mobility. He conceived the idea after observing the movements of a tomato worm in his garden, and the suit was usually referred to as the "tomato-worm suit." According to Colley: "I watched a tomato worm bend about 90 degrees, and the pressure in the worm did not change as far as I could see. It did not increase in diameter so I tried it on the suit."[78]

The Type XH-5 suit was constructed of laminated, rubberized fabric, with movement at the joints facilitated by ingenious ball-bearing fittings. It was provided with a self-sealing zipper from groin to neck ring, and was designed with detachable arms and legs to resolve the sizing problem. This feature also allowed for ease in dressing and undressing, and it was stated that the suit could be put on unassisted in four minutes and taken off in one minute. With its Plexiglas dome and all accessories, the XH-5 suit weighed a total of 20 pounds.

The suit was pressurized by means of an electrically driven 24-volt air compressor, weighing 8 pounds. It supplied 5 cubic feet of air per minute at 3 psi, at altitudes up to 80,000 feet. The air was led into the suit at the left side of the abdomen by a service assembly that also contained an oxygen feed, and microphone, headset, and electrically heated suit circuits. Pressure within the suit was regulated by means of an adjustable control valve, mounted on the left abdomen. A special demand-oxygen regulator and mask, or the Type A-14 demand mask, could be used.

One Type XH-5 pilot-altitude suit was ordered with special neck ring, for a price of $3,350, on April 10, 1943, and at least five others were subsequently obtained for test purposes. They were delivered to the Materiel Command in July, and tested in the high-altitude chamber by over thirty subjects to simulated altitudes up to 80,000 feet. In September, the suits were taken to Eglin Field and extensively flight-tested aboard a B-17F at altitudes up to 25,000 feet. Five flights were made, during which time all of the various crew functions in the aircraft were performed. Airmen participating in the tests found that the XH-5, like its predecessors, was uncomfortable because of inadequate ventilation, stiffness, and the fatigue caused by the effort required to move the body and limbs when the suit was pressurized. The test reports indicated that with an internal pressure of 3 psi, the wearer's ability to perform the normal duties required in military aircraft was approximately 25 percent of his ability when not wearing the suit. At 4 psi, the percentage of mobility was reduced to about 10 percent. It was not feasible to sight or operate the Norden bombsight or cameras adequately, and it would be necessary to adapt the aircraft controls and other instruments if the suit were to be used successfully. It was concluded that the latest model was airworthy, but those who flight-tested it definitely believed that the XH-5 was not suitable for use in combat.[79] During a review of the test results, the Materiel Command stated that the Goodrich Company was at least one year ahead of all other companies involved in the pressure-suit project.[80]

The disappointing results of the flight tests of the Goodrich Type XH-5 suit were an important factor in the final decision to terminate the entire full pressure suit-development program.

The Goodrich Type XH-5 was the most advanced full pressure suit developed during World War II. It was often called the "tomato-worm suit," because the individual arm and leg sections were inspired by the segments of a tomato worm's body. The rounded bellows and ball-bearing joints increased mobility, and made the 20-pound suit a big improvement over previous models. Note the individual air compressors (on the bench at right) used to pressurize each suit. In this photo, taken July 7, 1943, five volunteers are demonstrating the capability of the suit at simulated high altitude, in the low-pressure chamber at the Aero Medical Laboratory. Subsequent test flights aboard a B-17F in September 1943 proved that the XH-5 was airworthy; however, it was also stiff and exhausting to wear when pressurized, and greatly limited the flyer's ability to perform his duties. Neither the XH-5, nor any other suit developed during World War II, met the minimum requirements, and the AAF full pressure suit program was finally discontinued in October 1943. (SI Photo 84–10708)

The End of the AAF Full Pressure Suit Program

An event occurred on August 2, 1943, that had an adverse effect on the program to develop a practical full pressure suit. Maj. John G. Kearby, the dynamic project engineer, was killed in the crash of a Lockheed Hudson while returning to Wright Field after completing flight tests of an altitude suit. He was the first AAF officer to test a pressure suit in the altitude chamber and in actual flight. Between November 1942, and March 1943, he personally conducted extensive flight tests of several suits at Eglin Field, running risks which endangered his life. For his accomplishments, above and beyond the call of duty, Major Kearby was posthumously awarded the Legion of Merit.

Maj. John G. Kearby, pressure suit project engineer at Wright Field, wearing a small experimental oronasal demand-oxygen mask, designated as the A-6, constructed of transparent plastic. It is shown in this photo being worn during testing of the Goodrich Type 8-A suit at the Aero Medical Laboratory on April 2, 1942. Major Kearby was killed in the crash of a Lockheed Hudson, while returning to Wright Field on August 2, 1943. His tragic death not only brought a premature end to the promising career of this talented and dedicated officer, but also had an adverse impact on the future of the full pressure suit program in the AAF. (Courtesy USAF)

The months of diligent laboratory and flight testing wore on, and it became increasingly apparent that none of the full pressure suits met the minimum AAF performance specifications. The flight tests of the most advanced suit, the Goodrich Type XH-5, conducted in September 1943, proved discouraging to all concerned. The XH-5 was considered a remarkable improvement over the original full pressure suit of 1941, and it was capable of carrying an individual on a special mission to high altitude. However, officials concluded that neither this suit, nor any other, was sufficiently mobile for use in combat-crew positions. It was obvious that the full pressure suit had reached its

limit of development based on the state of the art at that time. These conclusions indicated that there were inherent difficulties in the use of a full pressure suit, which could not be overcome by any further mechanical refinement of the suits then available.[81]

According to Air Force Technical Report No. 5769, the design of full pressure suits had almost completely sacrificed mobility, in order to deliver air under pressure sufficient to maintain life at very high altitudes. The report stated that ". . . basically, all attempts to develop equipment around the principle of full pressurization for survival at altitude had failed because of the inability to resolve the fundamental paradox of adequate mobility at high pressure."[82]

At a meeting held on September 21, 1943, officials of the Materiel Command reviewed the full pressure-suit program and agreed that it was time to either buy the suits as they were or close the project. The full pressure-suit program, MX-117, was terminated in October 1943, and the various contractors concerned were notified of the decision of the Materiel Command to discontinue full pressure-suit development.[83]

The Emergency Partial Pressure Suit Program

The progress in jet- and rocket-powered aircraft development during the critical period of World War II made the need for some type of high-altitude protective garment even more urgent. On April 12, 1944, Brig. Gen. Franklin O. Carroll, Chief of the Engineering Division, Materiel Command, advised the Assistant Chief of the Air Staff in Washington, D.C., that the development of pressure-altitude suit equipment had resumed. The Aero Medical Laboratory was advised that a suit should be developed that could be used satisfactorily at altitudes of 55,000 to 60,000 feet.[84]

Because of the failure of the full pressure-suit program, an entirely different approach was needed. Fortunately, Dr. D. R. Drury and fellow scientists at the University of Southern California (USC) had for some months been investigating various factors concerned with personal protection during high-altitude flight. Their studies included pressure breathing and the efficiency of experimental counterpressure devices. Dr. James P. Henry and associates at USC developed a crude, but workable, emergency partial pressure suit, of new design, utilizing the pneumatic lever principle devised by Dr. Harold Lamport of Yale University. This became known as the "capstan principle." The suit was an ingenious combination of an inflatable vest and tubes, or capstans, along the sides of the arms, chest, and legs that pulled the suit's fabric tightly against the wearer's body, to apply mechanical counterpressure at high altitude against the internal expansion of gases and water vapor in the blood vessels and tissues.[85]

The emergency partial pressure suit, first conceived in December 1943, was a one-piece coverall fabricated of single-layer, porous, inelastic nylon, and was intended to be worn under regular flying clothing. As originally designed, it was cut to the sitting position in order to be pulled tight when counterpressure was required. Pneumatic levers were connected on the coverall's arms and legs to a pressure supply of 10 to 15 psi. The design of the partial pressure suit was based on the use of pressure breathing, pioneered during the war by A. Pharo Gagge of the Aero Medical Laboratory.[86] It was uninflated except in emergencies, such as the failure of cabin pressure at altitudes above 43,000 feet. A full face mask provided a satisfactory seal for high breathing pressures; the mechanical pressure exerted on the body balanced the breathing pressures and closely approximated ambient conditions at 40,000 feet.

The administration of required breathing pressures at extremely high altitudes was made possible by the use of a specially constructed helmet. During 1946, the Aero Medical Laboratory, working with the University of Southern California and the David Clark Company, managed to resolve problems with the helmet, and clear the way for production of an improved automatic emergency partial pressure suit and helmet under Project MX-829. Called the Type S-1, it was the first of a number of improved models, which eventually included the Type T-1 suit containing anti-G capability.

In a letter dated May 17, 1946, Brig. Gen. Lawrence C. Craigie, Chief of the Engineering Division, advised that the Air Materiel Command commended the University of Southern California Aeromedical Laboratory for its "foresight and ability" in significantly contributing to aeronautical science by developing the partial pressure high-altitude suit. Dr. James Henry, who joined the staff at Wright Field in 1946, was commended for "attacking the problems of development from a new point of view and for developing a successful high altitude suit." Dr. Henry also personally tested pressure-suit equipment, at considerable risk, in a low-pressure chamber up to a simulated altitude of 75,000 feet.[87]

In August 1947, Dr. Henry commented in connection with a proposed patent application that several others had contributed to the pressure-suit development, and that one or all of them could be named as co-inventors. The contributors included Dr. Henry C. Bazett, University of Pennsylvania, Dr. Alvin L. Barach, Columbia University, and Col. A. Pharo Gagge, Aero Medical Laboratory, Wright Field. Dr. Henry applied for a patent on the invention of the partial pressure suit in March 1948, and assigned the patent to the U.S. Government.[88]

Emergency partial pressure suits were used by all military services for many years while development was under way on the first practical full pressure suit. As a matter of interest, a successful full pressure suit was finally produced in the 1950s by a combination of innovative advances achieved through the cooperation of the U.S. Navy, the Aero Medical Laboratory, and private industry. Suit mobility was greatly enhanced by the use of narrow accordian-like pleats, which were a modification of the tomato-worm idea introduced by Russell Colley of Goodrich in 1943. Colley also developed an airtight metal joint that rotated on sealed-in bearings. Hans Mauch of the Aero Medical Laboratory contributed to the proper ventilation of modern pressure suits and space suits, by the development of a garment that was, in effect, an air-conditioning unit. It consisted of a multi-layered liner, resembling long-john underwear, that contained thousands of tiny holes, which allowed circulation of air from a blower around the wearer's body.[89] These concepts were among the first of many advanced techniques and materials used in pressure-garment design that led eventually to the Project Apollo space suits worn on the surface of the moon.

The world's first successful emergency partial pressure suit being worn by its inventor, Dr. James P. Henry, in 1946. The purpose of the partial pressure suit was to keep a flyer alive in the event of loss of cabin pressure, until he could bring his plane down below 40,000 feet. Development of the actual suit and helmet began at the University of Southern California, and continued at the Aero Medical Laboratory at Wright Field. The suit featured inflatable "capstan tubes" along the arms, legs, and chest, which pulled the suit's fabric tightly over the wearer's body to apply counterpressure against the expansion of body gases and water vapor. An oxygen mask was still used in this early version of the Type S-1 suit, but it was later replaced by an improved full-head helmet. Partial pressure suits were used by all services until after the full pressure suit was finally perfected in the late 1950s. (Courtesy USAF)

VI Survival Equipment

Under the broad title of survival equipment is included an almost endless variety of items, ranging from small waterproof containers of matches to huge air-rescue lifeboats equipped with provisions to sustain a number of people for weeks. Survival or rescue equipment can be placed in three general categories: that carried by the individual aviator on his person, that carried in each aircraft, and that used by rescue organizations in carrying out their missions. The purpose of this chapter is to survey the principal types of personal survival gear carried by or attached to the airman, and briefly mention larger equipment and the organization developed in connection with survival and rescue. It must be remembered that all types of survival and emergency equipment had to integrate with other items of flying clothing and gear, and within the constraints of aircraft design, capability, and mission requirements.[1]

The flyer who must abandon a disabled aircraft, whether by bailout or after a forced landing or ditching, may immediately find himself in a very serious situation. Survival conditions are often arduous, and space and weight considerations have always severely limited the type and amount of emergency equipment that can be carried. In case the flyer must abandon his aircraft in flight, he needs essential equipment and supplies attached to his person. If he brings his plane down on land or water, he must quickly retrieve his emergency gear, and in any event, must be trained in skills necessary to survive in the conditions he may encounter, be they arctic, jungle, desert, or sea. In addition to coping with difficult terrain, rough seas, and weather conditions, and his needs for food, water, and shelter, a downed aviator may find himself in a hostile area where he will have to evade capture and escape to friendly or neutral territory. Considering the obvious necessity for proper training, organization, and equipment for survival, in conditions which might threaten flyers' lives, it is surprising that so little emphasis was placed on these subjects prior to the outbreak of World War II.

During the first decade of military aviation, no serious throught was given to survival equipment or procedures. The U.S. Army aviators who flew with the 1st Aero Squadron during the Mexican Border Campaign in 1916 had no parachutes, survival kits, or special emergency equipment to carry with them on their flights over the rugged mountains of northern Mexico. They took along such available tools, rations, canteens of water, maps, money, a pocket compass, a pistol or rifle, and ammunition as could be carried, based on space and weight limitations. Common sense determined what emergency equipment was important, and still guides the development of survival gear today.

Army flyers with the American Expeditionary Forces in Europe during World War I had no need for elaborate survival equipment if they were forced down behind German lines; but a pocket compass, maps, and money were still essential if they were to have any hope of reaching the border of neutral Holland or Switzerland. Even though the population in German-occupied territory was largely friendly, Allied airmen were usually captured promptly by German troops and sent to a prisoner-of-war camp.

The Army Air Service that emerged from the demobilization after the Armistice soon began making cross-country flights over wilderness areas of the Western United States, Alaska, Panama, Hawaii, and the Philippines. The mission of the Army air arm during the 1920s called primarily for operations over land, while the U.S. Navy was mainly concerned with over-water flying. Nevertheless, flotation equipment was among the first types of survival gear obtained for Army aviators.

LIFE-PRESERVER VESTS

The need for a basic personal flotation device was recognized as soon as man began to fly over water. Nearly three-quarters of the globe is covered by water, and the unforgiving sea can deal swiftly and finally with human life, either through drowning or exposure. A kapok-filled life jacket for flyers, similar to the life jackets and vests then carried aboard ships, was offered for sale as early as 1912. The U.S. Navy experimented with various flotation coats, jackets, and suits during and after World War I, and by the early 1920s the Air Service was also testing similar models. To be practical for aviators, a life preserver must be compact for wear in a small cockpit, not interfere with the operation of the parachute during bailout, provide head-up buoyancy for a flyer burdened with very heavy clothing, and be durable and reliable.

Although inflatable rubber life vests were available commercially during the 1920s, kapok or cork vests were preferred by most airmen because they were considered foolproof, and did not require any action to provide buoyancy. The Army Air Service began testing a quilted-kapok life coat, specification 3017, in 1921, and finally standardized the design as the Type A-1 on September 30, 1931. It was redesignated as the Type A-1 life-preserver vest in the mid-1930s. An improved kapok life vest, without sleeves, the Type A-2, was adopted as limited standard on March 27, 1936, and both the A-1 and A-2 remained in limited use until declared obsolete on March 21, 1944. The kapok vests were dependable and durable, but bulky and uncomfortable to wear over flying clothing inside an airplane cockpit. Types A-1 through A-4 kapok-filled life-preserver cushions were also standardized for use between 1924 and 1932, and remained available for use in aircraft for many years. A flotation suit, called the Type C-1, was tested in the mid-1920s, and an improved model, the Type C-2, was standardized on October 23, 1928. The C-2 was never popular because of its bulk, but remained in limited use until finally declared obsolete on March 13, 1944.[2]

The development of pneumatic life preservers continued during the late 1920s, and they gradually gained favor with aviators as they were perfected. After testing and rejecting several U.S. Navy models, the Air Corps procured an air-inflated vest in July 1930, that had been adopted previously by the Navy Bureau of Aeronautics (BuAer). This first pneumatic vest for wear by Army flyers was intended for use in the Canal Zone. It was a commercially developed vest called "Airubber," and was made of rubberized fabric. The vest fit over the shoulders and was retained with an adjustable belt and crotch strap. It was inflated manually by blowing into two independent cells.[3]

In 1931, the Air Corps began testing an automatically inflated vest, using an easily replaceable carbon dioxide (CO_2) cylinder for each of the two compartments. It was adopted as substitute standard on April 11, 1932, despite objections by squadrons in the Hawaiian Islands. The units intended to benefit most from the lightweight, compact, pneumatic vest were concerned about the reliability of the inflation method and the durability of the rubber air cells.[4] The "Vest, Aircraft, Type B-1" was made of yellow rubberized drill, and two mouth valves for inflation were located in the neck of the vest, for emergency use. The B-1 was changed to limited standard on May 16, 1933, but not declared obsolete until March 13, 1944, long after all stocks were exhausted.[5]

An improved pneumatic vest, the Type B-2, was standardized for use on May 16, 1933. It incorporated leg straps, three separate air compartments, and an improved CO_2 cylinder located at the bottom of the vest. Like all pneumatic vests, it included mouth valves for emergency inflation. The B-2 was changed to limited standard on January 10, 1936, and finally declared obsolete on March 13, 1944.

Concerns about reliability persisted, leading to the development by the Equipment Branch of the sturdy Type B-3 pneumatic life vest, standardized on January 8, 1936. Although changed to substitute standard status on May 6, 1942, when the Type B-4 vest was adopted, the B-3 continued to see service until the end of World War II. It had two separate, but adjoining, latex-rubber air cells, with an outer casing of yellow cotton fabric. Buoyancy was provided in the ring around the neck as well as to the chest area. The B-3 was equipped with an automatic inflation system, using a small CO_2 cylinder for each bladder located at the bottom of the vest. To inflate, the wearer pulled down on cords attached to two small discharge levers. Separate mouth inflation tubes were also provided. Wearers were encouraged to inspect the CO_2 cylinders regularly to see if the caps were punctured, and check frequently for leaks in the vests themselves. Unfortunately, these safety measures were not always followed. The reliability of this vest eventually quieted most of the skeptics, but as late as 1937, crewmen were allowed the option of using either the pneumatic or kapok-type life-preserver vests while flying over water.[6]

With the onset of World War II, it soon became apparent that the few manufacturers of the Type B-3 vest would not be able to meet the increased demand. There was also a potential rubber shortage to consider because of the cut-off of supplies of natural rubber from Southeast Asia. The Spec. AN-V-18 pneumatic vest, used by the Navy, was tested extensively by the Equipment Laboratory in early 1942 and found to be satisfactory. It resembled the bladder-type B-3, but used less rubber, because it was constructed of superimposed pneumatic compartments made from rubber-coated yellow fabric. This vest was standardized for AAF use as the Type B-4 on May 6, 1942, to supplement procurement of the B-3 vest. Each of the two air compartments was provided with an automatic CO_2 inflation system, and with a separate mouth inflation tube.[7] The initial production of the vest was modified by the addition of a strap from the collar back to the rear of the belt, to prevent the wearer's head from slipping out of the collar opening. All B-3 and B-4 vests were eventually modified to include the strap, in accordance with Technical Order No. 13-1-17, dated May 25, 1944. Many were also modified in the field, by cementing a dye-marker packet between the cells.

On February 1, 1944, the AAF officially changed the nomenclature of the Type B-4 to Spec. AN-V-18, AN6519, as part of an effort believed to have been made to expedite mass production.[8] A vest imprinted "AN-V-18" was likely to have been procured originally by the Navy, a vest marked with the later standard AN designation "AN6519" or "AN6519-1" could have been procured by either the Navy or AAF, and a vest labeled "Type B-4" was procured only by the AAF. All three were identical, but represent different dates of manufacture. All saw extensive use through the end of the war.

In the spring of 1944, the Navy BuAer representative at Wright Field notified the Chief of the Personal Equipment Laboratory of reports that the standard AN life vest lacked sufficient buoyancy to support a heavily clothed airman in rough seas. The Laboratory had received no report of inadequate buoyancy from AAF sources, but by midsummer a project was opened to modify the Type B-4 or AN-V-18 vest, to make it capable of supporting an unconscious person with his face out of the water. An entirely new model was developed by the laboratory and tested in November by the AAF Proving Ground Command. The vest was considered to be a big improvement and was standardized for AAF use as the Type B-5 on December 12, 1944.[9] The Navy, in the meantime, was working independently to produce its own improved model, which was adopted as the MK II and used for over twenty years.

The Type B-5 life-preserver vest was a distinct departure from the conventional pneumatic life vest. It was more like a collar or halter; it was shorter, wider, and had an improved strap arrangement. The design also included pockets for shark-chaser (of dubious value) and dye-marker packets, a whistle on a string, and a Navy single-cell waterproof light carried in a pouch on the strap. Construction was similar to the old Type B-3, with black neoprene bladders encased in a yellow cotton vest. The two air compartments were equipped with separate mouth inflation tubes as a backup for the CO_2 inflation cylinders. The entire vest weighed approximately three pounds, compared to four pounds for the Types B-3 and B-4. The B-5 was very soft, pliable and comfortable, even when inflated, but most importantly it had greater buoyancy and provided much better support for the head. This was achieved through a wider collar area supporting the head, and by floating the wearer in a more nearly vertical position than was accomplished by other types of vests. The Type B-5 continued in service with the AAF, and later, in modified form, with the USAF, until the 1960s.

During World War II, a life vest, because of its shape when inflated, was usually called a "Mae West," after the famous and well-proportioned movie actress of the 1930s.

LIFE RAFTS

Survivors of a bailout or ditching at sea require a quick-to-deploy, seaworthy platform for survival until rescue is effected. The ready availability of food, water, and signal devices for day and night use is also of the utmost importance. The inflatable, pneumatic life boat or raft was perceived to be the answer for aviators because it was light in weight and could easily be carried in the limited space aboard aircraft.

A pneumatic life raft was invented by Ward T. Van Orman of the Goodyear Tire and Rubber Company in 1918, and similar rafts were tested by the U.S. Navy during the 1920s. The Army Air Corps was less concerned about using life rafts than the Navy; however, some Navy rafts were used by the Air Corps during this period.

The first pneumatic life raft to be adopted by the Air Corps was the Type A-1, standardized on November 20, 1928. This was a rather bulky commercial product, with a five-man, 1,000-pound capacity, which was practical only for use with large aircraft. Called an "Airaft," it had a rounded end, was made of formed rubber, and had two seats.[10]

In the early 1930s, the Air Corps concept was to provide pursuit aircraft in outlying United States possessions with rubberized, carbon dioxide gas-filled flotation bags, along with watertight flotation chambers, to keep the entire airplane afloat. However, when the Boeing P-26 pursuit appeared on the drawing board, floation installation presented serious technical problems and the concept was dropped by 1937.[11]

In 1931, a Navy pilot was rescued from a small, pneumatic life raft after several days adrift, following ditching in the Pacific off the coast of Panama. When Air Corps personnel heard of this event, the Materiel Division was requested to provide small life rafts for emergency use.

Three pneumatic life preservers used by the AAF during World War II. Left to right: Type B-3 with manufacturing date of March 1942, Type B-4 or AN6519–1 (AN-V-18), dated February 1945, and Type B-5, undated (c. 1945). The B-5 in the photo has a small pouch on the strap, for a single-cell identification light using the BA-30 battery. The lights usually had a large safety pin on the side for fastening to the life vest. (Courtesy Robert Lehmacher)

The potential of the life raft as an important item of survival equipment was recognized, and later that year thirty-six rafts, designated as the Type B-1, were sent to Hawaii for field testing in pursuit planes. The design was similar to the Type A-1, but it had only one seat, which could hold two men, and a 400-pound capacity. The B-1 raft, standardized on October 20, 1931, was found to be too bulky for convenient stowage in most small aircraft.

The limited funds and personnel available during the depression years led the Air Corps to concentrate on the development and procurement of multi-place pneumatic rafts. At times the Equipment Laboratory worked in conjunction with the Navy BuAer, Pan American Airways, and the manufacturers to produce improved models.

A collapsible pneumatic one-man airaft with a 250-pound capacity was designed and tested during 1935 and 1936. It was similar to the larger A and B types, but included changes in the method of flotation and other minor refinements. The design was standardized as the Type C-1 on April 13, 1937, but none was procured, because it required special storage space in the cockpit of the latest fighter planes and proved difficult to handle in an emergency. The Type C-1 design was declared limited standard on July 4, 1942, when the Navy AN-R-2 one-man raft was standardized and procured in quantity for AAF use. The C-1 design was declared obsolete on October 6, 1943.[12]

The beginning of hostilities brought extensive overwater flights, and the need for a suitable one-man life raft for AAF combat use became urgent. New construction methods and substitute materials had to be considered as a result of the rubber shortage and the requirement for mass production. In the meantime, actual combat experience was providing valuable lessons for designers and manufacturers. Attempts were made to standardize specifications where possible between the Army Air Forces, the U.S. Navy, and the British, who were also procuring rafts called "dinghies" in the United States. Conferences between the AAF and the Navy in February and March 1942 led to the conclusion that the existing Navy one-man raft was best for each crewman in planes having three or fewer seats. The Navy Spec. AN-R-2, AN6520 life raft was standardized for AAF use on July 4, 1942, and eventually replaced the two-man rafts of the B series.

One of the most important features of the one-man rafts used during World War II was that they could be carried on the person when flying and during bailout, and were available for immediate use as soon as the flyer reached the water. The AN-R-2 raft was made of yellow two-ply rubberized fabric, and was packed in a cloth container, which attached to the parachute harness. The packed container was approximately 15 × 14 × 3 ⅝ inches in size. When used with the seat-type parachute it was stowed between the parachute and the user's body, in place of the parachute cushion. Unfortunately, the hardness of the raft pack made it very uncomfortable on long missions.

The AN-R-2 container had a slot in the center through which the parachute-harness leg straps passed, when it was used as a seat pack. Having been designed for the Navy parachute, it did not mate very well with the later Army-Navy specification harness. A modification of the raft and container was introduced as the AN-R-2A, AN6520-1, on August 20, 1942.[13] The slot was eliminated and the case made more rectangular on the AAF version. The Navy solved the strap problem by retaining the leg-strap slot, but moving it two inches from the container edge, and designating it as the AN-R-2B raft.[14] However, the AAF also procured their raft in the Navy-designed case. The designation referred to the raft and the design of the case varied. Perhaps due to wartime demands for production, and also the need to integrate with a variety of parachutes, the raft container design was no indication of raft type or service. Generally rafts of this series were retained by tying them to the life preserver, chute container, or harness with a lanyard attached to the CO_2 cylinder of the raft. Inflation of the raft was accomplished by hand-turning a valve on the CO_2 cylinder. Inflated dimensions were approximately 66 × 40 × 12 inches.

By January 1943, contracts had been let for 15,000 AN-R-2A rafts with anticipated production to eventually reach 10,000 per month. The standardized raft was also referred to as the AN6520-1. Until June 1, 1943, production of life rafts was based on aircraft manufacturing schedules. After that date, the rate of production was increased to meet the issuing demand.

In the fall of 1943, a new raft, based on wartime experience, was designed by the Equipment Laboratory. It was slightly smaller but more stable than the previous type, was equipped with a spray shield, and had sailing ability. The container was distinctly different, a modification of that used with the RAF Type K dinghy. Snap hooks enabled easy attachment to the back of the parachute harness, and pockets were provided for additional survival components and accessories. Inflation was either by unscrewing the valve handle, or by pulling a ripcord to activate a lever, similar to that used with the Mae West. This raft was considered to be a vast improvement over the AN-R-2A. It was standardized on April 1, 1944, as the Type C-2, and placed in production.[15]

The final wartime development in one-man pararafts for the AAF was the Type C-2A, adopted as standard on May 21, 1945. The C-2A was the same as the C-2 except for minor improvements, including provision for a Corner Reflector MX-137, and a new type of paddle. Although late for World War II, this raft was to become the mainstay of the Korean conflict. It should be noted that in all series, the designation carried on the container referred to the raft. Early C-2 rafts were supplied in AN-R-2A style con-

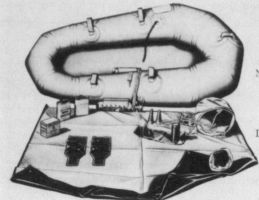

RAFT
ONE MAN PARACHUTE TYPE
PNEUMATIC LIFE
AN6520-1

NAMES: One man parachute type pneumatic life raft
Life raft
One man life raft
One man pneumatic raft
Parachute type life raft
Pneumatic life raft

DESCRIPTION: This life raft consists of a fabric floor cemented to a rubberized fabric flotation tube which is divided into two compartments by horizontal bulkheads.

The raft fits into a parachute pack which can be stowed on the pilot's seat or fastened to his parachute harness. It contains a rubber tube which is used for oral reinflation if the raft loses its buoyancy.

IT CONTAINS THE FOLLOWING ACCESSORIES:

One carbon dioxide inflation cylinder with hand operated valve
One sea anchor
One bailing cup
One pair of hand paddles
One can of drinking water

First aid kit
One pneumatic raft repair kit
One set of bullet-hole plugs
Sail
Three foot cotton cord
One can of sea marker

CHARACTERISTICS:

Raft capacity	approximately 250 pounds (1 person)
Total weight, with accessories	approximately 16 pounds
Raft dimensions, inflated	approximately 66 inches in length
Dimensions of parachute pack case	approximately 15^1_8 by 14^1_8 by 3^5_8 inches
Cylinder capacity	approximately $^3_4$ pound carbon dioxide (30.5 cubic inches)

ARMY

A. E. REFERENCE NUMBER: 45-8275
SPECIFICATIONS:
Detail AN-R-2a
Superseded AN-R-2
AN DRAWING NUMBER: AN6520
AN PART NUMBER: AN6520-1
A. S. C. STOCK NUMBER: 6600-660450
TECHNICAL ORDER NUMBER: 04-15-2
PRODUCTION STATUS: Under procurement.
SHIPPING DATA: Shipped complete with accessories.

NAVY

TYPE DESIGNATION: AN6520-1
SPECIFICATIONS:
General M-3Q
Detail AN-R-2A
Superseded AN-R-2
AN DRAWING NUMBER: AN6520
A. S. O. STOCK NUMBER: R83-R-15650
TECHNICAL NOTE NUMBER: 1-43
PROCUREMENT STATUS: Under procurement.

BRITISH

BRITISH REFERENCE NUMBER: 127C/81

The AN-R-2A, AN6520–1 one-man pneumatic life raft, widely used by AAF and Navy flyers during World War II. Note accessories including hand paddles and cone-shaped bullet-hole plugs. The raft container is at lower right. (This illustration reproduced from the "Index of Army-Navy Aeronautical Equipment: Miscellaneous," published by the AAF in 1943)

This 1944 photograph shows an AAF staff sergeant in khaki summer uniform, wearing the Type B-8 back parachute with snap-type harness strap fasteners. What appears to be a seat parachute is actually a Type C-2 pneumatic life raft. The lanyard from the neck of the raft's CO_2 bottle can be seen attached under the snap to his life vest. The white webbing on the C-2 raft container indicates that it is probably a prototype made in the Equipment Laboratory at Wright Field. Production C-2 rafts utilized olive-drab webbing. The staff sergeant is also believed to be wearing a Type B-4 pneumatic life vest and a Type C-1 survival vest. (SI Photo A4586E)

tainers and similarly, C-2A and later rafts could be found in non-typical containers.

It had been intended to provide one-man rafts only for smaller aircraft carrying one to three crewmen. Experience indicated that medium and heavy aircraft were safer to ditch and provided better floatability, which enabled the crew to deploy the bigger and better-equipped rafts carried in the larger airplanes. Bigger rafts were also favored because it was known that chances for survival and rescue at sea were greater when the crew stayed together. How-

ever, there were problems with the larger life rafts. Eighth Air Force crewmen found, among other problems, that if a large raft was upside down in the water, there was no way that they could turn it over. It was also impossible for those in the water, in winter flying clothing, to climb into the raft. Among many modifications were the hand patches cemented to the underside of the raft to enable it to be turned over, if it had been inflated upside down, and a short rope ladder was attached so that crewmen could climb into the raft.[16]

The Eighth Air Force, based on their own experience and that of the RAF, pressed for individual rafts for bomber crewmen. Authority was finally granted to major theater commanders to provide individual rafts.

Authorization for one-man rafts did not alter recommended escape procedures. Specific recommendations by type of aircraft were:[17]

All fighter aircraft:	Bail out where possible
A-20, A-26, P-61:	Bail out where possible
C-46, C-47, C-54:	Ditch where possible
B-17, B-25, B-29:	Ditch where possible
B-24, B-26:	Ditch or bail out

Each flyer was, of course, instructed in escape from his particular crew position in the aircraft in the event of bail-out. However, the inadequacy or omission of instruction in ditching procedure, the use of emergency equipment, and rescue techniques was a serious defect in the training of AAF crews during the early years of the war.[18]

Hundreds of airmen owe their lives to the successful use of life rafts during World War II. One of the best-known incidents occurred in October 1942, when Eddie Rickenbacker, famed World War I ace, was flying as a passenger in a B-17 that made a forced landing in the Pacific. He and seven men (one of whom died) were set adrift on Type A-2 rafts. Rickenbacker was rescued after 23 days, and his experience emphasized the need for development of improved survival gear and a more effective air-sea rescue system. In just a few short years, rapid evaluation of wartime experience produced less bulky, lighter rafts with more buoyancy. Pockets added to the bottom of the raft provided more stability and a sea anchor minimized drift. A spray shield protected the survivor from the brunt of the elements while a small sail was added to enable him to attempt controlled movement. The container developed from a simple fabric pack, stowed behind the aircraft seat, to a quick-release cushioned container. The early rafts had CO_2 cylinder valves which had to be unscrewed, but these were replaced with trigger-style valves, which could be activated automatically by the weight of the falling raft, when the crewman neared the water. The current raft design retains this feature.

Generally, the raft kit doubled as a seat cushion in the aircraft. At best, it was a firm, unyielding pack which was uncomfortable for long flights. The addition of survival components and accessories often caused more discomfort, so it was not unusual for the crewman to alter the composition of the kit. Components of newer raft kits were often used to update older kits.

Specific components for the AN-R-2 raft-and-container kit included two hand paddles, a sea marker, a can of drinking water, two bullet-hole repair plugs, and a repair kit. Attached to the raft were a bailing cup, a bucket sea anchor, and an air pump for topping-off the raft. In the AN-R-2A raft, the sea marker was deleted as this item was usually cemented between the cells of the B-4 life-preserver vest. A paulin (often referred to by civilians as a tarpaulin) was included, which could be used as a cover or sail. The envelope accessory flap of the Type C-2 pararaft contained the added signal flares, a sponge, a signal mirror, and a desalting kit to convert sea water for drinking. The Type C-2A pararaft had an inner, cloth, zippered bag, which held items developed late in the war. These included the MX-137 corner reflector which replaced the

sail. As search-and-rescue units began to use radar, the corner reflector was developed as a passive device designed to improve reflection of a radar signal.[19]

Larger rafts were equipped with an even more extensive selection of survival supplies and equipment, including fishing kits, the "Gibson Girl" emergency radio transmitter, and a Very pistol. Water is more essential than food for survival on land or at sea. The paulin supplied with the raft could be used not only as a sail or for supplying warmth, but could also be used to collect rain water for drinking. On later rafts, it was camouflaged on one side, for protection against sighting by enemy planes, while the other side was a signal panel for friendly aircraft.

All life rafts may be considered as survival equipment, but only the one-man pneumatic rafts are actually in the category of personal equipment for aviators. The following summary will account for all of the pneumatic life rafts, of various sizes, standardized for use by the Army Air Corps (from 1941, Army Air Forces), through the end of World War II:[20]

Five-man, 1,000-pound capacity

Type	Standardized	Obsolete
A-1	Nov. 20, 1928	Oct. 6, 1943
A-2	Apr. 9, 1937	May 6, 1944
A-3	Feb. 25, 1942	After 1945
A-3A	Jun. 20, 1944	After 1945

Two-man, 400-pound capacity (Also used in one-man aircraft)

B-1	Oct. 20, 1931	Apr. 10, 1941
B-2	Oct. 24, 1933	Oct. 6, 1943
B-3	Apr. 13, 1937	Feb. 24, 1944
B-4	Feb. 25, 1942	Jan. 28, 1944

One-man, 250-pound capacity

C-1	Apr. 13, 1937	Oct. 6, 1943 (Not procured, replaced by AN-R-2)
AN-R-2	Jul. 4, 1942	After 1945
AN-R-2A	Aug. 20, 1942	After 1945
C-2	Apr. 1, 1944	After 1945
C-2A	May 21, 1945	After 1945

Ten-man, 2,000-pound capacity

D-1	Experimental, service test from Nov 30, 1938	Aug. 6, 1940

Seven-man, 2,500-pound capacity (Type E-2, 12-man in emergency)

E-1	Jan. 22, 1943	After 1945
E-2	Mar. 20, 1943	After 1945
E-2A	Jun. 20, 1944	After 1945

PARACHUTE EMERGENCY KITS

The equipment covered thus far provided some of the tools needed for survival at sea. Other kits and components were developed to enable the downed airman to survive under different environmental conditions and situations.

During peacetime, the enemy was the environment, and airmen preparing for flight over isolated land areas gathered such items of Army field equipment, camping gear, and supplies as were available on base, and supplemented those with equipment purchased commercially or obtained from the U.S. Navy. Emergency kits improvised locally proved increasingly inadequate as aircraft capability and long-range operational activity expanded during the late 1920s. Only minimal research and development of survival equipment was carried out by the Materiel Division's Equipment Branch at Wright Field, and little actual procurement was made to fill the growing need.

In 1934, Air Corps units at Albrook Field, Canal Zone, requested that a parachute back pad be provided for attachment to the parachute harness that would contain pockets for carrying emergency jungle-survival items. The Equipment Branch designed a parachute seat kit to meet their needs, which was designated as the "Emergency Jungle Landing Kit." It consisted of the following components: 1 pistol, caliber .45, M1911, in leather holster; 20 rounds ball ammunition; 1 machete; 2 emergency rations; 1 pocket compass; 1 waterproof match box with matches; 1 vial iodine; 25 quinine tablets in metal container; and 1 mosquito headnet. A small quantity of these kits were assembled for use in Panama and the Philippine Islands; however, experience in the field showed them to be impractical, because the seat kit caused the heads of tall pilots to protrude over the windshield into the slipstream.

Late in 1936, the Equipment Laboratory, as it was then called, developed a parachute back-pad kit, but it initially positioned the pilot too far forward in his seat. In addition, it was too bulky and uncomfortable, and changes were eventually made to better distribute the components. These kits were tested and found satisfactory, and a small quantity was assembled at the Middletown Air Depot in Pennsylvania.[21]

As technology advanced and demands increased, the Equipment Laboratory again undertook the task of redesigning the back-pad kit. This time a pair of kits were developed, for both arctic and tropical use, that were externally identical but configured differently inside.[22] They were approximately 19 inches long, 17 inches wide, and 4 inches thick, were banjo-shaped like the previous kits, and similar in design to those developed by the U.S. Navy. Both types integrated with the parachute harness and formed the back pad for the seat-type parachute Type S-1.

They were interchangeable with the standard parachute back pad, and were a big improvement over previous designs.

The first of the pair, called the "Kit, Emergency, Type B-1, Alaskan Back Pad," was a limited procurement. Fifteen thousand kits were procured following standardization on August 7, 1941. The B-1 kit was changed to limited standard on October 7, 1942, and issued until stock was exhausted. The container was made of a horsehair-filled cushion, felt, and cotton duck. It is believed that the kit contained the bolo-type machete, Collins Model No. 18, which made the kit too rigid and caused complaints. Other components included emergency rations, pocket frying pan with fuel, gloves, compass, goggle, headnet, camphor gum, and caliber .45 ball pistol ammunition.

Considerably more attention was devoted to the development of the "Kit, Emergency, Type B-2, Jungle Back Pad." In December 1941, six jungle kits were sent to France Field, Canal Zone, for field testing. The B-2 kit was adopted as standard on January 16, 1942. The kit went into wartime production based on the prototype designed in 1938, utilizing the rigid bolo machete. The 1938 internal design was quickly modified, based on comments received from the Canal Zone, and the finished kit weighed

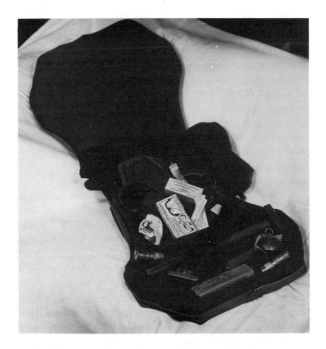

The Type B-2 Jungle Back Pad Emergency Kit of World War II. This photo of the parachute kit shows typical components including gloves, fishing kit, insect repellent, mosquito net, medical items, folding machete, pocket knife, red flare, compass, match container, and box of .45 caliber pistol ammunition. Rations are not shown. (Courtesy Robert Lehmacher)

10 pounds. About 335,000 Type B-2 kits were procured during the war, both as complete units and empty containers for depot assembly.

As originally produced by the contractors, the Type B-2 kit included the following components: folding machete with blade guard; pocket knife; sharpening stone; pocket compass; pair of mechanic's gloves; red fusee flare, commonly called a "railroad flare"; can of emergency rations; waterproof containers of matches, quinine, and calcium hypo-cholorite; 2 Carlisle first-aid packets; 6 Bandaids; tourniquet; box of ammonia aromatic spirits; 2 boxes of iodine; tube of tannic acid ointment; 2-ounce bottle of "Stay-Away" mosquito lotion; 10 yards of fishing line; 6 hooks and 6 flies; and a 20-round box of caliber .45 ball ammunition. A pistol was intended to be worn on the person.[23]

As the war progressed, technical advances and the changing needs of combat crewmen around the world dictated continuous alteration in the composition of the B-2 kit. Therefore, the B-2, the survival kit most commonly used during the war, was also the most modified. It would seem unlikely that this kit, with cut-out spaces for components, could be used with such a wide variety of non-conforming items; in practice, the neatly organized layout was soon discarded, with theater and local commanders tailoring the kits to their own special requirements. At least seven different component lists for the Type B-2 can be found and, unlike other kits, non-conformity was the rule. This makes documentation of the kit difficult, but in itself tells much about the constantly changing character of the war.[24]

A Type B-2 kit list from March 1945 indicated the following components retained from the original issue: folding machete; fishing kit; fusee flare; knife and sharpening stone; waterproof containers of matches and iodine; and the following added items: caliber .45 M15 shot ammunition; parachute rations; Type D-2 gloves; and the frying pan-insert first-aid kit.

As the stock of the Type B-1 Alaskan kit was depleted, the Type B-2 kit was to have been used universally. The B-2 kit was also placed in limited standard status as early as October 7, 1942, but because nothing else became available, it was used until finally declared obsolete on November 16, 1945. The Type B-2 kit was an available, if not a chosen, item.

The typical aircraft seat of the period was bucket-shaped. The seat portion could hold the seat parachute and perhaps a pararaft pack, and the back of the seat could accommodate the back-pad survival kit. With the increasing popularity of the back-type parachute, a new kit to be used as a seat cushion was needed. On June 12, 1942, the Type B-3 emergency-parachute kit was standardized for AAF use. The container was approximately 13 inches × 15 inches × 4 inches in size, and the components were intended to be the same as used in the Type B-2 kit. The adoption of the B-3 kit proved to be a non-event, because none were procured, in spite of the item being listed in the AAF Class 13 Supply Catalog.[25]

Throughout the war, improvements were made in survival equipment and techniques with the advice of explorers, backwoodsmen, and experienced hunters. Their suggestions were considered in conjunction with reports received from airmen in the field, and from the U.S. Navy, as well as research and testing at Wright Field, Ohio, Eglin Field, Florida, and Ladd Field, Alaska. As procurement of the B-2 kit continued, the Equipment Laboratory worked to develop a universal parachute-emergency kit. It would be configured for either the seat or back parachute, and outfitted with components for any war theater. A universal kit was developed as a result of recommendations and standardized as the "Kit, Emergency Parachute, Type B-4," on October 7, 1942.[26]

This new kit could be worn as a seat or back cushion, and featured components superior to those in earlier kits. Procurement was delayed, however, because of an unfortunate decision by supply officials. Technical Order Number 00-30-145 was issued on February 17, 1943, requiring that stocks of the earlier Types B-1 and B-2 kits be exhausted before new kits were released for issue.[27] A contract was let for 25,000 B-4 kits on June 4, 1943,

The Type B-4 parachute emergency kit, in a photo taken at Wright Field on May 19, 1943. The B-4 kit consisted of an olive-drab cotton duck container with felt padding and a zipper. Among the useful items in the kit can be seen a soft vinylite plastic canteen, shown under the gloves and mosquito headnet, a folding machete, plastic goggle, disk-shaped plastic frying-pan insert in pan containing a first-aid kit, sewing kit, and fishing kit, and a 15-minute signal flare at right. Two boxes of .45 caliber shot cartridges were usually included, but in this photo their place at the bottom is occupied by a fishing-kit tin usually found in the Type B-2 kit. The original kits had the metal tin of sealed rations, also used in the B-2. Later the D ration was used, and the fifteen-minute flare was replaced by two five-minute flares. Other later additions to the B-4 kit included the AAF survival manual and a multi-purpose poncho-quilt. (Courtesy USAF)

but not one had reached a combat theater by October. There was some controversy in regard to the delay in substituting the universal Type B-4 kit for the older kits then in use. The Chief of the Equipment Laboratory disagreed with the policy of not issuing B-4 kits until the supply of the older kits was exhausted. He said that there was considerable stock of the older kits, and their issue would cause personnel to continue to use inadequate material for an indefinite period.[28] Almost the entire 25,000 kits were in the various theaters of operation by the autumn of 1944, but the bulk went unissued, and large quantities were sold as surplus on the civilian market after the war and salvaged for their components.

The Type B-4 kit was about 15 inches × 12 inches × 4 inches in size, with an issue weight of 13 pounds. The container was made of cotton duck with felt padding and a zipper. The contents included: a folding machete; pocket knife and sharpening stone; 2 boxes of .45 caliber shot ammunition; matches in a waterproof container; signalling mirror; 2 flares; D ration; flexible plastic canteen; pocket compass; gloves; mosquito headnet; sun or snow goggles; oil; frying pan with cover and detachable handle; and a frying pan-insert kit. This was a disk-shaped plastic box for a wide variety of small medical and fishing items.[29]

About two years after its introduction, the Type B-4 kit was modified to include a copy of AAF Manual 21W dealing with jungle-desert-arctic-sea survival, and a very effective quilted poncho. This versatile item could be worn, lain on, slung as a hammock, and used as a litter, signal panel, or small "pup" tent. It also served to provide a welcome layer of cushioning to the kit container. This version of the kit was probably the type designated by the Materiel Command as the Type B-5 on April 12, 1944, but markings on surviving specimens continued to bear the B-4 designation. The "Kit, Parachute Emergency, Type B-5," is described and illustrated in Technical Order No. 03-1-46, July 10, 1945, which lists its status as "under procurement." According to the T.O.: "The Army B-5 kit is designed for use by all flyers who use a seat type parachute. When packed it appears to be a seat cushion and is worn directly above the seat type parachute. This kit contains a poncho quilt . . . other items in the kit are: wool socks, hood, and poncho carrying case." It is likely that the Type B-5 kit remained in service-test status and none were actually procured for standard issue before contracts were cancelled at the end of the war.[30]

SURVIVAL VESTS

By early 1943, work had begun on another new and unique survival kit and components, made in the form of a vest. Samples of what would become the "Vest, Emergency Sustenance, Type C-1," were completed in June.[31] In December, 3,000 vests, designated as "Vest Type Emergency Kit," were procured for combat testing by the Fifth, Tenth, Eleventh, and Fourteenth Air Forces and the Air Transport Command. Service tests were also conducted in Florida from January to June 1944. The vest was covered by specification 3206, established on January 11, 1944, and standardized on May 3. It was designed around very specific components, and only minor changes were made as a result of the tests completed on August 8. By December 1944, 200,000 Type C-1 vests were on order, with 16,000 units already delivered.

The design and configuration of the Type C-1 vest remained remarkably constant throughout its service life. It was well made, of dark olive-green tackle twill, with the AAF insignia printed in color on the upper left breast. The vest would not shrink and was very tough and durable. The front was secured with three buttons, and the back was adjustable with three tie strings, so one size would fit all. It was worn next to the flying clothing, under the Mae West life vest, parachute, and flyer's armor. The C-1 vest weighed 11 pounds with all components, and with its wide assortment of survival gear was intended to replace the parachute back-pad kits. It was also intended for use with the Type C-2 life raft, and components were designed to integrate well.[32]

The upper chest pockets of the C-1 vest, marked for personal items, were slanted outward on the prototype and some early contracted vests. The stenciled content markings varied among producers. Procurement was evidently enthusiastic, with no less than six different manufacturers producing the C-1 under at least nine contracts.[33] The vests were procured both complete and for local assembly. The construction of the vest provided sixteen pockets, each identified for specific items or kits. A holster for the M1911 or M1911A1 .45 caliber pistol was incorporated in the left underarm position. Components for the first time included an illustrated instruction booklet for the vest and its components, along with AAF Manual 21W on survival.

Among other components in the C-1 vest was a first-aid kit in a small plastic box, containing a morphine Syrette, along with other medical items and soap. This was located in pocket number 1 and, as issued, a red string was sewn between the pocket and flap and sealed with a spot of lead, to provide a visible check that the kit contents were not disturbed. Other pockets contained the following: two tins of emergency parachute rations; two red 5-minute fusee flares; a plastic box containing a 3-ounce oiler; 12 fire-starting tabs with a striking surface; a plastic whistle; razor and blades (or in its place a burning glass); large knife with 5-inch folding blade and folding saw blade; sharpening stone; mosquito headnet; fishing kit and instructions in a plastic box; spit and gaff hook assembly; emergency signaling mirror, ESM/1 or ESM/2; OD plastic

Front view of Type C-1 emergency sustenance vest, supplied to AAF flyers in case they were forced down in isolated areas. It was worn over flying clothing but under the Mae West and parachute harness. The adjustable 11-pound vest contained sixteen pockets, filled with items of equipment necessary or helpful for survival. Shown here are some of the components including a first-aid kit (upper left), large folding knife, box of .45 caliber shot cartridges, two cans of emergency parachute rations, ESM/2 signal mirror in packet (at right), and two five-minute red flares (bottom). (Courtesy Robert Lehmacher)

veloped for use in all parts of the world, it proved to be better suited to the tropics than to arctic regions.

Additional items were sometimes added to the C-1 vest by units in the field. In India, vests issued to B-29 crewmen contained a "Pointie Talkie" native phrase booklet, paper blood chits without serial numbers, probably printed in India, rayon-cloth maps, Chinese paper money, and on the front of the vest, on both sides of the opening, were two sewn-in rows of about forty Indian one-rupee silver coins. These vests were usually issued before a mission and turned in after the flight, along with the .45 caliber pistol.

A method was developed during World War II for adapting the standard musette bag as a quick-attachable container for the C-1 vest. This eliminated the need to wear the vest under other items of equipment. The canvas bag, containing the vest and contents, was attached only to the left side of the parachute harness to prevent entanglement with the Type C-2 life-raft static line.[36]

The Type C-1 vest, like the Type B-4 kit, met with difficulty in getting through the supply system and into combat usage. However, components unique to the C-1 quickly found their way into the Type B-2 back-pad kits still being used. Following the war, huge quantities of C-1

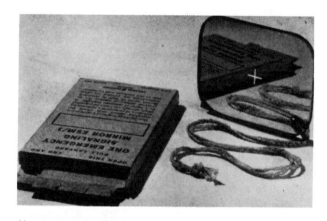

Next to a smoke signal, an emergency signalling mirror was the best daytime signal in World War II. Mirrors were included with several life rafts, the Type C-1 vest, and the Types E-5, E-11, and E-12 emergency kits. The mirror most widely used by the AAF was made by General Electric and known by the company designation ESM/1. It was made of mirrored tempered glass, with cross hairs in the center of the mirror for directing the beam. The ESM/1 was approximately 0.19 x 4 x 5 inches, and weighed 0.5 pound. It came with 4 feet of number 48 seine twine, used as a lanyard. Reports indicated a sight range of up to 18 miles, but considerable practice was needed if the user was to become proficient in signalling. A later, smaller model, the ESM/2, was made of tempered glass and mirrored on both sides with a clear cross in the center. Instructions on the back directed the user to superimpose the reflected cross upon the clear cross in the center of the mirror, and then view the object to be signalled through the two crosses. (Courtesy USCG)

waterproof container with 40 matches, a strip of flint along the side, and a compass in the top; a rain-sun hat and reversible OD/yellow gloves, usually Type D-3; box of 20 rounds .45 caliber M15 shot cartridges; waterproof soft-plastic holster or cover for the pistol; packets of gauze bandages; toilet paper; three-pint water container of soft vinylite plastic; and goggle Type III M1943.[34]

Each pocket was numbered in sequence and imprinted with the intended components. The sequence of the numbering was disrupted by the inclusion of pocket number 16 for insect repellent, which was added following the field tests conducted during the summer of 1944.

One item included in the initial production was deleted, based on service tests. This was a collapsible cooking utensil with a capacity of about one pint. This potentially hazardous item was made of asbestos with a neoprene coating inside, and was supported by a weak asbestos cord. It was rejected, because it proved to be unstable and the inside coating often caught fire, and not because the danger to health of asbestos was realized at that time.[35]

Except for the changes noted, the Type C-1 vest configuration remained constant until the spring of 1945, when more local option was authorized, and just one of the two emergency-parachute rations was required. Although de-vests were sold as surplus, and the completion of this kit is the quest of many of today's collectors of militaria.

Usage of the Type C-1 vest in World War II was rather limited, but the vest was put to good use during the Korean conflict, not only by U.S. Air Force flyers, but also Navy and Marine Corps fighter pilots. Reproductions were made in Vietnam tailor shops in the 1960s, sometimes of camouflage nylon, and the same concept continued with the standard American SRU-21/P nylon-mesh survival vest, introduced about 1966.

According to the Type Designation Sheets, another survival vest was placed in service-test status on May 21, 1945. This was the "Vest, Emergency Sustenance, Type C-2," which was described as "Similar to the Type C-1 except that some of the pockets are empty. Equipment will be placed in those pockets in the theater of operations to conform to the requirements of the particular theater involved."[37] It is not clear whether this vest was actually a separate experimental design, or just the Type C-1 vest with empty pockets that were filled locally. No examples of the Type C-2 vest or other information have been found and, in any event, development of survival vests was discontinued at the end of World War II and not resumed until the early 1960s.

SURVIVAL AND SUSTENANCE KITS

Prior to the war, a limited number of improvised emergency kits had been prepared and carried on cross-country flights in the United States and on missions in overseas U.S. possessions. The first standard emergency kit to be developed by the Materiel Division was the "Case, Emergency, Flyer's Sustenance, Type F-1." This kit was service-tested beginning in August 1939, and standardized on May 28, 1940. The F-1 kit was a "forced landing kit" stowed on board the airplane and did not attach to the pilot's personal equipment. The kit consisted of a silver-colored waterproof canvas bag with a carrying handle, approximately 13 inches × 8 inches × 2 inches in size. The case contained two tins of Air Corps emergency rations and one larger tin. The larger can contained a flash light, matches in a case, hunting knife, pocket compass, fishing line and hooks, two gauze bandages, iodine swabs, and a Carlisle first-aid dressing packet. The Type F-1 kit was changed to limited standard on April 29, 1943, when more suitable kits such as the Types E-1 and E-2 became available in quantity, and was declared obsolete on December 4, 1943.[38]

Active development of emergency or "E" kits began in the Miscellaneous Branch of the Equipment Laboratory in 1941. Most were elaborate, multi-man kits to be stowed onboard aircraft or airdropped by parachute and, as such, are beyond the scope of this study. However, within the

189

Compasses used by AAF flyers in survival situations during World War II included: Army Corps of Engineers type with canvas carrier (upper left), magnetic wrist-type, liquid-filled, (upper right), pocket type with lid and cloth pouch, included in Types B-1, B-2, B-4, E-5, E-10, and F-1 emergency kits (left), small brass survival compass (used in personal aids kits) which could be swallowed if required and retrieved later (center), waterproof match holder with compass on the side of the cover, carried in the Type C-1 vest (right center), and plastic button that could be sewn on uniform, used by Eighth Air Force airmen. When suspended by a thread, the dots on back pointed north (lower right). (Courtesy Robert Lehmacher)

Type E-1 through E-19 series were a few exceptions: Types E-3, E-3A, E-6, E-7, and E-17.[39]

The Types E-6 and E-7 kits were very simple containers: zippered pouches provided with three horizontal and vertical attachment straps and "D" rings for attachment on either side of the parachute harness. They were designated as "Kit, Emergency Sustenance," and both were standardized on November 27, 1942, and changed to limited standard on August 9, 1943. The Type E-6 kit held two boxes of Army K rations, and the Type E-7 held two cans of drinking water. They were sometimes referred to as the "Bailout Rations Kit," and "Bailout Water Kit."[40] The kits were apparently found to be unsatisfactory, and rather small quantities were procured and used during the war.

The Types E-3, E-3A and E-17 kits are more interesting. These kits were hidden, perhaps purposely, within the "E" series and often skipped over in period listings of emergency kits. Called "personal aids" kits, they were actually very small escape-and-evasion kits and were unique in that they were procured for the Army Air Forces by the Military Intelligence Service. The Type E-3 kit carried the usual identification data, but the Types E-3A and E-17 kits were devoid of any designation, contract information or origin, normally marked plainly on AAF equipment. This may indicate that the kits were also used by intelligence organizations.

The first design, Type E-3, was a pocket-sized escape kit, contained in a cloth sack with draw-strings and marked; "Kit, Emergency Sustenance (Type E-3), Spec. 94-40441, Mfg. by S. Buchsbaum & Co., Air Forces, U.S. Army."[41] Within the sack was a plastic box, which contained matches in a waterproof container; a tiny escape compass, which could be swallowed if necessary and retrieved later; a section of hacksaw blade; halazone water-purification tablets; adhesive tape; malted milk tablets; bouillon powder; and chewing gum. Only limited quantities are believed to have been procured after standardization on June 10, 1942, and the kit was changed to limited standard on April 6, 1945, when it was officially superseded by a totally different style of kit, the Type E-3A.

The Type E-3A kit, like the E-3, was intended to be carried in the flyer's pocket.[42] It was standardized on April

Type E-3A personal aids kit was a small escape-and-evasion kit, which could be carried in the flyer's pocket. It contained a variety of food and medical items as listed on the plastic flask, including matches in a waterproof case (upper left), and a small, brass compass, which could be swallowed if necessary and retrieved later (upper right below lid). (Courtesy Robert Lehmacher)

6, 1945, eight months after the Type E-17, but it appears that quantities of this kit were used by combat personnel. The kit consisted of a single flask of ethyl cellulose, similar to the Type E-17 flask, with directions for component use imprinted on the side. The flask top, secured to the body with tape, had an opening at one end covered with a waterproof screw cap. The empty flask could serve as a canteen.

Components in the tightly-packed Type E-3A flask were: matches in a plastic container; mini-compass; roll of adhesive tape; small hacksaw blade; 2 packets bouillon powder; two 2-ounce sweet chocolate bars; a box of caramels; 4 sticks of chewing gum; a tube of antiseptic ointment; a vial of benzedrine sulphate tablets; halazone tablets; and aspirin tablets. About 150,000 Type E-3 and E-3A kits are supposed to have been procured by the end of the war.

Pocket flasks identical to the E-3A have been found, but with a variation in the component list indicating Navy usage. Documentation of this flask has not been found but it is possible that the Navy mated the E-3 components with a modified E-17-type flask as their own, which was soon adopted by the AAF as the Type E-3A.

The Type E-17 kit was developed in April and standardized on July 31, 1944.[43] This lightweight kit used two transparent ethyl cellulose flasks, which listed components and instructions for use, but no manufacturer or contract information was printed on the side. The two flasks were carried, separated by an ESM/1 signal mirror, in an unmarked OD canvas pouch. The 6 × 4.5 × 3-inch pouch originally had only the wire pistol-belt hook, but most were modified later by the addition of belt loops. Lift-the-dot fasteners secured the pouch flap. The tops of the flasks were secured by a wire bail, and the opening screw cap was centered. It was intended that when needed, the components could be placed in pockets and the flasks used to carry drinking water. While the top screw cap had a watertight gasket, the telescoping top was secured with a wire bail, which did not make the flask really watertight. The E-17 was procured from at least two different manufacturers, so slight variations exist. Quantities in excess of 95,000 Type E-17 kits were said to have been procured prior to the end of the war.[44] This kit was still listed in USAF supply catalogs published in the 1950s.

The two flasks were packed in a manner that separated the contents broadly into categories as "general" and "medical." The first contained: Army chocolate ration; four 1-ounce Hershey bars; four sticks of chewing gum; two packets of bouillon powder; ten double-edge razor blades; fish hooks and line; leader; small compass; sewing kit; small hacksaw blade; box of three prophylactics; sharpening stone; and a round waterproofed container holding matches. The wooden match sticks were cut in

The Type E-17 was a more elaborate personal aids kit, for escape and evasion. It consisted of a heavy, OD canvas pouch, containing an ESM/1 signal mirror separating two plastic flasks packed with useful survival items, including food, medical supplies, small compass, sewing and fishing kits, matches, and even three prophylactics. (Courtesy Robert Lehmacher)

half so twice as many could be carried. Although the condom is well known as a device to prevent sexually transmitted diseases, its many uses in a survival situation are often overlooked. Since World War II, prophylactics have been included in almost all individual survival kits.

The other flask contained medical components consisting of the following tablets: sulfaguanidine; sulfadiazine; benzedrine sulfate; halazone; salt; and atabrine. Also included was sulfanilamide; iodine; ophthalmic ointment; adhesive compress; adhesive tape; tweezers; and a toothbrush.

The following is a brief summary of emergency kits in the "E" series as listed in the Type Designation Sheets, including dates of standardization.[45] Most were eventually changed to limited standard status, but only the Type E-13 kit was declared obsolete during the war (on March 13, 1944). The Type E-4 kit was not approved by AAF headquarters and was probably not procured; it was declared inactive on September 4, 1943. The Types E-10 and E-11 were also not approved and were placed on inactive status on August 31, 1943, when they were replaced by the Type E-14. However, 250 Type E-10 kits were prepared and sent to the CBI theater for special use.

Some more specialized survival and emergency kits were developed by the Materiel Command and by other organizations. These items included the Type A-1 emer-

AAF edged weapons (top to bottom): Emergency hand axe for multi-place aircraft, overall length 15.62 inches; bolo machete, Collins No. 18, 9.19-inch blade, and leather scabbard, found in prewar survival kits; hunting knife, 5-inch blade, with leather sheath, Great Western 1942 AAF contract (left); folding machete, 10-inch blade, with edge protector, carried in survival kits (right); M3 knife, 6.7-inch blade, with M8 scabbard, a trench knife but carried by some aviators (left); large folding knife with 4.75-inch blade, from C-1 vest (right); Boy Scout type 4-bladed pocket knife from C-1 vest (left); and Kingston 4-bladed pocket knife with aluminum sides, from B-2, B-4 kits, etc. (right). Note: Other hunting-type axes also were carried in multiplace planes and included survival kits. Many other types of personal knives were carried by flyers. (Courtesy Robert Lehmacher)

gency sea-rescue gear, consisting of a parachute and five interconnected containers of supplies, one of which held a modified Type A-3A life raft. The A-1 was placed on limited procurement on December 12, 1944. The Type PP-1 sea-rescue kit also consisted of five watertight containers, including one with a life raft. All five containers of supplies were connected together, forming a life line 200 feet long. The PP-1 was standardized on May 21, 1945. Special-purpose kits included the Type JJ-1 seawater desalting kit, standardized on October 17, 1944; the Type SS-1 fishing kit for multi-place life-rafts, standardized on August 31, 1945; and various emergency medical kits.

Type	Characteristics	Standardized
E-1	(Ration) Waterproof cardboard container with canvas cover, contained some equipment as well as food.	Mar. 23, 1942
E-2	(Sustenance) Metal box with canvas cover; equipment included stove, fishing gear, .22 cal.-.410 gauge combination gun.	Mar. 23, 1942
E-3	Pocket escape kit for rations ("personal aids" kit).	Jun. 10, 1942
E-3A	Pocket "personal aids" kit, replaced Type E-3.	Apr. 6, 1945
E-4	Small gasoline stove and 3 cooking utinsils.	Jan. 16, 1943
E-5	Waterproof container with rations, water, medical and signalling equipment, sufficient for five people. Supplemented rations listed for life raft on over-water flights.	Oct. 24, 1942
E-6	Bailout rations kit.	Nov. 27, 1942
E-7	Bailout water kit.	Nov. 27, 1942
E-8	Desert and tropical implements kit, weighing 29 pounds, included .22 cal.-.410 gauge combination gun.	Nov. 27, 1942
E-9	Desert and ocean rations (aircraft or aerial delivery).	Nov. 27, 1942
E-9A	Similar to Type E-9 but improved container, 35 pounds (aircraft or aerial delivery).	Apr. 11, 1944
E-10	Desert and tropical emergency sustenance (aerial delivery). Superseded by E-14.	Nov. 27, 1942
E-11	Shipwreck, emergency sustenance, buoyant (aerial delivery). Superseded by E-14.	Nov. 27, 1942
E-12	Arctic emergency sustenance, 200 pounds, food, equipment, including .22 cal.-.410 combination gun or .30 cal. M1 carbine.	Feb. 3, 1943
E-13	Ocean emergency sustenance, cancelled because of similarity to E-5 and E-11 kits (aerial delivery).	May 25, 1943
E-14	Desert and tropical emergency sustenance, 80 pounds, food and equipment, including .22 cal.-.410 combination gun (aircraft or aerial delivery). Superseded E-10 & E-11.	Aug. 19, 1943
E-15	Ocean emergency sustenance, 90 pounds, buoyant container (aerial delivery). Superseded E-12.	Aug. 19, 1943
E-16	Northern area ration-replenishing kit, superior to Type E-1. Metal container, 35 pounds (aerial delivery).	Mar. 29, 1944
E-17	Emergency-escape kit, medical and misc. items for use in case of forced landing in enemy territory.	Jul. 31, 1944
E-18	Aluminum airtight container with suitable components for emergency survival of 3 men including .22 cal.-.410 combination gun (with Type G-8 parachute for aerial delivery).	Jul. 19, 1945
E-19	Ocean use, buoyant, food, water desalting kit, for 60 man-days (aerial delivery).	Jul. 19, 1945

AAF edged weapons (top to bottom): vinyl-covered OD scabbard marked "U.S., 1945;" machete for above, 18-inch, marked "Collins, U.S., 1942;" machete scabbard with AAF insignia impressed in rigid OD plastic; machete, unmarked, parkerized finish, with black plastic grips, pictured in several "E" type emergency airdrop kits; and leather scabbard for above. (Courtesy Robert Lehmacher)

ESCAPE AND EVASION (BARTER) KITS

In addition to the Types E-3, E-3A, and E-17 "personal aids" kits discussed previously, which were actually small survival kits, special escape and evasion (E and E) kits were developed and used during the war. More commonly referred to as "barter kits," they were issued to certain flyers, for use in case of an emergency landing in an unfriendly or primitive area overseas. Some airmen were able to barter their way out of difficult situations by the use of these E and E kits. Others were simply robbed by the natives of all valuables. Because of their high value, the kits were accountable, and airmen had to sign for them upon issue and return them as instructed.

The contents of the sealed plastic E and E kits, developed for use in Europe and the Pacific varied, but the following is a description of two typical kits, believed to date from World War II.[46] The "Atlantic Kit" for use in the European theater consisted of 15/100 troy ounces of fine

gold in the form of three rings, two British or South African half-sovereign coins, and one British or one South African sovereign (pound) coin, French 20-franc coin and 10-franc coin. All the coins in the kit examined appear to date prior to 1945.

The "Southeast Asia Kit" contained 1.08 troy ounces of fine gold consisting of two rings, a chain section with four links, a gold-embossed pendant, and a 21-jewel Swiss calendar watch with cloth band.

Other simpler packets, intended for jungle natives in remote areas, included colorful plastic beads, pins, mirrors, and trinkets, and several Indian silver rupee coins. These were listed in the revisions of April 1, 1944, to the AAF illustrated Class 13 catalog as "Kit, Flyer Trading Packet, Spec. 40685."

A special "kit" that had some of the characteristics of both a survival kit and an E and E barter kit was developed for flying personnel of the Fourteenth Air Force in China. This kit was made in the CBI in the form of a money belt, and was rather crudely fabricated of green canvas-like cloth with strings for tieing behind. It contained Chinese paper money, a pocket compass, and halazone tablets. The money-belt kit was strictly controlled, and airmen had to sign for it before a mission and return it upon landing.[47]

Another type of AAF individual escape and evasion "kit" was often issued to flyers in the European and Pacific theaters. This kit consisted of a small waterproof pouch, normally worn around the neck, with contents especially intended for the area or country over which the airman would fly. It usually contained one or two silk-finish rayon maps, printed in color, and a small compass, which could be swallowed if necessary for later retrieval. Local paper money was often included, and perhaps a native phrase booklet called a "Pointie Talkie." One of the better-known components was the escape flag or blood chit, in various forms, which was often included in the envelope or, like the Pointie Talkie, issued separately to flyers in various war zones.

BLOOD CHITS

The "Blood Chit" was the aviator's IOU, an agreement or pledge of payment or reward for the safe recovery of the bearer.[48] Since it could be exchanged by a native for payment, it was an accountable item, serially numbered, and usually issued and signed for by the airman. The flag-type blood chits were carried mainly in China and Southeast Asia. The blood chit originated with the "Flying Tigers," the American Volunteer Group, operating in China from late 1941 until July 1942. A serially numbered section of linen-type cloth bore the flag of the Republic of China in color, the promise of a reward in Chinese, and the official mark or "chop" of the Aeronautical Commission in

World War II escape and evasion aids: "Blood Chits," CBI theater with Republic of China flag, type produced in U.S. with "W" before serial number (left); SEA type in several languages, with American flag (right); vinyl pouch containing folded map and small compass (lower left); and "Pointie Talkie" native phrase booklet with cover open (lower right); all displayed on typical rayon escape map. (Courtesy Robert Lehmacher)

Chungking. A similar chit was made in the United States for flying personnel of the U.S. Army Air Forces, who began arriving in the China-Burma-India theater of operations in the spring of 1942. It was printed on waterproof silk-finish cloth, and the "W" preceding the serial number

indicated that the chit was procured from Washington, D.C. The chop in this case was that of the Chinese Embassy in Washington.

The flag-type blood chits were worn according to unit policy or the fancy of the airman. Some men sewed their chit on the back of their flying jacket, however, it was found that wearing the chit with the Chinese Nationalist flag displayed was dangerous if forced down in communist-held territory. Many flyers then sewed the chit inside their jacket for use as a pocket, or carried it hidden on their person, in a packet around the neck, or in a survival kit. The original type of chits used by the Flying Tigers or the AAF in China were copied by local craftsman in India, using more attractive and durable leather. These were sold to American airmen during the war, and reproductions are being made in Asia today for sale to collectors.

Cloth blood chits, with the American flag in color, were prepared by the Military Intelligence Service, G2 Section, U.S. War Department. The promise of a reward for helping the flyer was printed on the fabric section in several different Asian languages, and the chits were issued in the appropriate locations. New versions were prepared when the war moved into new areas.

In the European and Mediterranean theaters, the RAF incorporated safe-conduct messages along the margin of flight maps, and some of these were used by American airmen. Cloth flight maps of Asia were later published by the AAF Aeronautical Chart Service, with a strip on the right side bearing a safe-conduct message in seven languages, including English. Calling-card and passport-type blood chits were used in North Africa, with a message in Arabic and English from the President of the United States. It also included a list of helpful words in Arabic, French, Spanish and Portuguese.

A folder, featuring a large picture of an American flag, was issued to AAF personnel operating near or over Soviet-occupied territory. A problem developed with the first issue, because of the instruction that the bearer should present it to any Russian troops he encountered. When the downed airman reached in his pocket for the safe conduct pass, he was shot by the edgy Russian soldiers. A second version was quickly issued, instructing the user to keep his hands high and not attempt to remove the booklet from his pocket, where it would no doubt be found when he was searched.

The precedent set by the blood chits used in World War II continued after the end of that conflict, and variations were carried during the Korean and Vietnam wars. The actual value of the blood chit is debatable. Airmen who flew in the various wars have mixed opinions; some feel that they were a useful item to carry, while others believe they were (and are) useless, especially in Asia and the Middle East, for a variety of reasons.

THE AIR RESCUE SYSTEM

Having discussed briefly the development of survival technology through World War II, mention must be made of the other and equally important function: search and res-

cue. Prior to the war, little consideration had been given by the Army to locating and rescuing missing airmen. Downed flyers were searched for in a rather haphazard fashion, utilizing the available resources of local bases and units and, if over water, those of the U.S. Navy and Coast Guard. An organized rescue program or organization was not thought to be necessary, until the advent of large fleets of American aircraft operating over vast areas of the globe.[49]

The unprecedented expansion of Army Air Forces activity after Pearl Harbor, including long overwater flight operations, created a critical need for an effective worldwide air rescue system. Not only was the rescue of highly trained airmen essential to the war effort, but the maintenance of morale would also be greatly enhanced by the knowledge that all flyers could expect to be saved if they were forced down. Because much of the flying during the war was over water, the concepts and capabilities of rescue were developed primarily for recovering airmen from the sea. By 1945, however, efforts were also underway to rescue downed flyers from behind enemy lines on land.

Even before the United States entered the war, the mechanics of search and rescue were being perfected by the Germans and British. A great deal of effort was expended in Europe in establishing an organization utilizing the grid method of search, and specially trained and equipped to rescue downed flyers. Early AAF attempts at air-sea rescue leaned heavily upon the RAF for guidance and support, and British rescue-control centers served as models for those established by the AAF.[50]

In the immense areas of the Pacific, little aid could be expected from the British and, for that reason, the greatest amount of AAF air-sea rescue effort was concentrated in that region, including operations in enemy-held waters. It was realized early on that time was of primary importance in rescue work, as was cooperation between the AAF and the U.S. Navy. The Navy utilized many aircraft and surface vessels for search and rescue, but in March 1943 they also began to employ submarines in the rescue role.

During the summer of 1943, Army Air Forces planners prepared a worldwide rescue plan, which was approved by Gen. Henry H. Arnold, the commanding general. The program was implemented by the newly established AAF Flight Control Command, but progress towards completion was slowed by lengthy arguments over areas of jurisdiction and responsibilities.[51] Overall AAF responsibility was eventually assigned to the new Emergency Rescue Branch, subordinated to the Assistant Chief of the Air Staff for Operations, Commitments, and Requirements, in Washington, D.C.[52] By 1944, control centers were being opened, and better coordination was established between the AAF, Navy, and Coast Guard. In February 1945, an AAF regulation was published, which included a uniform plan for air-sea rescue in the United States, overseas theaters, and on air transport routes.[53]

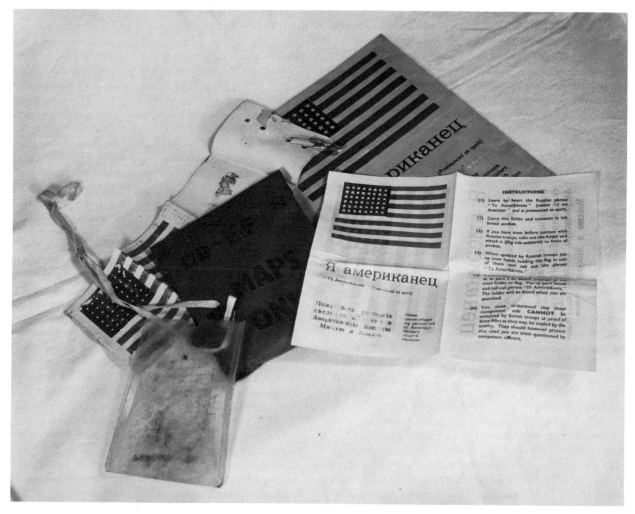

Typical AAF Mediterranean theater escape kit. This kit, usually worn around the neck, consisted of a plastic pouch containing an American flag-arm band of the type worn on D-Day by invasion forces (left), a safe conduct message in Russian with American flag (upper right), and a packet of rayon maps (center). A small escape compass and foreign paper money were sometimes included (not shown). (Courtesy Robert Lehmacher)

In 1943, increased emphasis was placed on survival training and rescue techniques for all aircrew members, utilizing many excellent publications and films produced by the AAF Training Command. Percentages of successful rescues in every theater rose, not only through the use of improved equipment and procedures, and increased numbers of rescue personnel, but also because aircrewmen became aware of the importance to them of their own actions before, during, and after abandoning their aircraft.[54] Notwithstanding this progress, inadequate training, shortages of equipment, and the lack of proper organization for air rescues hindered efforts until rather late in the war. Equipment and supplies, including survival gear,

were often shared by AAF and Navy units in the field, especially in combat zones. A limited number of items of Army-Navy "AN" standard survival equipment were available for procurement by both services but, unfortunately, materiel adopted by one branch or service seldom found any other users. Greatly improved survival and rescue equipment became available by mid-1945.[55]

Specialized search-and-rescue units were formed in accordance with the AAF rescue plan, and outfitted with a variety of equipment. The equipment included rescue boats, L-5 liaison planes, and amphibians of the OA-10 series, the AAF version of the Navy PBY-5 "Catalina." Pilots and maintenance personnel of AAF rescue units were trained in seaplane operations, at the Naval Air Station, Pensacola, Florida. B-17H (SB-17) and later, faster and longer-ranged B-29 (SB-29) aircraft were modified to drop the "Lifeboat, Airborne, Type A-1" by parachute. Experiments were not completed in time for SB-29s with the A-1 lifeboat to see action before the Japanese surrender. This boat, designed about May 1944, was 27 feet long and could accommodate 12 men for 20 days. The sturdy, wooden-hulled craft weighed 3,250 pounds when fully outfitted with survival equipment and supplies. Its two air-cooled engines gave it a speed of eight knots and a cruising range of 500 miles. This was a big improvement over the pneumatic life rafts.

The importance of radio-homing aids in rescue operations was also emphasized, and many missing aircraft were located through preliminary radio search from direction-finder stations. The need for recovering flyers down in difficult terrain and stranded behind enemy lines led to the development of the helicopter for rescue purposes. Sikorsky R-6 helicopters made their appearance in the Pacific in the last months of the war, but the small number available was confined chiefly to land-rescue and-evacuation duties, mainly in the China-Burma-India theater.

An Arctic, Desert and Tropic Information Center (ADTIC) was established by the AAF in 1943, to study and disseminate new survival information of importance to airmen flying in all parts of the world. Numerous ADTIC bulletins, manuals, and films were prepared and distributed during the course of the war.

The Air Sea Rescue Agency was organized in Washington, D.C. in the spring of 1944, to help coordinate air-sea rescue activities between the services, and provide the latest information on survival equipment and techniques. The Agency was under the jurisdiction of the Coast Guard, which in wartime was under the control of the Navy. The staff included representatives from all services, but the Agency was basically occupied with advisory and liaison functions. Publications included the *Air Sea Rescue Bulletin,* prepared monthly for the Agency by the Coast Guard, beginning in July 1944. The *ASR Bulletin* provided valuable information on new survival equipment and procedures. The "Air-Sea Rescue Equipment Guide," first published in 1945, was a handbook constantly updated by supplements. It furnished details on Navy, AAF, and Allied survival gear.[56]

Inter-service cooperation was recognized early as essential to efficient rescue operations. It was often achieved between operational units and sometimes even at higher command levels, but during all of World War II effective planning was hampered by the failure of the Army and Navy to agree on rescue responsibility. The basic question of inter-service responsibility for rescue operations was not settled until the AAF delegated its responsibility for rescue to the Air Transport Command (ATC), on April 1,

1946. The Air Rescue Service (ARS) which was then formed gradually extended its range until it became an effective, worldwide organization.[57]

THE SUCCESS OF AIR RESCUE OPERATIONS

Air rescue operations in World War II achieved varying degrees of success according to the theater of operation, the climatic conditions, and period of the war.[58] Aircrews in the Eighth Air Force were assured a one-in-three chance of rescue from the sea, but most of those who bailed out or made a forced landing in enemy-controlled territory were captured and sent to a prisoner-of-war camp. By 1945, distressed crews in the Far East Air Force were rescued in more than 50 percent of the cases. Across the wide Pacific, the chance of rescue varied according to the area and command. Rescue efforts on the long bombing routes to Japan were almost 80 percent successful in some months, but in the Southwest Pacific such results were never attained. In other areas—such as the continental United States, Alaska, the Caribbean, the North Atlantic, and the South Atlantic—the probability of rescue also varied, but an upward trend toward the end of the war was consistent.[59] The situation had improved to the extent that by 1945, combat crews could reasonably expect to be picked up if they were shot down.[60] This was a testimony to the improvement in equipment, training, technique, inter-service cooperation, and the overall rescue program.

Despite all difficulties, the lives of nearly 5,000 Army Air Forces flyers were saved through the use of survival equipment and techniques, and the dedicated efforts of air rescue personnel on both land and sea.[61] Perhaps the most important factor of all was the courage and ingenuity of the American airman in a survival situation.

# Miscellaneous Equipment

A common complaint voiced by the flyer, concerning the equipment used during World War II, was that he felt like a Christmas tree when fully equipped, with items dangling everywhere.[1] An examination of aviation-supply catalogs published from World War I through World War II discloses a substantial growth in the number of items of clothing and personal gear available to the airman, but also a significant increase in the sophistication of the equipment. The development of equipment and procedures has traditionally been tied closely to advances in aircraft technology. Providing the most modern and efficient personal gear for the aviator has always been a challenge, and this situation is unlikely to change in the foreseeable future.

Several major categories of personal equipment have been discussed in previous chapters. The following is, by necessity, only a small selection of some of the more important types of miscellaneous flight materiel used by Army aviators.

WATCHES FOR AVIATORS

Military operations are keyed to correct, or at least, standard time, and synchronized time is particularly important to the airman. Army pocket watches normally were of two types; Grade I (railroad grade), and Grade II; the grade being determined by the requirements for accuracy. Wrist watches were issued at least as early as 1912, and during World War I the Signal Corps procured wrist watches from the Hampden Watch Company, the Illinois Watch Company, and the Elgin Watch Company. A seven-jewel movement was adopted as standard for issue to authorized enlisted personnel and a fifteen-jewel movement for sale to officers. All had a waterproof case bearing the serial number of the movement on the outside. The Army Air Service issued a time and stop watch (navigation timer), made in Switzerland. It was a fifteen-jewel pocket watch with a white dial face marked "Allion a Versailles, U.S. Air Service, Importe de Suisse." The gun-metal case was trimmed with gold plate and the hands were gilt. Many flyers provided their own personal watches, rather than use the standard Army watches, which became a responsibility of the Ordnance Department during the 1920s.

The installation of timepieces in aircraft, for general flight and navigation purposes, became common during the early 1920s. These clocks, with various features, were usually of American manufacture. According to a report by the U.S. Bureau of Standards in 1923, any sturdy, reliable make of clock could be used. The only clocks peculiar to Army aircraft at that time were reversing stopwatches used in bombing. These were so constructed that, when the stem was pressed for the second time, the pointer started to move back to zero instead of stopping as in a stopwatch of the usual type.[2]

Accuracy was essential in the timepieces and stopwatches required for use in working complex navigation problems. By the early 1930s, watches procured by the Air Corps had become an item of issue for use in aerial navigation. The "hack watch" was a particular kind of wristwatch, used especially by navigators, so constructed that the movement stopped when the winding knob was disengaged, allowing accurate setting. The hack watch could be "hacked," or stopped, and set to within a second, meaning that the second hand could be synchronized with the minute hand.[3]

The first watch to be standardized by the Air Corps was designated as the Type A-1. Intended for use with the ground speed drift-indicator, it entered service-test status in June 1926, and was finally standardized for use on March 29, 1930. It was changed to limited standard on March 28, 1936, but was not declared obsolete until January 21, 1944, long after stock was exhausted.[4]

The Type A-2 was a Swiss Wittnauer watch set, adopted as limited standard on January 8, 1932, after only six months of service-testing. The A-2 was designed as a master timepiece, from which the navigator could set his wristwatch. It consisted of one solar and one sidereal watch mounted in a wooden case. A movable lid on the case provided a means of covering the face of either watch, to avoid the mistake of taking time from the wrong watch. Solar time is the apparent time, while sidereal time is time measured by reference to the apparent motion of the first point of Aries. The A-2 was finally declared obsolete on November 22, 1943.

Another watch, the Type A-3, was also adopted as limited standard on January 8, 1932, after the same period of service-testing as the A-2. This was a Wittnauer wristwatch with a sweep second hand. It incorporated a special inner dial, which could be rotated for the second setting. It was used with the sextant for astronomical observations, and was declared obsolete at the same time as the Type A-2.

The next watch set to be procured by the Air Corps was designated as the Type A-4, and adopted as limited standard on October 12, 1934, after eighteen months of testing. It consisted of one Waltham solar and one sidereal watch with a white face, mounted in a wooden case, and could be rotated for record setting. It was often referred to as an "avigation" watch. The A-4 was used for navigation purposes, and was not declared obsolete until March 14, 1942.

The Type A-5 watch was a George H. Adamson product, with a Waltham Company movement. It consisted of a black 24-hour dial, and indicated in arc and time. Service testing began on April 16, 1934, but it was placed in-active status on July 19, 1937, and reworked into the Type A-9.

Most watches, beginning with the Type A-6, were built according to Air Corps specifications. The Type A-6 was designed as a master timepiece, to keep the solar and sidereal time during navigation missions. It consisted of two standard white-face railroad watches, mounted in a vibration-proof wooden case, which incorporated a win-

The Type A-6 sidereal watch in vibration-proof wooden case. De-signed as a master timepiece, it was accompanied by a solar watch to accurately keep the solar and sidereal time during navigation missions. This photo dated July 15, 1934, shows the A-6 sidereal with the case open. (Courtesy U.S. Army)

The Type A-4 sidereal "avigation" watch, made by the Waltham Company, was adopted by the Air Corps as limited standard issue on October 12, 1934. It was fitted in a wooden case with a solar watch, and used for navigation purposes, until finally declared obsolete in 1942. (Courtesy U.S. Army)

dow to permit observation. It was similar to the Type A-4 except that the second-hand setting position was now obtained by the use of a secondary stopwatch. A limited procurement, probably because of budgetary constraints, was made on August 22, 1934. The A-6 was changed to limited standard on May 1, 1940, and declared obsolete on November 26, 1943, along with most of the older types of watches.

The Type A-7 hack watch was a secondary timepiece, set from a master watch and incorporating stopwatch mechanism. This photo taken on July 15, 1934, shows the original version procured in October 1934, with a white face but changed to black by 1940. The A-7 was replaced by the A-11, and declared obsolete in November 1943. (Courtesy U.S. Army)

color was changed to black by 1940.[5] A limited procurement was made on October 2, 1934, and probably another small quantity in the late 1930s. It was made limited standard on May 1, 1940, and declared obsolete on November 26, 1943.

According to the Type Designation Sheets, the Type A-8 was never standardized officially, although a limited procurement was made on October 12, 1934, and another on May 28, 1940. It evidently proved quite satisfactory, because it continued in production during World War II. The A-8 was a stopwatch, designed for timing ground-speed meters for determining the velocity of aircraft relative to the ground. It was a pocket type, incorporating a continuous running movement with one sweep hand. One revolution of the hand was equivalent to ten seconds of time. The face was white on watches manufactured by the Wittnauer Watch Company before the war, but changed to black on Waltham models made in 1940 and later.

The Type A-9 watch was modified from the Type A-5 by reworking the dial and hands to indicate time on a twenty-four-hour face, and by the addition of a sweep second hand. A device to stop the movement to permit

The Type A-8 was a pocket stopwatch procured by the Air Corps in limited quantities in 1934 and 1940, and in considerable numbers during World War II. This photo from July 15, 1934, shows the original Wittnauer ten-second timer with a white face. The A-8 watches procured in 1940 and later had a black face. (Courtesy U.S. Army)

The Type A-7 was designed as a secondary timepiece or hack watch, the time being set from a master watch and incorporating stopwatch mechanism. It could be attached to the wrist with a brown leather band, or carried in the pocket. The A-7 originally had a white face but the

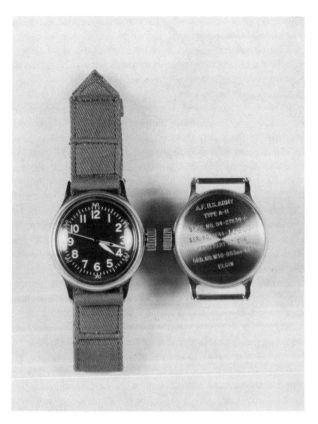

1938, and adopted as limited standard on May 1, 1940. It was a wrist type with a twenty-four-hour dial, and operated as a stopwatch by manipulating the stem. It was declared obsolete on November 26, 1943, after stock was exhausted.

The Type A-13 was a master, similar to the A-9 except for incorporation of a start-and-stop feature in the stem. It was tested from September 22, 1938, and standardized on May 1, 1940. It was changed to limited standard on October 20, 1941, and declared obsolete on November 26, 1943.

The Type A-14 designation was not assigned, and the Type A-15 was service-tested but declared obsolete on June 4, 1945. The A-15 was a seventeen-jewel Bulova wrist type, with a sweep second hand incorporating a rim accumulator.

The last watch to be adopted by the AAF during World War II was the Type A-16, designated as substitute standard on March 24, 1945. It was similar to the A-11, except that temperature-rate tolerances were doubled and luminous markings and a twenty-four-hour dial were added.

Watches produced for use by both the Army and Navy under the "AN" standardization system were procured by the AAF beginning in 1942. Of particular interest is the AN5740 master navigational watch. This pocket-type watch had a black face and a twenty-four-hour dial. It was made

The Type A-11 wrist watch was carried by thousands of Army flyers, after standardization on May 1, 1940. The example in this photo, dated September 28, 1944, was made by the Elgin Watch Company and has the normal fabric band. The back shows the typical AAF markings. The A-11 hack watch proved to be an accurate, dependable timepiece for navigators and other aviators flying in every theater of operations. (Courtesy USAF)

setting was incorporated in the twenty-four-hour movement. A limited procurement of the A-9 was made on July 19, 1937, it was adopted as limited standard on May 1, 1940, and declared obsolete on November 26, 1943.

The Type A-10 watch is believed to have been an experimental design in 1937 that was discontinued.

The Type A-11 was the first watch since the A-1 to actually have been standardized for Air Corps use. Testing began on October 6, 1937, and the watch was standardized on May 1, 1940. It was a wrist-type hack watch with a fifteen-jewel movement, had a black face, and was provided with a sweep second hand. It was normally issued with a brown fabric band, but it can also be found with a brown leather band. The A-11 was built in large quantities during the war by several manufacturers, including Elgin Waltham, and Bulova, and is perhaps the best known of all AAF watches.

An Elgin-designed hack watch designated as the Type A-12 was placed in service-test status on September 22,

The AN5740 master navigational watch used by both AAF and Navy navigators during World War II. This photo shows a specimen from the NASM Collection of an AN5740 made by the Hamilton Watch Company, in its special metal carrying case from the George H. Adamson Company. The watch was cushioned by springs inside the case, to reduce the amount of vibration and shock to which it was subjected in normal use. Also shown is the original box with markings and an instruction leaflet. (SI Photo 85–6744)

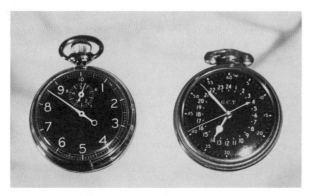

Type A-8 pocket stopwatch of wartime manufacture, with black face (left); and AN5740 master navigational watch, shown without case (right). (Courtesy Robert Lehmacher)

by the Hamilton Watch Company and possibly other manufacturers, and was used in quantity. The AN5740 watch was installed in a special metal carrying case from the George H. Adamson Company, and was suspended inside by springs to minimize shock and vibration.

A number of other watches were tested over the years but not adopted for aviation use for one reason or another. A model called a "pilot's watch" received the B-1 type designation late in 1944. It was service-tested beginning on January 5, 1945, and declared obsolete on June 4 of that year.

Aviators require accurate, dependable timepieces, especially in wartime. The sturdy watches produced by American industry performed outstanding service for all branches of the armed forces, under the most difficult conditions, in every corner of the globe.[6]

SIGNAL PISTOLS AND PROJECTORS

Pistols

Signal pistols, also known as pyrotechnic pistols, Very pistols, and flare guns, proved to be important items of equipment for all military personnel, including flyers. This equipment was intended primarily to send prearranged or emergency signals that required immediate action, and to provide illumination.

Signalling by means of colored lights goes back a long way in history, and military pyrotechnics, which are specialized fireworks, were used by the U.S. Army during the Civil War. When the United States entered World War I, both the Army and the Navy were using the Mark III 10-gauge Very pistol, first introduced in 1914. This was an improved version of the signal pistol originally patented by Lt. Edward W. Very of the U.S. Navy on May 1, 1877.

The Mark III was a sturdy steel and brass, single-action, single-shot pistol with wooden grips and no trigger guard. It was 12.37-inches long and weighed about 2.5 pounds. The Mark III fired the Mark II signal-light cartridge, available in red, green, and white. The pistol action was top-break and similar to that of a shotgun, and the cartridges also resembled shotgun shells in appearance, although containing Roman candle balls instead of lead shot.[7] The star ignited as it left the barrel, and burned as it rose to a height of almost 200 feet.

The American Expeditionary Forces arriving in France in 1917 were equipped mainly with the weapons of the Allies. It was soon decided that the 10-gauge signal cartridge was too small for effective signalling under wartime conditions, and the Army adopted the very efficient French signal system. This simplified supply and improved signal communication with the French. The decision involved a change in caliber to 25 mm (1 inch) and the adoption of a French signal pistol, which was placed in production in the United States as the "Very Pistol, Mark IV." The new 25 mm pistol was similar in operation to the Mark III. It was single-action, constructed of brass, about 7.75-inches long overall, and weighed 2 pounds. The Mark IV was carried in the Very pistol holster, M1917. Cartridges included the Very star, Mark I, and the Very parachute cartridge, Mark I, both with a variety of colors and number of stars. The old Mark III 10-gauge pistols were returned to the United States for use in training.[8] In order to obtain a longer range, some of the Mark IV pistols were modified by giving the 4-inch barrel an 8.875-inch long lining of brass alloy .125-inch thick. This reduced the caliber to 12-gauge, and the modified pistol then had an overall length of 12.5 inches.[9]

Aviators used pyrotechnic pistols for signalling between aircraft in flight, and between aircraft and personnel on the ground. Ground personnel also used them for signalling aircraft. Flyers forced down behind enemy lines

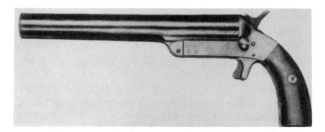

The durable Mark III 10-gauge Very pistol served from World War I through the end of World War II. Although intended primarily for U.S. Army ground forces and Navy personnel, it was also used at times by aviators for emergency signalling. The approximate height of the pyrotechnic signal trajectory was 200 feet. (Courtesy USCG)

also found the pistols effective for setting their aircraft on fire. Efforts were made to equip all planes with a signal pistol, attached by clips in the pilot's cockpit.[10]

During 1918, the Army Air Service found that a larger signal was desirable for use with airplanes, and the French 35 mm Model 1917 Chobert St. Étienne pistol was adopted as the "U.S. Signal Pistol, 35 mm, Mark I, Aviation." The cartridge, in a variety of colors and types, contained a larger quantity of pyrotechnic material, for better visibility aloft, and the propelling charge of powder was only sufficient to carry the illuminant clear of the wings of the plane. The Mark I was a single-action pistol made of aluminum, with an overall length of 10 inches, and a weight of 2 pounds. Manufacture of the Mark I began in the United States, but only one complete pistol was delivered by the time of the Armistice.[11]

Large stocks of pyrotechnic materiel were on hand after the war and remained in service, despite the recommendation of the Army Pyrotechnic Board that new equipment be developed.[12] The Mark III pistol continued as standard issue in the Navy and Marine Corps, while the Mark III and Mark IV pistols remained in use by ground personnel of the Army and National Guard. The Mark IV was still shown as standard issue as late as 1929.[13] It was finally phased out during the 1930s, but the old Mark III continued in service with the new lightweight M5 10-gauge Very pistol. Both the Mark III and the M5 pistols were changed to limited standard status for ground use during World War II, after the AN-M8 pyrotechnic pistol was adopted for standard use by all branches of the armed forces.

Pyrotechnic pistols and other devices were widely used on Army air fields, for communicating with aircraft in the days before radios entered general use. They were used frequently during World War II for signalling to or between aircraft, when radios were out of operation, or when radio silence had to be maintained. Pyrotechnics were also included in survival kits and life rafts for signalling during emergencies.

After World War I, the Army Air Service standardized on the "35mm Signal Pistol, Mark I, Aviation," for use aboard aircraft. Its main purpose was the projection of signals and flares from aircraft in flight. Instructions specified that a holster and ammunition holder be installed in the cockpit, within easy reach of either the pilot or observer.[14] During the mid-1930s, the Army Air Corps adopted a new pyrotechnic pistol, designated the M2, as a replacement for the Mark I pistol. Although developed commercially by the International Flare-Signal Company, the M2, like other signal pistols and ammunition, was the responsibility of the Army Ordnance Department.

The M2 was an awkward-looking, double-action, muzzle-loading brass pistol with no trigger guard, designed to be operated by one hand wearing a heavy glove. The handle

U.S. Signal Pistol, 35 mm, Mark I, Aviation, adopted by the Army Air Service in 1918 for use aboard aircraft. A single-action, top-break pistol of aluminum construction, it weighed 2 pounds and fired the larger 35 mm pyrotechnic cartridges in a variety of types and colors. (Reproduced from "Handbook of Aircraft Armament," Air Service, Washington, D.C., 1918)

had Bakelite grips bearing the manufacturer's name, and the military nomenclature was stamped on the short barrel. The M2 had a bore diameter of 1.56 inches, an overall length of 5.4 inches, a barrel length of only 2.15 inches, and a weight of 3.1 pounds.[15] A safety latch protruded on the rear of the grip, which was depressed automatically when the pistol was held for firing. The M2 had a strong recoil, and it was recommended that it be held with both hands when discharged. A lanyard was attached to the butt, which could be fastened to the plane.

The range of the M2 was about 200 feet, and a variety of rimless ammunition was available, including the M11 red star parachute-distress signal. The later rimmed signal cartridges for the AN-M8 pistol would not function in the M2 because it was muzzle-loaded, and the rim at the base of the cartridges was considerably larger in diameter than the cartridge cases themselves. Like the Mark III, the M2 was also sold commercially, and variations exist. The M2 was changed to limited standard early in 1943, when the AN-M8 pyrotechnic pistol entered service, and was declared obsolete by 1945.[16]

The AN-M8 pyrotechnic pistol was developed during 1942 as a replacement for all other types of signal pistols. It was originally designed to be the standard model for use by all branches of the armed forces, and continued in service for many years after the end of World War II. The AN-M8 was designed as a double-action, breech-loading, top-break pistol. It had plastic grips and, unlike the M2, it was equipped with a trigger guard. The pistol had a bore diameter of 1.58 inches, was 8.2 inches in overall length (9.9 inches with the M1 mount), and weighed 2.1

204

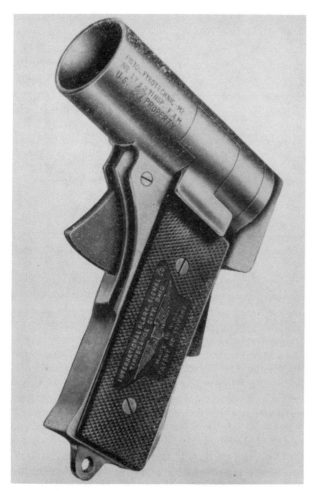

coded messages could be sent with pyrotechnic signals. The various colored signals that were available for use with the M2 and AN-M8 pyrotechnic pistols were assigned different meanings under a code that was changed at frequent intervals in each edition of the Signal Operation Instructions. The M11 red star parachute signal, however, was always used as a distress signal to be fired from the ground or from a life raft.[18] Ammunition was usually carried in the Types A-5, A-6, or A-7 canvas containers.

Hand Projectors

World War II generated an urgent requirement for large quantities of pyrotechnic equipment. Most of the current production of signal pistols and many of the older types were needed for use aboard aircraft or by ground personnel. This urgency stimulated the development of a new type of signalling device: the hand-held signal projector. These small, simple, inexpensive devices were lightweight, and fit easily in a survival kit, life raft, or pocket. They were not intended for use aboard aircraft in flight, but replaced many of the pyrotechnic pistols in rafts and emergency kits. Separate designs were developed by the

The M2 double-action, muzzle-loading, pyrotechnic pistol was used to project flares and signals from aircraft in flight. Introduced in the mid-1930s, it had a bore diameter of 1.56 inches, and weighed just over 3 pounds. A variety of rimless ammunition was available including an aircraft parachute flare, single- or double-star aircraft signals, blinker or cluster signals in red, yellow, or green, with or without parachutes, and the M11 red star parachute distress signal. (Courtesy USCG)

pounds. It was often issued with the M1 spring-recoil mount, which attached to the barrel and could be fastened to the airplane fuselage by machine bolts. It could, of course, be fired without the mount. The pistol and mount became standard equipment on bombers and were also carried on some fighters and other types of aircraft.[17] The AN-M8 was provided with the Type A-2 canvas holder.

A large variety of flare and signal ammunition was available for use including some parachute types. Cartridge-type (rimmed) signals could be loaded by inserting them through the breech end of the barrel. Rimless signals were loaded either through the breech or muzzle end. Brief,

The AN-M8 double-action, breech- or muzzle-loading, pyrotechnic pistol was introduced during World War II as the standard signal pistol for use by all branches of the armed forces. It had a bore diameter of 1.58 inches and weighed 2.1 pounds. The AN-M8 was a top-break design, and fired both the rimmed types of flares and signal ammunition and the rimless ammunition used with the M2 pistol. It could be fired by hand or from the M1 mount, shown here attached to the barrel. The disk on the chain is a clamp-on muzzle cover. (Author's Collection)

Army and Navy, but as the war progressed, some of the projectors were used by both branches for emergency signalling.[19]

The "Projector, Pyrotechnic, Hand, M9," was standard equipment in the Army during, and for many years after, World War II. It consisted of a short steel barrel with hinged breech, which housed the firing mechanism. The M9 had an overall length of 7.6 inches, and weighed only 14 ounces. The bore diameter was 1.56 inches, and many of the same signal rounds used in the M2 and AN-M8 pistols could be fired from the M9, including the M11 distress signal. The projector, like the pistol, could

The M9 pyrotechnic projectors were used widely during World War II, instead of signal pistols, in life rafts and emergency kits. The M9 was a small, simple device, consisting of a tube, held in the hand, from which a signal was fired by striking the firing-pin handle with the palm of the other hand, or hitting it against the ground or an oar. A safety clip was secured to the firing mechanism by a chain. The M9 was issued in a protective pouch with several signal rounds. (Courtesy USCG)

fire a signal to an altitude of about 200 feet. It was discharged by removing a safety clip attached to the end of a chain, and striking the firing pin handle with the palm of the hand, or hitting it against the ground, or an oar. The M9, like the signal pistols, normally came in a kit consisting of a moisture-resistant pouch with several signal rounds.[20]

The U.S. Navy developed the hand projector, Mark 3, a 10-gauge device that was eventually superseded by the Mark 4 model. Both were basically similar in operation to the M9, except that they were discharged by pulling and releasing the spring-loaded firing pin.[21]

"Signal, Flare, 2-Star Hand Held, M-75 (T-49)," was the official nomenclature for another pyrotechnic device introduced for AAF use during the latter part of the war. It was probably also used by the Navy along with the M9 in life-raft kits. The M-75 signal was cylindrical in shape, 5 inches long, 1.18 inches in diameter, and weighed 6 ounces. It was an expendable red star distress flare projector for one-time use at night, and could be carried in life-raft kits along with smoke grenades and signals.[22]

Other Pyrotechnic Equipment

Signal flares were included in certain Army and Navy survival kits. These included beacon flares in the Types E-10 and E-12 emergency kits, Coston-type flares in the Type E-5 kit, and 15-minute red fusee flares in the Types B-2, B-4, B-5, and E-11 kits. Two 5-minute red fusee flares were carried in the Type C-1 sustenance vest. The red fusee flares were similar to those used on railroads, but did not have the sharp nail in one end of the tube for making them fast and in an upright position. By the end of the war, the fusee flares were being replaced by the M-75 and Navy Mark I signals.[23]

Other items of pyrotechnic equipment were pressed into use by the AAF at the height of the war, for operational and emergency signalling. These included some Navy Mark III and Mark V pistols, and the Army M5, 10-gauge Very pistols. The Navy Mark V was a later model of the old Mark III, and was lighter, with a shorter barrel. AN-M3, AN-M8, or M18 smoke grenades, or the Navy Mark I Mod 0 hand-held distress signal, were included in most life-raft kits, or carried aboard aircraft for daytime emergency signalling. The Mark I Mod 0 had an illuminating flare on one end for night use, and on the opposite end generated smoke for day use.

RAF pyrotechnic signal equipment was issued to some Eighth Air Force units, for life-raft use during 1942–43, including the British "Signal Pistol, 1-inch, No. 2, Mark V," which operated much like the U.S. AN-M8 pistol. The British pistol was usually loaded with the T-51 emergency signal. The RAF, as well as many AAF experts, believed it preferable for survival purposes to have more shells of a lower candlepower than a few of great brilliance.[24]

FLASHLIGHTS

The first tubular electric hand torch or flashlight was manufactured in the United States in 1898. The Army found the flashlight to be a useful article of equipment, and various sizes and styles using two or more dry-cell batteries eventually became common items of issue. Flashlights and batteries were the responsibility of the Signal Corps. A two-cell flashlight was listed as standard equipment in Signal Corps Manual No. 3, 1916, and saw extensive use during and after World War I.[25] Another Army light was box-shaped and featured a magnifying lens.

The Air Corps procured the Type A-1, the first flashlight of its own design, during the mid-1920s. It was a two-cell, 3 volt, tubular type of conventional design.[26]

The Type A-2 was a commercial product, tested by the Air Corps between May 16, 1928, and June 3, 1930, but not adopted. It was similar to the A-1, except that the light was reflected at a right angle to the body. This design was probably quite similar to a standard Signal Corps type.

Standard Army flashlights were utilized by the Air Corps during the depression years of the 1930s, and a special design for aviation use was not standardized until August 20, 1941. This was the Type A-3, a headlight type for aircraft-maintenance purposes. It was changed to limited standard on February 15, 1944, and used through the end of World War II.

The Type A-4 was a three-cell type of flashlight, designed for use by crews in signalling taxiing airplanes at night. Although standardized on August 20, 1941, none was procured.

The Type A-5 was a special two-cell flashlight, with a flexible arm used for airplane-inspection purposes. It was standardized on August 20, 1941, and used in quantity well into the postwar period.

The next flashlight to be standardized for AAF use was the Type A-6, a handy pen light for illumination of maps and airplane equipment in flight. It was standardized on January 16, 1942, changed to limited standard on April 29, 1943, and used through the end of the war. It was replaced in production by the Type A-6A, which was the same as the A-6 except that it was made of plastic Tenite II material, and had a removable red color-filter so that use of the light would not interfere with night vision. It was standardized on April 29, 1943, and changed to limited standard on March 8, 1944. The Type A-6B was similar to the A-6A but the selective red filter was not detachable. The A-6B was standardized on March 8, 1944, changed to limited standard on July 18, 1945, and like the A-6 and A-6A, used in quantity through the end of the

conflict. The A-6B was officially superseded by the AN8023-1 flashlight on July 18, 1945. This standard model for all services consisted of a housing for two size "AA" batteries, with a lamp head designed with a selective red filter. The housing also had an attached combination switch and pocket clip.

The Type A-7 was a special lamp assembly, which was actually a waterproof floating identification light, for fastening by a cord to a multi-place life raft. It was standardized on June 22, 1942, and remained in use throughout the war, although the AAF intended to replace the A-7 with a hand-energized flashlight. The A-7 should not be confused with another floating identification lamp, the Type A, Signal Corps Type LM35, contained in the Type E-11 kit, or the Navy attachable life-jacket light, some of which were procured by the AAF in 1945 for use with the Type B-5 life vest.[27]

The Type A-8 was another pocket-type three-cell flashlight which was 4 × 5 inches in size. It was standardized on July 30, 1942, and changed to limited standard on April 10, 1945.

The Type A-9 saw considerable use in survival kits after its standardization on May 12, 1944. It was included in the Types E-2, E-5, and E-10 kits, and life rafts Type A-3A and E-2A. It was also useful for other tasks, because no batteries were required. The A-9 was a hand-energized type activated by squeezing the handle. It had a large reflector with a concentrated beam, and superseded a similar Navy hand-generating model with a smaller lens, also standardized by the AAF on May 12, 1944, as the Type A-10.

The last of the AAF flashlights of World War II was the Type A-11. It was a two-cell, signalling flashlight, with a luminous wand for directing aircraft while taxiing at night. The A-11 was originally standardized on July 8, 1944, but was not approved, and placed in inactive status on November 8. However, according to the Type Designation Sheets, the design was again standardized for use on April 2, 1945.

AAF flashlights were of a non-sparking or anti-static electricity design. In addition to the flashlights listed above, adopted by the AAF for use, standard flashlights and lamps developed by the Army Signal Corps were also used in quantity. Perhaps the best known was the Army TL-122-B flashlight. It was a two-cell type, with a head at right angles to the tube, and could be carried on the belt or pocket by a metal hook attached to the back of the OD plastic case. This "gooseneck" flashlight could also be used for signalling with a variety of colored lenses.

Although not a flashlight as such, the Signal Lamp, M-227, was often used on airfields and control towers. It was shaped like a submachine gun and had a metal skeleton-shoulder stock and pistol grip. It was a powerful multi-cell lamp, with several colored lenses, which pro-

AAF flashlights and signal equipment (from top): Signal light, M-227; Type A-1 air-drop message container, a weighted packet with 72-inch bright-yellow fabric streamer; single-cell light for B-5 life vest (laying on streamer). Bottom row, left to right: Type A-9 hand-energized flashlight; Army TL-122-B flashlight; typical small commercial flashlight carried by many airmen; Type A-7 floating identification light for life rafts; Navy Mark 1, Mod 0 distress smoke signal, also used by AAF, and signal mirrors ESM/1 and ESM/2. (Courtesy Robert Lehmacher)

jected a beam that could be controlled by a trigger to send Morse code signals.

FLYERS' CLOTHING BAGS

The Army has always been well supplied with special containers, bags, and kits for almost every purpose, and clothing was no exception. Since World War I, officers in transit had carried their clothing in an olive-drab or khaki canvas clothing roll with handle, and shipped their other gear in a footlocker. A musette bag with shoulder strap was available for carrying personal items. When not car-

rying a pack or haversack in the field, traveling enlisted personnel traditionally used a denim barracks bag for their belongings. The barracks bag was replaced, by World War II, with the larger olive-drab canvas duffel bag, required by troops going overseas. The sturdy, water-repellent duffel bag included a carrying strap, and could be secured with a padlock. The old barracks bag was then used as a laundry bag. Clothing carried in either bag developed what was known as "barracks bag press."

A compact container was considered more suitable for flying personnel, because of their frequent trips, the limited space available in the aircraft, and their need to have a "Class A" or service uniform available with as few wrinkles as possible for immediate wear at their destination. Special clothing bags, actually folding canvas suitcases, were provided for use by all aviators, beginning in 1931. The number of models and modifications shows that even this seemingly simple, low-priority item received considerable study on the part of Wright Field technical personnel and the manufacturers.

The first clothing bag designed specifically for Army aviators was the Type B-1, which entered test status on February 19, 1930, and was standardized for use on January 4, 1931.[28] It was provided with an attachment for hanging in the aircraft fuselage during cross-country flights, and could also be folded for carrying by the handle. The B-1 was changed to limited standard on January 6, 1932, when the Type B-2 bag was adopted, but was not declared obsolete until December 15, 1943. This was long after stocks were exhausted, but the durable bags could survive many years of hard usage.

The Type B-2 bag was an improved B-1, made with a cotton-duck outer shell. It was standardized on January 6, 1932, changed to limited standard on March 21, 1933, and finally declared obsolete on March 31, 1944. The Type B-2A was a modification standardized on March 21, 1933. Improvements were made to the hanger compartment, overall length was increased, and extra pockets were added. The B-2A was in turn changed to limited standard on May 16, 1936, but was not declared obsolete until February 15, 1946.

Additional minor refinements were made to the design of the Type B-2A, which resulted in the standardization of a new clothing bag on May 16, 1936. The Type B-3 was externally similar to the B-2A, but two outside pockets closed by zippers were added, and three metal coat hangers were provided. The B-3 was changed to limited standard on November 9, 1939, but remained in service until after the end of the war. Both the B-3 and its successor, the B-4, were listed in the AAF Class 13 Illustrated Supply Catalog dated September 30, 1943.[29]

Development of the ideal flyer's clothing bag continued, finally resulting in the standardization of the famous Type B-4 bag on November 9, 1939. This sturdy, virtually waterproof, OD duck folding suitcase is well-known to every veteran flyer of World War II. It continued in use for many years after the end of the conflict, and modern nylon versions are still produced today. The B-4 bag was similar to the B-3, but had simplified construction of the seams, heavy-duty zippers, and improved hanger design. It also had a metal ring for suspending the open bag. Both the B-3 and B-4 bags were the same size: 24 × 18 × 4 inches when closed and empty. The excellent design allowed a surprisingly large amount of clothing to be packed inside.

The diverse needs of the aviator were not overlooked even at the height of the war, as evidenced by the development of a medium-size canvas clothing bag, the Type

AAF airmen carried the popular Type B-4 flyer's clothing bag to every part of the world where U.S. troops saw service during World War II. The heavy olive-drab duck suitcase could be unzipped and opened out flat for packing. It had a stiffener on top and bottom, and a leather carrying handle. Hangers were provided, and it even had a snap partition inside for shoes. External pockets on each side were closed by strong zippers, and a metal ring was furnished for suspending the open bag. (SI Photo 85–3103)

B-5, standardized on January 25, 1945. It was not as large and heavy as the standard B-4, but was otherwise similar in design.

The last of the "B" series bags developed during the war was the Type B-6, an experimental design that was type-designated on July 15, 1944, but not adopted for use. The B-6 was a modification of the successful B-4 bag but tests showed that it did not represent any marked improvement.

Less well known is the Type C-1 clothing bag standardized on November 16, 1932. It was an olive-drab, cotton-duck bag, with a zipper top-closure and two handles. The C-1, which somewhat resembled a satchel, was designed to carry incidental articles of flying gear. It was changed to limited standard on October 21, 1941, when a modification, the Type C-2, was standardized, and finally declared obsolete on December 15, 1943. The Type C-2, however, was never procured, because it was decided that its function could be performed by the Type A-3 kit bag, normally used to carry parachutes. The C-2 design was declared obsolete on March 21, 1944. The Type A-3 kit bag is described in Chapter III.

FIRST AID EQUIPMENT

Flight surgeons were first assigned, during World War I, to care for the special medical needs of aviators, with general support and treatment provided by the Army Medical Department.[30]

One of the first special items of medical equipment to be developed, specifically for use by aviators, was a small first-aid kit for aircraft introduced in October 1934. By World War II, several first-aid kits were in use, and special types were developed for inclusion in survival kits and life rafts. The contents of the kits, although standardized initially by the Medical Department, were often modified by the flight surgeons to meet local needs.[31]

The kits included the widely used "Kit, First Aid, Aeronautic," installed in all combat, cargo, transport, training, and glider aircraft, as well as in the Types E-8, E-11, and E-12 emergency kits. They were also originally included in life rafts but were superseded by a special waterproof life raft first-aid kit. Four kits were normally placed aboard bombers, and one in each fighter plane; however, the inclusion of this type of first-aid kit in fighters was discontinued during the war. The compact, canvas, zipper-bound kit carried aboard combat aircraft normally contained the following: three small first-aid dressings, one tourniquet, one bottle halazone tablets, one box adhesive bandages, one 4-inch scissors, iodine applicators, two morphine Syrettes, two tubes sulfadiazine (later twelve tablets), one box sulfanilamide, and an eye-dressing unit. One tube of burn ointment was added later. The morphine Syrettes, sulfa, and halazone tablets were removed from kits carried on training planes in the Zone of Interior.[32]

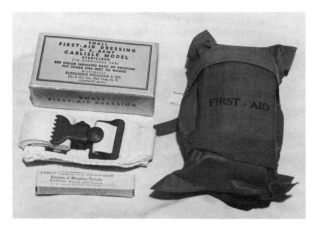

The Packet, First Aid, Parachute, consisted of a waterproof, olive-drab cloth pouch, containing a small first-aid dressing, morphine Syrette, and field tourniquet. It was provided with tie strings so that it could be fastened to the life vest, the right side of the parachute harness, or in or near a crew position in the aircraft. (Courtesy USAF)

The "Packet, First Aid, Individual Aircrew Member" was designed for issue to each airman. It was used primarily by fighter pilots after the "Kit, First Aid, Aeronautic" was removed from fighter planes during the war. It contained a small dressing, wound tablets (sulfabizine), and other medications, and nine safety pins.[33]

An improved version of the individual aircrew packet was developed by the Aero Medical Laboratory at Wright Field in 1944. This was designated as the "Packet, Aircrew, Individual, First Aid, Type A-1," and was standardized on March 26, 1945. It contained medications similar to those in the original packet.[34]

Another widely-used item was the "Packet, First Aid, Parachute." The waterproof packet contained a small Carlisle first-aid dressing, a morphine Syrette, and a field tourniquet. The packet was normally fastened to the parachute harness, on the right lift web opposite the ripcord grip, by ties attached to the olive-drab cloth cover. It was sometimes tied to the life vest, or to a convenient part of the airplane structure near a crew position, or in a gun turret or other cramped location.[35]

The "Kit, First Aid, Parachute (Frying Pan Insert)" was a different kit, supplied with the emergency parachute kits Types B-4 and B-5. The medical items were sealed in a circular plastic container carried in the frying pan of the emergency kits, and included sterile compresses, sulfa drugs, benzedrine, salt tablets, atabrine, halazone tablets, and boric acid ointment.[36]

A standard first-aid kit for life rafts, with A.E. reference number 45-8397, was introduced for AAF use during the war. It contained waterproof packages of first-aid supplies bound together in a paper wrapper. U.S. Navy kits were

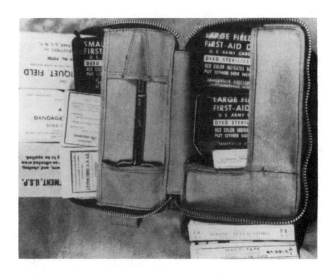

The Kit, First Aid, Aeronautic, showing the contents of the zipper-bound canvas case. Components included various bandages, medicines, and tourniquet (left), scissors (center), and dressings and medicines (right). This kit was installed in all AAF gliders, combat, cargo, transport, and training aircraft, as well as in survival kits and life rafts. It was later replaced aboard fighters and life rafts by other kits, but thousands continued to perform valuable service through the end of the war. (Courtesy USAF)

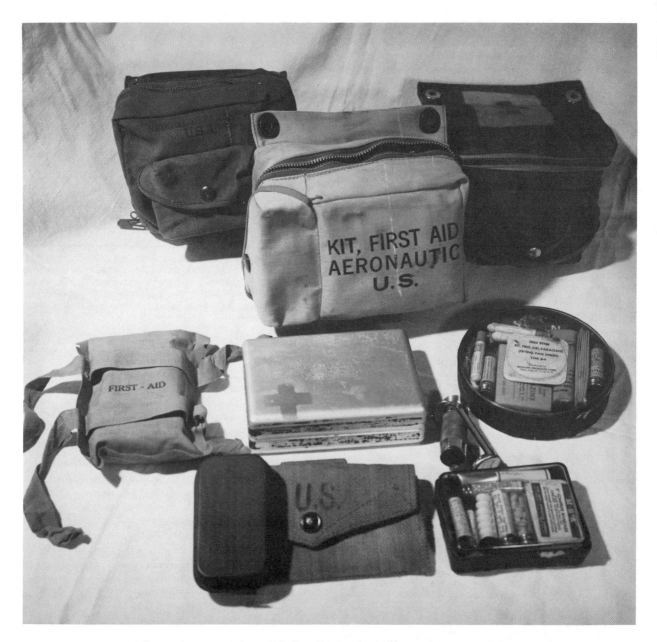

First-aid kits used by AAF. (Top row): three variations of Kit, First Aid, Aeronautic. (Center row, left to right): Packet, First Aid, Parachute; individual aircrew member kit; match safe as used for medical components in Types B-2 and B-4 emergency kits; and frying pan insert kit for B-4 emergency kit. (Bottom row, left to right): Field dressing with pouch marked "USAC 1944, British Made," (reverse lend-lease), C-1 vest kit. (Courtesy Robert Lehmacher)

also used, including "First Aid Kit, Camouflaged (Aviation Individual)" worn on the belt.[37]

Larger medical kits were developed for war service and were especially intended for bomber, cargo, and transport airplanes, flying over arctic or jungle areas. They were designated as "Kit, First Aid, Arctic" and "Kit, First Aid, Jungle" and contained a large variety of appropriate medicines, compresses, and small medical items. Both of these kits came in the form of a chest with a carrying handle, and were well marked for identification.[38]

The Gallagher medical kit, introduced early in 1945, represented a new departure in first-aid treatment during flight at high altitude. Developed by Col. John L. Gallagher, MC, it consisted of a plastic case curved to fit the contours

The bombardier's kit consisted of a Type E-1 fabric case, containing hand computers and other items also used by navigators and pilots. This photo from the "Bombardier's Information File," March 1945, shows the equipment and working materials for use in maintaining bombing records and calculations. The kit was provided for every student and graduate bombardier through regular supply channels. It included: Types C-2, G-1, J-1, and E-6B computers; a set of dropping angle charts, for use with the E-6B; a Type A-8 stopwatch and Type A-11 wrist (hack) watch; pen-type flashlight; bombing flight-record holder; tools; drafting pencils; eraser; dividers; Weems plotter; parallel rule; transparent triangles; and bombing tables (fluorescent). Other kits were provided for navigators, gunners, etc. (Author's Collection)

of bomber and transport fuselages. If a plane were forced down at sea, the container would act as a self-sealing, buoyant life raft, which could support the weight of an average man for some time. A feature of the Gallagher kit was the "pressure bandage," an easily handled gauze pad stuffed with packing material with bandage roll attached, which formed a pliant but firm covering for large and small wounds and eliminated the need for a conventional tourniquet. Morphine was kept in a special, heated compartment with a built-in lock, and the kit also included sulfa drugs, standard dressings, and a safety knife to facilitate the slitting of heavy clothing. The Gallagher kit was successfully used by the Eighth Air Force, and was adopted for all B-29 aircraft.[39]

Notes

INTRODUCTION

1. George W. Gray, *Science at War* (N.Y., 1943), p. 224.
2. Dr. W. R. Lovelace, Lt. Col. A. P. Gagge and Dr. C. W. Bray, *Aviation Medicine and Psychology,* Headquarters, Air Materiel Command, Wright Field, Ohio, 1946, p. 1.
3. Gray, *Science at War,* p. 225.

I HUMAN ENGINEERING

1. Lt. Col. C. L. Beaven, "A Chronological History of Aviation Medicine," mimeographed reference guide prepared by the School of Aviation Medicine, Randolph Field, Texas, 1939, pp. 4–6.
2. Brig. Gen. Theodore C. Lyster, MC, not only strove during World War I to establish proper physical and mental standards for aviators, but also worked towards the eventual establishment of a separate medical service responsible to an independent air force. He is considered the father of aviation medicine.
3. For a detailed study of U.S. military flying clothing from World War I through 1945, see C. G. Sweeting, *Combat Flying Clothing: Army Air Forces Clothing During World War II* (Washington, D.C., 1984).
4. Beaven, p. 13. For a detailed account of aviation-medicine research in World War I, see *Air Service Medical,* published by the Air Service, Division of Military Aeronautics, U.S. War Department (Washington, D.C., 1919).
5. Harry G. Armstrong, *Principles and Practice of Aviation Medicine* (Baltimore, Md., Third Edition, 1952), p. 41; a classic study, first published in 1939.
6. Mae Mills Link and Hubert A. Coleman, *Medical Support of the Army Air Forces in World War II,* Office of the Surgeon General, USAF (Washington, D.C., 1955), p. 13.
7. Beaven, p. 15.
8. Ibid., p. 16. Supercharging, or turbocharging, increases air pressure by compressing air before it reaches the intake manifold of the engine, to prevent power loss at higher altitudes.
9. Beaven, p. 16.
10. Link and Coleman, p. 972. The Air Force Aerospace Medical Research Laboratory building (Building 29), at Wright-Patterson AFB, Ohio, was named in honor of Maj. Gen. Harry G. Armstrong on June 1, 1985.
11. Link and Coleman, p. 971. Maj. Gen. Malcolm C. Grow, MC, was also honored for his work during World War II in developing body armor for aviators. He was appointed the first Surgeon General of the U.S. Air Force in 1949.
12. "Functions of the Activities of the Materiel Division, Wright Field," Memorandum Report No. 50–63, Materiel Division,

Wright Field, Ohio, Mar. 3, 1934, and Addendum 1, Feb. 4, 1935. See also "Materiel Division Number," *Air Corps News Letter.* Vol. XX, No. 1, Jan. 1, 1937.
13. Irving Brinton Holley, Jr., *Buying Aircraft: Materiel Procurement for the Army Air Forces,* Office of the Chief of Military History, U.S. Army (Washington, D.C., 1964), p. 463.
14. Link and Coleman, p. 975.
15. Holley, p. 558.
16. Ibid., p. 470.
17. Edward O. Purtee, "Development of AAF Clothing and Other Personal Equipment Peculiar to Air Operations," (Three-volume unpublished study, number 204, prepared for the Air Technical Service Command, Wright Field, Ohio, May 22, 1945), vol. I, p. 16 (hereafter cited as ATSC Study).
18. Charles A. Dempsey, *50 Years of Research On Man in Flight,* Aerospace Medical Research Laboratory, (Wright-Patterson AFB, Ohio, 1985), p. 28.
19. "The Personal Equipment Laboratory, Its Mission and Function," *The Personal Equipment Officer,* vol. II, no. 1, (c. 1946), p. 28.
20. "History of the AAF Materiel Command," Headquarters, Materiel Command, Wright Field, Ohio, 1943, pp. 24–25.
21. John A. Miller, *Men and Volts at War: The Story of General Electric in World War II* (N.Y., 1947), pp. 98–99.
22. "High Altitude Flight Testing of Flyers' Personal Equipment in Specially Engineered B-17E No. 41-2407," Memorandum Report No. ENG-49-697-1H, by Lt. Col. W. Randolph Lovelace II, Aero Medical Laboratory, Engineering Division, Materiel Command, Wright Field, Ohio, Mar. 20, 1944.
23. Type Designation Sheets were documents maintained as part of the type designation system for aeronautical cothing and equipment from the mid-1920s until the early 1950s. The original collection of documents is now part of the archives of the National Air and Space Museum, Smithsonian Institution, and located at the NASM Archival Support Center, Paul E. Garber Facility, Silver Hill, Md. See also Sweeting, *Combat Flying Clothing.*
24. Maj. Samuel R. M. Reynolds, "Human Engineering in the Army Air Forces," *The Personal Equipment Officer,* vol. II, no. 1 (c. 1946), p. 3.
25. From a speech by Brig. Gen. David N. W. Grant, Air Surgeon, in 1943, quoted by Major Reynolds and others including Morris Fishbein (Ed.), *Doctors at War* (N.Y., 1945), pp. 278–79.
26. Reynolds, p. 4.
27. Ibid., p. 5.
28. "Physiology of Flight: Human Factors in the Operation of Military Aircraft," AAF Manual No. 25-2, Headquarters, Army Air Forces, Washington, D.C., Mar. 15, 1945, p. 88. The first edition of this manual was produced by the Aero Medical Laboratory in 1941.
29. Ibid., p. 88.

1. "Physiology of Flight," AAF Manual No. 25-2, p. 18.
2. Douglas H. Robinson, M.D., *The Dangerous Sky: A History of Aviation Medicine* (Seattle, Wash., 1973), pp. 9–10.
3. L. T. C. Rolt, *The Aeronauts: A History of Ballooning, 1783–1903* (N.Y., 1966), pp. 199–200.
4. "Draeger-Hoehenatemgeraet fuer Ballon, Flugzeug, Luftschiff und fuer Hochgebirgsforschung," catalog of the Draegerwerk, Lübeck, 1936, pp. 3–4.
5. "The Medical Aspects of the National Geographic Society—U.S. Army Air Corps Stratosphere Flight of Nov. 11, 1935," Memorandum Report no. Q-54-9, prepared by Capt. Harry G. Armstrong, Equipment Branch, Engineering Section, Materiel Division, Wright Field, Ohio, Feb. 3, 1936; and Robinson, p. 36.
6. Robinson, p. 69.
7. Douglas H. Robinson, M.D., *The Zeppelin in Combat* (Sun Valley, Calif., 1966), pp. 211–12.
8. "Oxygen Apparatus Draeger Type B of German Origin Found on Board a Zeppelin," Stencil No. 931 (JNRR), Office of the Chief Signal Officer, War Department, Washington, D.C., Feb. 8, 1918.
9. Maj. Georg P. Neumann, *Die deutschen Luftstreitkraefte im Weltkriege* (Berlin, 1920), pp. 215–16.
10. "Instruction sur L'Appareil Respiratoire Automatique pour vols à Hautes Altitudes," Ministère de la Guerre, Section Technique de L'Aeronautique Militaire, Paris, 1918.
11. "History of the Bureau of Aircraft Production," Historical Study No. 198, Vol. VIII, Chapter XLVI, Oxygen Equipment, Washington, D.C., n.d., c. 1920, p. 2279.
12. *Air Service Medical*, pp. 429–30.
13. Ibid., p. 428, and "History of the Bureau of Aircraft Production," p. 2278.
14. Benedict Crowell, *America's Munitions, 1917–1918*, Office of the Assistant Secretary for War, Director of Munitions (Washington, D.C., 1919), p. 320. See also "History of the Bureau of Aircraft Production," p. 2278.
15. "Dreyer's Oxygen Inhaling Apparatus," Stencil No. 734 (JNRR), Office of the Chief Signal Officer, War Department, Washington, D.C., Dec. 10, 1917.
16. Col. G. W. Mixter and Lt. H. H. Emmons, *United States Army Aircraft Production Facts* (Washington, D.C., 1919), p. 5.
17. "History of the Bureau of Aircraft Production," p. 2279.
18. Ibid., p. 2280.
19. Ibid., p. 2282.
20. Ibid., p. 2286.
21. Ibid., p. 2287.
22. "Report on American Made Dreyer Apparatii," by Capt. Paul Pleiss. Technical Section, U.S. Air Service, A.E.F., (France), Jun. 4, 1918. See also "History of the Bureau of Aircraft Production," p. 2289.
23. "History of the Bureau of Aircraft Production," pp. 2293–94.
24. Ibid., p. 2294. As far as is known, only one example of the complete American-built Dreyer Oxygen System has survived. It is in the collection of the National Air and Space Museum, Smithsonian Institution.
25. Maurer Maurer (Ed.), *The U.S. Air Service in World War I*, Office of Air Force History, Headquarters, USAF (Washington, D.C., 1978), vol. I, p. 125.
26. "Use of Oxygen Equipment by U.S. Aviators in France, 1917–18," Memorandum for Record, National Air and Space Museum, Smithsonian Institution, Washington, D.C., Nov. 20, 1984.
27. Robinson, *The Dangerous Sky*, p. 81, quoting B. J. Silly in *R.A.F. Quarterly*, Mar. 1931.
28. Brig. Gen. Harold R. Harris, USAF (Ret.), Falmouth, MA., letters to the author May 6, and May 21, 1984.
29. See Note 23, Chapter I, for information on the Air Corps type designation system.
30. "Oxygen Instruments," Report No. 130, by Franklin L. Hunt, Aeronautic Instruments Section, U.S. National Bureau of Standards, Washington, D.C., 1921, pp. 744–45.
31. Ibid., pp. 745–47. See also "Oxygen Control Regulator for Airplanes," War Department Document No. 924, Prepared in the Office of the Director of Air Service, Washington, D.C., Jul. 31, 1919, and "Field Test of Prouty Oxygen Apparatus," Equipment Section Test Report No. 51, Air Service Engineering Division, McCook Field, Dayton, Ohio, Sep. 24, 1919.
32. "Oxygen Instruments," Report No. 130, Bureau of Standards, 1921, p. 739.
33. "Liquid Oxygen Apparatus," drawing and specifications, Bureau of Standards, Washington, D.C., n.d., c. 1922.
34. "Apparatus, Oxygen, Prouty Type," U.S. Army Air Service Specification No. 27,104-A, Jun. 6, 1922, and No. 98-27,104-B, Apr. 10, 1923, McCook Field, Ohio. See also "Description and Adjustment of Prouty Oxygen Gas Apparatus," *Air Service Information Circular*, vol. II, no. 174, Washington, D.C., Jan. 15, 1921.
35. Type Designation Sheets.
36. *Handbook of Instructions for Airplane Designers*, Air Service Engineering Division (Dayton, Ohio, Third Edition, June 1922), p. 251.
37. "Practical Field Service Use of Oxygen," *Air Service Information Circular*, vol. VI, no. 543, Washington, D.C., Nov. 1, 1925, p. 1.
38. "Oxygen Apparatus—General Instructions," Technical Order No. 03-10, Office of the Chief of the Air Corps, Washington, D.C., Nov. 5, 1927.
39. "Oxygen Apparatus—Modifications," Technical Order No. 03-10-1, Office of the Chief of the Air Corps, Washington, D.C., June 30, 1928.
40. "The Use of Gaseous and Liquid Oxygen in the Service," Air Corps Technical Report No. 3443, by P. N. Sutton, Equipment Branch, Materiel Division, Wright Field, Ohio, Apr. 28, 1931. Also reprinted as *Air Corps Information Circular*, vol. VII, no. 667, Washington, D.C., June 30, 1932.
41. "Aircraft Instruments," Technical Regulations No. 1170-50, Air Corps, War Department, Washington, D.C., Nov. 1, 1929.
42. Letter to NACA from Maj. C. W. Howard, Chief, Experimental Engineering Section, Materiel Division, Wright Field, Ohio, June 2, 1930.
43. Robinson, *The Dangerous Sky*, p. 119.
44. "Trip to Washington, D.C.," Memorandum Report No. X-54-203, by Capt. Harry G. Armstrong, Equipment Branch, Engineering Section, Materiel Division, Wright Field, Ohio, Apr. 1, 1935.
45. "A Study of the Merits of Liquid and Gaseous Oxygen for Air Corps Use at High Altitudes," Memorandum Report No. X-54-231, Equipment Branch, Engineering Section, Materiel Division, Wright Field, Ohio, Mar. 12, 1935.
46. "Oxygen Masks," Memorandum Report No. Q-54-40-A1, by Dr. J. W. Heim, Equipment Laboratory, Engineering Section, Materiel Division, Wright Field, Ohio, May 2, 1938.
47. "Development of Gas-Oxygen Light Weight Cylinders, Gas-Oxygen Regulators and Valves, and an Oxygen Mask," Memorandum Report No. X-54-203, by Capt. Harry G. Armstrong, Equipment Branch, Engineering Section, Materiel Division, Wright Field, Ohio, Sep. 25, 1936. See also Harry G. Arm-

strong, *Principles and Practice of Aviation Medicine* (Baltimore, Md., 1939), pp. 309–10.

48. "Outline of Course of Instruction in High Altitude Physiology," Aero Medical Research Unit, Equipment Laboratory, Experimental Engineering Section, Materiel Division, Wright Field, Ohio, Jan.-Mar. 1941, p. 44.

49. Armstrong, *Principles and Practice of Aviation Medicine*, 1939, pp. 310–11, and "Oxygen in Aviation," *Journal of Aviation Medicine*, Dec. 1938, p. 172. It should be noted that Dr. W. Randolph Lovelace II, one of the inventors of the B.L.B. oxygen mask, left the Mayo Foundation in 1941, was commissioned in the Air Corps, and joined the staff of the Aero Medical Laboratory, where he eventually became director.

50. "Oxygen Mask," Memorandum Report No. EXP-54-660-1, by Capt. Harry G. Armstrong, Equipment Laboratory, Experimental Engineering Section, Materiel Division, Wright Field, Ohio, Oct. 19, 1939.

51. Armstrong, *Principles and Practice of Aviation Medicine, 1939, pp. 316–17.*

52. "General-Oxygen Equipment," Technical Order No. 01-1H-1B, Air Corps, War Department, Washington, D.C., Apr. 20, 1938.

53. "Annual Report of the Chief, Materiel Division, FY 1939," Wright Field, Ohio, 1939, pp. 30–31. See also Armstrong, *Principles and Practice of Aviation Medicine*, 1939, pp. 319–21.

54. "Outline of Course of Instruction in High Altitude Physiology," pp. 50–52.

55. Col. A. Pharo Gagge, Ph.D. USAF (Ret.), New Haven, CT., letter to the author, Apr. 23, 1986. According to *The Official Pictorial History of the AAF,* by the Historical Office, AAF (N.Y., 1947), p. 155, 22,900 AAF aircraft were destroyed on combat missions during World War II, of which about 8,300 were lost in the presence of enemy planes, the remainder to AAA fire. About 20,700 more AAF planes were lost overseas from other causes, including accidents.

56. Link and Coleman, p. 257. As a matter of interest, Henry Seeler, who designed the Draeger demand valve used in German oxygen regulators, came to the United States after World War II, and joined the staff of the Aero Medical Laboratory at Wright Field in 1947.

57. Link and Coleman, p. 257.

58. Carl R. Thompson, Denton, Texas, former captain assigned to the 368th Bombardment Squadron, 306th Bombardment Group (H), Thurleigh, England, letter to the author, Nov. 25, 1985.

59. Link and Coleman, p. 652.

60. Fred Huston, Follett, Texas, formerly assigned to the 337th Bombardment Squadron, 96th Bombardment Group (H), letter to the author, Nov. 12, 1985.

61. "Handbook of Instructions with Parts Catalog for Type A-10 Revised Oxygen Mask," Technical Order No. 03-50B-1, published by the Air Service Command, Patterson Field, Fairfield, Ohio, Feb. 5, 1943. See also "Reference Manual for Personal Equipment Officers," AAF Manual No. 55-0-1, Headquarters, Army Air Forces, Washington, D.C., June 1, 1945, pp. 4-B-3-4-B-4.

62. "Freezing Tests on the A-10R and A-10A Demand Type Oxygen Masks," Memorandum Report No. ENG-49-660-39-R, Aero Medical Laboratory, Engineering Division, Materiel Command, Wright Field, Ohio, Apr. 10, 1944.

63. Link and Coleman, p. 257.

64. "Handbook of Instructions with Parts Catalog for Type A-14 Demand Oxygen Mask," Technical Order AN 03-50B-6, Headquarters, Army Air Forces, Washington, D.C., July 20,

1943, p. 8. See also AAF Manual 55-0-1, June 1, 1945, p. 4-B-4.

65. Link and Coleman, p. 653.

66. Fred Huston, Follett, Texas, letter to the author, Nov. 12, 1985.

67. "Visual Field Restrictions by a Face-Oxygen Mask Cover," Memorandum Report No. ENG-49-695-37G, Aero Medical Laboratory, Engineering Division, Materiel Command, Wright Field, Ohio, June 6, 1944.

68. Col. A. Pharo Gagge, Ph.D. USAF (Ret.), letter to the author, Apr. 23, 1986. The figure of 43,000 feet often cited in various histories is incorrect. See Link and Coleman, pp. 265–66. Colonel Gagge was awarded the Legion of Merit decoration in 1944 for his accomplishments in developing the pressure-breathing oxygen system.

69. Col. A. Pharo Gagge, Ph.D., USAF (Ret.), letter to the author, Apr. 23, 1986.

70. "Personal Flying Equipment as Used in Central and Western Pacific Areas," Memorandum Report No. TSEAL-3-695-52, by Lt. Col. A. P. Gagge, Chief, Biophysics Branch, Aero Medical Laboratory, Engineering Division, Air Technical Service Command, Wright Field, Ohio, May 18, 1945. See also Link and Coleman, p. 267.

71. Lt. Col. Donald S. Lopez, USAF (Ret.), Deputy Director, National Air and Space Museum, Washington, D.C., letter to the author, Jan. 31, 1986. Former Captain Lopez (5 victories, CBI), used both the Type A-13A and A-15A masks, while flying P-47N aircraft with the 611B Fighter Test Squadron at Eglin Field, Fla., during testing of the Type A-15A mask in the summer of 1945. For the test program the squadron flew at 42,000 or 43,000 feet. Captain Lopez also flew unpressurized early models of the P-80 jet while at Eglin. Later P-80s and subsequent jet fighters had pressurized cockpits, and pressure-breathing equipment was only needed as a backup. According to Col. A. P. Gagge, some of the communication problems were caused by personnel, who were improperly trained in the use of the pressure-breathing oxygen system.

72. "Masks, Pressure Demand Oxygen," Project No. 3926C452.17, Report of the Army Air Forces Board, Orlando, Fla., on Tests Conducted by the AAF Proving Ground Command, Eglin Field, Fla., Mar. 13, 1945.

73. "Use of Oxygen and Oxygen Equipment," Technical Order No. 03-50-1, Prepared by the Aero Medical Research Laboratory, Engineering Division, Materiel Command, Wright Field, Ohio, July 1, 1943. Other editions of this T.O. also provide valuable information, particularly that of Nov. 9, 1942. See also AAF Manual 55-0-1, June 1, 1945, pp. 4-B-4— 4-B-8.

74. "Underwater Use of Portable Oxygen Walk-Around Assembly by Personnel in Escape from Submerged Aircraft," Memorandum Report No. TSEAL-3-660-68-A, Oxygen Branch, Aero Medical Laboratory, Engineering Division, Air Technical Service Command, Wright Field, Ohio, Nov. 20, 1944.

75. "Review of the Status of Oxygen Equipment with Reference to Information Gathered in a Visit to USSTAF," Memorandum Report No. TSEAL-3-660-53-F-1, Oxygen Branch, Aero Medical Laboratory, Engineering Division, Air Technical Service Command, Wright Field, Ohio, Dec. 31, 1944, p. 6.

76. "Emergency Oxygen Unit for Use in Parachute Escape or in Case of Failure of Regular Oxygen Supply at High Altitude," *The Journal of Aviation Medicine*, vol. II, no. 2, June 1940, pp. 59–66.

77. "Type H-2 Emergency Oxygen Cylinder Assembly," Memorandum Report No. ENG-49-660-14-S-9, Aero Medical Lab-

216

oratory, Engineering Division, Air Technical Service Command, Wright Field, Ohio, Sep. 23, 1944, p. 1.

78. "Physiology of Flight," AAF Manual 25-2, pp. 75–78.
79. "Parachute Descent From a Pressure Altitude of 39,750 Feet (Density Altitude, 40,200 Feet)," by Lt. Col. W. Randolph Lovelace II, MC, Memorandum Report No. ENG-49-695-1K, Aero Medical Laboratory, Engineering Division, Materiel Command, Wright Field, Ohio, July 9, 1943. See also "Bail-Out at 40,000 Feet," Air Force, Oct. 1943, pp. 24–25, 48.
80. "Emergency Oxygen Cylinder Assembly (Bail-Out)," Expenditure Order No. 660-98, Extracted from Research and Development Projects, Engineering Division, Air Technical Service Command, July 1, 1945, pp. 205–06.
81. "Combination Mask and Helmet: Mask, Oxygen, Type C-1, For Use With Demand Oxygen Systems," (Restricted), U.S. Army Air Forces Instruction Booklet, n.p., n.d. (c. 1942).
82. "Progress of Project Conducted On Expenditure Order No. 660-81," Memorandum Report No. ENG-49-660-51, Aero Medical Laboratory, Engineering Division, Materiel Command, Wright Field, Ohio, Aug. 21, 1943.
83. Dempsey, p. 33.
84. Link and Coleman, p. 654.
85. Ibid., p. 655.

III MILITARY PARACHUTES

1. "Wearing of Parachutes," Bulletin No. 12, Headquarters, McCook Field, Dayton, Ohio, Mar. 29, 1922. Maj. Thurman H. Bane, Commanding Officer, ordered the wearing of parachutes by McCook Field pilots during test flights or combat practice, after the tragic death of Lt. Frederick W. Niedermeyer, Jr. in a crash on Mar. 13, when he was not wearing a parachute.
2. Brig. Gen. Harold R. Harris, USAF (Ret.), Falmouth, Mass., letter to the author, Jan. 27, 1986. His jump is also described in many publications including "Supplement to Parachute Manual," Engineering Division, Air Service, McCook Field, Ohio, Feb. 1925, p. 4.
3. Ibid., "Supplement to Parachute Manual," p. 4.
4. Circular No. 6, Office of the Chief of Air Service, War Department, Washington, D.C., Jan. 15, 1923.
5. ATSC Study, vol. III, pp. 2–3. For details on the technical aspects and aerodynamics of the parachute, see W. D. Brown, Parachutes (London, 1951, and later editions).
6. For a typical account see The Encyclopaedia Britannica, vol. 17, (Chicago, 1943), p. 252. The information from the Aero Club of Poland was provided by David Gold, parachute engineer and historian, in a letter to the author, Feb. 1, 1979; it was obtained originally through correspondence by Sidney Jackson, Chief of Research and Development, Irvin Industries, Great Britain, from the Aero Club of Poland, Warsaw.
7. ATSC Study, vol. III, p. 3.
8. Ibid., pp. 4–5.
9. "Parachute Jump From Aeroplane is Successful," Aero Magazine, vol. III, no. 23, Mar. 9, 1912. This historic jump is described in many references, but full details are presented in this account.
10. Charles deForest Chandler and Frank P. Lahm, How Our Army Grew Wings (N.Y., 1943), p. 277.
11. David Gold, Early Development of the Manually Operated Personnel Parachute, 1900–1919 (Newbury Park, CA., 1968), p. 2.
12. "Stevens 'Life Pack,'" Aeronautics, Oct. 1912.

13. ATSC Study, vol. III, pp. 5–6.
14. Ibid., p. 6.
15. Gen. der Kavallerie von Hoeppner, Deutschlands Krieg in der Luft (Leipzig, 1921), p. 59.
16. Crowell, p. 343.
17. Ibid., p. 341.
18. ATSC Study, vol. III, p. 7.
19. "The Balloon Jumpers of the World War," Air Corps News Letter, published by the Chief of the Air Corps, War Department, Washington, D.C., Aug. 29, 1928. This article quotes from the Report of the Balloon Section, U.S. Army, vol. I, (1919).
20. Crowell, p. 342. Also mentioned in Mixter, United States Army Aircraft Production Facts, pp. 104–05.
21. Gold, p. 7.
22. Der Fallschirm Heinecke, illustrated factory handbook published by Schroeder & Co., G.m.b.H. (Berlin, n.d., c. 1918), p. 13.
23. Ibid., p. 11. See also description and illustrations in Neumann, pp. 217–227.
24. ATSC Study, vol. III, p. 8, quoting "Parachute Progress Report," Technical Section, U.S. Air Service, Nov. 20, 1918.
25. Alex Imrie, Pictorial History of the German Army Air Service, 1914–1918 (Chicago, 1971), p. 165.
26. Gold, pp. 8–9.
27. ATSC Study, vol. III, p. 10, quoting report by the U.S. Air Service, A.E.F., France, Nov. 15, 1918.
28. Ibid., p. 11, quoting "Airplane Parachute Progress Report No. 7," by the Airplane Division, A.E.F., Nov. 29, 1918.
29. Ibid., pp. 42–43. See also Barry Gregory and John Batchelor, Airborne Warfare, 1918–1945 (London, 1979), p. 11.
30. ATSC Study, vol. III, p. 12, quoting "Reporting on Parachute Development, Wilbur Wright Field," by 2nd. Lt. S. W. Wilcok, A.S., Dec. 1918.
31. "Parachute Manual," prepared by Parachute Branch, Equipment Section, McCook Field, Ohio, Oct. 1920, p. 13. This first Air Service airplane parachute manual contains details on all parachutes tested by the Air Service during 1918–19, as well as the new Army Type "A" parachute.
32. Gold, p. 13. Gold personally interviewed Irvin concerning his role in developing the Type "A" parachute.
33. Ibid., p. 13.
34. ATSC Study, vol. III, p. 15.
35. "Parachute Manual," Oct. 1920, p. 30.
36. Ibid., pp. 39–40.
37. Ibid., p. 42. The loads and speeds in tests were, of course, greatly increased during the following years.
38. Ibid., p. 47.
39. See Note 1.
40. See Note 4.
41. Don Glassman, Jump!: Tales of the Caterpillar Club (N.Y., 1930), and "Firsts Among the Parachute Jumpers," Air Corps News Letter, published by the Office of the Chief of the Air Corps, War Department, Washington, D.C., vol. XVII, issue no. 5, May 29, 1933, pp. 109–113.
42. "Parachute Manual," 3rd ed., Oct. 1924, p. 32.
43. Ibid., p. 32.
44. "1926 Collier Trophy," Aero Digest, Mar. 1926, p. 118. For a description of the presentation by President Calvin Coolidge at the White House on Feb. 7, 1926, see The New York Times, Feb. 8, 1926, p. 25:7.
45. ATSC Study, vol. III, pp. 20–21.
46. Ibid., p. 22.
47. Ibid., p. 23, quoting contract W535 AC-1402 with Irving Air Chute Company, Buffalo, N.Y., June 2, 1928, in the Wright Field contract files.

48. "The Parachute Rigger," Training Manual No. 2170-72, Chief of the Air Corps, War Department, Washington, D.C., June 29, 1929. This manual also provided information on construction principles, specifications for materials, packing, maintenance, repair instructions, and details on the use of the parachute.

49. See Note 23, Chapter I.

50. ATSC Study, vol. III, p. 23, quoting letter from Maj. Leslie MacDill, Chief, Experimental Engineering Section, Materiel Division, Wright Field, Ohio, to Chief, Army Air Corps, Washington, D.C., Mar. 16, 1928.

51. *Manual for All Models of Switlik Safety Chutes,* Switlik Parachute and Equipment Company (Trenton, N.J., n.d., c. 1935); *Irvin Air Chutes, Symbols of Safety,* Irving Air Chute Company, Inc. (Buffalo, N.Y., n.d., c. 1934); and Floyd Smith, *Coming Down,* Illustrated Manual of the Switlik Manufacturing Company (Trenton, N.J., n.d., c. 1932).

52. ATSC Study, vol. III, pp. 26–27.

53. *Safe! The Triangular Parachute,* booklet published by the Triangle Parachute Company (Cincinnati, Ohio, n.d., c. 1931).

54. ATSC Study, vol. III, pp. 24–25, and "Parachutes–Triangular Types–Construction, Maintenance, Storage, and Use," Technical Order No. 13-5-1, Office of the Chief of the Air Corps, Washington, D.C., May 17, 1934.

55. ATSC Study, vol. III, p. 25.

56. Ibid., p. 26. See also "The Development and Procurement of Parachutes for the Army Air Forces," AFLC Historical Study No. 246, by Virginia G. Toole, Headquarters, Air Materiel Command, Wright-Patterson AFB, Ohio, Dec. 1948, p. 17. (hereafter cited as AFLC Study 246)

57. Ibid., p. 26.

58. See Note 54, T.O. No. 13-5-1, May 17, 1934.

59. "Parachutes—Construction, Maintenance, Storage, and Use," Technical Order No. 13-5-2, Office of the Chief of the Air Corps, Washington, D.C., June 15, 1933.

60. See Note 23, Chapter I. The Type A-1 quick-attachable chest parachute utilized a triangular canopy.

61. "Clothing, Parachutes, Equipment and Supplies," AAF Illustrated Catalog, Class 13, Headquarters, Army Air Forces, Washington, D.C., Sep. 30, 1943, pp. 14–16. Revised pages issued Apr. 1, 1944.

62. ATSC Study, vol. III, p. 29.

63. Ibid., p. 30.

64. Ibid., pp. 30–31.

65. AFLC Study 246, pp. 22–23.

66. David Gold, "Milestones in the History of Parachute Development," unpublished research paper prepared by Gold, former senior project engineer, Irvin Industries, Inc., c. 1980, pp. 4–5, and letters to the author, various dates.

67. Ibid., p. 5.

68. AAF Manual No. 55-0-1, June 1, 1945, p. 12-A-1. See also AAF Illustrated Catalog, Class 13, Sep. 30, 1943, pp. 76–77; and "Pilot's Information File," AAF Regulation No. 62-15, Headquarters, Army Air Forces, Washington, D.C., Apr. 9, 1943, as amended, pp. 8-4-1 thru 8-4-9. Note: there were also similar handbooks for bombardiers and navigators, and each provided details on bailing out of aircraft and general parachuting procedures in wartime.

69. AFLC Study 246, pp. 23–24.

70. Ibid., pp. 23–24. See also AAF Illustrated Catalog, Class 13, Sep. 30, 1943, pp. 76–77; "Pilot's Information File;" and "Hitting the Silk: A Manual on the Care and Use of the Parachute," AAF School of Applied Tactics, Orlando, Fla., Nov. 1944, p. 12. The last two references cited also provide details on escape from aircraft and general parachuting procedures and techniques for combat flyers.

71. "Reference Manual for Personal Equipment Officers," AAF Manual No. 55-0-1, pp. 12-A-1 thru 12-D-1.

72. ATSC Study, vol. III, p. 33, quoting *Guardian Angel Parachute Book,* by the E. R. Calthrop Company, England, Mar. 1919.

73. Ibid., pp. 33–34.

74. Ibid, p. 35. The tests were completed in May 1937. See also AFLC Study 246, pp. 23–24.

75. Ibid., p. 35, quoting Aero Medical Laboratory Memorandum Report No. EXP-M-54-670-411, Aug. 27, 1941.

76. Ibid., p. 36, quoting AML Memorandum Report No. ENG-M-54-670-57, Apr. 10, 1943.

77. Ibid., p. 36, quoting AML Memorandum Report No. GEMS-MX-43-23, Apr. 29, 1943.

78. Ibid., pp. 36–37, quoting report; "Observations on Air Force Personnel Equipment in U.K. and Africa," by Col. John Hargraves, MC, Sep. 4, 1943.

79. Ibid., p. 37, quoting AAF Proving Ground Report No. 3-43-126, Eglin Field, Fla., Nov. 17, 1943.

80. Ibid., p. 39. See also "Case History of Quick Release Parachutes," AFLC Historical Study No. 128, compiled by the Historical Division, Headquarters, Air Technical Service Command, Wright Field, Ohio, May 1945.

81. "Pilot's Information File," Apr. 9, 1943, amended, p. 8-4-9.

82. "Reference Manual for Personal Equipment Officers," AAF Manual No. 55-0-1, p. 12-C-3.

83. ATSC Study, vol. III, p. 32.

84. "Enemy Air-Borne Forces," Special Series No. 7, Military Intelligence Service, War Department, Washington, D.C., Dec. 2, 1942. For further details on military parachuting, training, aircraft and combat operations, see such books as John Weeks, *The Airborne Soldier* (Poole, England, 1982).

85. ATSC Study, vol. III, p. 32.

86. AFLC Study 246, p. 36.

87. Ibid., pp. 36–39. See also ATSC Study, vol. III, pp. 32–33, and Type Designation Sheets.

88. ATSC Study, vol. III, pp. 46–47.

89. Ibid., p. 47, quoting AML Memorandum Reports ENG-54-671-29D, May 7, 1942, and ENG-54-670-53A, Dec. 14, 1942.

90. Ibid., pp. 47–50. See also AFLC Study 246, pp. 30–33, and the Type Designation Sheets.

91. AFLC Study 246, pp. 33–36.

92. "Handbook of Aircraft Armament," Bureau of Aircraft Production, Air Service, U.S. Army, Washington, D.C., 1918, pp. 88–89.

93. ATSC Study, vol. III, pp. 42–43.

94. "Bombs for Aircraft," Technical Manual No. 9-1980, War Department, Washington, D.C., Nov. 15, 1944.

95. ATSC Study, vol. III, p. 46.

96. AFLC Study 246, pp. 41–45.

97. "Report of Aircraft Accident," AAF Form No. 14, Lt. Col. Melbourne W. Boynton, at Wilmington, Ohio, 19 Aug. 1944, and Col. A. Pharo Gagge, Ph.D., USAF (Ret.), letter to the author, Aug. 14, 1986. See also Link and Coleman, pp. 340–343.

98. ATSC Study, vol. III, pp. 39–40. See also "The Aneroid-activated Parachute Opening Device," Memorandum Report No. TSEAL5B-696-66A, Aircraft Laboratory, Engineering Division, Air Technical Service Command, Wright Field, Ohio, Sep. 5, 1945.

99. "Effects of Interference on the Accuracy of an Aneroid-activated Parachute Opening Device," Memorandum Report No. TSEAL2-696-4-1, Aircraft Laboratory, Engineering Division, Air Technical Service Command, Wright Field, Ohio, Nov. 21, 1945.

100. Col. A. Pharo Gagge, Ph.D., USAF (Ret.), letter to the author, July 22, 1986.

1. "Helmets and Body Armor," Office of the Chief of Ordnance, U.S. Army, Washington, D.C., June 1, 1945, p. 19.; an important reference.
2. Harry P. Judson, *Caesar's Army* (Boston, 1888), pp. 32–33. See also Auguste Demmin, *An Illustrated History of Arms and Armour* (London, 1877), pp. 117–119.
3. Terence Wise, *Medieval Warfare* (N.Y., 1976), pp. 38–40. See also Claude Blair, *European Armour, Ca. 1066 to Ca. 1700* (London, 1958), p. 33.
4. Roy C. Laible, *Ballistic Materials and Penetration Mechanics* (N.Y., 1980), p. 18.; this book provides a good summary of the development and use of armor from earliest times to the present.
5. Comdr. Frederick J. Lewis, USN, et al, *Military Helmet Design*, Research Project NM810109.1, Naval Medical Field Research Laboratory (Camp Lejeune, N.C., 1958), p. 6.
6. Harold L. Peterson, *Arms and Armor in Colonial America, 1526–1783* (N.Y., 1956).
7. Bashford Dean, *Helmets and Body Armor in Modern Warfare* (New Haven, Conn., 1920), p. 52.; this is the classic work on personal armor in World War I.
8. Ibid., pp. 59–60.
9. Ibid., pp. 289–291.
10. Lewis, p. 10.
11. Ibid.
12. Col. James B. Coates, Jr. and Maj. James C. Beyer, (Eds.), *Wound Ballistics*, Office of the Surgeon General, Dept. of the Army (Washington, D.C., 1962), p. 661. See also Dean, *Helmets and Body Armor in Modern Warfare.*
13. Coates and Beyer p. 661.
14. K. N. Finne, *Russkiye Vozdushnyye Bogatyri I. I. Sikorsky* (Russian Air Knights of I. I. Sikorsky), (Belgrade, 1930), p. 36.
15. "Engins D' Armement," Section Technique de L' Aeronautique Militaire, Imp. Catala Frères, Paris, 3 Feb. 1917, p. 341-000 St. Aé.
16. Dean, p. 228. See also Crowell, p. 226, and Lewis, pp. 27–30.
17. Dean, p. 231.
18. Coates and Beyer, p. 663. See also Col. Otis O. Benson, Jr. and Lt. Col. I. Louis Hoffman, "A Study of Wounds in Combat Crews With Certain Recommendations for Prevention," *Air Surgeon's Bulletin*, July 1944, p. 1. This article quotes a Twelfth Bomber Command study covering the period Feb. 1 to Oct. 29, 1943, showing that approximately 60 percent of wounds in the Mediterranean area were caused by antiaircraft fire. The proportion of wounds caused by flak varied widely with the different types of aircraft. As would be expected, only 23.3 percent of the wounds among fighter pilots were the result of flak. In Europe, the proportion of bomber-crew casualties from flak increased towards the end of the war as the number of Luftwaffe fighter attacks decreased due to American air superiority. AA fire in the Pacific was generally not as intense as it was in Europe.
19. Coates and Beyer p. 664.
20. Link and Coleman, p. 622.
21. Coates and Beyer, p. 672. Unless otherwise indicated, data on standardized armor are those shown in this reference. For additional information on items see "Helmets and Body Armor," in "Record of Army Ordnance Research and Development, Helmets and Body Armor," June 1, 1945, volume 2, book 1, section 3, Office of the Chief of Ordnance, Research and Development Service, Washington, D.C., Jan.

1946, and AAF Manual 55-0-1, June 1, 1945, pp. 9-A-1 thru 9-G-1.
22. Coates, and Beyer, pp. 668–69.
23. Link and Coleman, p. 624.
24. Ibid., p. 631, quoting interview with Brig. Gen. Malcolm C. Grow by H. A. Coleman, Apr. 4, 1946.
25. Ibid., p. 623.
26. Ibid., p. 623.
27. "Records of Army Ordnance Research and Development, Helmets and Body Armor," Jan. 1946, p. 167.
28. Coates and Beyer, p. 684.
29. Carl R. Thompson, Denton, Texas, letter to the author, Nov. 25, 1985.
30. Coates and Beyer, p. 657. See also "Record of Army Ordnance Research and Development, Helmets and Body Armor," Jan. 1946, p. 153.
31. Lewis, p. 42.
32. "Helmet, Flyer's, Armored—2nd Supplement (Final Report)," Project No. (M-4) 155b, Report of the Army Air Forces Board, Orlando, Fla., Sep. 5, 1944, on Tests Conducted by the AAF Proving Ground Command, Eglin Field, Fla., Aug. 18, 1944.
33. Coates and Beyer, p. 659.
34. Robert Lehmacher, Burbank, Ill., letter to the author, Nov. 10, 1983. This helmet is in the Lehmacher collection of aviation memorabilia. Note that the word "flak" was misspelled on the label. The term is an abbreviation of the German "Flugabwehrkanone," or antiaircraft gun.
35. "Record of Army Ordnance Research and Development, Helmets and Body Armor," Jan. 1946, p. 155. The surviving M4A2E1 helmet is now in the collection of the National Air and Space Museum.
36. Ibid., p. 157. See also Coates and Beyer, p. 659.
37. Production figures were compiled from various official sources cited in this chapter but do not necessarily represent final Ordnance Department compilations.
38. Link and Coleman, p. 632.
39. Brig. Gen. Malcolm C. Grow and Lt. Col. Robert C. Lyons, MC, "Body Armor, A Brief Study on the Development," *Air Surgeon's Bulletin*, vol. II, Jan. 1945, p. 10.
40. Coates and Beyer, p. 664.
41. Ibid. See also "Body Armor for Modern Battle," by Col. Rene R. Studler, *Army Ordnance*, Jan.-Feb. 1946, pp. 59–61.

V   ANTI-G GARMENTS AND PRESSURE SUITS

1. Brig. Gen. Charles E. "Chuck" Yeager, USAF (Ret.), talk presented at the National Air and Space Museum, Smithsonian Institution, Washington, D.C., Oct. 17, 1985. The anti-G suits tested were the Franks Flying Suit (FFS) and probably the AAF Type G-2.
2. "Handbook of Protective Equipment," Air Force Manual 64-4, Department of the Air Force, Washington, D.C., Nov. 15, 1968, pp. 31–32, and edition of Nov. 29, 1974, pp. 4-1 to 4-2.
3. John R. Poppen and Cecil K. Drinker, "Physiological Effects and Possible Methods of Reducing the Symptoms Produced by Rapid Changes in the Speed and Direction of Airplanes as Measured in Actual Flight" *Journal of Applied Physiology*, Oct. 1950, p. 204.
4. J. H. Doolittle, M.I.T., "Accelerations in Flight," Report No. 203, National Advisory Committee for Aeronautics (N.A.C.A.), Washington, D.C., 1925.

5. Poppen and Drinker, p. 215. See also "Design and Use of Anti-G Suits and Their Activating Valves in World War II," by Maj. George A. Hallenbeck, MC, AAF Technical Report No. 5433, Aero Medical Laboratory, Engineering Division, Headquarters, Air Materiel Command, Wright Field, Ohio, Mar. 6, 1946, p. 31.; an important study, hereafter cited as the Hallenbeck Report.

6. H. G. Armstrong and J. W. Heim, "The Effect of Acceleration on the Living Organism," *Journal of Aviation Medicine,* 1938, 9:, pp. 199–214. See also Armstrong, 1939, pp. 390–417.

7. "The Effect of Taping the Body on "G" Tolerance in Man," by Capt. G. L. Maison, et al, Aero Medical Laboratory, Wright Field, Report No. 204 for the National Research Council, Division of Medical Sciences, Committee on Aviation Medicine, Sep. 29, 1943. Japanese aviator abdominal belts were originally obtained from downed Japanese pilots in the Pacific theater during World War II. Examples are in the collection of the National Air and Space Museum, along with standard types of U.S. anti-G garments and experimental items such as the Lamport Pneumatic Lever Suit.

8. J. P. Lawrie, "Aviation and Medical Research," from a paper presented to the Tenth International Congress of Military Medicine and Pharmacy, vol. 2, Proceedings, Washington, D.C., 1939. Reprinted in *Aircraft Engineering,* June 1940, pp. 164–70.

9. Lt. Gen. Adolf Galland, German Air Force (Ret.), interview with the author, Feb. 10, 1981. See also Dr. Siegfried Ruff, "German Acceleration Research," *Aircraft Engineering,* June 1940, pp. 166–170. For a detailed account of wartime developments, see *German Aviation Medicine in World War II,* vols. I and II, prepared under the auspices of the Surgeon General, U.S. Air Force (Washington, D.C., 1950).

10. J. P. Lawrie, "Aviation and Medical Research," *Aircraft Engineering,* June 1940, p. 164.

11. "Status of Development of the Hydrostatic Suit," Memorandum Report No. EXP-M-54-660-11C, by Maj. Otis O. Benson, Jr., Aero Medical Research Unit, Equipment Laboratory, Materiel Division, Wright Field, Ohio, Sep. 25, 1941.

12. Hallenbeck Report, p. 31. See also "Evaluation of Anti-G Suits," by Capt. George L. Maison, MC, Aero Medical Laboratory, Wright Field, Ohio, Report No. 309 for the National Research Council, Division of Medical Sciences, Committee on Aviation Medicine, Apr. 18, 1944. In addition to preference for the air-operated device, pilots of P-51 aircraft were more anxious to obtain anti-G protection than pilots of P-47s, because the P-51 was more maneuverable than the P-47 at ordinary altitudes. The P-51s were often used for deep-penetration escort missions involving aerial combat with enemy fighters.

13. "The Cotton G-Suit," Memorandum Report No. EXP-M-54-660-11D, by Maj. D. B. Dill, Aero Medical Research Unit, Equipment Laboratory, Materiel Division, Wright Field, Ohio, Dec. 22, 1941.

14. Hallenbeck Report, p. 33. See also "Present Position of Anti-G Suits," Report F. R. 93, by Sq. Ldr. A. K. McIntyre, RAAF, Flying Personnel Research Committee, Sydney, Australia, June 1944.

15. Hallenbeck Report, p. 33. See also "Preliminary Report on K.O.P. Anti-G Suits," Report F. R. 92, by Sq. Ldr. A. K. McIntyre, RAAF, Flying Personnel Research Committee, Sydney, Australia, June 1944.

16. Hallenbeck Report, p. 34. See also Link and Coleman, p. 287, and "Evaluation of Anti-G Suits, Report No. 1," Memorandum Report No. ENG-49-696-51A, by Capt. George L. Maison, MC, Aero Medical Laboratory, Engineering Division, Materiel Command, Wright Field, Ohio, Sep. 29, 1943.

17. Hallenbeck Report, p. 34.

18. Ibid., p. 38.

19. Ibid., p. 42. See also "Evaluation of Anti-G Suits," by 1st. Lt. George A. Hallenbeck, et al, Aero Medical Laboratory, Wright Field, Ohio, Report No. 254 for the National Research Council, Division of Medical Sciences, Committee on Aviation Medicine, Dec. 12, 1943.

20. Hallenbeck Report, p. 42.

21. Ibid., p. 44. See also "Evaluation of Anti-G Suits," by Capt. C. A. Maaske, Capt. G. A. Hellenbeck, and 1st. Lt. E. E. Martin, Aero Medical Laboratory, Wright Field, Ohio, Report No. 348 for the National Research Council, Division of Medical Sciences, Committee on Aviation Medicine, June 10, 1944.

22. Type Designation Sheets.

23. Hallenbeck Report, p. 44. See also "Evaluation of Anti-G Suits, Report No. 5," Memorandum Report No. ENG-49-696-51E-1, by Capt. George L. Maison, MC, et al, Aero Medical Laboratory, Engineering Division, Materiel Command, Wright Field, Ohio, Aug. 11, 1944.

24. Hallenbeck Report, p. 50.

25. "Final Report on Anti "G" Flying Suits—Comparative Test of Clark and Berger Models," Report No. 3-44-77, by Capt. P. F. Scholander, AAF Proving Ground Command, Eglin Field, Fla., Sep. 1, 1944.

26. Hallenbeck Report, p. 54. See also AAF Manual 55-0-1, June 1, 1945, pp. 6-A-1 thru 6-F-1.

27. "Use, Maintenance and Storage of Fighter Pilot's Pneumatic Suit (Anti-G) Types G-3 and G-3A," Technical Order No. 13-1-23, Headquarters, U.S. Air Force, Washington, D.C., July 1, 1949. This T.O. states that all Type G-3 suits are obsolete and will be condemned.

28. Hallenbeck Report, p. 56. See also "Evaluation of Anti-G Suits, Report No. 6," Memorandum Report No. TSEAL3-696-51F, by Capt. Clarence A. Maaske, et al, Aero Medical Laboratory, Engineering Division, Air Technical Service Command, Wright Field, Ohio, Nov. 16, 1944.

29. Hallenbeck Report, p. 59.

30. "Determination of the Effect of Time of Inflation on the G Protection Gained From the Clark G-4 Suit," by J. P. Henry, et al, Aeromedical Laboratories, University of Southern California, Los Angeles, Report No. 398 for the National Research Council, Division of Medical Sciences, Committee on Aviation Medicine, Dec. 1, 1944; and "Comparison of the Protective Value of an Anti-Blackout Suit on Subjects in an A-24 Airplane and on the Mayo Centrifuge," by E. H. Lambert, M.D., Mayo Aero Medical Unit, Memorandum Report to AAF Materiel Center, Series B, No. 2, Oct. 1945.

31. "Use, Maintenance and Storage of Fighter Pilot's Pneumatic Suit (Anti-G) Type G-4A," Technical Order No. 13-1-41, Headquarters, U.S. Air Force, Washington, D.C., Mar. 14, 1951, and Type Designation Sheets.

32. Hallenbeck Report, p. 61. See also "Pneumatic Anti-Acceleration Suits, A New Design Applying the Principle of the Pneumatic Lever," by Dr. Harold Lamport, et al, Interim Report, Contract OEMMcmr-199, Sup. 1, Committee on Medical Research, Office of Scientific Research and Development, Apr. 5, 1943.

33. Capt. George L. Maison, MC, et al, "Acceleration and the G Suit," *Air Surgeon's Bulletin,* Jan. 1945, p. 7. See also AAF Manual 55-0-1, June 1, 1945, p. 6-D-1.

34. Hallenbeck Report, p. 128.

35. "Installation of Anti-G Equipment in the Eighth Air Force Fighter Groups," Memorandum Report No. TSEAL3-696-51K, by 1st. Lt. Kenneth E. Penrod, Aero Medical Laboratory, Engineering Division, Air Technical Service Command, Wright Field, Ohio, Apr. 10, 1945.

220

36. "The Introduction of Anti-"G" Equipment Into the MTO," Memorandum Report No. TSEAL3-696-51N, by Capt. George A. Hallenbeck, Aero Medical Laboratory, Engineering Division, Air Technical Service Command, Wright Field, Ohio, May 12, 1945.

37. "A Report on the Introduction of Anti-"G" Equipment to FEAF and a Survey of Aero-Medical Problems in SWPA Including Continental Australia," Memorandum Report No. TSEAL3-696-51H, by Capt. Clarence A. Maaske, Aero Medical Laboratory, Engineering Division, Air Technical Service Command, Wright Field, Ohio, Feb. 24, 1945. See also Link and Coleman, pp. 836–37.

38. "Personal Flying Equipment as Used in Central and Western Pacific Areas," Memorandum Report No. TSEAL3-695-52, by Lt. Col. A. P. Gagge, Aero Medical Laboratory, Engineering Division, Air Technical Service Command, Wright Field, Ohio, May 18, 1945, p. 45.

39. Armstrong, 1939, p. 330.

40. "High Altitude Pressure Suits," by J. Allen Neal, volume IV, section VIII, History of Wright Air Development Center 1 July–31 December 1955, Wright-Patterson AFB, Ohio, 1956, p. 4.

41. Helen W. Schultz, "Case History of Pressure Suits," Historical Study No. 126, Headquarters, Air Materiel Command, Wright-Patterson AFB, Ohio, May 1951, p. 3., an important reference, hereafter cited as Schultz Study. For reasons unknown, the Wiley Post suits were not mentioned.

42. U.S. Patent No. 1,991,601 for a "Stratosphere Flying Suit," filed Nov. 28, 1932, by Cecil F. De Lasaux of Milwaukee, Wis., patented Feb. 19, 1935, at the U.S. Patent Office, Washington, D.C.

43. Stanley R. Mohler and Bobby H. Johnson, Wiley Post, His Winnie Mae, and the World's First Pressure Suit (Washington, D.C., 1971), p. 71.

44. Ernest "Ernie" H. Shultz, Burbank, Cal., telephone interview with the author, Jan. 24, 1987.

45. Russell S. Colley, Pinehurst, N.C., letter to the author, Feb. 5, 1987.

46. "Test of Oxygen Pressure Flying Suit for High Altitude Flying," Memorandum Report No. I-54-431, by F. G. Nesbitt, Equipment Branch, Engineering Section, Materiel Division, Wright Field, Ohio, June 21, 1934, with report of test results, Memorandum Report No. I-54-431-A1, June 23, 1934.

47. Mohler and Johnson, p. 84, based on a communication from Russell S. Colley.

48. "Test of Oxygen Pressure Flying Suit for Use at High Altitudes," Memorandum Report No. I-54-458, by F. G. Nesbitt, Equipment Branch, Engineering Section, Materiel Division, Wright Field, Ohio, Aug. 27, 1934.

49. Charles L. Wilson, "Wiley Post: First Test of High Altitude Pressure Suits in the United States," Archives of Environmental Health, vol. 10, May 1965, pp. 805–10.

50. Ibid., p. 809. See also T. W. Walker, "The Development of the Pressure Suit for High Altitude Flying," The Project Engineer, May 1956. This article also provides information on early foreign pressure suits.

51. Mohler and Johnson, p. 84. Post's third pressure suit and helmet and the Winnie Mae are on display in the National Air and Space Museum, Smithsonian Institution, Washington, D.C. The helmet used with Post's first and second pressure suits is also in the NASM collection.

52. Mohler and Johnson p. 83.

53. See Jane's All the World's Aircraft, and the Aircraft Year Book annual editions from the 1920s and 1930s for information on official altitude records. According to the 1981 edition of the Guiness Book of World Records, the greatest

recorded height reached by any pilot without a pressure cabin or pressure suit was 49,500 feet, achieved by RAF Squadron Leader G. W. H. Reynolds, in a Spitfire Mark VC over Libya in 1942.

54. Jane's All the World's Aircraft and the Aircraft Year Book. A new world altitude record of 59,445 feet was established by the British, flying a jet-powered De Havilland Vampire in March 1948.

55. T. W. Walker, The Project Engineer, May 1956, p. 6.

56. "Development of Sub-Stratosphere Pressure Suits in the German Air Force," Memorandum Report No. TSEAL-3-660-48-M, by V. J. Wulff and Col. W. R. Lovelace II, Aero Medical Laboratory, Air Technical Service Command, Wright Field, Ohio, Aug. 11, 1945. See also German Aviation Medicine in World War II.

57. Lloyd Mallan, Suiting Up for Space: The Evolution of the Space Suit (N.Y., 1971), p. 53, quoting Maj. Charles L. Wilson, USAF. See also Eloise Engle and Arnold S. Lott, Man in Flight: Biomedical Achievements in Aerospace (Annapolis, Md., 1979), pp. 223–26.

58. Schultz Study, p. 3.

59. Ibid., p. 3.

60. Ibid.

61. Ibid., p. 4.

62. "Pressure Suits and Anti-Blackout Suits," extracted from Report of Research and Development Projects, July 1, 1942, prepared by the Engineering Division, Materiel Center, Wright Field, Ohio, p. 583.

63. Schulz Study, p. 6.

64. "The Altitude Pressure Suit," Memorandum Report No. ENG-49-660-11-C-1, by Capt. Waring L. Dawbarn, Aero Medical Laboratory, Engineering Division, Materiel Command, Wright Field, Ohio, Oct. 11, 1943.

65. Mallan, p. 105.

66. Schulz Study, p. 6.

67. U.S. Patent No. 2,390,233 for a "Sealed Aviator's Suit and Helmet and Means for Controlling Gas Pressure and Oxygen Delivery Therein," filed Dec. 17, 1941, by John D. Akerman, Walter M. Boothby, Arthur H. Bulbulian, and William R. Lovelace II, patented Dec. 4, 1945, at the U.S. Patent Office, Washington, D.C. Note that Boothby, Bulbulian and Lovelace, then of the Mayo Clinic, invented the "B.L.B.," the first modern American oxygen mask.

68. Schultz Study, Document Digest, p. 7.

69. U.S. Patent No. 2,390,233.

70. U.S. Patent No. 2,404,020 for a "Pressure-Applying Aviator's Suit With Helmet," filed Mar. 10, 1943, by John D. Akerman, patented July 16, 1946, at the U.S. Patent Office, Washington, D.C.

71. Schulz Study, Document Digest, p. 18.

72. Ibid., Document Digest, p. 10.

73. Ibid., Document Digest, p. 11.

74. Ibid., Document Digest, p. 15. See also "Report on Pressure Suit, High Altitude, Goodyear Tire & Rubber Co., Test Of," Test TED No. NAF 2597, Aeronautical Materials Laboratory, Naval Air Experimental Station, Philadelphia, Penn., Sep. 3, 1943.

75. "Pressure Suit—Type BABM," Memorandum Report No. ENG-49-M-660-11-X, by 1st. Lt. Waring L. Dawbarn, Aero Medical Laboratory, Engineering Division, Materiel Command, Wright Field, Ohio, Apr. 21, 1943. See also Schulz Study, Document Digest, pp. 17–18.

76. Schulz Study, Document Digest, pp. 3–4.

77. Ibid., Document Digest, pp. 9–10.

78. Russell S. Colley, Pinehurst, N.C., letter to the author, Feb. 5, 1987. Colley filed a patent application for this suit design

on Aug. 3, 1943, listing Carroll P. Krupp and Donald H. Shook as co-inventors. U.S. Patent number 2,410,632 was granted on Nov. 5, 1946. As is usually the case, they were assignors to their parent firm, the B. F. Goodrich Company.

79. AML Memorandum Report No. ENG-49-660-11-C-1, Oct. 11, 1943, Note 64. See also "Pressure Altitude Suit Equipment," by Maj. J. A. Roth, MC, Report of the Army Air Forces Board, Project No. (M-4) 314, Orlando, Fla., Jan. 17, 1944.
80. Schulz Study, Document Digest, p. 19. An example of the improved Goodrich Type XH-1 suit is in the collection of the National Air and Space Museum.
81. AML Memorandum Report No. ENG-49-660-11-C-1, Oct. 11, 1943, p. 3.
82. "The Development of High Altitude Oxygen Helmets," Air Force Technical Report No. 5769, Aero Medical Laboratory, Wright-Patterson AFB, Ohio, Mar. 1949. See also Schulz, Document Digest, pp. 49–51.
83. Schulz Study, p. 7.
84. Ibid., Document Digest, p. 21.
85. Ibid., Document Digest, p. 28.
86. Ibid., p. 2.
87. Ibid., Document Digest, pp. 30–31.
88. Ibid., Document Digest, pp. 39–40.
89. Mallan, p. 150.

VI SURVIVAL EQUIPMENT

1. For information on this subject, see Sweeting, *Combat Flying Clothing*, pp. 15–16.
2. Ibid., pp. 60–61. See also Type Designation Sheets.
3. Raymond J. Snodgrass, "Development of Survival and Rescue Equipment for the Army Air Forces," Study 272, Air Technical Service Command, Wright Field, Ohio, May 22, 1945, p. 132., hereafter cited as Study 272.
4. Ibid., p. 133.
5. Type Designation Sheets.
6. Study 272, p. 134. See also AAF Manual 55-0-1, June 1, 1945, p. 13-L-1, and "Air-Sea Rescue Equipment Guide," NAVCG-117, published by the U.S. Coast Guard for Air Sea Rescue Agency, Washington, D.C., 1945, p. 59. "AN" or Army-Navy standard items were available for use by all services and many were supplied to the Allies.
7. Study 272, p. 59.
8. Type Designation Sheets. See also AAF Manual 55-0-1, June 1, 1945, p. 13-L-1; NAVCG-117, 1945, p. 59; and "Index of Army-Navy Aeronautical Equipment: Miscellaneous," Technical Order No. 03-1-46, Fairfield Air Technical Service Command, Patterson Field, Ohio, July 10, 1945, p. 62. An unnumbered edition of this illustrated catalog was published in 1943, and superseded by a numbered T.O. on June 20, 1944, as amended.
9. Type Designation Sheets. See also AAF Manual 55-0-1, June 1, 1945, p. 13-L-1.
10. Type Designation Sheets.
11. Study 272, p. 75.
12. Type Designation Sheets.
13. Study 272, p. 96. For details of rafts and accessories, see AAF Manual 55-0-1, June 1, 1945, pp. 13-H-1–13-J-5; T. O. 03-1-46, July 10, 1945, pp. 48–61; NAVCG-117, 1945, pp. 59–60; and "Miscellaneous Aircraft Equipment," Technical Manual 1-416, War Department, Washington, D.C., Mar. 22, 1944, pp. 1–15. TM 1-416 has interesting coverage of carbon dioxide-inflation systems including valves.
14. Study 272, p. 96.
15. Ibid., p. 98, and Type Designation Sheets. See also AAF Manual 55-0-1, June 1, 1945, p. 13-H-4; NAVCG-117, 1945, pp. 60–61; and T. O. 03-1-46, July 10, 1945, p. 58.
16. W. L. Warren, Penrose, N.C., letter to the author, Jan. 31, 1987. Former First Lieutenant Warren was the Personal Equipment Officer for the 327th Bombardment Squadron, 92nd Bombardment Group (H), Podington, England, during 1944–45.
17. AAF Manual 55-0-1, June 1, 1945, p. 13-C-1.
18. Frank E. Ransom, "Air-Sea Rescue 1941–1952," Historical Study No. 95, prepared for USAF Historical Division, Air University, Maxwell AFB, Ala., Aug. 1954, p. 42., hereafter cited as USAF Study 95. Survival following a bailout or ditching and subsequent rescue depended on many factors, including the skill and composure of the individual, his physical conditions, weather conditions, ditching characteristics of the aircraft, and even luck.
19. AAF Manual 55-0-1, June 1, 1945, p. 13-H-5.
20. Type Designation Sheets. See also AAF Manual 55-0-1, June 1, 1945; NAVCG-117, 1945; and T.O. 03-1-46, July 10, 1945.
21. Study 272, p. 154.
22. Ibid., p. 155. See also Type Designation Sheets; AAF Manual 55-0-1, June 1, 1945, p. 14-D-6; and NAVCG-117, 1945, p. 68. Note: the AAF Class 13 supply catalog shows a different configuration for the B-1 kit than Study 272, including a folding machete. It is believed that Study 272 is correct and the B-1 carried the bolo-type Collins Model No. 18 machete.
23. Study 272, p. 155. See also Type Designation Sheets; NAVCG-117, 1945, p. 68; "Pilot's Information File," AAF Regulation No. 62–15, edition of Oct. 1943; and Robert Lehmacher, Burbank, Ill., letter to the author, Dec. 13, 1986.
24. Robert Lehmacher, Burbank, Ill., letter to the author, Dec. 13, 1986.
25. "AAF Illustrated Catalogs, Clothing, Parachutes, Equipment and Supplies," Class 13; and Robert Lehmacher, Burbank, Ill., letter to the author, Dec. 13, 1986.
26. Study 272, p. 159; and Type Designation Sheets. See also NAVCG-117, 1945, pp. 69–70.
27. Study 272, p. 160. See also Technical Order No. 00-30-145, Headquarters, Army Air Forces, Washington, D.C., Feb. 17, 1943.
28. Study 272, p. 160.
29. Ibid., p. 161. See also Type Designation Sheets; AAF Manual 55-0-1, June 1, 1945, p. 14-D-6; NAVCG-117, 1945, pp. 69–70.
30. Type Designation Sheets; and Robert Lehmacher, Burbank, Ill., letter to the author, Dec. 12, 1986. See also T.O. 03-1-46, July 10, 1945, p. 45.
31. Study 272, pp. 161–62.
32. Although designed to integrate, the type designations of the C-1 vest and C-2 raft were coincidental. The Type C-2 pararaft was the second Army one-man raft design.
33. Robert Lehmacher, Burbank, Ill., letter to the author, Dec. 12, 1986. This information was based on the examination of dozens of Type C-1 vests produced during World War II.
34. Study 272, p. 164. See also AAF Manual 55-0-1, June 1, 1945, pp. 14-D-1–14-D-6; NAVCG-117, 1945, pp. 66–68; T.O. 93-1-46, July 10, 1945, p. 45; "Instructions for the Use of Emergency Sustenance Vest, Type C-1," booklet prepared by the Arctic-Desert-Tropic Branch, Headquarters, Air Force Tactical Center, included with each vest; and study of actual specimens of the C-1.
35. Study 272, p. 164.
36. AAF Manual 55-0-1, June 1, 1945, p. 14-D-3.
37. Type Designation Sheets.
38. Type Designation Sheets; and Study 272, p. 171.

222

39. Study 272, pp. 42 and 167; and Type Designation Sheets. See also AAF Manual 55-0-1, June 1, 1945, p. 14-D-8.
40. Type Designation Sheets, and Study 272, p. 167.
41. Ibid.
42. Study 272, p. 167. See also AAF Manual 55-0-1, June 1, 1945, pp. 14-D-7–14-D-8; and Type Designation Sheets.
43. Study 272, p. 167. See also AAF Manual 55-0-1, June 1, 1945, pp. 14-D-14–14-E-1; and Type Designation Sheets.
44. Study 272, p. 167.
45. Type Designation Sheets. See also AAF Manual 55-0-1, June 1, 1945, pp. 14-D-7–14-E-2; and NAVCG-117, 1945, pp. 70–77.
46. E&E kits described in sealed bid brochure, sale no. 01-9001, Aug. 1, 1979, offered by the Defense Logistics Agency, Battle Creek, Michigan. Specimens of E&E kits are included in the collection of the National Air and Space Museum, Smithsonian Institution.
47. Lt. Col. Donald S. Lopez, USAF (Ret.), interview with the author, Mar. 27, 1987. Former First Lieutenant Lopez flew with the 75th Fighter Squadron, (5 victories), in China during 1943–44, and was issued the money-belt kit.
48. *Air Sea Rescue Bulletin,* No. 11, May 1945, pp. 13–19. See also Sweeting, *Combat Flying Clothing,* pp. 57–58. Specimens are included in the National Air and Space Museum collection, including Blood Chit number 0001, issued to Maj. Gen. Claire L. Chennault, Commander of the "Flying Tigers." Former 1st. Lt. Donald S. Lopez does not remember signing for the Blood Chit he received upon arrival in China. He kept it as a souvenir when he returned to the U.S.
49. USAF Study 95, p. 1.
50. Ibid., p. 2.
51. "Saving Air Crews," *Flying,* Oct. 1943, p. 158. See also *AAF: The Official Guide to the Army Air Forces* (N.Y., 1944).
52. Capt. Earl H. Tilford, "The Development of Search and Rescue: World War II to 1961," *Aerospace Historian,* Winter, Dec. 1977, pp. 232–233.
53. AAF Regulation 20-54, dated Feb. 3, 1945, cited in USAF Study 95, p. 9.
54. USAF Study 95, p. 140. See also AAF Manual 55-0-1, June 1, 1945.
55. *Aerospace Historian,* Dec. 1977, p. 233.
56. See Note 6.
57. See Study 272, p. 2. See also Woodford Agee Heflin (Ed.), *The United States Air Force Dictionary* (Washington, D.C., 1956). The ARS is now the Aerospace Rescue and Recovery Service (ARRS).
58. *Aerospace Historian,* Dec. 1977, p. 233.
59. USAF Study 95, p. 175.
60. *Aerospace Historian,* Dec. 1977, p. 233. See also USAF Study 95; and Wesley F. Craven and James L. Cate, *The Army Air Forces in World War II* (Chicago, 1948–1955), vol. VII, pp. 478–479 and 481–482.
61. Ibid., p. 233.

VII MISCELLANEOUS EQUIPMENT

1. Link and Coleman, p. 832.
2. "Aeronautic Instruments," by Franklin L. Hunt, Technologic Papers of the Bureau of Standards No. 237, U.S. National Bureau of Standards, Washington, D.C., May 16, 1923, p. 508.
3. *U.S. Air Force Dictionary,* p. 243.
4. Type Designation Sheets.
5. "Aircraft Instruments—Aircraft Clocks," Technical Manual No. 1-413, Chief of the Air Corps, War Department, Washington, D.C., Nov. 7, 1940, pp. 167–70, and revised edition dated Feb. 2, 1942, pp. 163–64.
6. For general repair instructions for various types of standard Army watches, see "Ordnance Maintenance; Wrist Watches, Pocket Watches, Stop Watches, and Clocks," Technical Manual No. 9-1575, War Department, Washington, D.C., Apr. 6, 1945.
7. Crowell, p. 219.
8. *History of Military Pyrotechnics in World War,* War Department Document No. 2031, prepared by the Ordnance Department, U.S. Army (Washington, D.C., 1920), p. 20.
9. G. B. Christensen, "American Signal Pistols, 1846–1918," *Guns Review,* undated, p. 18.
10. "Handbook of Aircraft Armament," 1918, pp. 87–88.
11. *History of Military Pyrotechnics in World War,* p. 21. See also *Handbook of Ordnance Data,* War Department Document No. 1861, prepared by the Ordnance Department, U.S. Army (Washington, D.C., 1919), p. 291. Mark II and Mark III experimental 35 mm aviation signal pistols were tested during 1918 but not adopted.
12. Maj. LeRoy Hodges, *Notes on Post-War Ordnance Development* (Richmond, Va., 1923), pp. 94–95. Fund reductions during this period prevented production of many improved weapons and items of equipment desired by the Army in the 1920s.
13. Capt. Arthur R. Wilson, *Field Artillery Manual* (Menasha, Wis., 3rd Edition, 1929), vol. I, chapter XVIII, pp. 2–3. The Mark IV 25 mm Very pistol was included in the Army Ordnance Department "Standard Nomenclature List No. B-12," Washington, D.C., Jan. 15, 1926.
14. *Handbook of Instructions for Airplane Designers,* June 1922, pp. 216–19. See also "Pyrotechnics," by Capt. Ira Crump, Ordnance Department, *Army Ordnance,* vol. VII, no. 37, Jul.-Aug. 1926.
15. "Small Arms, Light Field Mortars and 20mm Aircraft Guns," Technical Manual No. 9-2200, War Department, Washington, D.C., Oct. 11, 1943, pp. 134–35. See also "Standard Nomenclature List No. B-18," Army Ordnance Department, July 29, 1936; "Handbook of Ordnance Materiel," OS 9-63, vol. 1, The Ordnance School, Aberdeen Proving Ground, Md., June 1944, p. 23; AAF Manual 55-0-1, June 1, 1945, p. 13-I-6; and NAVCG-117, 1945, p. 119. For details on pyrotechnic ammunition, see "Ammunition, General," Technical Manual No. 9-1900, War Department, Washington, D.C., July 3, 1942, pp. 91–98; and "Military Pyrotechnics," Technical Manual No. 9-981, War Department, Washington, D.C., May 30, 1942.
16. AAF Manual 55-0-1, June 1, 1945, p. 13-I-6. See also "Pilot's Information File," May 1, 1943, p. 8-5-1.
17. AAF Manual 55-0-1, June 1, 1945, pp. 13-H-6 and 13-I-6; and "Pilot's Information File," May 1, 1943, p. 8-5-1. See also NAVCG-117, 1945, p. 119; and TM 9-2200, Oct. 11, 1943, p. 67.
18. "Pilot's Information File," May 1, 1943, p. 8-5-1. See also "Ammunition, General," Technical Manual No. 9-1900, War Department, Washington, D.C., June 18, 1945, pp. 162-68; and TM 9-981, May 30, 1942.
19. NAVCG-117, 1945, pp. 119-21. See also AAF Manual 55-0-1, June 1, 1945, pp. 13-H-6, 13-I-6, and 13-I-7.
20. AAF Manual 55-0-1, June 1, 1945, p. 13-H-6. See also TM 9-2200, Oct. 11, 1943, p. 141. For details on pyrotechnic pistol holder, Type A-2, see Technical Order No. 03-1-46, July 10, 1945, p. 13.

21. NAVCG-117, 1945, pp. 120–21. See also AAF Manual 55-0-1, June 1, 1945, p. 13-I-6.
22. AAF Manual 55-0-1, June 1, 1945, p. 13-H-6.
23. Ibid., p. 13-I-7. See also NASVCG-117, 1945, pp. 39 and 48.
24. Ibid., p. 13-I-7. See also NAVCG-117, 1945, pp. 122-138 for details on British pyrotechnic equipment.
25. ''Technical Equipment of the Signal Corps, 1916,'' Signal Corps Manual No. 3, War Department Document No. 541, War Department, Washington, D.C., 1917.
26. Type Designation Sheets.
27. AAF Manual 55-0-1, June 1, 1945, p. 13-L-1.
28. Type Designation Sheets.
29. AAF Illustrated Supply Catalog, Class 13, Sep. 30, 1943, p. 5. See also Type Designation Sheets.
30. See Chapter I.
31. AAF Manual 55-0-1, June 1, 1945, p. 11-A-1.
32. Ibid., pp. 11-A-1–11-A-2. See also ''Pilot's Information File,'' Oct. 1, 1943, pp. 8-13-1–8-13-3; and Technical Order No. 03-1-46, Apr. 1, 1945, p. 51.
33. AAF Manual 55-0-1, June 1, 1945, p. 11-C-2.
34. Type Designation Sheets.
35. AAF Manual 55-0-1, June 1, 1945, p. 11-C-1. See also ''Pilot's Information File,'' Apr. 1, 1944, p. 8-13-3.
36. AAF Manual 55-0-1, June 1, 1945, p. 11-C-1. See also NAVCG-117, 1945, pp. 37–38.
37. Ibid., p. 13-H-9. See also NAVCG-117, 1945, p. 5, and Technical Order No. 03-1-46, Apr. 1, 1945, p. 51.
38. AAF Manual 55-0-1, June 1, 1945, pp. 11-C-1–11-C-2.
39. *Air Force,* March 1945, p. 53.

Glossary of Abbreviations

Most of the following abbreviations are used in the text and reference sections of this book. Other abbreviations listed are frequently encountered by historians and collectors and are included for their assistance.

AA	Antiaircraft
AAA	Antiaircraft Artillery
AAC	Army Air Corps
AAF	Army Air Forces
AAFld	Army Air Field
AAFSAT	Army Air Forces School of Applied Tactics
AC	Air Corps
A/C	Aviation Cadet
Actg.	Acting
Adm.	Admiral
ADTIC	Arctic, Desert, and Tropic Information Center
A.E.F., AEF	American Expeditionary Forces (WW I)
Aero Med.	Aeronautical Medical
AFB	Air Force Base
AFLC	Air Force Logistics Command
AG	Adjutant General
AGF	Army Ground Forces
AM	Air Medal
AMC	Air Materiel Command
AML	Aero Medical Laboratory
AN, A-N	Army-Navy
ANC	Army Nurse Corps
AOS	Arterial Occlusion Suit
APG	Air Proving Ground
APO	Army Post Office
AR	Army Regulation
ARC	American Red Cross
ARRS	Aerospace Rescue and Recovery Service
ARS	Air Rescue Service
AS	Air Service
ASC	Air Service Command
ASF	Army Service Forces
A.S.S.C.	Aviation Section, Signal Corps
Asst.	Assistant
Assy.	Assembly
ATC	Air Transport Command
ATSC	Air Technical Service Command
AUS	Army of the United States
Aux.	Auxiliary
AVG	American Volunteer Group (Flying Tigers)
Avn.	Aviation
Bd.	Board
Bomb.	Bombardment
Br.	Branch
Brig. Gen.	Brigadier General
BuAer	Bureau of Aeronautics (U.S. Navy)
BuOrd	Bureau of Ordnance (U.S. Navy)
C.	Centigrade or Celsius
c.	circa
CAA	Civil Aeronautics Administration
C.A.A.G.	Cotton Aerodynamic Anti-G (suit)
CAP	Civil Air Patrol
Capt.	Captain
CBI	China-Burma-India theater of operations (WW II)
CF	Central Files
CG	Commanding General
Chem.	Chemical
Cir.	Circular
CIOS	Combined Intelligence Objectives Sub-Committee
Civ.	Civilian
Clo	"Clo" is a unit of measurement used to determine the insulation afforded by clothing.
cm	centimeters
Co.	Company
CO	Commanding Officer
CO_2	Carbon Dioxide
Col.	Colonel
Comd.	Command
Comdr.	Commander
Comm.	Communications
Corp.	Corporation
Cpl.	Corporal
cu.in.	cubic inches
Dep.	Deputy
Dept.	Department
DFC	Distinguished Flying Cross
Dia.	Diameter
Dir.	Director
Div.	Division

Dr.	Doctor	Lg	Large
DSC	Distinguished Service Cross	Lib.	Library
DSM	Distinguished Service Medal	LM	Legion of Merit
E&E	Escape and Evasion	Lt.	Lieutenant
Elect.	Electric	Lt. Col.	Lieutenant Colonel
EM	Enlisted Man	Lt. Comdr.	Lieutenant Commander (Navy)
Eng.	Engineering	Lt. Gen.	Lieutenant General
E.O.	Engineering Order	Ltr.	Letter
Equip.	Equipment	M	Master, Medium, Model
ETA	Estimated time of arrival	Maint.	Maintenance
ETD	Estimated time of departure	Maj.	Major
ETO	European theater of operations	Maj. Gen.	Major General
Exec.	Executive	Mat.	Materiel
Exp.	Experimental	MC	Medical Corps or Materiel Command
F.	Fahrenheit		
F.A.I.	Fédération Aéronautique Internationale	MD	Materiel Division
		MD or M.D.	Doctor of Medicine
FCC	Flight Control Command	Mech.	Mechanic
FEAF	Far East Air Force	Med.	Medium
FFS	Franks Flying Suit	Memo	Memorandum
Flak	AA shell fire or fragments (from a German term)	MG	Machine Gun
		MH, MOH	Medal of Honor
Fld.	Field	Mil.	Military
FM	Field Manual	Misc.	Miscellaneous
F/O	Flight Officer	M.I.T.	Massachusetts Institute of Technology
fpm	feet per minute		
fps	feet per second	mm	Milimeters
ft.	feet	MOS	Military Occupational Speciality
FTC	Flying Training Command	MP	Military Police
Ftr.	Fighter	mph, m.p.h.	miles per hour
FY	Fiscal Year	M/Sgt.	Master Sergeant
GAF	German Air Force	MTO	Mediterranean theater of operations
G, g	gravity	NAAF	Northwest African Air Forces
G.E.	General Electric Company	NACA, N.A.C.A.	National Advisory Committee for Aeronautics
Gen.	General		
GHQ	General Headquarters	NAF	Naval Aircraft Factory, Philadelphia, Pa.
GI, G.I.	Government Issue		
GO	General Order	NASM	National Air and Space Museum
Gp.	Group	NCO	Noncommissioned Officer
G.P.O., GPO	U.S. Government Printing Office	NDRC	National Defense Research Committee
GPS	Gradient Pressure Suit		
GSC	General Staff Corps	NG	National Guard
HE	High Explosive	NRC	National Research Council
Hist.	History, Historical	OCAC	Office, Chief of Air Corps
hp	horsepower	OCQM	Office of the Chief Quartermaster
HQ, Hq.	Headquarters	OC(S)	Officer Candidate (School)
Ind.	Indorsement (on military correspondence)	O.D., OD	Olive drab
		Off.	Officer, Official, Office
IG	Inspector General	O.G., OG	Olive green
Info.	Information	ONI	Office of Naval Intelligence
K.O.P.	Kelly One-Piece (suit)	OPM	Office of Production Management
L	Large or light	Ops.	Operations
Lab.	Laboratory	OQMG	Office of the Quartermaster General
lbs.	Pounds		

ORC	Officers' Reserve Corps	Sm.	Small
Ord.	Ordnance	SM	Soldier's Medal
Org.	Organization(al)	SO	Special Orders
OSRD	Office of Scientific Research and Development	SOP	Standard Operating Procedure
OTU	Operational Training Unit	SOS	Services of Supply, or an international distress signal
p., pp.	page, pages	Spec.	Specification
par.	paragraph	Sq., Sqrd.	Squadron
para.	parachute	SR	Special Regulations
PEL	Personal Equipment Laboratory	S/Sgt.	Staff Sergeant
PEO	Personal Equipment Office(r)	Std(s).	Standard(s)
per., pers.	personnel	Sup.	Supply
Pfc.	Private first class	Supv.	Supervisor
PGC	Proving Ground Command	SWPA	Southwest Pacific Area
PH	Purple Heart	T., Tech.	Technical
PhD	Doctor of Philosophy	Tac., Tact.	Tactical
POW	Prisoner of War	TCC	Troop Carrier Command
pr.	pair	TI	Technical Instruction
Prod.	Production	TM	Technical Manual
Prof.	Professor	Tng.	Training
psi, p.s.i.	pounds per square inch	T.O., TO	Technical Order
Pur.	Purchasing	T/O	Table of Organization
PX	Post Exchange	TR	Training Regulations
QM	Quartermaster	Trans.	Transport(ation)
QMC	Quartermaster Corps	T/Sgt.	Technical Sergeant
RA	Regular Army	TTC	Technical Training Command
RAAF, R.A.A.F.	Royal Australian Air Force	TWX	Teletypewriter Exchange Message
RAF, R.A.F.	Royal Air Force (Great Britain)	U.K., UK	United Kingdom
RCAF, R.C.A.F.	Royal Canadian Air Force	UR	Unsatisfactory Report
R&D	Research and Development	USAC	United States (Army) Air Corps
Rear Adm.	Rear Admiral	USAAC	United States Army Air Corps
Reg.	Regulation	USAAF	United States Army Air Forces
Res.	Reserve, research	USAF	United States Air Force
Ret.	Retired	USCG	United States Coast Guard
RFC, R.F.C.	Royal Flying Corps (Great Britain)	USMA	United States Military Academy (West Point, N.Y.)
RN, R.N.	Royal Navy (Great Britain), or Registered Nurse	USMC	United States Marine Corps
RNAS, R.N.A.S.	Royal Naval Air Service (Great Britain)	USN	United States Navy
		USNA	United States Naval Academy (Annapolis, Md.)
RNZAF, R.N.Z.A.F.	Royal New Zealand Air Force	USSAFE	United States Strategic Air Forces in Europe
rpm, r.p.m.	revolutions per minute		
Rpt.	Report	USSBS	United States Strategic Bombing Survey
S	Small		
S., St.	Staff	USSR, U.S.S.R.	Union of Soviet Socialist Republics
SAAF, S.A.A.F.	South African Air Force	USSTAF	United States Strategic Air Force
SAM	School of Aviation Medicine	Univ.	University
SEA	Southeast Asia	UXB	Unexploded bomb
Sect.	Section	ZI	Zone of Interior (by inference, the continental United States)
Serv., Sv.	Service		
Sgt.	Sergeant		
SHAEF	Supreme Headquarters, Allied Expeditionary Forces (Europe)		
SI	Smithsonian Institution		
SigC, SC	Signal Corps, U.S. Army		

Bibliography

GENERAL

AAF: The Official Guide to the Army Air Forces, a Directory, Almanac and Chronicle of Achievement. Published for the Army Air Forces Aid Society. New York, 1944.

Air Corps News Letter. Publication of the Office of the Chief of the Air Corps, War Department. Washington, D.C., Aug. 1926–Aug. 1941.

Air Force. Official service journal of the U.S. Army Air Forces. New York, Dec. 1942–through World War II, (now published by the Air Force Association).

Air Forces News Letter. Publication of the Office of the Chief of the Air Corps, War Department. Washington, D.C., Sep. 1941–Nov. 1942.

Air Service Journal. Publication of the Gardner-Moffat Company. New York, 1917–20.

Air Service Medical. Published by the Air Service, Division of Military Aeronautics, War Department. Washington, D.C., 1919.

Air Service News Letter. Publication of the Office of the Chief of the Air Service, War Department. Washington, D.C., Sep. 1918–Jul. 1926.

Air Surgeon's Bulletin. Publication of the Office of the Air Surgeon, AAF. Headquarters, Army Air Forces. Washington, D.C., 1944–45.

Armstrong, Harry G. *Principles and Practice of Aviation Medicine.* Baltimore, Md., 1939 and 1952 editions.

Beaven, Lt. Col. C. L. "A Chronological History of Aviation Medicine." Mimeographed reference prepared by the School of Aviation Medicine. Randolph Field, Texas, 1939.

Benford, Col. Robert, M.D. *Doctors in the Sky.* Springfield, Ill., 1955.

"Bombardiers' Information File," AAF Regulation No. 62–15, Headquarters, Army Air Forces. Washington, D.C., Mar. 1945, as amended. The "BIF" was a loose-leaf handbook that included subjects of importance to all aircrew members.

Chandler, Charles deForest, and Lahm, Frank P. *How Our Army Grew Wings.* New York, 1943.

"Clothing, Parachutes, Equipment and Supplies," AAF Illustrated Catalog, Class 13. Headquarters, Army Air Forces. Washington, D.C., Sep. 30, 1943. Revised pages issued Apr. 1, 1944.

Craven, Wesley, and Cate, James L. (eds.) *The Army Air Forces in World War II.* Chicago, Ill., 7 vols., 1948–58.

Crowell, Benedict. *America's Munitions, 1917–1918.* Report of the Assistant Secretary of War, Director of Munitions. Washington, D.C., 1919.

Dempsey, Charles A. *50 years of Research On Man in Flight.* Aerospace Medical Research Laboratory. Wright-Patterson AFB, Ohio, 1985.

Goldberg, Dr. Alfred. "History of the United States Air Force." Air Training Command Pamphlet No. 190–1. Randolph AFB, Texas, 1961.

Gray, George W. *Science at War.* New York, 1943.

Grow, Lt. Col. Malcolm C., and Armstrong, Capt. Harry G. *Fit To Fly: A Medical Handbook for Fliers.* New York, 1942.

Heflin, Woodford Agee (ed.). *The United States Air Force Dictionary.* Washington, D.C., 1956.

"Index of Army-Navy Aeronautical Equipment: Miscellaneous." Technical Order No. 03–1–46. Fairfield Air Technical Service Command. Patterson Field, Ohio, Jul. 10, 1945.

Journal of Aviation Medicine. Publication of the Aero Medical Association of the United States. St. Paul, Minn., 1930–

Link, Mae Mills, and Coleman, Hubert A. *Medical Support of the Army Air Forces in World War II.* Report of the Office of the Surgeon General, USAF. Washington, D.C., 1955.

Lovelace, Dr. W. R., Gagge, Lt. Col. A. P., and Bray, Dr. C. W. *Aviation Medicine and Psychology.* Publication of the Air Materiel Command, AAF. Wright Field, Ohio, 1946.

Maurer, Maurer (ed.). *The U.S. Air Service in World War I.* Office of Air Force History, Headquarters USAF. 4 vols. Washington, D.C., 1978.

230 "Miscellaneous Aircraft Equipment." Technical Manual No. 1–416. War Department. Washington, D.C., Mar. 22, 1944.

"Navigator's Information File," AAF Regulation No. 62–15. Headquarters, Army Air Forces. Washington, D.C., Nov. 24, 1944. The "NIF" was a loose-leaf style handbook with much information on equipment and procedures of importance to the military aviator.

"Physiology of Flight: Human Factors in the Operation of Military Aircraft." AAF Manual No. 25–2, Headquarters, Army Air Forces. Washington, D.C., Mar. 15, 1945.

"Pilot's Information File," AAF Regulation No. 62–15. Headquarters, Army Air Forces. Washington, D.C., Apr. 9, 1943, as amended. The "PIF" was a very useful general reference containing much valuable information.

Purtee, Edward O. "Development of AAF Clothing and Other Personal Equipment Peculiar to Air Operations." 3 vols. Unpublished study no. 204, prepared for the acting director of the Air Technical Service Command. Wright Field, Ohio, May 22, 1945. Important reference on Army flying clothing and equipment.

"Reference Manual for Personal Equipment Officers." AAF Manual No. 55–0–1. Headquarters, Army Air Forces. Washington, D.C., Jun. 1, 1945. Another useful official reference covering the World War II period.

Robinson, Douglas H., M.D. *The Dangerous Sky: A History of Aviation Medicine*. Seattle, Wash., 1973.

Sweeting, C. G. *Combat Flying Clothing: Army Air Forces Clothing During World War II*. Washington, D.C., 1984.

The Official Pictorial History of the AAF. Prepared by the Historical Office of the Army Air Forces. New York, 1947.

The Personal Equipment Officer. Publication of the Personal Equipment Laboratory, AAF. Wright Field, Ohio, 1945–46.

Type Designation Sheets. Documents recording information on aviation clothing and equipment maintained by the Materiel Division, Wright Field, Ohio, from the mid-1920s until the early 1950s. They cover almost every item of aeronautical equipment. Now in the archives of the National Air and Space Museum, Smithsonian Institution.

I HUMAN ENGINEERING

Beaven, Lt. Col. C. L. "A Chronological History of Aviation Medicine." Mimeographed reference prepared by the School of Aviation Medicine. Randolph Field, Tex., 1939.

Crowell, Benedict. *America's Munitions, 1917–1918*. Report of the Assistant Secretary of War, Director of Munitions. Washington, D.C., 1919.

Dempsey, Charles A. *50 Years of Research on Man in Flight*. Aerospace Medical Research Laboratory. Wright Patterson AFB, Ohio, 1985.

Link, Mae Mills, and Coleman, Hubert A. *Medical Support of the Army Air Forces in World War II*. Report of the Office of the Surgeon General, USAF. Washington, D.C., 1955.

"Materiel Division Number." *Air Corps News Letter*. Jan. 1, 1937.

"Officers' Directory," Wright Field, Dayton, Ohio, including Materiel Command, Signal Corps Aircraft Agency and U.S. Navy. Various dates, 1939–44.

"Physiology of Flight: Human Factors in the Operation of Military Aircraft." AAF Manual No. 25–2, Headquarters, Army Air Forces. Washington, D.C., 1945.

Purtee, Edward O. "Development of AAF Clothing and Other Personal Equipment Peculiar to Air Operations." 3 vols. Unpublished Study no. 204, prepared for the acting director of the Air Technical Service Command. Wright Field, Ohio, May 22, 1945.

Sweeting, C. G. *Combat Flying Clothing: Army Air Forces Clothing During World War II*. Washington, D.C., 1984.

"Your Body in Flight," Technical Order No. 30–105–1, Prepared by the Aero Medical Laboratory, Engineering Division, ATSC, Wright Field, Ohio, Sep. 30, 1944. This handbook superseded T.O. No. 30–25–13, Jul. 20, 1943.

II OXYGEN EQUIPMENT

"Aircraft Instruments," Technical Regulations No. 1170–50. Air Corps, War Department, Washington, D.C., Nov. 1, 1929.

Air Service Medical. Published by the Air Service, Division of Military Aeronautics, War Department. Washington, D.C., 1919.

Armstrong, Harry G. *Principles and Practice of Aviation Medicine*. Baltimore, Md., 1939 and 1952 editions.

Armstrong, Harry G. "Oxygen Mask." Memorandum Report No. EXP-54–660–1. Equipment Laboratory, Experimental Engineering Section, Materiel Division. Wright Field, Ohio, Oct. 19, 1939.

"A Study of the Merits of Liquid and Gaseous Oxygen for Air Corps Use at High Altitudes." Memorandum Report No. X–54–231. Equipment Branch, Engineering Section, Materiel Division. Wright Field, Ohio, Mar. 12, 1935.

Crowell, Benedict. *America's Munitions, 1917–1918*. Report of the Assistant Secretary of War, Director of Munitions. Washington, D.C., 1919.

"General—Oxygen Equipment." Technical Order No. 01–1H–1B. Air Corps, War Department. Washington, D.C., Apr. 20, 1938.

"Handbook of Instructions: Low-Pressure Oxygen Cylinders Types A–4, D–2, F–1 and G–1." AN 03–50C–3. Headquarters, Army Air Forces. Washington, D.C., Jun. 25, 1943.

Heim, Dr. J.W. "Oxygen Masks." Memorandum Report No. Q–54–40–A1. Equipment Laboratory, Engineering Section, Materiel Division, Wright Field, Ohio, May 2, 1938.

"History of the Bureau of Aircraft Production." Historical Study No. 198, vol. VIII, chapter XLVI, Oxygen Equipment. Washington, D.C., n.d., c. 1920.

Hunt, Franklin L. "Oxygen Instruments." Report No. 130. Aeronautic Instruments Section, U.S. National Bureau of Standards. Washington, D.C., 1921.

Lovelace, Dr. W. R., Gagge, Lt. Col. A. P., and Bray, Dr. C. W. Aviation Medicine and Psychology. Publication of the Air Material Command, AAF. Wright Field, Ohio, 1946.

"Masks, Pressure Demand Oxygen." Project No. 3926C452.17. Report of the Army Air Forces Board. Orlando, Fla., Mar. 13, 1945.

"Oxygen Equipment," Handbook M–42–3, Department of Mechanics, Air Corps Technical School. Wright Field, Ohio, Oct. 30, 1936.

Pleiss, Paul. "Report on American Made Dreyer Apparatii." Technical Section, U.S. Air Service, A.E.F., Jun. 4, 1918.

"Pressure Breathing." Memorandum Report No. TSEAL–3C–695–1CC. Aero Medical Laboratory, Engineering Division, Air Technical Service Command. Wright Field, Ohio, Dec. 20, 1944.

"Reference Manual for Personal Equipment Officers." AAF Manual No. 55–0–1. Headquarters, Army Air Forces. Washington, D.C., Jun. 1, 1945.

"Report on Pressure Breathing Mission." Formerly secret report from Headquarters, 7th Photo Reconnaissance Group, APO 634, N.Y., to Commanding General, Materiel Command, Attn: Lt. Col. A. P. Gagge, Aero Medical Laboratory, Wright Field, Ohio, May 13, 1944.

"Review of the Status of Oxygen Equipment with Reference to Information Gathered in a Visit to USSTAF." Memorandum Report No. TSEAL–3–660–53–F–1. Oxygen Branch, Aero Medical Laboratory, Engineering Division, Air Technical Service Command. Wright Field, Ohio, Dec. 31, 1944.

Robinson, Douglas H., M.D. The Dangerous Sky: A History of Aviation Medicine. Seattle, Washington, 1973.

Robinson, Douglas H., M.D. The Zeppelin in Combat. Sun Valley, Cal., 1966.

Rolt, L. T. C. The Aeronauts: A History of Ballooning, 1783–1903. New York, 1966.

"The Oxygen Mask and Goggle Assembly as a Substitute for Gas Masks." Memorandum Report No. ENG–49–660–58. Aero Medical Laboratory, Engineering Division, Materiel Command. Wright Field, Ohio, Mar. 1, 1944.

"Use of Oxygen and Oxygen Equipment." Technical Order No. 03–50–1. Aero Medical Laboratory, Engineering Division, Materiel Command. Wright Field, Ohio, Jul. 1, 1943, and other editions.

III MILITARY PARACHUTES

"Clothing, Parachutes, Equipment and Supplies." AAF Illustrated Catalog, Class 13. Headquarters, Army Air Forces. Washington, D.C., Sep. 30, 1943.

Brown, W. D. Parachutes. London, 1951.

"Case History of Quick Release Parachutes." AFLC Historical Study No. 128, Compiled by the Historical Division, Headquarters, Air Technical Service Command. Wright Field, Ohio, May 1945.

Devlin, Gerald M. Paratrooper! New York, 1979.

Dixon, Charles. Parachuting. London, n.d., c. 1930.

Gavin, Lt. Gen. James M. On to Berlin. New York, 1978.

Glassman, Don. Jump. New York, 1930. Best source of early history of the Caterpillar Club.

Gold, David. Early Development of the Manually Operated Personnel Parachute, 1900–1919. Newbury Park, Cal., 1968.

Graham, Lloyd. Ripcord. Buffalo, N.Y., 1936.

Greenwood, James R. The Parachute. New York, 1964.

Gregory, Barry, and Batchelor, John. Airborne Warfare, 1918–1945. London, 1979.

"Hitting the Silk: A Manual on the Care and Use of the Parachute." AAF School of Applied Tactics. Orlando, Fla., Nov. 1944.

Irvin Air Chutes, Symbols of Safety. Illustrated factory manual of Irving Air Chute Company, Inc. Buffalo, N.Y., n.d., c. 1934, and another, c. 1937.

Lucas, John. The Big Umbrella. London, 1973.

MacDonald, Charles. Airborne. New York, 1970.

Manual for All Models of Switlik Safety Chutes. Illustrated manual of Switlik Parachute and Equipment Company. Trenton, N.J., n.d., c. 1935.

232

Mazer, Lt. "Airplane Parachutes." National Advisory Committee for Aeronautics Technical Memorandum No. 322. Washington, D.C., Aug. 1925. Translated from *Bulletin Technique,* Aug. 1924, of the Service Technique de L' Aéronautique, Paris, France.

"Parachutes and Aircraft Clothing." Technical Manual No. 1–440. War Department. Washington, D.C., Jun. 1945.

"Parachutes-Construction, Maintenance, Storage, and Use." Technical Order No. 13–5–2. Office of the Chief of the Air Corps. Washington, D.C., Jun. 15, 1933. This T.O. deals only with circular parachutes, their inspection, repair, packing, etc.

"Parachute Manual." Prepared by the Parachute Branch, Equipment Section, McCook Field. Dayton, Ohio, 1920. Also editions of 1923, 1924, and supplement, 1925.

"Parachutes-Triangular Types-Construction, Maintenance, Storage, and Use." Technical Order No. 13–5–1. Office of the Chief of the Air Corps. Washington, D.C., May 17, 1934.

"Pilot's Information File." AAF Regulation No. 62–15. Headquarters, Army Air Forces. Washington, D.C., Apr. 9, 1943, as amended.

Purtee, Edward O. "Development of AAF Clothing and Other Personal Equipment Peculiar to Air Operations." Vol. 3. Unpublished study no. 204, prepared for the acting director of the Air Technical Service Command. Wright Field, Ohio, May 22, 1945.

Safe! The Triangular Parachute. Booklet published by the Triangle Parachute Company. Cincinnati, Ohio, n.d., c. 1931.

Smith, Floyd. *Coming Down.* Illustrated manual of the Switlik Manufacturing Company. Trenton, N.J., n.d., c. 1932.

Switlik Safe-T-Chutes. Illustrated factory manual of the Switlik Parachute Company. Trenton, N.J., 1945.

"The Parachute Rigger." Training Manual No. 2170–72. Chief of the Air Corps, War Department. Washington, D.C., Jun. 29, 1929.

Toole, Virginia G. "The Development and Procurement of Parachutes for the Army Air Forces." AFLC Historical Study No. 246. Headquarters, Air Materiel Command. Wright-Patterson AFB, Ohio, Dec. 1948.

Weeks, John. *The Airborne Soldier.* Poole, England, 1982.

Zim, Herbert S. *Parachutes.* New York, 1942.

Zweng, Charles A. *Parachute Technician.* No. Hollywood, Cal., 1944.

IV ARMOR FOR AVIATORS

Ashdown, Charles H. *European Arms and Armour.* New York, 1967.

Benson, Col. Otis, Jr., and Hoffman, Lt. Col. I., "A Study of Wounds in Combat Crews With Certain Recommendations for Prevention." *Air Surgeon's Bulletin,* Jul. 1944.

Blair, Claude. *European Armour, Ca. 1066 to Ca. 1700.* London, 1958.

Boutell, Charles. *Arms and Armour in Antiquity and the Middle Ages.* London, 1907.

Coates, Col. James B., Jr., and Beyer, Maj. James C. (eds.). *Wound Ballistics.* Office of the Surgeon General, Department of the Army. Washington, D.C., 1962. Important reference on armor.

Crowell, Benedict. *America's Munitions, 1917–1918.* Report of the Assistant Secretary of War, Director of Munitions. Washington, D.C., 1919.

Dean, Bashford. *Helmets and Body Armor in Modern Warfare.* New Haven, Conn., 1920. Standard reference on armor development in World War I.

Demmin, Auguste. *An Illustrated History of Arms and Armour.* London, 1877.

Grow, Brig. Gen. Malcolm C., and Lyons, Lt. Col. Robert C., MC. "Body Armor, A Brief Study on the Development." *Air Surgeon's Bulletin,* vol. II, Jan. 1945.

"Helmets and Body Armor." Office of the Chief of Ordnance, U.S. Army. Washington, D.C., Jun. 1, 1945. Useful reference.

Judson, Harry P. *Caesar's Army.* Boston, Mass., 1888.

Laible, Roy C. *Ballistic Materials and Penetration Mechanics.* New York, 1980. Important study of ancient and modern armor.

Lewis, Comdr. Frederick J., et al. *Military Helmet Design.* Research Project NM810109.1. Naval Medical Field Research Laboratory. Camp Lejeune, N.C., 1958.

Link, Mae Mills, and Coleman, Hubert A. *Medical Support of the Army Air Forces in World War II.* Report of the Office of the Surgeon General, USAF. Washington, D.C., 1955.

Morrison, Sean. *Armor.* New York, 1963.

Nickel, Helmut. *Warriors and Worthies: Arms and Armor Through the Ages.* New York, 1969.

Oakeshott, R. Ewart. *The Archaeology of Weapons.* New York, 1960.

Peterson, Harold L. *Arms and Armor in Colonial America, 1526–1783.* New York, 1956.

"Record of Army Ordnance Research and Development, Helmets and Body Armor." Vol. 2, book 1, section 3. Office of the Chief of Ordnance, Research and Development Service. Washington, D.C., Jan. 1946. Important, detailed study of armor in World War II.

Stone, George Cameron. *A Glossary of the Construction, Decoration and Use of Arms and Armor, in All Countries and in All Times.* New York, 1934.

Studler, Col. Rene R. "Body Armor for Modern Battle." *Army Ordnance.* Jan.-Feb. 1946.

Wise, Terence. *Medieval Warfare.* New York, 1976.

V ANTI-G GARMENTS AND PRESSURE SUITS

Anti-G Garments

"A Report on the Introduction of Anti-'G' Equipment to FEAF and a Survey of Aero-Medical Problems in SWPA Including Continental Australia." Memorandum Report No. TSEAL3–696–51H, by Capt. Clarence A. Maaske. Aero Medical Laboratory, Engineering Division, Air Technical Service Command. Wright Field, Ohio, Feb. 24, 1945.

Armstrong, Harry G. *Principles and Practice of Aviation Medicine.* Baltimore, Md., 1939 and 1952 editions.

Armstrong, H. G., and Heim, J. W. "The Effect of Acceleration on the Living Organism." *Journal of Aviation Medicine,* 1938: 9.

Doolittle, James H. "Accelerations in Flight." National Advisory Committee for Aeronautics (N.A.C.A.) Report No. 203. Washington, D.C., 1925.

"Evaluation of Anti-G Suits." By 1st. Lt. George A. Hallenbeck, et al. Aero Medical Laboratory. Wright Field, Ohio. Report No. 254 for the National Research Council, Division of Medical Sciences, Committee on Aviation Medicine, Dec. 12, 1943.

"Evaluation of Anti-G Suits." By Capt. C. A. Maaske, Capt. G. A. Hallenbeck, and 1st. Lt. E. E. Martin. Aero Medical Laboratory. Wright Field, Ohio. Report No. 348 for the National Research Council, Division of Medical Sciences, Committee on Aviation Medicine, Jun. 10, 1944.

"Evaluation of Anti-G Suits." By Capt. George L. Maison. Aero Medical Laboratory. Engineering Division. Wright Field, Ohio. Report No. 309 for the National Research Council, Division of Medical Sciences, Committee on Aviation Medicine, Apr. 18, 1944.

"Final Report on Anti 'G' Flying Suits—Comparative Test of Clark and Berger Models." Report No. 3–44–7, by Capt. P. F. Scholander. AAF Proving Ground Command. Eglin Field, Fla., Sep. 1, 1944.

German Aviation Medicine in World War II. 2 vols. Prepared under the auspices of the Surgeon General, USAF. Headquarters, U.S. Air Force. Washington, D.C., 1950.

Hallenbeck, Maj. George A., MC. "Design and Use of Anti-G Suits and Their Activating Valves in World War II." AAF Technical Report No. 5433. Aero Medical Laboratory, Engineering Division, Headquarters, Air Materiel Command. Wright Field, Ohio, Mar. 6, 1946. Important, detailed study.

"Handbook of Protective Equipment." Air Force Manual No. 64–5. Department of the Air Force. Washington, D.C., Nov. 15, 1968.

"Installation of Anti-G Equipment in the Eighth Air Force Fighter Groups." Memorandum Report No. TSEAL3–696–51K, by 1st. Lt. Kenneth E. Penrod. Aero Medical Laboratory, Engineering Division, Air Technical Service Command. Wright Field, Ohio, Apr. 10, 1945.

Lawrie, J. P. "Aviation and Medical Research." *Aircraft Engineering.* June 1940.

Maison, Capt. George L., MC, et al. "Acceleration and the G Suit." *Air Surgeon's Bulletin.* Jan. 1945.

"Personal Flying Equipment as Used in Central and Western Pacific Areas." Memorandum Report No. TSEAL–3–695–52, by Lt. Col. A. P. Gagge. Aero Medical Laboratory, Engineering Division, Air Technical Service Command. Wright Field, Ohio, May 18, 1945.

Poppen, John R., and Drinker, Cecil K. "Physiological Effects and Possible Methods of Reducing the Symptoms Produced by Rapid Changes in the Speed and Direction of Airplanes as Measured in Actual Flight." *Journal of Applied Physiology,* Oct. 1950.

"Preliminary Report on K.O.P. Anti-G Suits." Report F. R. 92, by Sq. Ldr. A. K. McIntyre, RAAF. Flying Personnel Research Committee. Sydney, Australia, Jun. 1944.

"Reference Manual for Personal Equipment Officers." AAF Manual No. 55–0–1. Headquarters, Army Air Forces. Washington, D.C., Jun. 1, 1945.

"Status of Development of the Hydrostatic Suit." Memorandum Report No. EXP–M–54–660–11C, by Maj. Otis O. Benson, Jr. Aero Medical Research Unit, Equipment Laboratory, Materiel Division. Wright Field, Ohio, Sep. 25, 1941.

"The Cotton G-Suit." Memorandum Report No. EXP–M–54–660–11D, by Maj. D. B. Dill. Aero Medical Research Unit, Equipment Laboratory, Materiel Division. Wright Field, Ohio, Dec. 22, 1941.

"The Introduction of Anti-'G' Equipment into the MTO." Memorandum Report No. TSEAL3–696–51N, by Capt. George A. Hallenbeck. Aero Medical Laboratory, Engineering Division, Air Technical Service Command. Wright Field, Ohio, May 12, 1945.

"Use, Maintenance and Storage of Fighter Pilot's Pneumatic Suit (Anti-G) Types G–3 and G–3A." Technical Order No. 13–1–23. Headquarters, U.S. Air Force. Washington, D.C., Jul. 1, 1949.

"Use, Maintenance and Storage of Fighter Pilot's Pneumatic Suit (Anti-G) Type G–4A." Technical Order No. 13–1–41. Headquarters, U.S. Air Force. Washington, D.C., Mar. 14, 1951.

"Development of Sub-stratosphere Pressure Suits in the German Air Force," Memorandum Report No. TSEAL–3–660–48–M, by V. J. Wulff and Col. W. R. Lovelace II, Aero Medical Laboratory, Air Technical Service Command, Wright Field, Ohio, Aug. 11, 1945.

Engle, Eloise, and Lott, Arnold S. *Man in Flight: Biomedical Achievements in Aerospace.* Annapolis, Md., 1979.

German Aviation Medicine in World War II. 2 vols. Prepared under the auspices of the Surgeon General, USAF. Headquarters, U.S. Air Force. Washington, D.C., 1950.

"High Altitude Pressure Suits." By J. Allen Neal. Vol. IV, section VIII, History of Wright Air Development Center, 1 Jul.-31 Dec. 1955. Wright-Patterson AFB, Ohio, 1956.

Mallan, Lloyd. *Suiting Up For Space: The Evolution of the Space Suit.* New York, 1971.

Mohler, Stanley R., and Johnson, Bobby H. *Wiley Post, His Winnie Mae, and the World's First Pressure Suit.* Washington, D.C., 1971.

"Pressure Altitude Suit Equipment." Report of the Army Air Forces Board, Project No. (M-4) 314, by Maj. J. A. Roth, MC. Orlando, Fla., Jan. 17, 1944.

Schultz, Helen W. "Case History of Pressure Suits." Historical Study No. 126. Headquarters, Air Materiel Command. Wright-Patterson AFB, Ohio, May 1951. Important, detailed study.

"Test of Oxygen Pressure Flying Suit for High Altitude Flying." Memorandum Report No. I–54–431, by F. G. Nesbitt. Equipment Branch, Engineering Section, Materiel Division. Wright Field, Ohio, Jun. 21, 1934, with report of test results, Memorandum Report No. I–54–431–A1, Jun. 23, 1934.

"Test of Oxygen Pressure Flying Suit for Use at High Altitudes." Memorandum Report No. I–54–458, by F. G. Nesbitt. Equipment Branch, Engineering Section, Materiel Division. Wright Field, Ohio, Aug. 27, 1934.

"The Altitude Pressure Suit." Memorandum Report No. ENG–49–660–11–C–1, by Capt. Waring L. Dawbarn. Aero Medical Laboratory, Engineering Division, Materiel Command. Wright Field, Ohio, Oct. 11, 1943.

"The Development of High Altitude Oxygen Helmets." Air Force Technical Report No. 5769. Aero Medical Laboratory. Wright-Patterson AFB, Ohio, Mar. 1949.

Walker, T. W. "The Development of the Pressure Suit for High Altitude Flying." *The Project Engineer,* May 1956.

Wilson, Charles L. "Wiley Post: First Test of High Altitude Pressure Suits in the United States." *Archives of Environmental Health.* Vol. 10, May 1965.

VI SURVIVAL EQUIPMENT

Air Sea Rescue Bulletin. Publication of the Air Sea Rescue Agency. Washington, D.C., 1944–c. 1946.

"Air-Sea Rescue Equipment Guide." NAVCG-117. Published by the U.S. Coast Guard for the Air Sea Rescue Agency. Washington, D.C., 1945.

"Clothing, Parachutes, Equipment and Supplies." AAF Illustrated Catalog, Class 13. Headquarters, Army Air Forces. Washington, D.C., Sep. 30, 1943.

"Index of Army-Navy Aeronautical Equipment: Miscellaneous." Technical Order No. 03–1–46. Fairfield Air Technical Service Command. Patterson Field, Ohio, Jul. 10, 1945.

"Miscellaneous Aircraft Equipment." Technical Manual No. 1–416. War Department. Washington, D.C., Mar. 22, 1944.

"Pilot's Information File." AAF Regulation No. 62–15. Headquarters, Army Air Forces. Washington, D.C., Apr. 9, 1943, as amended.

Ransom, Frank E. "Air-Sea Rescue 1941–1952." USAF Historical Study No. 95. USAF Historical Division, Air University. Maxwell AFB, Ala., Aug. 1954.

"Reference Manual for Personal Equipment Officers." AAF Manual No. 55–0–1. Headquarters, Army Air Forces. Washington, D.C., Jun. 1, 1945.

Snodgrass, Raymond J. "Development of Survival and Rescue Equipment for the Army Air Forces." Study 272. Air Technical Service Command. Wright Field, Ohio, May 22, 1945. Excellent reference, also containing information on aircrew and emergency rations.

"Survival on Land and Sea." AAF Manual 21W. Prepared by the Arctic, Desert, and Tropic Information Center, New York, N.Y., Jul. 1944. Revised edition, AAF Manual 64–0–1. Published by Headquarters, Army Air Forces. Washington, D.C., Jun. 1945. Later renumbered as AAF Manual 64–5. A number of other survival publications were produced by the AAF Arctic, Desert, and Tropic Information Center.

The Personal Equipment Officer. Publication of the Personal Equipment Laboratory, AAF. Wright Field, Ohio, 1945–46.

Tilford, Capt. Earl H. "The Development of Search and Rescue: World War II to 1961." *Aerospace Historian.* Winter, Dec. 1977.

Type Designation Sheets. Records of aeronautical clothing and equipment maintained by the Materiel Division. Wright Field, Ohio, mid-1920s until the early 1950s.

VII MISCELLANEOUS EQUIPMENT

"Aeronautic Instruments." Technologic Papers of the Bureau of Standards, No. 237, by Franklin L. Hunt. Washington, D.C., May 16, 1923.

"Aircraft Instruments—Aircraft Clocks." Technical Manual No. 1–413. Chief of the Air Corps, War Department. Washington, D.C., Nov. 7, 1940, and revised edition, Feb. 2, 1942. Also includes watches.

"Air-Sea Rescue Equipment Guide." NAVCG–117. Published by the U.S. Coast Guard for the Air Sea Rescue Agency. Washington, D.C., 1945.

"Automatic Pistol Cal. .45 M1911 and M1911A1." Field Manual No. 23–35. War Department. Washington, D.C., Apr. 30, 1940.

"Binoculars, Field Glasses, and B.C. Telescopes, All Types." Technical Manual No. 9–1580. War Department. Washington, D.C., Apr. 6, 1942, and revised edition, Mar. 15, 1945.

"Bombardier's Information File." AAF Regulation No. 62–15. Headquarters, Army Air Forces. Washington, D.C., Mar. 1945.

"Clothing, Parachutes, Equipment and Supplies." AAF Illustrated Catalog, Class 13. Headquarters, Army Air Forces. Washington, D.C., Sep. 30, 1943.

Crowell, Benedict. *America's Munitions, 1917–1918*. Report of the Assistant Secretary of War, Director of Munitions. Washington, D.C., 1919.

Crump, Capt. Ira. "Pyrotechnics." *Army Ordnance*. Vol. VII, no. 37, Jul.-Aug. 1926.

"Gunner's Information File: Flexible Gunnery." AAF Manual No. 20, Headquarters, Army Air Forces. Washington, D.C., May 1944, as amended.

"Handbook of Aircraft Armament." Bureau of Aircraft Production, Air Service, U.S. Army. Washington, D.C., 1918.

"Index of Army-Navy Aeronautical Equipment: Miscellaneous." Technical Order No. 03–1–46. Fairfield Air Technical Service Command. Patterson Field, Ohio, Jul. 10, 1945.

"Miscellaneous Aircraft Equipment." Technical Manual No. 1–416. War Department. Washington, D.C., Mar. 22, 1944.

"Navigator's Information File." AAF Regulation No. 62–15. Headquarters, Army Air Forces. Washington, D.C., Nov. 24, 1944.

"Pilot's Information File." AAF Regulation No. 62–15. Headquarters, Army Air Forces. Washington, D.C., Apr. 9, 1943, as amended.

"Pistols and Revolvers." Technical Manual No. 9–1295. War Department. Washington, D.C., Nov. 9, 1942.

"Reference Manual for Personal Equipment Officers." AAF Manual No. 55–0–1. Headquarters, Army Air Forces. Washington, D.C., Jun. 1, 1945.

"Small Arms Materiel and Associated Equipment." Technical Manual No. 9–2200. War Department. Washington, D.C., Oct. 11, 1943.

Sweeting, C. G. *Combat Flying Clothing: Army Air Forces Clothing During World War II*. Washington, D.C., 1984.

"Technical Equipment of the Signal Corps, 1916." Signal Corps Manual No. 3, War Department Document No. 541. War Department. Washington, D.C., 1917.

Technical Orders. Hundreds of T.O.s and amendments pertaining to individual items of personal equipment were published by the Air Service, Air Corps, and Army Air Forces after the system originated in October 1918. They provided details of maintenance, repair, and use of flying equipment.

The Personal Equipment Officer. Publication of the Personal Equipment Laboratory, AAF. Wright Field, Ohio, 1945–46.

Type Designation Sheets. Records maintained by the Materiel Division on almost every type of aeronautical equipment. Wright Field, Ohio, mid-1920s until the early 1950s.

"Wrist Watches, Pocket Watches, Stop Watches, and Clocks." Technical Manual No. 9–1575. War Department. Washington, D.C., Apr. 6, 1945.

Index

Page references to illustrations are printed in **boldface**.